WordPerfect® 6 for Windows™ QuickStart

Greg Harvey

que®

WordPerfect® 6 for Windows™ QuickStart

Library of Congress Catalog No.: 93-85726

ISBN: 1-56529-463-7

95 94 93   6   5   4   3   2   1

Interpretation of the printing code: the rightmost double-digit number is the year of the book's printing; the rightmost single-digit number, the number of the book's printing. For example, a printing code of 93-1 shows that the first printing of the book occurred in 1993.

Screen reproductions in this book were created with Collage Plus from Inner Media, Inc., Hollis, NH.

WordPerfect 6 for Windows QuickStart is based on WordPerfect 6.0 for Windows.

Publisher: David P. Ewing

Associate Publisher: Rick Ranucci

Director of Publishing: Michael Miller

Managing Editor: Corinne Walls

Marketing Manager: Ray Robinson

Composed in *Garamond* and *MCPdigital* by Que Corporation.

About the Author

Greg Harvey is a well-known computer consultant and author of training manuals and user guides. Besides WordPerfect, Greg has written books on popular PC software packages such as Lotus 1-2-3 and WordStar, and on Macintosh packages such as HyperCard and PageMaker.

Publishing Manager
Charles O. Stewart, III

Acquisitions Editor
Thomas F. Godfrey III

Product Director
Jim Minatel

Editors
Sara Kurtz Allaei

Sara Black

Thomas Hayes

Patrick Kanouse

Barbara K. Koenig

Susan Ross Moore

Christine Prakel

Joy Preacher

Pamela Wampler

Technical Editor
Michael Watson

Book Designer
Amy Peppler-Adams

Cover Designer
Tim Amrhein

Production Team
Angela Bannan

Danielle Bird

Ayrika Bryant

Charlotte Clapp

Brook Farling

Teresa Forrester

Joelynn Gifford

Michelle Greenwalt

Heather Kaufman

Tim Montgomery

Caroline Roop

Dennis Sheehan

Sue VandeWalle

Mary Beth Wakefield

Donna Winter

Lillian Yates

Indexers
Joy Dean Lee
Suzanne Snyder

Acknowledgments

I want to take this opportunity to thank all of the many talented people who contributed so much to the success of this project:

At Harvey and Associates: Jane Vait, for her diligence in editing my raw manuscript, checking over figures, and generally paying attention to all the details that might otherwise have been overlooked in the rush. Shane Gearing, for his unflagging behind-the-scenes support of this project.

At Que Corporation: Chuck Stewart, for his help in getting this book revision off the ground and helping me focus on how to make this book better. Tom Godfrey, for all his help in keeping the project on track and on time. Jim Minatel, for his insight and helpful ideas for improving this edition of the book. Thanks Jim! Pamela Wampler, for her excellent copy editing and general good humor (it's always a pleasure to work with you!). Barbara Koenig, for her invaluable production skills and for being so much fun to work with (let's do it again sometime).

And elsewhere: George Beinhorn, for his work in revising the text and figures in some of the early chapters. George, I couldn't have done it without you. Rene Pate at WordPerfect Corporation, for allowing me the privilege of Beta testing this awesome version of WordPerfect for Windows.

Trademark Acknowledgments

All terms mentioned in this book that are known to be trademarks or service marks have been appropriately capitalized. Que Corporation cannot attest to the accuracy of this information. Use of a term in this book should not be regarded as affecting the validity of any trademark or service mark.

Microsoft is a registered trademark and Windows is a trademark of Microsoft Corporation.

WordPerfect is a registered trademark of WordPerfect Corporation.

Contents at a Glance

Introduction 1

1 An Overview of WordPerfect 6.0 for Windows 9

2 Getting Acquainted with WordPerfect
   for Windows 25

3 Getting Started 65

4 Editing a Document 107

5 Proofreading Text 141

6 Formatting Paragraphs and Characters 167

7 Formatting Pages 213

8 Printing a Document 249

9 Managing Files in WordPerfect 265

10 Creating Macros 295

11 Using Merge for Mass Mailings 317

12 Sorting and Selecting Data 341

13 Outlining 361

14 Annotating a Document 375

15 Creating Tables 405

16 Using Columns and Graphics 445

17 Creating and Using Button Bars 475

Index 495

Table of Contents

Introduction 1

    What Does This Book Contain? 2

    Who Should Use This Book? 4

    What Is New in WordPerfect for Windows? 4

    Where to Learn More about WordPerfect for Windows 5

    Where to Find More Help 6

    Conventions Used in This Book 6

1   An Overview of WordPerfect for Windows 9

    The Benefits of Using WordPerfect 6.0 for Windows 11

        Using Icons 12

        Using the Mouse 14

        Using the Keyboard 15

        Understanding the Object-Action Model 16

    WordPerfect 6.0 for Windows Graphical Features 17

        The Ruler 19

        The Power Bar 20

        The Button Bar and Feature Bars 20

    File Compatibility with Other Versions of WordPerfect 22

    Summary 23

2   Getting Acquainted with WordPerfect for Windows 25

    Understanding the WordPerfect Program Window 27

        The Title Bar 28

        The Menu Bar 28

        The Power Bar 30

        The Status Bar 30

        Customizing the Status Bar 31

        The Button Bar 32

Understanding the Components of a Document Window 35

    Scroll Bars..36

    The Ruler Bar 38

    The Reveal Codes Window 39

Using the Mouse 41

    Selecting Menu Commands with the Mouse 43

    Choosing QuickMenu Commands with the Mouse 45

    Selecting Text with the Mouse 45

    Sizing and Moving a Window with the Mouse 47

Learning the Keyboard 50

    The Function Keys 51

    The Alphanumeric Keys 54

    Selecting Pull-Down Menu Commands with the Mnemonic Keys 54

    The Shortcut Keys 55

    The Cursor-Movement Keys 57

Getting On-Line Help 58

    Getting Context-Sensitive Help 59

    Using the Help Menus 59

    Using the Help Command Buttons 61

    Searching for a Help Topic 61

    Using the Coaches 62

    Exiting Help 63

Summary 63

3   Getting Started **65**

Starting WordPerfect for Windows 67

    Starting WordPerfect from the Program Manager 67

    Starting WordPerfect with the Windows File Run Command 68

    Opening a Document When You Start WordPerfect 69

    Starting WordPerfect from the File Manager 70

Creating a New Document 71

    Selecting a Template for the New Document 72

    Understanding WordPerfect's Default Settings 73

    Changing WordPerfect's Default Settings 75

    Entering Document Text 75

      Seeing Placement of Formatting Characters 77

    Choosing Draft Mode 78

    Creating a Business Letter 79

    Creating an Envelope 80

Moving the Cursor 82
   Moving the Cursor with the Mouse 83
   Moving the Cursor with the Keyboard 83
   Using the Arrow Keys 83
   Using the PgUp and PgDn Keys 84
   Using the Home and End Keys 85
   Using the Go To Key 85
Choosing WordPerfect Commands 87
   Choosing Menu Options 87
   Choosing QuickMenu Options 88
   Choosing Options in Dialog Boxes 89
   Canceling Command Selections 94
Saving a Document 94
   Naming Files 96
   Associating Files with WordPerfect for Windows 97
   Saving the Document under a New Name 98
   Using the Backup Features 99
   Closing Document Windows and Exiting WordPerfect 101
Using WordPerfect in the Windows Environment 103
   Returning to Windows without Exiting WordPerfect 103
   Switching between WordPerfect and Other Programs 103
   Copying and Pasting Text between Programs 104
Summary 106

4   Editing a Document 107

Opening Documents for Editing 108
   Viewing the Contents of Documents 111
   Choosing Open File Options 112
   Using QuickList 113
Working with Multiple Documents 114
   Opening a New File 115
   Retrieving One File into Another File 115
   Opening Multiple Documents in One Step 116
   Viewing More than One Document Window 116
   Switching between Cascaded or Tiled Windows 116
   Closing Document Windows 118
Inserting Text 118
   Adding Text in Insert Mode 119
   Replacing Text in Typeover Mode 119

Replacing Text in Insert Mode 119

Using Abbreviations to Insert Text 121

Inserting Spaces 123

Inserting Tabs 123

Inserting Blank Lines 123

Deleting Text 124

Selecting Text with the Keyboard 124

Deleting Text with Keyboard Shortcuts 124

Undoing a WordPerfect Command 125

Restoring Deleted Text 126

Cutting, Copying, and Pasting Text 127

Copying or Moving Text in the Same Document................................ 128

Using Drag-and-Drop Editing 130

Copying or Moving Text between WordPerfect Documents 132

Editing in the Reveal Codes Window 132

Working with Hidden Codes 133

Deleting Hidden Codes 135

Marking Proposed Changes with Redline or Strikeout............................. 135

Choosing the Redline Method 136

Marking Text with Redline or Strikeout 137

Removing Redline and Strikeout Markings... 138

Summary 139

5 Proofreading Text **141**

Locating Text with the Find Feature 142

Performing a Search 142

Using Wild-Card Characters 147

Replacing Text and Codes with the Replace Feature 148

Replacing a String 148

Performing a Global Find and Replace 150

Correcting Errors with the Speller 151

Checking a Word, Page, Document, or Selection 152

Selecting an Alternative Spelling 153

Using the Other Speller Options 154

Ignoring Words with Numbers... 155

Eliminating Double Words 156

Correcting Irregular Case 156

Replacing Misspelled Words Automatically 157
Using a Document Dictionary 157
Finding the Right Word with the Thesaurus 157
Displaying Synonyms and Antonyms 158
Looking Up More Alternative Words 159
Using the Look Up Option 161
Using the Grammar Checker 161
Starting Grammatik 162
Choosing Grammatik Options 164
Summary 166

6 **Formatting Paragraphs and Characters 167**
Changing the Units of Measurement 169
Understanding the Ruler 170
Adjusting the Left and Right Margins 171
Auto Code Placement 174
Tab Settings in WordPerfect 176
The Tab Ruler 177
Deleting Tabs 177
Changing the Type of Tab 178
Adding Tabs 178
The Tab Set Dialog Box 179
Deleting All Tabs 179
Setting Uniform Tabs 180
Setting Nonuniform Tabs 181
Changing Dot Leader and Align Characters 181
Indenting Paragraphs 182
Indenting the First Line of a Paragraph 182
Indenting a Paragraph on the Left 182
Indenting a Paragraph on the Left and Right 183
Creating a Hanging Indent 184
Changing the Type of Justification 185
Aligning Text 188
Centering a Line between Margins 188
Centering Text on a Specific Point 189
Aligning Flush Right 190
Aligning Text on a Decimal or Other Characters 191
Using the Decimal Align Key Combination, Alt+Shift+F7 191
Changing the Alignment Character 192

Understanding Fonts 193
    Choosing a Font 197
    Applying Attributes to Text 199
    Using Bold, Italics, and Underlining in the Text 199
    Superscripting and Subscripting Text 200
Converting Text to a Different Case 201
Changing the Line Spacing 201
Adjusting the Line Height 203
Formatting Text with QuickFormat 204
    Formatting Text with Bullets and Numbers 205
Using Special Characters 206
Controlling Line Breaks... 208
    Keeping Text Together with Hard Spaces 208
    Hyphenating Text Manually 209
    Using the Hyphenation Feature 209
Summary 212

7   Formatting Pages 213

Choosing the Paper Size 215
    Using Envelopes 216
    Creating a New Paper Definition 218
    Specifying Binding Offset 220
Changing the Top and Bottom Margins 221
Centering Top to Bottom 222
Positioning Text on the Page with Advance 223
Using Headers and Footers 224
    Creating a Header or Footer 226
    Inserting a Page Number in a Header or Footer 227
    Placing Headers and Footers on Odd or Even Pages ... 228
    Inserting the File Name in a Header or Footer 228
    Editing a Header or Footer 228
    Discontinuing a Header or Footer 229
    Adding a Watermark to a Document 229
Numbering Pages 232
    Formatting Page Numbers 232
Suppressing Page Formats... 234
Controlling Page Breaks 235
    Inserting Hard Page Breaks 236

Keeping Text Together on a Page 236

Using Block Protect 237

Using Conditional End of Page 238

Using Widow/Orphan Protection 239

Forcing a Page to Be Odd or Even 239

Using Subdivide Page 240

Formatting a Document with Styles.. 242

Defining a Style Using Quick Create 243

Creating or Editing a Style with the Styles Editor 245

Managing Styles 246

Applying a Style 247

Summary 248

8   Printing a Document **249**

Selecting a Printer 250

Installing a Printer Driver 252

Adding a Printer 253

Choosing a Printer Initial Font 254

Using WordPerfect Printer Setup Options 255

Updating Printer Drivers 257

Copying or Deleting a Printer Driver 257

Testing Your Printer 257

Printing Your Documents 259

Printing the Current Page or Entire Document 259

Previewing a Document Before Printing 264

Summary 264

9   Managing Files in WordPerfect **265**

Saving a Document with a Password 266

Assigning a Password 267

Opening a Password-Protected File 268

Deleting or Changing a Password 269

Creating a Document Summary 269

Entering Document Summary Information 270

Printing and Saving a Document Summary 272

Printing a Document Summary and a File 273

Saving a Document Summary in a File 274

Setting the Document Summary Preferences 275

Using QuickLists to Identify Directories 276
   Editing or Creating a QuickList 276
   Displaying Files with QuickList 279
Using File Management Options 280
Using QuickFinder to Locate Files 285
   Indexing Files with QuickFinder 286
   Editing an Existing Index 288
   Managing QuickFinder Indexes 288
   Searching with QuickFinder 289
   Using Search Operations 292
Summary 294

10 Creating Macros **295**

Understanding Macros 297
Recording a Macro 297
   Pausing the Recording of a Macro 299
   Using the Mouse When Recording a Macro 300
Playing a Macro 300
Using Other Ways to Play Macros 301
   Assigning a Macro to the Macro Cascading Menu 301
   Assigning a Macro to the Button Bar 304
   Assigning a Macro to the Keyboard 306
Editing a Macro 308
Creating a Library of Useful Macros 310
   A Macro for Entering the Company Name and Address 311
   A Macro for Capitalizing Each Word in a Line 312
   A Macro for Transposing Two Characters 312
   A Macro for Starting a New Letter 313
Summary 314

11 Using Merge for Mass Mailings **317**

Understanding the Merge Operation 318
   Creating a Table Data File 320
   Creating a Text Data File 323
   Entering Information in a Data File 325
   Editing Records in the Data File 326
   Creating a Form File 327

Merging the Form and Data Files 329
    Selecting the Records to Merge 333
    Addressing Envelopes 337
    Printing Mailing Labels 338
Summary 340

12 Sorting and Selecting Data **341**

Understanding Sorting 342
    Choosing the Kind of Sorting 343
    Selecting the Sort Order 345
    Defining the Sort Keys 346
    Selecting the Type of Sort Key 346
Performing the Sort 348
    Specifying Keys for Sorting Lines 351
    Specifying Keys for Sorting Paragraphs 353
    Specifying Keys for Sorting Merge Records in Text Data Files 354
    Specifying Keys for Sorting Table Rows 355
    Specifying Keys for Sorting Parallel Columns 356
Selecting Records 357
    Specifying the Selection Statement 357
    Creating a Global Selection Statement 359
Summary 360

13 Outlining **361**

Understanding Outlining in WordPerfect 6.0 for Windows 362
Creating an Outline 365
Editing an Outline 369
Understanding the Outline Feature Bar 370
    Collapsing and Expanding the Outline 370
    Moving Outline Headings 372
Summary 374

14 Annotating a Document **375**

Numbering Lines 377
Adding Comments to a Document 380
    Editing a Comment 383
    Converting a Comment to Text 383
    Converting Text to a Comment 384

Adding Sound Clip Comments 384

Playing a Sound Clip 385

Recording Sound Clips 387

Creating Bookmarks 388

Using the QuickMark Feature 389

Using Hypertext to Jump from Bookmark to Bookmark 390

Making Hypertext Jumps 392

Editing a Hypertext Link 394

Adding Footnotes and Endnotes 395

Creating a Footnote or an Endnote 395

Editing a Footnote or an Endnote 397

Deleting a Footnote or an Endnote 398

Changing the Footnote or Endnote Numbering 398

Using Footnote and Endnote Options 399

Changing the Location of Endnotes in the Document 403

Using WordPerfect's Other Reference Features 404

Summary 404

15 Creating Tables **405**

Understanding Table Basics 407

Creating a Table 408

Moving in a Table 410

Entering Text in a Table 411

Editing Text in a Table 413

Selecting Cells with the Mouse 413

Selecting Cells with the Keyboard 415

Cutting and Copying Cells 415

Using Drag and Drop to Cut and Copy 418

Deleting a Table 419

Editing the Table Structure 420

Changing the Column Widths 421

Inserting Columns and Rows 423

Deleting Columns and Rows 424

Joining Cells 424

Splitting a Joined Cell 426
Joining or Splitting Tables 426
Modifying the Border Lines or Fill Patterns 427
Formatting the Table 430
Selecting Fonts for a Table 430
Formatting Cells 431
Formatting Columns 433
Formatting Rows 435
Formatting the Entire Table 436
Performing Calculations in a Table 438
Using Data Fill 441
Using the Sum Function 442
Summary 443

16 Using Columns and Graphics 445
Defining Columns 447
Defining Columns in the Columns Dialog Box 449
Adjusting Widths of Newspaper Columns from the Ruler 451
Entering Text in Columns 453
Understanding Graphics in WordPerfect 454
Inserting a Graphics Image into a Document 458
Repositioning a Graphics Image 460
Resizing a Graphics Image 462
Adding a Caption to a Graphics Image 464
Editing a Graphic with the Image Tools Palette 465
Scaling or Cropping a Graphics Image 466
Rotating or Flipping a Graphics Image 467
Using Borders and Graphics Lines 469
Adding Borders to a Document 469
Creating Horizontal and Vertical Graphics Lines 470
Summary 473

17 Creating and Using Button Bars 475
The Button Bars in WordPerfect for Windows 476
Editing a Button Bar 478

Creating a Button Bar 483

Creating a Library of Custom Button Bars 484

   The Editing Button Bar 485

   The Bookmark Button Bar 487

   The Document Button Bar 489

   Linking the Button Bars 491

Summary 493

Index **495**

Introduction

If you are new to WordPerfect 6 for Windows or are upgrading from an earlier DOS or Windows version, this book is for you. *WordPerfect 6 for Windows QuickStart* will help you grasp the basics of using WordPerfect for Windows, enabling you to create your own documents (or modify existing documents created by others) with a minimum of effort. You don't even need to be familiar with Windows or mice—all the basics are covered.

WordPerfect 6 for Windows QuickStart uses a tutorial approach, taking you through important concepts step-by-step, describing all the fundamentals you need to know about the program. The text supplies essential information and provides comments on what you see. Many illustrations help guide you through procedures and clarify new concepts.

Learning any new program can be an intimidating experience. *WordPerfect 6 for Windows QuickStart* is designed to help shorten your learning curve by allowing you to learn basic concepts quickly. Whether you are completely new to WordPerfect or are already a user of an earlier DOS- or Windows-based version, you will find *WordPerfect 6 for Windows QuickStart* an efficient method for learning the fundamentals of this new version of the graphical WordPerfect.

What Does This Book Contain?

The chapters in *WordPerfect 6 for Windows QuickStart* take you from basic information to more sophisticated tasks, including creating macros and customizing the Button Bar.

Chapter 1, "An Overview of WordPerfect for Windows," shows you the wide range of WordPerfect's capabilities and gives you valuable information on the benefits of using WordPerfect under the graphical user interface provided by Windows. Compatibility with other versions of WordPerfect is also discussed.

Chapter 2, "Getting Acquainted with WordPerfect for Windows," introduces you to the parts of the WordPerfect window and document windows, using the mouse and keyboard, and accessing WordPerfect's on-line Help window.

Chapter 3, "Getting Started," teaches you how to start WordPerfect for Windows and open document files. You also learn how to navigate the document window, select WordPerfect commands in pull-down menus and dialog boxes, save your document files, exit WordPerfect, and switch between WordPerfect and other programs that you run under Windows.

Chapter 4, "Editing a Document," teaches you how to open documents for editing and perform such standard operations as inserting, deleting, and cutting and pasting text. Working with multiple documents and understanding the Reveal Codes window are also covered in this chapter.

Chapter 5, "Proofreading Text," shows you how to use the Search and Replace features to find and replace text and codes; to check for spelling errors with the Speller; to look up synonyms with the Thesaurus; and to check for proper grammar with Grammatik.

Chapter 6, "Formatting Paragraphs and Characters," explains how to format lines and paragraphs in a document. You learn how to change the left and right margins, set tabs, indent text, align text, select new fonts, change the line spacing, insert special characters, and hyphenate text.

Chapter 7, "Formatting Pages," focuses on formatting operations that affect the entire document. Here, you learn, among other things, how to select a new paper size, change top and bottom margins, create headers and footers, number pages, control page breaks, and use styles to format the document.

Chapter 8, "Printing a Document," shows you how to select a printer, preview the printout, and print your documents. Installation of a WordPerfect printer driver is also covered here.

Chapter 9, "Managing Files in WordPerfect," describes how to use passwords to protect your documents, create QuickLists and QuickFinder to locate files, and use the WordPerfect file management options included in the Open File dialog box to perform such routine housekeeping chores as copying and moving files.

Chapter 10, "Creating Macros," teaches you how to record and play back macros. This chapter includes macros you can use to start your own macro library.

Chapter 11, "Using Merge for Mass Mailings," explains how to use the Merge feature to perform typical mail merge operations. You learn how to set up form letters and data files, and perform the merge to the screen or directly to the printer. You also learn how to use the Merge feature to address envelopes and print mailing labels.

Chapter 12, "Sorting and Selecting Data," explains how to rearrange and select the text you want to use. You learn how to sort lines, paragraphs, merge records, and rows of a table.

Chapter 13, "Outlining," teaches you how to use WordPerfect 6 for Windows' new outlining feature to set up formal outlines as well as organize reports that use a series of main and subordinate headings.

Chapter 14, "Annotating a Document," teaches you how to note special conditions in your document with comments and sound clips, locate your place quickly in a document with bookmarks and Hypertext links between these bookmarks, as well as how to reference your sources in a document with footnotes and endnotes.

Chapter 15, "Creating Tables," teaches you to create and edit tables in WordPerfect. You also learn how to enter formulas in tables.

Chapter 16, "Using Columns and Graphics," teaches you how to set up text columns and import graphics into your documents. The chapter also teaches you how to add borders to your document, draw graphics lines, and edit graphics images with the new Image Tools palette.

Chapter 17, "Creating and Using Button Bars," teaches you how to modify the Button Bars supplied with the program. You learn how to create custom Button Bars of your own.

Who Should Use This Book?

WordPerfect 6 for Windows QuickStart is designed as an introductory guide for new WordPerfect users. Whether you are sitting down with WordPerfect for Windows for the first time or upgrading from an earlier version of WordPerfect, *WordPerfect 6 for Windows QuickStart* contains the information to get you going quickly. The book highlights important concepts and takes you through important procedures by providing steps and explanations interwoven with numerous examples and illustrations.

What Is New in WordPerfect for Windows?

Although WordPerfect 6 for Windows offers essentially the same nucleus of features as version 5.2 of WordPerfect for Windows, it also contains many new features, including the following:

- *Bookmarks.* You can add bookmarks that mark a particular place in the document and then return to it by selecting the bookmark name.

- *Bullets and Numbers.* You create bulleted or numbered lists by selecting the type of bullets or numbers and then typing your list. You can set the list up so that each time you press Enter to start a new line, WordPerfect inserts another bullet or the next number and indents the line until you turn off the Bullets and Numbers feature.

- *Coaches.* You can use this new on-line Help feature to have WordPerfect walk through each step required to complete a new task.

- *Envelope.* You can use this feature to address envelopes for your letters. WordPerfect will automatically copy the mailing address you have typed in the letter and use it as the mailing address in the new envelope you're creating.

- *Feature Bars.* Several WordPerfect commands now lead directly to the display of Feature Bars rather than the opening of a dialog box, as soon as you select the command. Features bars consist of a series of buttons that perform related tasks or open dialog boxes where you can select further options. Unlike the Power Bar (also appearing in this list), Feature Bar buttons can be accessed either by clicking them with the mouse or by pressing Alt+Shift plus the mnemonic letter (hot key) shown on the button.

- *Graphics borders.* You can now add borders around paragraphs, pages, or between or around columns in a document.

- *Power Bar.* Replacing the ribbon in earlier releases of WordPerfect for Windows, the Power Bar consists of a series of buttons that perform the most commonly used tasks such as opening or saving a new document, selecting a new font or font size, or changing the justification of the text. Unlike Feature Bars, however, you must use the mouse to click the buttons on the Power Bar.

- *QuickMenus.* Many objects in the WordPerfect for Windows screen (including the left margin, the document itself, and the top and bottom areas of the document where headers and footers appear) are now associated with QuickMenus (mini-menus containing only the commands that you would normally use when working with that particular object). To open a QuickMenu, you click the secondary mouse button (the right button when you use the mouse as a right-handed person would, or the left button when you use the mouse as a left-handed person would).

- *Templates.* Each document you create is formatted according to a Standard template. In addition to the Standard template, WordPerfect 6 for Windows supplies you with a variety of other templates that you can select for formatting special documents (such as memorandums or expense reports). In addition to these predefined templates, you can also create your own custom templates. Templates in WordPerfect for Windows not only control what format settings are applied to the new document but also which macros, Feature Bars, custom Button Bars, and the like are available.

This book introduces you to all these exciting new features and more!

Where to Learn More about WordPerfect for Windows

After you learn the fundamentals presented in this book, you may want to learn more advanced applications of WordPerfect. Que Corporation has several WordPerfect for Windows books you can use:

Using WordPerfect 6 for Windows, Special Edition, is a reference book that provides comprehensive coverage of all aspects of using WordPerfect 6 for Windows. A quick command reference and tear-out command chart are included with this book.

WordPerfect 6 for Windows Quick Reference is an affordable, compact reference of the most commonly used WordPerfect 6 for Windows commands and functions. This is a handy book to keep near your computer when you need to quickly find the purpose of a command and the steps for using the command.

You can find both of these books in better bookstores worldwide. In the United States, you can call Que Corporation at 1-800-428-5331 to order books or obtain further information.

Where to Find More Help

You can use the context-sensitive Help feature to answer some of your questions while working with WordPerfect 6 for Windows. The Help feature is explained and illustrated in chapter 2, "Getting Acquainted with WordPerfect for Windows." Also, you can refer to the appropriate sections of the WordPerfect documentation provided with the WordPerfect for Windows program.

Should all else fail, contact WordPerfect Customer Support. For information on installation, call 1-800-228-6076. For information on features, call 1-800-228-1029. Assistance is available Monday through Friday, from 7:00 a.m. to 6:00 p.m., Mountain Time.

For more information on how to use Windows 3.0 or 3.1, consult Que's *Using Windows 3.1,* Special Edition.

Conventions Used in This Book

A number of conventions are used in *WordPerfect 6 for Windows QuickStart* to help you learn the program. This section provides examples of these conventions so that you can distinguish among the different elements in WordPerfect for Windows.

Direct quotations of words that appear on-screen are spelled as they appear on-screen and are printed in a special typeface, as in Macro Record.

Information you are asked to type is printed in blue, as in type a:install.

The mnemonic letter (or hot key) you can type after pressing the Alt key to activate a menu or to select a menu command or a dialog box option appears in boldface, as in **File Save As** or **Edit Undelete**.

Within the step-by-step procedures and tables, many keys appear as blue keyboard character icons (pictures similar to the actual keys on the keyboard), as in Alt + ◆Backspace or ◆Backspace .

When two keys appear together separated by a + (plus), as in Ctrl+Del or Alt+Backspace, you press and hold down the first key as you also press the second key. When two keys appear together *without* a plus sign between them, such as Home Home, the first key is pressed and released before the second key is pressed.

When three keys appear together separated by a + (plus), as in Alt+Shift+F3, you press and hold down the first key as you also press the second and third keys.

Features that are new to Version 6 of WordPerfect for Windows are indicated by this icon in the margin:

When you can use a QuickMenu during a procedure, a QuickMenu icon appears in the margin:

An Overview of WordPerfect for Windows

The benefits of WordPerfect 6.0 for Windows

WordPerfect 6.0 for Windows' graphical features

Compatibility with other versions of WordPerfect

Before you pick up the mouse and start using WordPerfect 6.0 for Windows, you need to know the range of capabilities this new graphical version of WordPerfect offers. Both beginning and experienced WordPerfect users will profit from the general information in this chapter—information about how WordPerfect uses the Windows environment and the benefits of using WordPerfect under the Windows graphical user interface.

Unlike WordPerfect 5.1 and 6.0 for DOS, which both run as DOS character-based programs under Windows without supporting the Windows environment, WordPerfect for Windows offers a 100-percent Windows-compliant application. This application combines the best of the Windows user interface with the most advanced generation of WordPerfect technology. Better yet, WordPerfect for Windows provides complete file compatibility with earlier DOS-based versions.

In this chapter, you see how WordPerfect 6.0 for Windows operates under Windows, and you learn what the program can do for you.

Key Terms in This Chapter

CUA   Common User Access. Refers to the common menu structure, keystroke shortcuts, and methods of working that the Windows graphical user interface offers.

GUI   Graphical User Interface (pronounced "gooey"). Refers to operating environments (such as Windows and OS/2 on IBM-compatible computers or the Macintosh operating environment) that rely more on manipulating symbolic graphic elements than on typed commands. These environments also provide a standard menu structure.

Icons   Symbols that represent a program, file, or function. An icon's graphic suggests its function. WordPerfect for Windows uses a special set of icons on the Button Bar; you can click these icons to select commands.

Mouse   A hand-held device used to select data, menu commands, and options in Windows programs.

Non-Windows program   A program that can run with or without Windows and that is not necessarily CUA-compliant.

Windows   A graphical user interface (GUI) built on the DOS operating system that provides a common user access (CUA) to all the applications that run under it.

Windows program   A program, such as WordPerfect for Windows, that does not run without Windows and that makes full use of the Windows GUI environment.

Whether you are an experienced computer user who is new to WordPerfect or a first-time computer user, you can quickly grasp the fundamentals of WordPerfect for Windows. If you start by learning the most basic concepts of WordPerfect and gradually build on your knowledge and experience, you will be amazed at your rapid progress.

This book uses an easy, step-by-step approach to teach you the fundamental WordPerfect tasks. Many of the techniques you use in WordPerfect 6.0 for Windows are common to all Windows applications; most of the fundamentals you learn while mastering WordPerfect will carry over to other Windows programs.

The Benefits of Using WordPerfect 6.0 for Windows

To understand the benefits of using WordPerfect for Windows, you need to understand the general advantages of operating a computer program under a graphical user interface (GUI—pronounced "gooey"). Windows was developed by Microsoft Corporation, an industry leader both in developing operating systems and in developing application programs for the IBM and Macintosh computers. According to Microsoft, a true GUI environment meets several specific criteria. The following are among the most important of these criteria:

- The computer screen displays a true representation of how the printed document will appear.

- The user interface is graphically oriented and makes extensive use of *icons* (symbols that graphically represent a document, program, or command).

- The user interface provides standard elements in all applications, including menus, dialog boxes, and windows. For example, after you learn to print with the **Print** command on the **File** menu in WordPerfect for Windows, you know how to print with every other Windows program.

- The user interface enables you to manipulate the screen directly. For example, you can move a window containing a WordPerfect document across the screen by using the mouse to drag the window in the direction you prefer.

- The user interface uses the *object-action* model; you select the object you want to affect before you select the command you want to apply to the object.
- The user interface supports multiple applications.
- The user interface is easy to install and use.

WordPerfect 6.0 for Windows supports all these GUI criteria. The program gives you freedom to work the way you want to work, while providing a standardized user interface that is intuitive and fun to use.

Because WordPerfect for Windows is significantly easier to learn and use than its non-Windows counterparts, you can learn faster and, consequently, be more productive with the program. With the CUA (Common User Access) supported by WordPerfect for Windows, you also will find learning other Windows programs easier. In no time, you will be able to work with several programs simultaneously and transfer information between the programs at will—even if you have never used a computer program.

Using Icons

By now, you surely realize that graphics are important in Windows programs such as WordPerfect. You will encounter several standard graphic elements in WordPerfect for Windows and in all Windows programs.

One of the most basic graphic elements is the *icon*. Icons are small symbols that represent a program, file, or function. An icon's graphic suggests its function. Some icons represent their function better than others. Icons representing simple actions fare better than those depicting more complex operations.

For example, look at the icon used in the Print button on the Power Bar.

The icon contains a printer and piece of paper. The icon suggests the function of sending a document to the printer. Now look at the Copy to Clipboard button on the Power Bar.

This icon shows an arrow pointing towards a small picture of a Clipboard, denoting the addition of information to the Clipboard. Although some icons might be harder to figure out than others, with just a little familiarity, you can recognize the function of all WordPerfect for Windows icons.

Windows also represents application programs with icons (at least until you open them). The Windows File Manager program icon, for example, is a filing cabinet, which suggests its function as a file management program. The WordPerfect 6.0 for Windows program icon uses the initials WP with the nib of a pen below, suggesting the program's writing functions.

Program icons change into larger Windows. When you position the mouse pointer on the WordPerfect icon and click the primary mouse button twice in rapid succession (a technique known as *double-clicking*), the WordPerfect program starts.

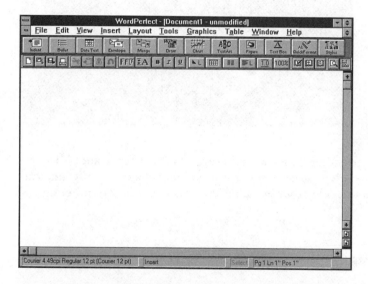

When the program finishes loading, WordPerfect for Windows opens in a full-screen window.

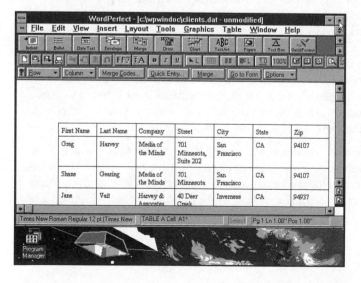

By clicking a button, you can reduce this full-screen program window to a smaller version on the Windows desktop.

By clicking a
different button,
you can reduce a
program to its
program icon—
even while the
program is run-
ning.

WordPerfect icon

Besides icons, WordPerfect for Windows uses several other important GUI
elements. Before you explore these elements in the next chapter, however, you
need to learn more about one other element: the *pointer*, or, more precisely,
the *mouse pointer*.

Using the Mouse

The *pointer* is a free-floating cursor that indicates your current position on-
screen; its usual shape is an arrowhead (pointing toward the left). The pointer
changes shape, however, to indicate a change in function. For example, when
you position the pointer somewhere within the WordPerfect menu bar or on a
Button Bar or scroll bar, the pointer maintains the shape of an arrowhead.
When you move the pointer somewhere within a document window, the
pointer immediately changes shape from the arrowhead to an I-beam shape.
This I-beam shape enables you to select the text you want to edit, or to reposition the *insertion point* (also known as the cursor) in the text.

You move the pointer with the *mouse,* a hand-held device whose movements
on your desk correlate with the movement of the pointer on-screen. The mouse
may be the most difficult aspect of mastering WordPerfect for Windows. Many
users initially find working with the mouse more difficult than anticipated and

14

more tiring than using the keyboard. The *point-and-click, drag,* and *double-click* techniques used by WordPerfect for Windows do require some time and effort to master. With a little perseverance, however, you will find using the mouse as natural as typing with the keyboard.

> *Note:* The best way to become proficient with the mouse is to play Solitaire, the card game included with Windows. In this game, you learn to point-and-click, drag, and double-click while you are entertained.

Although you can do almost everything you need in WordPerfect 6.0 for Windows without the mouse, you have little incentive to do so. Because the Windows environment is set up for direct manipulation of the screen, you will find that the mouse provides, if not the ideal tool, a much better tool than the keyboard for performing many of WordPerfect's routine tasks. After you master the mouse techniques for selecting pull-down menu commands and dialog box options, you will use the same techniques throughout the program. This consistent way to access program features is especially helpful because it enables you to give your full attention to the WordPerfect command or procedure you are learning.

Using the Keyboard

Despite the advantages of using the mouse, the keyboard still has a place in WordPerfect 6.0 for Windows. Windows programs always enable the user to select commands and dialog box options with an Alt+letter key combination. Whenever possible, the designers of WordPerfect have assigned mnemonic combinations that use the first letter of each command, such as Alt+F+P to choose the **File Print** command. Be aware, however, that such combinations are not always possible. The **Edit** menu, for example, has three options that begin with the letter C: Cu**t**, **C**opy, and Convert Case. You press Alt+E+C to copy text, Alt+E+T to cut text, and Alt+E+V to access a menu where you can convert selected text to all upper- or lowercase letters.

If you feel more comfortable using the keyboard to accomplish a particular operation in WordPerfect, you have no reason not to do so. As you become more experienced with WordPerfect for Windows, you will start mixing keyboard and mouse techniques, depending on the task and your degree of familiarity with the procedure.

Note: WordPerfect for Windows, like its DOS counterparts, has function-key equivalents for most important commands. The program offers two function key arrangements: the CUA keyboard and the WordPerfect DOS keyboard. Both keyboards use the 12 function keys alone and in combination with Shift, Ctrl, Ctrl+Shift, Alt, and Alt+Shift. The CUA keyboard maintains the CUA standard for keystroke movement. The WordPerfect DOS keyboard attempts to maintain as much keystroke compatibility as possible with WordPerfect 5.1 and 6.0 for DOS. If you are new to WordPerfect, do not burden yourself with learning all these function-key assignments when you need to concentrate on learning new commands. Stick with the pull-down menus that you can access with the mouse or the keyboard. If you have experience with WordPerfect 5.1 or 6.0, select the WordPerfect DOS keyboard and decide which system you want to use as you become familiar with the new interface.

Understanding the Object-Action Model

Before you start looking at the major functions of the WordPerfect 6.0 for Windows program in more detail, you should examine one more aspect of working with a Windows program. Recall that earlier, in recounting the major features of a true GUI, the object-action model was mentioned as one of the important aspects of the user interface. Windows programs as a whole (including WordPerfect for Windows) consistently follow this pattern in which you select the items you want to affect before you select the command.

In WordPerfect for Windows, you routinely select the block of text (the object) before you choose the command you want to apply to the block (the action). Although in the DOS-based WordPerfect, you routinely mark a block of text before you apply an attribute (such as underlining) to the block, the object-action model is not as prominent or consistently adhered to as in WordPerfect 6.0 for Windows (and all other Windows programs).

The major benefit of the object-action model is that it enables you to perform a series of actions on a single block of text without having to select the block each time (as with WordPerfect for DOS). To format a heading in a document so that it is in bold and italic type, for example, you select the heading, choose the **Bold** and **Italic** options in the Font dialog box (or press Ctrl+B or Ctrl+I), and you're done!

WordPerfect 6.0 for Windows Graphical Features

As you would expect, the most exciting and powerful features in WordPerfect 6.0 for Windows are graphical in nature. Your work is done in what is now commonly referred to as WYSIWYG (What-You-See-Is-What-You-Get) mode. In WYSIWYG mode, text always appears in the font, size, and attribute you assign, and graphics in the document are shown at all times. Not only that, but WordPerfect for Windows shows you the page borders and elements like page numbers and headers and footers that you put on the top and bottom of the page.

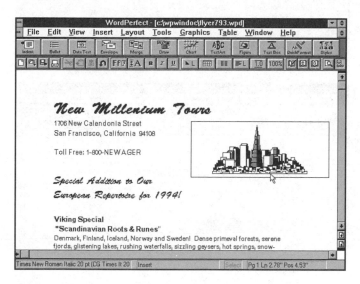

Here is an example of a document in WordPerfect 6.0 for Windows. WYSIWYG shows you all text attributes as they will print as well as the contents of any graphics you use.

Not only are graphics always visible in a document window, but they also are simple to reposition and resize. To move a graphic image in WordPerfect for Windows, use the mouse to select and drag the image to its new place on the page. When you release the mouse button, text immediately reformats and wraps around the graphic's boundaries.

To resize a graphic, click one of its borders to select the graphic. Then click one of the sizing handles (the rectangles that appear around the frame of the graphic), and drag the mouse until the graphic is the correct size.

This graphic is ready for resizing. Note the sizing handles that appear around it.

Here, by clicking one of the corner sizing handles and dragging, the graphic is resized.

The desktop publishing aspects of WordPerfect for Windows make creating documents such as flyers and newsletters easier. Creating these documents in character-based versions of WordPerfect is tedious at best.

The Ruler

Even if you don't need graphics in your documents, you will benefit from the graphical interface of the Ruler. The Ruler is one of WordPerfect for Windows' most powerful and easy-to-use features.

You can use the Ruler to accomplish most, if not all, routine formatting that your documents will require.

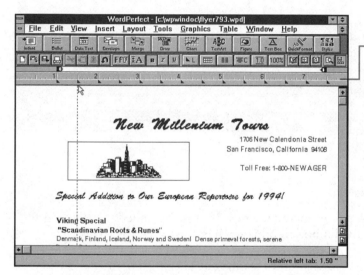

The Ruler

The Ruler enables you to change the margins and tabs by manipulating the icons directly. You also can change the font, style, justification, or line spacing with special buttons.

If positioning tabs directly on the Ruler is too imprecise for your needs, you can access the Tab Set dialog box quickly by clicking the Ruler with the secondary mouse button, then selecting **T**ab Set command on the QuickMenu that pops up rather than using the pull-down menus.

If you need, for example, to set accurate left and right margins that are beyond your abilities to pinpoint with the mouse on the Ruler, you can choose the **M**argins command on the Ruler's QuickMenu and then enter the values in the Margins dialog box. This procedure is much faster than choosing the **La**yout menu and selecting the **M**argins command on the regular pull-down menus.

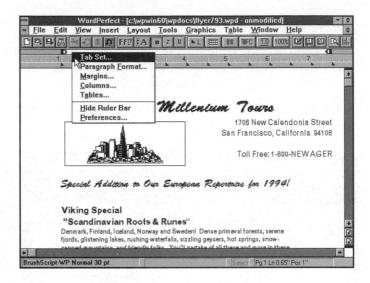

You can use the QuickMenu commands that appear when you click the Ruler with the secondary mouse button to display dialog boxes associated with setting tabs and margins.

The Power Bar

WordPerfect 6.0 for Windows includes a new Button Bar called the *Power Bar* (this feature replaces the Ribbon in previous Windows versions). This bar contains a series of buttons that enable you to quickly choose the most commonly used WordPerfect for Windows features by clicking a particular button with the mouse. For example, this bar contains buttons for creating a new document, opening an existing document, saving changes, printing the document, and cutting, copying, and pasting text to new areas in the document. If this is not enough, you also can use the Power Bar to select a new font and font size, create columns, change the justification, and zoom in and out on the document text.

The Button Bar and Feature Bars

In addition to the Power Bar, WordPerfect 6.0 for Windows includes other Button Bars that are routinely displayed in the WordPerfect program window. These bars include the Button Bar and Feature Bars. The Button Bar is displayed by choosing the **B**utton Bar command on the View pull-down menu (or clicking the Button Bar button—the last one—on the Power Bar). Feature Bars are automatically displayed as soon as you undertake a task like creating an outline or creating a formula in the cell of a WordPerfect for Windows table.

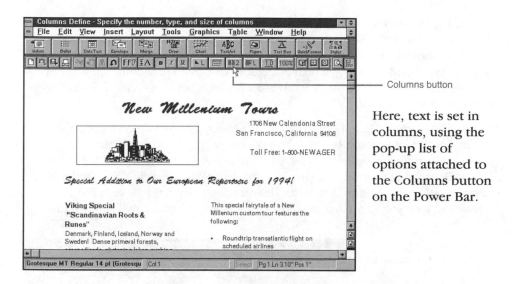

Columns button

Here, text is set in columns, using the pop-up list of options attached to the Columns button on the Power Bar.

The Button Bar contains a series of buttons, each of which has an icon with a word describing its function. (If you want to fit more buttons on the screen, you can have just the icon or just the text appear on the buttons.) To perform the WordPerfect command attached to each button on the Button Bar, you must use the mouse to click the button. The Button Bar grants you immediate access to commonly used commands, and you don't have to remember where the command is located on the WordPerfect menu bar.

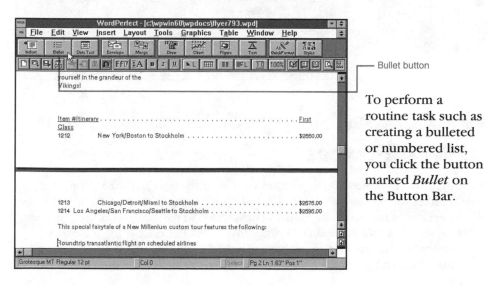

Bullet button

To perform a routine task such as creating a bulleted or numbered list, you click the button marked *Bullet* on the Button Bar.

Unlike the Power Bar, the Button Bar is fully customizable. You can reposition the Button Bar at the bottom of the window or on either side of the window. As you will learn in chapter 17, "Creating and Using Button Bars," you can create Button Bars containing any WordPerfect for Windows command you want, in any sequence. Therefore, you can create a Button Bar for every special task you perform in WordPerfect.

Feature Bars are designed to help you with specific tasks like creating an outline or entering formulas into the cells of a table. As such, Feature Bars appear automatically when you start a particular task. Feature Bars are like the Power Bar in that they are not customizable. You can, however, access their buttons either by clicking them with the mouse (as with the Button Bar or Power Bar), or you can select them by using predefined keystroke shortcuts.

Outline Feature Bar —

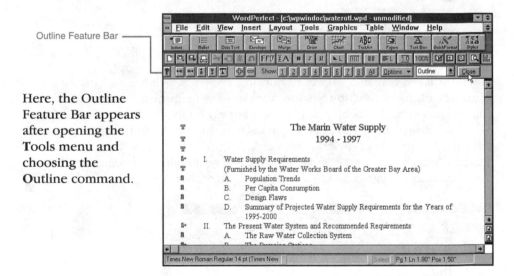

Here, the Outline Feature Bar appears after opening the **Tools** menu and choosing the **Outline** command.

File Compatibility with Other Versions of WordPerfect

Although, WordPerfect 6.0 for Windows uses a different file format from WordPerfect for Windows 5.1 and 5.2 and WordPerfect 5.1 and 6.0 for DOS, the latest version of the program ensures complete compatibility with these earlier versions of the Windows and DOS programs. WordPerfect 6.0 for Windows automatically converts files from these other DOS and Windows WordPerfect versions when you open the files with the **Open** command on the **File** menu.

WordPerfect for Windows performs this automatic conversion for numerous text and word processing formats. This feature makes it easy to open and edit a document created in another word processor, such as Microsoft Word for Windows 2.0, Ami Pro 3.0, or another version of WordPerfect for DOS or Windows. You can save your edits in the original word processing file format by selecting the appropriate file format in the Save File as **Type** drop-down list box when you save the document with the Save **As** command on the **File** menu.

Summary

In this overview of WordPerfect 6.0 for Windows, you were introduced to the program's special capabilities. You also learned how WordPerfect for Windows uses the Windows graphical environment to provide a program that is easy to learn and use. You were introduced to the prominent graphical aspects of WordPerfect for Windows such as drag-and-drop graphics, the Ruler, Power Bar, Feature Bars, and Button Bar and how they can help you complete your work.

You now are ready to begin learning specific features and commands in Word-Perfect 6.0 for Windows. In the next chapter, you will begin your mastery of WordPerfect by learning your way around the WordPerfect window, which is where you do all your work.

Getting Acquainted with WordPerfect for Windows

Understanding the WordPerfect program window

Understanding document windows

Using the mouse

Learning the keyboard

Getting on-line Help

This chapter explains how WordPerfect 6.0 presents information and interacts with you under Windows. As a part of the explanation, this chapter includes a complete description of the graphical elements used by WordPerfect for Windows. In addition to familiarizing you with the basic components of the windows used by WordPerfect, this chapter also shows you how to use the mouse and the keyboard and how to obtain on-line Help at any time while using the program.

If you already have used Windows programs and are eager to get started with WordPerfect, you may want to scan the sections on Windows in WordPerfect before jumping ahead to the next chapter. In that chapter, you will learn how to start the program and use WordPerfect commands.

Key Terms in This Chapter

Document window

Smaller window within the WordPerfect program window. The document window contains each document you have open. Each document window has its own title bar at the top of the window and contains the text of your document. WordPerfect for Windows enables you to have open up to nine document windows at one time.

Menu bar

The second bar at the top of the WordPerfect program window. The menu bar contains the WordPerfect pull-down menus.

Mouse pointer

Pointer with an arrow or I-beam shape you move with the mouse. The pointer assumes the shape of an arrow when you select WordPerfect commands and options or scroll the document. The pointer assumes the shape of an I-beam when you move it over text in your document.

Power Bar

The third bar at the top of the WordPerfect program window. The Power Bar contains a series of buttons that perform the most common tasks when you click them.

Scroll bars

Vertical and horizontal bars located on the right and bottom of the document window. These bars are preceded by arrows and contain a single box. Scroll bars are used to bring into view new parts of the document in the document window.

Title bar

The first bar in the program or document window. The title bar displays the name of the program or the path and file name of the active document. If the document has not yet been saved, the title bar contains a default file name such as `WordPerfect - [Document1]`.

WordPerfect program window

Framed area on-screen that contains the WordPerfect program. Consists of program title bar, menu bar, Power Bar, all document windows you have open, and the status bar.

Understanding the WordPerfect Program Window

Before you begin to use WordPerfect, take a few moments to become familiar with the various components of the *WordPerfect program window,* the name given to the window that contains all the WordPerfect commands, on-screen prompts, and documents you create. The WordPerfect program window appears full-size whenever you start the program. The WordPerfect window contains these components: title bar, menu bar, Power Bar, document window with a horizontal and vertical scroll bar, and status bar. The WordPerfect program window can also display another component called a *Button Bar,* and each document window can contain its own ruler bar.

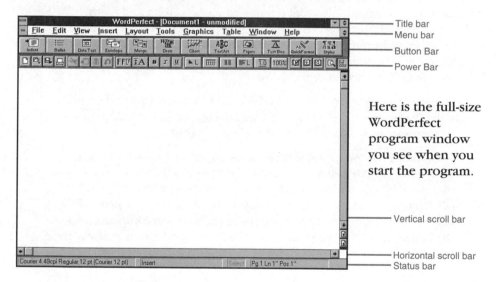

Title bar
Menu bar
Button Bar
Power Bar

Here is the full-size WordPerfect program window you see when you start the program.

Vertical scroll bar

Horizontal scroll bar
Status bar

When you first start the program right after installing it, the WordPerfect window contains only the title bar, menu bar, and Power Bar at the top, a full-size blank document called [Document1 - unmodified] in the middle, and the status bar at the bottom. The untitled document window contains scroll bars at the bottom and right that enable you to move through text quickly.

The Title Bar

The program title bar is the top line of the WordPerfect program window. This title bar is made up of the following components:

- *The program Control menu box.* Click this box (or press Alt+space bar) to display the program Control menu. You can use this menu to move or resize the WordPerfect program window, access the Program Manager in Windows, or close the WordPerfect program window and thereby exit WordPerfect.

- *The program name (WordPerfect).* When the active, or current, document window is full-size, the document's file name is displayed in square brackets following the program name. Each document is given a default file name, such as Document1, Document2, and so on until you save the document. Also, the document name is followed by the word "Unmodified" until you add some text to a new document or edit an existing document. When you resize the active document window, the file name disappears from the program title bar and appears in the title bar of the file's document window.

- *The Minimize button.* Click the Minimize button to shrink the entire WordPerfect program window (including all open documents) to a program icon at the bottom of the Windows desktop.

- *The Restore button or Maximize button.* Click the Restore button to reduce the WordPerfect program window in the Windows desktop so that the window no longer takes up the entire screen. When you use the Restore button to reduce the size of the WordPerfect program window, the Restore button changes to the Maximize button. Click the Maximize button to return the WordPerfect program window to full-size.

The Menu Bar

The second line of the WordPerfect program window holds the *menu bar*. The menu bar consists of pull-down menus that contain the program command options you select to perform various operations as you write and edit a document. When the active, or current, document window is full-size, the doc-menu bar also contains the document's Control menu box at the far left and the ment's Restore button at the far right. (These features disappear from the menu bar as soon as you reduce the size of the document window.)

To select a menu on the menu bar, you can click the menu name with the mouse. Or, you can press Alt and the letter in the menu name that is underlined. For example, Alt+F opens the File menu in the menu bar.

You also can activate the menu bar with the keyboard by pressing the function key, F10. Then use the arrow keys to move to the menu command and press Enter to select the command.

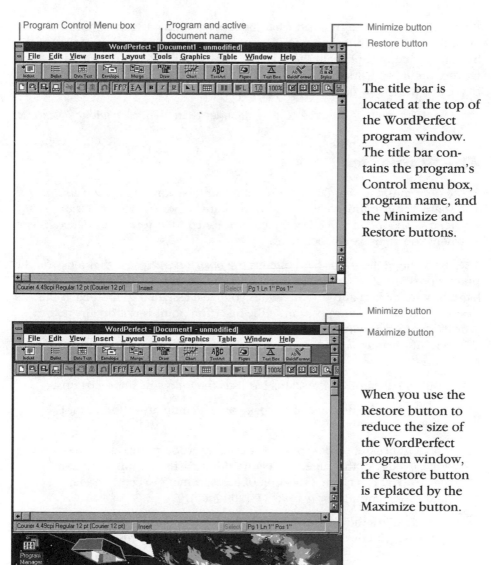

Program Control Menu box — Program and active document name — Minimize button — Restore button

The title bar is located at the top of the WordPerfect program window. The title bar contains the program's Control menu box, program name, and the Minimize and Restore buttons.

Minimize button — Maximize button

When you use the Restore button to reduce the size of the WordPerfect program window, the Restore button is replaced by the Maximize button.

The Power Bar

Right below the menu bar, you find the Power Bar. The Power Bar contains a variety of buttons useful for performing common tasks such as opening, saving, and printing your document. To use a button on the Power Bar, you must position the mouse pointer somewhere on the button, and then click the primary mouse button.

If you're not sure from the icon what the function of a particular button is, just position the mouse pointer on the button and a short description of the button's function appears in the title bar. For example, if you position the pointer on the very first button on the Power Bar (the icon with the blank sheet of paper), the following message appears in the title bar:

```
New Document - Create a new document in a new window - Ctrl+N
```

The Status Bar

At the bottom of the WordPerfect program window, you find the *status bar*. The status bar gives information about the status of your document. For example, it keeps you informed of the current font and font size of the text as well as where you are in your document.

The right side of the status bar contains the *position indicator* that tells you the precise position of the insertion point in your document. The left side of this bar tells you the font and text attributes you have assigned to the text at the insertion point's present position. If the insertion point is not on any text, WordPerfect lists the initial font used by your printer in this area. Sometimes this font information is temporarily replaced with information about the operation the program is currently performing (such as saving a file).

The position indicator on the status bar uses the following abbreviations:

- Pg tells you the number of the page on which the insertion point is located.

- Ln identifies the vertical position of the insertion point, measured from the top edge of the page. By default, this measurement is shown in inches. You can change this unit of measurement to centimeters, millimeters, points, or *w* units (1/1200 inch).

- Pos identifies the horizontal position of the insertion point, measured from the left edge of the page. As with Ln, by default this measurement is given in inches and can be changed to any of the other units of measurement mentioned previously.

- Col tells you which column is current when your document uses more than one column. If your document uses a single column, Col does not appear as part of the position indicator.

- Cell tells you which column and row is current in a WordPerfect table. When the insertion point is not in any of the cells of a table, Cell does not appear as part of the position indicator.

> *Tip:* By choosing **P**references on the **F**ile menu and selecting **P**references and **D**isplay in the Preferences dialog box, you can customize many aspects of WordPerfect's screen display with the options in the Display Preferences dialog box. To change the units of measure shown on the status bar, for example, select the Status Bar/Ruler Display option. To change which units are displayed in dialog boxes, change the Units of Measure option.

In between the font and position indicator information on the status bar, you see a Select indicator in light gray. This indicator remains dimmed until you select text with the mouse or press F8 (Select); then, Select appears as normal text, indicating that Select mode is on.

Customizing the Status Bar

Getting the Status Bar the Way You Want It

1. Open the **F**ile menu and choose **P**references. The Preferences dialog box appears.

2. Choose **P**references and **S**tatus Bar. The Status Bar Preferences dialog box appears.

3. To add a new item to the status bar, select its option in the Status Bar Items list box. When you select the option, an X appears in the option's check box.

4. To remove an existing item from the status bar, select its option to remove the X from the check box. Alternately, you can click the item directly on the status bar and then drag it off the status bar. When you release the mouse button, WordPerfect will delete the item.

continues

continued

5. To resize an item on the status bar, position the mouse pointer on one of the item's edges. When the pointer changes to a double-headed arrow, drag to the left or right (depending upon whether you want to make the item smaller or larger).

6. To rearrange the items on the status bar, click the mouse pointer on an item and then drag the item's outline to the new position.

7. To change the appearance of the information in each item or the item itself on the status bar, choose the **O**ptions button. The Status Bar Options dialog box appears. Select a new font, font size, or other appearance options. When you have finished, choose OK to return to the Status Bar Preferences dialog box.

8. When the status bar looks the way you want it to, choose the OK button. Remember that if you change your mind, you can always return the status bar to its default configuration by choosing the **D**efault button in the Status Bar Preferences dialog box.

WordPerfect for Windows lets you customize the information that appears on the status bar. This means that if don't want to see the Select indicator on the status bar, you can remove it. Likewise, if you want the Position indicator to be the first thing you see in the status bar and the Font indicator the last, you can reverse their positions.

The Button Bar

Displaying the Button Bar the Way You Want It

1. To display the WordPerfect Button Bar if it's not already showing, open the **V**iew menu and choose **B**utton Bar. Or you can click the Button Bar button on the Power Bar.

2. To select another Button Bar (see chapter 17 for details on how to create your own), click the secondary mouse button (the one opposite of the one you normally use to select items in WordPerfect for Windows) to open the Button Bar QuickMenu and then select the name of the Button Bar you want to use in the list. (To learn about QuickMenus, see "Choosing QuickMenu Commands with the Mouse," later in this chapter.)

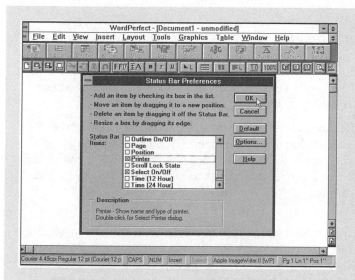

Here you see the status bar after customizing its items to include the CAPS, NUM, Insert mode, and Printer indicators.

3. To move the Button Bar to a new position in the WordPerfect program window, position the mouse pointer on one of the gray spaces between the buttons; then, when the pointer changes to a cupped hand, drag the outline of the Button Bar to its new position.

If you release the mouse button when the outline is somewhere within the document window, the Button Bar will become a palette of buttons that floats in its own dialog box in the document window (you can resize and shape this palette as you see fit). If you drag the outline of the Button Bar to the horizontal scroll bar and release the mouse button, WordPerfect for Windows will position the Button Bar at the bottom of the WordPerfect program window. If you drag the outline to the vertical scroll bar, the program will position the Button Bar on the right side of the WordPerfect window with the buttons arranged vertically. If you position the outline of the Button Bar on the left edge of the document window and release the mouse button, WordPerfect will position the Button Bar on the left side of the WordPerfect program window (again, in a vertical arrangement).

4. If you want to change the appearance of the buttons in the Button Bar or the Button Bar itself, click the Button Bar with the secondary mouse button and choose **Preferences** on the Button Bar Quick-Menu. Then choose the **Options** button to open the Button Bar Setup dialog box.

continues

33

continued

> You can use the options in this dialog box to select the new font and font size for the text in the buttons; increase or decrease the number of rows used by the Button Bar; select between displaying only **Text**, **P**icture, or **P**icture and **T**ext (the default); and select a new location for the Button Bar (**L**eft, **R**ight, **T**op, **B**ottom, or **P**alette).
>
> 5. When you have finished changing the appearance options in the Button Bar Setup dialog box, choose the OK button to return to the Button Bar Preferences dialog box. Then choose the Close button in the Button Bar Preferences dialog box to close it and return to your document window.

The WordPerfect Button Bar is a series of buttons that you can use instead of the pull-down menus to select particular WordPerfect commands. To select a command from the WordPerfect Button Bar, simply position the mouse pointer on the button and click the primary mouse button. If you use the mouse regularly, you will find that using the Button Bar is the easiest way to select the WordPerfect commands you commonly use while creating and editing documents.

WordPerfect for Windows makes it easy to move the Button Bar to different positions around the WordPerfect program window. Simply drag the Button Bar to its new position around the borders of the WordPerfect program window or somewhere within the current document window.

Button Bar ———

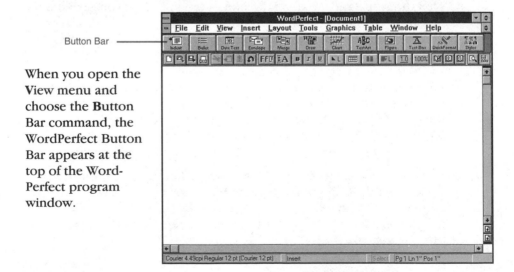

When you open the View menu and choose the **B**utton Bar command, the WordPerfect Button Bar appears at the top of the Word-Perfect program window.

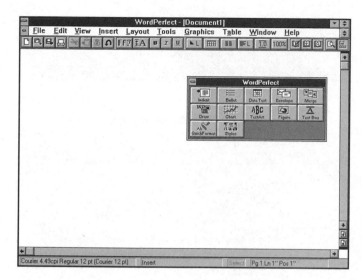

When you drag the Button Bar into the current document window, it becomes a palette of icons appearing in its own dialog box.

You can resize and reshape this Button Bar palette by dragging the appropriate side of its dialog box. If you make the dialog box too small to display all the buttons, WordPerfect for Windows will add a scroll bar to the palette so that you can use it to select buttons that no longer appear in the dialog box. To move the Button Bar palette within the document window, drag it by its title bar. To remove the display of the Button Bar palette altogether, click the Control button in the upper left corner of its dialog box.

> *Tip:* You can easily customize the contents of the WordPerfect Button Bar and even create Button Bars of your own. For complete information on how to create and edit Button Bars, see chapter 17.

Understanding the Components of a Document Window

WordPerfect can handle up to nine different documents at one time. Each document you work on is placed in a separate document window. As with the WordPerfect window, every document window has its own Control menu box, title bar, and Size buttons (Minimize and Maximize or Restore).

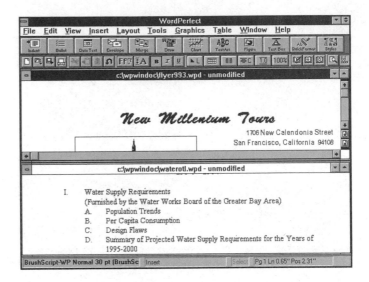

Here, two document windows are open in the WordPerfect program window.

Scroll Bars

A document window also contains some elements not found in the WordPerfect window. One of the most prominent of these unique elements is the scroll bars that appear at the bottom and far right of the document window.

When the active document window is full-size, the scroll bars appear to be part of the WordPerfect window itself.

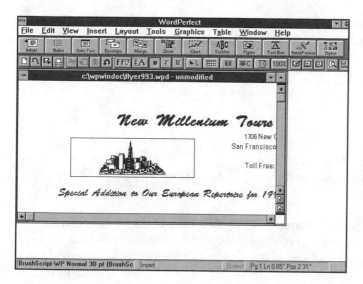

When you reduce the size of the document window, you can tell that the horizontal and vertical scroll bars are not a part of the WordPerfect window.

Because only a very small part of any document can be seen at one time in a document window, WordPerfect offers several methods for viewing new parts of the document you're working on in the document window. The horizontal and vertical scroll bars provide one of the easiest ways to bring new parts of a document into view.

You can use the following techniques when you use a scroll bar:

- To scroll up or down the document several lines at a time, click the up or down scroll arrow in the vertical scroll bar. To scroll left or right, click the left or right scroll arrow in the horizontal scroll bar.

- To scroll up or down the document one window-length at a time, click the vertical scroll bar once above or below the scroll box (the box right below the scroll arrow pointing upward). To scroll left or right one window-width at a time, click the horizontal scroll bar ahead or behind its scroll box.

- To scroll up or down the document one page at a time, click the up or down scroll arrow inside the document window at the very bottom of the vertical scroll bar.

- To scroll the document continuously (either vertically or horizontally), click the appropriate scroll arrow and hold the mouse button down until the part of the document you want to see comes into view, and then release the mouse button.

- To scroll to a particular position in the document, drag the scroll box to the approximate position on the vertical scroll bar before you release the mouse button. For example, to scroll to the middle of the document, drag the scroll box to the middle of the vertical scroll bar.

The Ruler Bar

Turning the Ruler On and Off

Open the **View** menu and choose **Ruler**; or press Alt + ⇧Shift + F3.

The Ruler Bar is an optional element of the document window. You can display the Ruler Bar when you need to change some of the formatting of your document. The Ruler Bar is one of the most handy editing tools in WordPerfect for Windows. You can use the Ruler Bar to change the left and right margins or modify your tab settings.

When you turn on the Ruler Bar display, the Ruler appears at the top of the current document window.

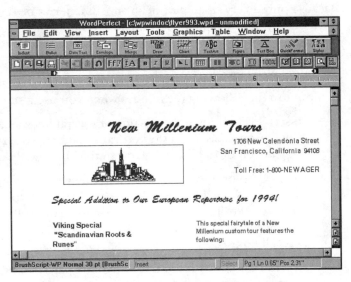

The **Ruler** command is a toggle. To turn off the Ruler Bar, you select the command sequence a second time. When you turn on the Ruler Bar in a document, WordPerfect does not turn on the Ruler Bar in any other document window you have open. To display the Ruler in another document window, make that window active by selecting the document in the **Window** pull-down menu, and then select the **Ruler** command on the View menu. Or press Alt+Shift+F3.

Tip: To have WordPerfect for Windows automatically display the Ruler Bar in all document windows that you open, open the **File** menu and choose **P**references, and then choose **D**isplay under Preferences. Choose the **R**uler radio button, and then choose the Show Ruler on New and Current Document option to place an X in its check box. Note that at this point, you can also change the way the Ruler Bar appears by selecting any of the Ruler Options (**T**abs Snap to Ruler Grid, Show Ruler Bar Guides, and Sculptured Ruler Bar) to remove the X from its check box.

The Reveal Codes Window

Opening and Closing the Reveal Codes Window

1. To open the Reveal Codes window, open the View menu and choose Reveal Codes; or press Alt + F3. To open the Reveal Codes window with the mouse, drag the Reveal Codes split bar either at the bottom or the top of the vertical scroll bar until the Reveal Codes window is the size you want, and then release the mouse button.

2. To close the Reveal Codes window, open the View menu and choose Reveal Codes; or press Alt + F3 a second time. To close the Reveal Codes window with the mouse, click the Reveal Codes window with the secondary mouse button, and then select Hide Reveal Codes in the QuickMenu. Or you can drag the border separating the Reveal Codes and the document window all the way up or down to the very top or bottom of the document window, and then release the mouse button.

As you select various editing commands in WordPerfect for Windows, the program inserts formatting codes into the document. These codes tell your printer how to produce the various formatting effects. Normally, these codes are hidden in the document (thus their name, *hidden codes*). You can, however, split the document window and reveal these codes (thus the name, *Reveal Codes*).

WordPerfect offers a couple of methods for splitting the active document window and displaying Reveal Codes. When the document window is split, the regular text without codes appears in the upper pane and the text with the hidden formatting codes appears in the Reveal Codes window in the lower pane.

You can open the Reveal Codes window with the mouse or keyboard. When you open this window with the mouse, you decide how large to make the window. The first time you open this window with the keyboard, WordPerfect splits the document window so that the Reveal Codes window takes up about a quarter of the screen. If you then size the Reveal Codes window with the mouse, the Reveal Codes window retains this size when you open it with the keyboard.

Drag the Reveal Codes window split bar up or down to open the Reveal Codes window.

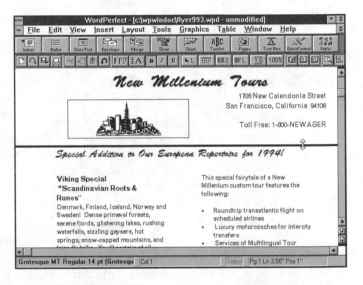

When you release the mouse button, WordPerfect for Windows splits the document window, placing the Reveal Codes window at the bottom.

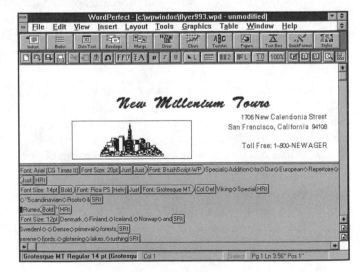

Tip: To have WordPerfect for Windows automatically display the Reveal Codes window in all the document windows that you open, open the File menu, choose Preferences, and then choose Display under Preferences. Next, choose the Reveal Codes radio button, and then choose the Show Reveal Codes on New and Current Document option to place an X in its check box. Note that at this point, you can also change the way the size and the codes appear in the Reveal Codes window. You can modify such things as the font and font size shown in the codes, the color of the text and background of the Reveal Codes window, and whether or not the hidden codes appear sculptured and display such details as their current settings.

Using the Mouse

As you learned in chapter 1, under the GUI (Graphical User Interface) provided by Windows, the mouse provides the most natural way to select menu options or elements in the document. Even the most diehard keyboard enthusiasts may use the mouse to select document text, as well as to select, move, and size document windows and graphics in WordPerfect for Windows. Although some users at the outset (especially those upgrading from WordPerfect 5.1 under DOS) may choose WordPerfect menu options with the quick function key equivalents, many users may find themselves in time using the mouse even to make menu selections.

WordPerfect for Windows supports either a two-button mouse (like the Microsoft mouse) or a three-button mouse (like the Logitech mouse). Most program functions are accessed by using the *primary mouse button* (this is the left button when you use the mouse on the right side of the keyboard as a right-handed person would normally do, and the right button when you have switched the mouse buttons and use the mouse on the left side of the keyboard as a left-handed person would normally do). You use the *secondary mouse button* (the right button for you right-handed people and the left button for you southpaws) only when you need to display a QuickMenu (the menu of options attached to a particular object in WordPerfect for Windows like the Power Bar, Button Bar, scroll bars, document text, and so on).

Note, however, that it makes no difference whether your mouse has two or three buttons because WordPerfect usually uses only the primary mouse button. Because WordPerfect has no use for the middle button and only one function for the secondary button on a mouse, whenever you see an instruction that says "click the mouse" in this book, you know to click the primary mouse button (anytime you have to click the secondary mouse button to get something done, this will be stated explicitly in the text).

WordPerfect for Windows relies on the primary mouse button except when opening QuickMenus with the secondary button.

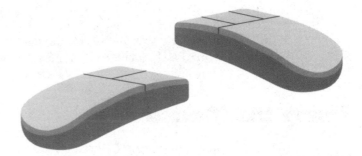

To use the mouse to select pull-down menus and QuickMenus, dialog box options, and text, you need to master three basic mouse-button techniques in WordPerfect for Windows. These techniques include:

- *Clicking.* Pressing and then immediately releasing the mouse button.

- *Double-clicking.* Clicking the mouse button twice in rapid succession. The timing of the clicks is crucial in double-clicking. If you wait too long between clicks, WordPerfect interprets your action as two clicks instead of one double-click. WordPerfect for Windows also supports triple-clicking (three rapid clicks in a row) and quadruple-clicking (four rapid clicks in a row) when selecting sections of text with the mouse!

- *Dragging.* Clicking and holding the mouse button as you move the mouse.

Tip: You can adjust the double-click and tracking speed of your mouse in Windows. To adjust these items, select the Main group window, double-click the Control Panel icon to open the Control Panel window, and then double-click the Mouse icon to open the Mouse window and select options. Here's also where you lefties can switch the primary and secondary mouse buttons so that the primary (right) button corresponds to the inside button and the secondary (left) button corresponds to the outside button when you position the mouse on the left side of the keyboard (a much more natural arrangement for us southpaws).

Selecting Menu Commands with the Mouse

The WordPerfect pull-down menus (**File** through **Help**) are normally displayed in the menu bar at the top of the WordPerfect program window. Each menu contains various options that appear as soon as you open the menu by selecting it from the menu bar.

In addition to the WordPerfect pull-down menus, you also can access the Control menu, a standard Windows menu. The Control menu's options enable you to switch between programs and minimize or restore the WordPerfect document window. To access this menu, click the Control menu box (the box with the line in its center located in the upper left corner of the WordPerfect document window). When selecting the Control menu, be careful not to double-click the Control menu box; this action closes the WordPerfect document window instead of displaying the Control menu options.

To select a WordPerfect pull-down menu, position the mouse pointer on the menu name and click the primary mouse button. The menu name becomes highlighted, and opens to display all the options available on that menu. If you forget which menu contains the option you want, you can locate the option by dragging the mouse across the menus on the menu bar. As you drag the mouse over each menu name, the program displays the menu options and a description of the menu's purpose appears in the title bar of the WordPerfect program window.

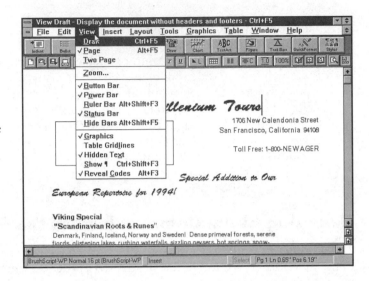

To open the View menu with the mouse, position the pointer on View, and then click the primary mouse button.

To choose a command from a selected menu, click the command name. If you already know which menu contains the command you want to use and you want to select the command quickly, you can save time by dragging to that menu and then continuing to drag down until the option is selected (indicated by highlighting) before you release the primary mouse button. To close a menu without making a selection, click outside the menu, or press Esc until you have backed out of all the options.

If a menu command appears dimmed (in light gray letters), the command is not currently available for selection. If a check mark appears in front of a command, the command can be toggled on and off. When a key combination follows an option, you can use that keyboard shortcut to select the command without accessing the pull-down menus at all.

If a menu option is followed by ellipses (three dots, as in the case of the Font command [Font...] on the Layout menu), a dialog box with more options appears as soon as you select the option. If an option is followed by a triangle pointing to the right (▶), a cascading menu containing more options appears to the right of the option as soon as you click the command or drag to it. After a cascading menu is displayed, you can choose any of its options as you normally would.

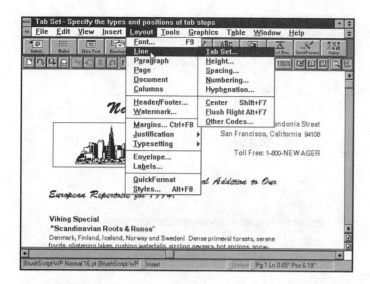

The **Line** command on the **Layout** pull-down menu is attached to a cascading menu that opens as soon as you select it.

Choosing QuickMenu Commands with the Mouse

In addition to the pull-down menus that open from the menu bar at the top of the screen, WordPerfect 6.0 for Windows includes a set of QuickMenus that appear directly from on-screen objects such as the Power Bar, Button Bar, scroll bars, and the status bar. To open a QuickMenu, click the object with the secondary mouse button (the right mouse button—unless you have switched the mouse buttons in Windows). When a QuickMenu is open, you choose a command the same way you choose a command on a WordPerfect pull-down menu: either by clicking the command or dragging to it.

Selecting Text with the Mouse

In a WordPerfect document, you must select the text you want to modify before you can choose an editing command. WordPerfect displays the text you select by highlighting it (that is, showing the text in inverse video).

A line of text is
selected.

Whenever you move the mouse pointer over text, the pointer changes from
an arrowhead to an I-beam shape. To select text with the mouse, position the
I-beam immediately in front of the first character you want to include, and then
drag the mouse until all the remaining text is highlighted. To select several
words on a single line of text, drag to the right until all the words are highlighted. To select several lines of text, drag across the line and then down until
all the lines are highlighted. To select a paragraph of text, drag diagonally from
the upper left corner to the lower right corner.

When selecting text with a mouse, you can use shortcuts that don't involve
dragging. These shortcuts are explained in table 2.1.

Table 2.1   Shortcuts for Selecting Text with a Mouse

Selection	Shortcut
Single word	Double-click somewhere in the word. WordPerfect selects all the characters in the word plus the space following the word.
Sentence	Triple-click (three rapid clicks in a row) somewhere in the sentence. WordPerfect selects all the text in the sentence plus the space following the period (or other punctuation such as a question mark or exclamation mark).

Selection	Shortcut
Paragraph	Quadruple-click (four rapid clicks in a row) somewhere in the paragraph.
Any amount of text	Position the I-beam pointer in front of the first character and click. Press and hold down ⌈⊹Shift⌉, and then position the I-beam right after the last character, and click again (this technique is known as the *Shift+click method*). If you ever select text in error, click the mouse again to deselect the text before you choose any WordPerfect commands that would act on the highlighted text.

You can also select a sentence, paragraph, or all text in the document with the mouse without having to click or drag through the text. Instead, use the QuickMenu attached to the left margin of the document. To open this Quick-Menu, click the secondary mouse button in the left margin on the line containing the sentence or paragraph you want to select (anywhere will do when selecting all the text). Then select the command you want to use: Select **Sen**tence to select the sentence on the current line, Select **P**aragraph to select the current paragraph, or Select **A**ll to select all text in the entire document.

Sizing and Moving a Window with the Mouse

The WordPerfect window and each document window you open contain two Size buttons located in the upper right corner: a Minimize button (downward pointing arrow) followed by a Restore (double-headed arrow) or Maximize button (upward pointing arrow). Click the Minimize button on the title bar of the WordPerfect window to reduce the entire WordPerfect program to a program icon at the bottom of the Windows desktop.

Here, you see the WordPerfect program window as it appears when you reduce the program to the WP program icon in Windows.

To restore the WordPerfect program window to its previous size, double-click the WP program icon; or, click the icon and select the **R**estore command on the Control menu that appears. If the WordPerfect window was not full-size when you clicked the Minimize button, a Maximize button replaces the Restore button. You then can click the Maximize button to enlarge the window so that the program takes up the entire screen.

To reduce the active document window to an icon in the WordPerfect window, choose the **Mi**nimize command on the document Control menu (opened by clicking the Control menu box that appears on the line with menu bar to the immediate left of the **F**ile menu).

To restore the document window to its previous size, double-click the document icon; or, click the icon and then select the **R**estore command on the Control menu that appears. If the document window was not full-size when you clicked the Minimize button, you then can click the Maximize button to enlarge the window so that the document program fills the entire work area in the WordPerfect window.

To size the WordPerfect program window or a document window somewhere between full-size and an icon, click the Restore button at the far right of the title bar. After a window is sized between these two extremes, you can easily change the size and shape of the window with the mouse.

To change the size, position the pointer on the frame of the active document window until the pointer changes to a double-headed arrow. Then drag the mouse to resize the window. You can resize a window in the following ways:

- To make the window shorter from the bottom, position the pointer on the bottom side. When the pointer changes to a double-headed arrow pointing up and down, drag the mouse upward. To make the window taller, click the same side but drag the mouse downward instead.

- To make the window wider from the right, position the pointer on the right side. When the pointer changes to a double-headed arrow pointing left and right, drag the mouse to the right. To make the window narrower, drag the mouse to the left.

- To make the window smaller by shortening it from the bottom and narrowing it from the right, position the pointer on the lower right corner. When the pointer changes to a double-headed arrow pointing diagonally up to the left and down to the right, drag up toward the left. To make the window larger, drag the mouse down toward the right. You also can resize a window in a single direction by clicking the top or left frame. You can resize a window in two directions by dragging from any of the other three corners as well.

When the document window is the size and shape you want, simply release the mouse button.

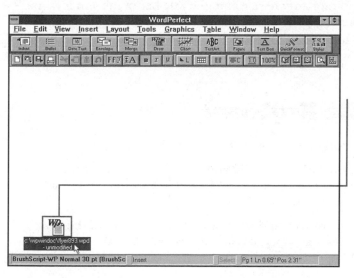

Here, you see a document window after reducing it to a document icon in the WordPerfect program window.

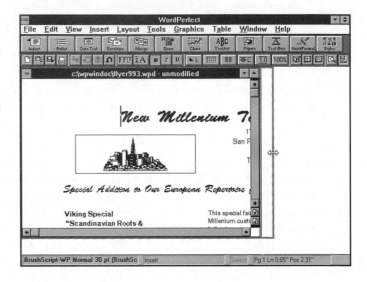

In this example, you make the document window wider by dragging the mouse pointer to the right.

Moving the WordPerfect window in the Windows desktop or a document window in the WordPerfect window is a snap with the mouse. You simply position the mouse pointer anywhere within the title bar of the window you want to move, and then drag the mouse in the direction where you want to move the window. When the window is positioned where you want it on the screen, release the left mouse button.

Learning the Keyboard

WordPerfect uses the following areas of the keyboard:

- The function keys labeled F1 to F12 and located at the top of the enhanced keyboard, or labeled F1 to F10 and located on the left side of the Personal Computer AT keyboard.

- The alphanumeric, or "typing," keys located in the center of the keyboard. This area includes special keys such as Esc, Ctrl, Alt, Shift, Backspace, and Enter.

- The numeric and insertion point keypads on the right side of the keyboard. On the enhanced keyboard, these keypads are separate. In the original keyboard design, the keypads are combined.

This is an AT keyboard.

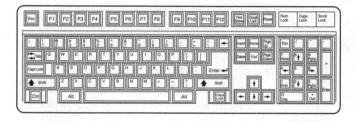

This is an Enhanced Keyboard.

The Function Keys

When using WordPerfect for Windows, you can select many commands either with the pull-down menus or function key equivalents. WordPerfect assigns up to six functions to the function keys F1 to F12, depending on whether or not the key is used alone or in combination with Shift, Alt, Alt+Shift, Ctrl, or Ctrl+Shift. Table 2.2 shows you the default function key assignments in WordPerfect 6.0 for Windows. This keyboard arrangement is called the *CUA (Common User Access) keyboard.* This keyboard is used throughout the book.

	Alone	⇧Shift	Alt	Alt + ⇧Shift	Ctrl	Ctrl + ⇧Shift
F1	Help	Help: What Is?	Thesaurus	Grammatik	Speller	*****
F2	Find	Find Next	Find Previous	*****	Replace	*****
F3	Save As	Save	Reveal Codes	View Ruler	Redisplay	Show Symbols
F4	Open	New	Exit	*****	Close	Clear
F5	Print	Full Page View	Page View	Hide Bars	Draft View	*****
F6	Next Pane	Previous Pane	Next Window	Previous Window	Next Document	Previous Document
F7	Indent	Center	Flush Right	Decimal Tab	Hanging Indent	Double Indent
F8	Select	Select Cell	Styles	*****	Margins	*****
F9	Font	Merge	Sort	*****	Generate	*****
F10	Menu	Repeat	Macro Play	Feature Bar	Macro Record/Stop	*****
F11	Figure	Text Box Edit	Text Box Create	*****	Horizontal Line	Vertical Line
F12	Table	Table Lines/Fill	Table Number	*****	Table Format	Table Data

If you are familiar with the function keys in WordPerfect 5.1 or 6.0 for DOS, you will quickly discover that almost none of the function key assignments you know are used in the CUA keyboard! Don't despair, however. WordPerfect for Windows supplies a special DOS keyboard file that converts the function key assignments back to those used in WordPerfect 5.1 and 6.0.

To select this keyboard file and restore the WordPerfect 5.1 and 6.0 function key assignments, follow these steps:

1. Open the **File** menu, and then select the Preferences option. The Preferences dialog box appears.

2. Choose **Preferences** followed by **Keyboard** command in the Preferences dialog box. The Keyboard Preferences dialog box appears.

3. Highlight <WPDOS Keyboard> in the **Keyboards** list box.

4. Choose the **Select** button in the Keyboard Preferences dialog box, or press Enter to make your selection and close the Keyboard Preferences dialog box.

5. Choose the Close button or press Enter to close the Preferences dialog box and return to the current document window.

The WordPerfect 5.1 and 6.0 function key assignments you are familiar with are now active in WordPerfect 6.0 for Windows. Note, however, that because of differences between the DOS and Windows interface, you will find that some of the 5.1 and 6.0 function keys are no longer needed and are reassigned.

When you are ready to learn the standard CUA keyboard, you can turn off the WordPerfect DOS keyboard by opening the Keyboard Preferences dialog box, highlighting <WPWin 6.0 Keyboard>, and then choosing the **Select** button.

The function key assignments for both the CUA and DOS keyboards are written on either side of the plastic WordPerfect template that comes with the software. The assignments are color coded as follows:

- Black means that the function key is used alone.

- Green means that you must hold down Shift as you press the function key.

- Blue means that you must hold down Alt as you press the function key.

- Blue with a green dot after it means that you must hold down Alt+Shift as you press the function key.

- Red means that you must hold down Ctrl as you press the function key.

- Red with a green dot after it means that you must hold down Ctrl+Shift as you press the function key.

The Alphanumeric Keys

The alphanumeric keys are similar to those on a typewriter. In addition to the number, letter, and punctuation keys in the standard QWERTY arrangement, the alphanumeric keys include Tab↹, Caps Lock, ←Backspace, ⏎Enter, ⇧Shift, Ctrl (Control), and Alt (Alternate).

The Tab key inserts a tab stop to indent the first line of a paragraph. You also can use this key to move to the next set of options in a dialog box. On the IBM keyboard, the combination of Shift+Tab is referred to as *Back Tab*. You use Back Tab in a WordPerfect document as the Margin Release to move the insertion point one tab stop to the left. In a dialog box, pressing Back Tab takes you to a previous set of options.

The Backspace key (abbreviated BkSp in Windows programs) deletes the character immediately to the left of the insertion point. Don't confuse this key with the left-arrow key (←) located on the cursor keypad, which is marked identically. The left-arrow key is nondestructive; it simply moves the insertion point one character to the left.

The Enter key is used to insert a carriage return (referred to more often as a *hard return* in WordPerfect). Press this key to end a paragraph or a short line of text, such as the name and address in the return address portion of a business letter.

The Shift key is used to create uppercase letters or access the shifted character on keys that combine two different characters (such as the @ symbol on the 2 key and the ? character on the / key). Note that pressing the Caps Lock key produces only uppercase letters; it does not access the shifted character on such keys.

The Shift, Ctrl, and Alt keys also are used in combination with the function keys to access particular WordPerfect commands.

Selecting Pull-Down Menu Commands with the Mnemonic Keys

You can press the Alt key to access the WordPerfect menu bar if you don't use the mouse. If you know which menu you want to use, you can press Alt plus the letter that is underlined in the menu name (referred to as the *mnemonic key*). For example, to display the options on the File menu, you can press Alt+F. After a WordPerfect pull-down menu is displayed, you can select a command simply by typing its mnemonic letter (that is, the one that is underlined in the command). To save changes to your document, you can select the **S**ave command on the **F**ile menu by pressing Alt+F, then pressing S. When you learn the command, you can accelerate the key sequence by pressing Alt+F+S to save changes to your document.

Note: Remember that in this book, the mnemonic keys are indicated by boldface rather than underline. (A boldface character is easier to see on a printed page than a single underlined character.)

The Shortcut Keys

In addition to the function keys, WordPerfect offers several shortcuts that use the Ctrl key in combination with a single letter for selecting commonly used WordPerfect commands. Some of these shortcut keys, such as Ctrl+X for **E**dit Cu**t** and Ctrl+V for **E**dit **P**aste, are common to most Windows programs. Other shortcut keys, such as Ctrl+G for **E**dit **G**o To and Ctrl+W for **I**nsert **C**haracter are unique to WordPerfect for Windows.

Table 2.3 shows the shortcuts in WordPerfect and describes the WordPerfect command that each shortcut performs.

Table 2.3   The Shortcut Keys in WordPerfect 6.0 for Windows

Shortcut Keys	*Function*
Ctrl + A	Abbreviations
Ctrl + B	Bold
Ctrl + ⇧Shift + B	Bullets and Numbers
Ctrl + C	Copy to Clipboard (same as Ctrl + Ins)
Ctrl + D	Date text
Ctrl + ⇧Shift + D	Date code
Ctrl + E	Center

continues

Table 2.3   Continued

Shortcut Keys	Function
Ctrl + G	Go To
Ctrl + I	Italics
Ctrl + J	Full justification
Ctrl + K	Convert case
Ctrl + L	Left justification
Ctrl + N	New Document
Ctrl + Q	Find QuickMark
Ctrl + Shift + Q	Set QuickMark
Ctrl + O	Open document
Ctrl + Shift + O	Outline styles
Ctrl + P	Print page
Ctrl + Shift + P	Page number display
Ctrl + R	Right justification
Ctrl + S	Save
Ctrl + T	Templates
Ctrl + U	Underline
Ctrl + V	Paste from Clipboard
Ctrl + W	WordPerfect characters
Ctrl + X	Cut to Clipboard

Shortcut Keys	Function
Ctrl + Z	Undo
Ctrl + ⇧Shift + Z	Undelete

The Cursor-Movement Keys

The insertion point is the flashing vertical bar (referred to as the *cursor* in DOS programs) that marks the place where the next character you type appears in a document. The insertion point also marks the location of hidden formatting codes that control the final appearance of the document when you select various formatting commands, such as a tab indent with Tab or boldfacing text with Ctrl+B.

In a WordPerfect document, you can use the direction keys on the cursor-movement keypad to move the insertion point through text. Note, however, that pressing one of these keys has no effect any place in a document where you haven't yet entered text.

The numeric keypad on the keyboard contains both direction and numeric keys. To move the insertion point with these keys, the Num Lock key must not be engaged. If Num Lock is engaged, WordPerfect will enter numbers in your document instead of moving the insertion point. To disengage Num Lock so that you can move the insertion point instead of enter numbers, press the Num Lock key in the upper left corner of the numeric pad. If you have an enhanced keyboard, you can use the separate cursor-movement keypad to move the insertion point even when Num Lock is engaged.

> *Tip:* For complete information on which keys to use to move the insertion point in the document, see tables 3.1 and 3.2 in the next chapter.

Getting On-Line Help

WordPerfect 6.0 for Windows offers extensive on-line Help in a special Help window you can access at any time while using the program. You even can keep the Help window displayed by resizing and rearranging both the WordPerfect and Help windows so that they are side-by-side (a process known as *tiling* in Windows). With tiling, you can get help on a particular procedure and keep those instructions displayed on-screen in the Help window as you perform the procedure in a nearby document in the WordPerfect window.

You also can get help by choosing the **Help** menu and selecting one of the Help commands listed in table 2.4.

Table 2.4   The Help Menu Commands in WordPerfect for Windows

Option	Function
Contents	Displays an alphabetical list of all Help topics. To get information about a particular topic, select the appropriate cross-reference.
Search for Help On	Lets you search for a particular Help topic.
How Do I	Displays an alphabetical list of commonly performed tasks (such as Move a section of text or Change line spacing) arranged by categories (such as Edit and Format). To get information on how to perform a particular task, click the task, or select the task and press Enter.
Coach	Leads you through each of the steps necessary to complete the task. As WordPerfect for Windows coaches you through the required steps, you are actually performing the task in the current document.
Tutorial	Lets you run an on-line tutorial that teaches you the basics of using WordPerfect for Windows.

Option	Function
About WordPerfect	Displays the About WordPerfect dialog box that contains the program's license number and release date. When using WordPerfect's free customer support telephone lines, you often need to have this information handy.

Most Help topics contain cross-references indicated by an underlined keyword or phrase in the Help text (and shown in green on a color monitor). Each cross-reference leads to related Help topics that can give you more Help information.

To select a cross-reference and display a related Help topic with the mouse, position the mouse pointer somewhere on the cross-reference until the pointer changes into the hand icon with the index finger pointing up. Then click the mouse button.

You also can select a cross-reference with the keyboard. Simply press Tab until the appropriate cross-reference is highlighted, and then press Enter.

Getting Context-Sensitive Help

To get context-sensitive help that is directly related to the action you are performing, open the **Help** menu and choose the **What Is** command, or press the Shift+F1 (What Is Help) key. The program then adds a question mark enclosed in a bubble to the mouse pointer. While the pointer assumes this shape, you can get help on any pull-down menu or menu option by selecting the menu or option with the mouse, or on any key or key combination by pressing the key or keys.

Using the Help Menus

The WordPerfect Help window has its own menu bar that contains the **File**, **Edit**, **Bookmark**, and **Help** menus. When this window is displayed, you can choose any of these Help menus just as you would a WordPerfect menu on the menu bar in the WordPerfect window.

The **File** menu enables you to open other Help files (the WPWP60US.HLP is the main Help file used by the program) with the **Open** command, print the currently displayed Help topic with the **P**rint Topic command, select your printer with the **P**rinter Setup command, or close the WordPerfect Help menu with the E**x**it command.

The **E**dit menu in the WordPerfect Help window contains two options: **C**opy and **A**nnotate. You can use the **C**opy command to copy to the Clipboard the text of the currently selected Help topic. After the text is copied to the Clipboard, you can paste this Help information into a document by first selecting the document window and then choosing the **P**aste command on the **E**dit menu in the WordPerfect program window.

You can use the **A**nnotate command to add your own comments and notes to a particular Help topic. Select the topic you want to annotate, and then choose the **A**nnotate command on the **E**dit menu of the WordPerfect Help window. Type your comments in the Annotation list box, and then select the OK button. When the program closes the dialog box, a paper clip appears to the left of the Help topic heading to remind you of the attached note. To display your comments in the Help Annotation box, simply click the paper clip.

The **B**ookmark menu contains a single command, **D**efine. You can use this command to mark your place in the Help topics you refer to frequently so that you can return to them quickly.

To mark a Help topic for speedy retrieval, select it with the Help Index or select one of the commands on the WordPerfect **H**elp menu. Then choose the **D**efine command on the **B**ookmark menu in the WordPerfect Help window. The program places the name of the currently selected Help topic in the Bookmark Name text box. If you want to name the bookmark something else, type the new name in this box. Otherwise, select the OK button. WordPerfect will number the bookmark name you assign and add it to the Boo**k**mark menu. To return to a Help topic, select the Bookmark name from this menu (click it with the mouse or type its number with the keyboard).

The **H**elp menu in the WordPerfect Help window has three commands: How to Use **H**elp, Always on **T**op, and **A**bout Help. Select the How to Use **H**elp command to obtain general information about using the Microsoft Help system (which WordPerfect uses along with all other Windows programs). Select the Always on **T**op command to ensure that Microsoft Help window is always on top of any other window that you have open. Select the **A**bout Help command to display a dialog box that shows the version and copyright notice for Microsoft Help.

Using the Help Command Buttons

In addition to the pull-down menus, the WordPerfect Help window contains five command buttons you can use to navigate through Help topics. These Help command buttons perform the tasks listed in table 2.5.

Table 2.5   The Help Command Buttons

Help Button	Function
Contents	Activates the WordPerfect Help contents command described earlier in this chapter.
Search	Enables you to search for specific Help topics that contain keywords.
Back	Displays the most recent Help topic you selected. You can use this button to continue to move back through the topics you have reviewed. When you reach the first topic you looked at, this button becomes dimmed.
History	Displays the Windows Help History dialog box listing previously viewed Help topics. The most recently viewed topic is listed first. To redisplay a topic, double-click it.
Print	Prints the current Help topic.

Searching for a Help Topic

Using Keywords to Search for a Help Topic

1. Select the Search button.

2. Type the first few letters of the keyword until it is selected in the list of keywords displayed in the list box; or, scroll through this list until you highlight the desired keyword.

3. Click the Show Topics button or press ⏎Enter to search the Help topics.

continues

61

continued

> WordPerfect indicates the number of topics found and displays them in the list box at the bottom of the dialog box.
>
> 4. Select the Help topic you want to view in the list box at the bottom of the dialog box, and then select the Go To button. If you decide that you don't want to review any of the Help topics, select the Close button or press Esc to return to the WordPerfect Help window.

The Search command button in the WordPerfect Help window enables you to select a keyword and then search for all Help topics that contain that keyword. After you have located all topics containing the keyword, you can select a topic and display its Help information in the Help window.

 ## Using the Coaches

Performing a New Task with a Coach

1. Open the Help menu and choose the Coach command. The Coach dialog box appears.

2. Select the task in the dialog box, and then choose the OK button. The Coach instructions appear on-screen.

3. Choose the Continue button to walk through the steps. When the Coach instructs you to do something, you can perform the action or you can choose the Show Me button; when you choose Show Me, WordPerfect shows you the action to be performed. To get more information about a particular step, choose the Hint button.

4. When you are ready to return to the document and quit Coach, choose the Quit button.

In WordPerfect 6.0 for Windows, you can use the Coach feature to get step-by-step instructions for performing common tasks such as creating bulleted lists or adding a header or footer to your document. After you select the task for which you need help in the Coach dialog box, the program displays a series of dialog boxes that "coach" you through each step necessary to perform the task. Sometimes the program may give you a choice between choosing the commands or performing the action via a Show Me button. You can quit the Coach feature at any time prior to completing the entire task by choosing the Quit button.

Exiting Help

To exit Help, you need to close the Help window. You can either open the File menu and choose the Exit command in the WordPerfect Help window menu bar or press Alt+F4, or you can simply double-click the Help window's Control menu box. Note that you cannot close the WordPerfect Help window by pressing the Esc key.

Summary

In this chapter, you learned how WordPerfect presents information on the screen, how to identify the components of the windows used by WordPerfect, and how you can use the mouse and keyboard. Next, you learned how Word-Perfect uses the various parts of the keyboard, including the alphanumeric keys, numeric keypad, and function keys. Finally, the chapter introduced you to WordPerfect's comprehensive on-line Help system and showed how you can use it to obtain help at any time when using the program.

In the next chapter, you will begin learning how to use WordPerfect. You will learn how to start the program, open a new document, select WordPerfect commands, save your document, and exit the program. As part of this process, you also will learn how to open other programs in addition to WordPerfect and transfer information between WordPerfect and the other programs you have open.

Getting Started

3

Starting WordPerfect for Windows

Creating a new document

Moving the cursor

Choosing WordPerfect commands

Saving a document

Using WordPerfect in Windows environment

This chapter introduces you to the fundamentals of starting and using WordPerfect for Windows. Here, you become acquainted with the operation of WordPerfect under Windows and learn basic word processing skills, including how to position and size the document window, select menu options, start a new document, save your work, and exit WordPerfect.

If you are upgrading from WordPerfect for DOS, you will want to pay particular attention to the sections in this chapter that explain how to move the cursor in a document and select text with the keyboard. You will find that most of the techniques you are familiar with for these procedures have changed in WordPerfect for Windows.

Key Terms in This Chapter

Clipboard

A special area of computer memory that holds the text or graphics you cut or copy. You can paste data you moved to the Clipboard into different documents in WordPerfect or in different applications.

Cursor (insertion point)

The flashing, vertical marker that indicates where the next character will be inserted when you type. To move the cursor, use the cursor keys or position the I-beam pointer in the text and click the left mouse button.

File name

A descriptive name you give your document when you save it. The file name can be up to eight characters with a three-character extension and is always displayed in the title bar.

Hard return

The code that WordPerfect inserts when you press the Enter key to end a paragraph of text.

Soft return

The code that WordPerfect inserts at the end of a line after word wrap occurs.

Word wrap

The word processing feature that automatically moves a word to the beginning of the next line if the word won't fit at the end of the line within the current margin settings. With word wrap, you don't have to press the Enter key except at the end of a paragraph.

Starting WordPerfect for Windows

You have several alternatives for starting WordPerfect. This section on starting WordPerfect assumes that you have already successfully installed the program onto your hard disk.

Starting WordPerfect from the Program Manager

Starting WordPerfect from the Program Manager

1. Start Windows at the C:\> prompt in DOS by typing win and pressing ⏎Enter.

2. If you can't see the WordPerfect group window in the Program Manager, choose the **W**indow menu, and then choose either the **C**ascade option (or press ⇧Shift + F5) or the **T**ile option (or press ⇧Shift + F4).

   Locate the WordPerfect group window in the Program Manager window. This window contains the WordPerfect program icon.

3. Position the mouse pointer on the WordPerfect program icon and double-click the left mouse button to start the program.

When you start Windows by typing win in DOS, you are immediately placed in the Program Manager. The easiest way to start WordPerfect from the Program Manager is to activate the WordPerfect group window and then select the WordPerfect program icon.

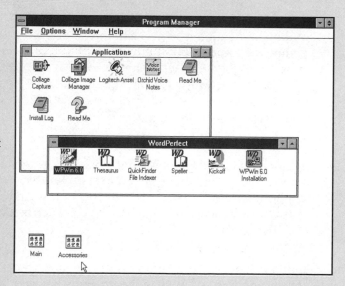

Note that you also can start the program by clicking the WordPerfect program icon to select it (the title bar containing WordPerfect becomes highlighted) and then either pressing Enter or choosing **O**pen from the File menu.

Starting WordPerfect with the Windows File Run Command

Starting WordPerfect from Windows' File Menu

1. Open the **F**ile menu and choose **R**un.

2. Type the following start-up command for WordPerfect in the Command Line text box of the Run dialog box:

    wpwin.exe

This is the Run
dialog box after
you type wpwin.exe
in the **C**ommand
Line text box to
start WordPerfect
for Windows.

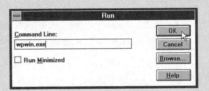

During installation, you may have prevented WordPerfect from adding the location of the directory that contains the WordPerfect program to the PATH command in your AUTOEXEC.BAT file. If this is the case, in the text box of the Run dialog box, you must precede the start-up command with the path name that indicates the disk drive and directory path, as in

    c:\wpwin\wpwin.exe

3. Position the mouse pointer on the OK button and click the left mouse button (or press ↵Enter) to start WordPerfect. If you want the application to shrink to the WordPerfect program icon as soon as the program starts, click the Run **M**inimized check box before you click the OK button.

This method for starting WordPerfect doesn't require you to have the WordPerfect group window open in the Program Manager. Instead, you type the WordPerfect start-up command in a dialog box.

If you make an error when entering the WordPerfect start-up command, Windows will display an Application Execution Error dialog box that contains the following message:

```
Cannot find file; check to ensure the path and filename are
correct
```

If this dialog box appears, click the OK button in the center of the dialog box (or press Enter). Repeat the preceding steps to edit the Command Line text box in the Run dialog box.

Note: You also can start Windows and WordPerfect at the same time from DOS. Simply type win, press the space bar, and type wpwin at the C:\> prompt. As soon as the Program Manager is loaded, Windows will immediately start WordPerfect.

Opening a Document When You Start WordPerfect

You can open a document at the same time that you start WordPerfect. To do this, enter the WordPerfect start-up command in the Command Line text box of the Run dialog box; then press the space bar and type the path and file name of the document in which you want to work. For example, to open a document called JONES.LTR in a WordPerfect directory named LETTERS, you would enter wpwin.exe letters\jones.ltr in the Command Line text box of the Run dialog box.

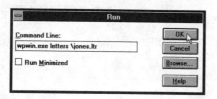

Here, the start-up command is followed by a document name. The document will open at the same time WordPerfect starts.

Tip: You also can start Windows and WordPerfect and open an existing WordPerfect document at the same time from DOS. To do this, type the Windows start-up command, press the space bar, type the WordPerfect start-up command, press the space bar, and then type the name of the document. For example, to open a document named JONESLTR located in the C:\WPWIN\DOCS directory of your hard disk at the time you start WordPerfect, enter win wpwin c:\wpwin\docs\jonesltr at the C:\> prompt.

Starting WordPerfect from the File Manager

Starting WordPerfect from the File Manager

1. To start the File Manager from the Program Manager in Windows, open the Main group window and double-click the File Manager icon (the two-drawer filing cabinet).

2. Use the vertical scroll bar to display the WPWIN folder in the Directory Tree window, and then double-click this folder; or press `PgDn` until you select the WPWIN folder, and then press `⏎Enter` to open it.

3. Double-click the WPWIN.EXE file icon; or use the arrow keys to select the file (shown by a dotted line around the icon and file name) and press `⏎Enter` to start WordPerfect.

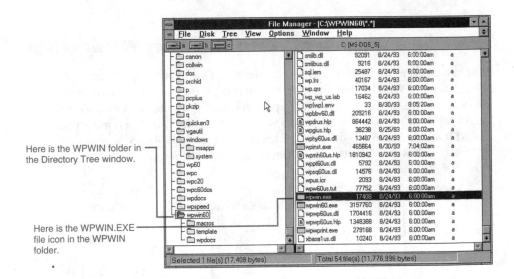

Here is the WPWIN folder in the Directory Tree window.

Here is the WPWIN.EXE file icon in the WPWIN folder.

Note: Remember that when you quit WordPerfect, you will return to the File Manager if that's the place in Windows where you launched the program. To get back to the Program Manager, quit the File Manager by opening the File menu and choosing the Exit option. When the Exit File Manager dialog box appears, click the OK button or press Enter.

You also can start WordPerfect from the File Manager by double-clicking a document that is "associated" with WordPerfect. This will open the document at the same time WordPerfect is started. See "Associating Files with WordPerfect for Windows," later in this chapter, for more information about file association.

Creating a New Document

Creating a New Document

> Begin typing in the WordPerfect for Windows document screen.
>
> or
>
> To open a new document in a separate WordPerfect window, open the File menu and choose New.

When you start WordPerfect for Windows without also selecting a document to open, the program displays a blank, full-size document window in which you can enter the text for your new document. WordPerfect automatically assigns the temporary name DOCUMENT1 to the first open document window until you use the **File Save** or **File Save As** command to name and save the file. This temporary name appears in the title bar of the document window. If you already have document windows open, such as DOCUMENT1 and DOCU-MENT2, WordPerfect assigns the next available numbered name to your document window, in this case DOCUMENT3.

If you ever need to start a new document while you still have one or more existing documents open, you can open a new document window. To open a new document window, open the File menu and choose the New option. The new document window becomes the active one and is assigned the next available default file name.

Remember that WordPerfect enables you to have up to nine documents open at one time, provided that your computer has sufficient memory.

Selecting a Template for the New Document

Retrieving a Template for an Open Document

1. Open the File menu and choose Template; or press Ctrl + T.

WordPerfect for
Windows displays
the Templates
dialog box.

2. Highlight a template from the Document Template to Use list.

   To view a template before retrieving it, choose the View button. WordPerfect for Windows displays the template in a separate Viewer window, where you can use the arrow keys and scroll bars to view more of the template. To exit the Viewer and return to the Templates dialog box, double-click the Viewer windows' Control menu box; or press Alt + F4.

3. Choose OK to retrieve the template you selected.

WordPerfect for Windows comes with over 40 document templates. A *template* is a ready-made document that may contain text, formatting settings, View options (such as hiding or displaying the Button Bar and Power Bar), and graphic images. The supplied templates provide attractive and useful document designs that can save you a great deal of time. You can also design and save your own templates. When you open a new document, WordPerfect for Windows automatically applies the Standard template.

Understanding WordPerfect's Default Settings

Whenever you start WordPerfect, the program puts into effect a number of *default settings* (or simply *defaults*). These default settings affect the way the program interacts with you, the way the program displays information, and the initial formatting used in each new document you create.

Typical program default settings determine the location of different types of files created by WordPerfect, when backups of documents are made, how and what information is displayed on-screen, the initial print settings, and which keyboard is loaded each time you start WordPerfect.

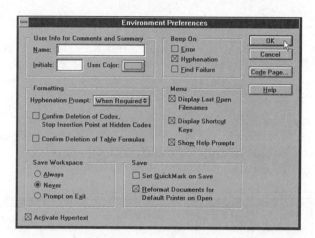

To see or change program default settings that determine the way WordPerfect interacts with you, display the Environment Preferences dialog box by choosing the File Preferences Environment command.

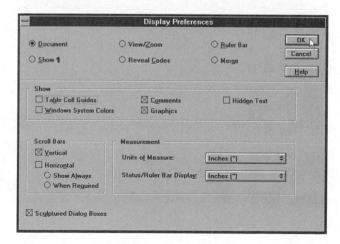

To see or change program default settings that determine the way information is displayed on-screen, display the Display Preferences dialog box by choosing the File Preferences Display command.

Typical document defaults determine such things as the margins; line spacing; type and justification; and the number, type, and spacing of preset tabs in a new document. Depending on the type of document you are creating, you may have to alter some or all of these default settings to correctly format the document. WordPerfect enables you to modify a default setting either just for the documents you are currently creating or for all documents you create in the future.

> *Note:* Remember that the changes you make in the Preferences dialog box affect the documents you create in the future, not just the current document.

To see the Ruler, choose the View **R**uler command or press Alt+Shift+F3. The Ruler shows the margins and tabs in effect. To see the Power Bar, choose the View **P**ower Bar command. The Line Spacing button on the Power Bar shows line spacing, and the Justification button shows the current justification.

To change the format settings only for the document you are working on, choose the new format settings you want from the Ruler, the Power Bar, or the **L**ayout menu. Changing the format settings for all future documents is explained in the next section.

Power Bar

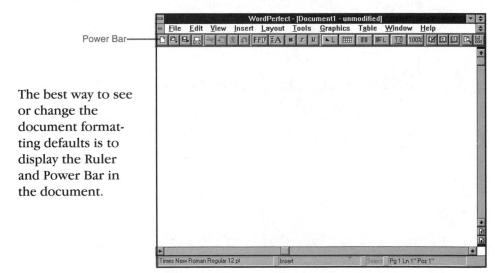

The best way to see or change the document formatting defaults is to display the Ruler and Power Bar in the document.

Changing WordPerfect's Default Settings

Changing Formatting Defaults

1. Open the Layout menu, choose Document, and then choose Initial Codes Style.

2. Make any desired formatting changes in the Styles Editor.

3. Choose Close to return to the document window.

   You will learn about editing styles in chapter 7, "Formatting Pages."

When you choose a new document setting from the pull-down menus, Power Bar, or Ruler, WordPerfect inserts the appropriate formatting code in the Reveal Codes window. For example, if you make full-justification the new default justification (instead of left-justification) by choosing the Layout Justification Full command, the program inserts [Just:Full] in the Reveal Codes window.

When you return to the active document, your changes are in effect in the document, from the cursor's present position on. When you open a new document, the new format settings also are in effect for that entire document.

Entering Document Text

To begin entering text for a new document, simply start typing. As you type, characters appear at the location of the cursor (insertion point), and the Pos measurement in the status bar increases. When you reach the end of the line, the program's word wrap feature automatically moves the cursor to the next line and inserts a soft return code, [SRt], in the Reveal Codes window to mark the place where the line breaks.

When you want to end a paragraph, press Enter; WordPerfect inserts a hard return at that location and moves the cursor to the beginning of the next line. To insert a blank line in the text, press Enter without entering any text on that line.

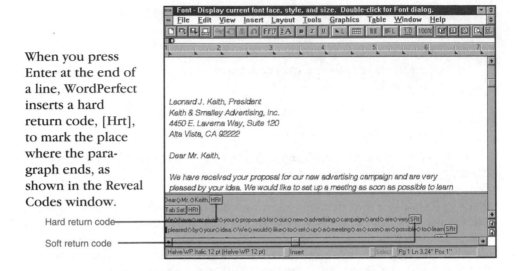

When you press
Enter at the end of
a line, WordPerfect
inserts a hard
return code, [Hrt],
to mark the place
where the para-
graph ends, as
shown in the Reveal
Codes window.

Hard return code

Soft return code

If you later add text to a line or delete text from a line in a paragraph,
WordPerfect adjusts the placement of the soft return code in each line to suit
the edit. WordPerfect does not, however, adjust the placement of the hard
return code.

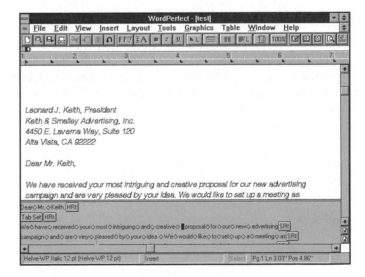

Here you see the
same paragraph
after editing its text.
Notice that the
position of the soft
return code at the
end of each line has
changed. Notice,
too, that the
placement of the
hard return codes
has not changed.

To join two paragraphs or to delete a blank line in the document, you need to delete the hard return at the end of the line. Normally, hard returns are not visible in the regular document window. You can, however, delete them "blindly" by positioning the cursor at the beginning of the first line of the paragraph you want to join and pressing Backspace, or by positioning the cursor at the beginning of the blank line you want to remove and pressing Del.

Seeing Placement of Formatting Characters

Displaying Formatting Codes

1. Open the **File** menu, choose **Preferences**, and then choose **Display**. WordPerfect displays the Display Preferences dialog box.

2. Choose **Show**.

3. Choose Show Symbols on New and Current Document, and then mark the check boxes for the formatting symbols you want displayed in the document screen.

4. Choose **OK** to close the Display Preferences dialog box, and then choose **Close** to return to the document window.

   The formatting codes in your document are now represented by the characters you selected in the Display Preferences dialog box.

   You can also toggle the display of formatting symbols on and off by choosing View, **Show**; or press Ctrl + Shift + F3.

To see the placement of hard returns, spaces, tabs, and other formatting characters in the text of your document, you can assign to each feature a character that you can see in the normal document window.

Choosing Draft Mode

In Page mode, a document that uses a number of proportionally spaced fonts in different sizes can be harder to read than a document that displays all text in one font. To overcome this problem, you can change from the default Page mode to *Draft mode* by opening the View menu and choosing **D**raft, or by pressing Ctrl+F5.

In Draft mode, WordPerfect displays all text in the document window in a uniform, monospaced font, regardless of the font and type size you assign to the text. However, any graphics in the text disappear. They either are not visible at all in the regular document or are simply represented by empty graphics boxes that show the graphics' placement but not their contents, depending on whether **G**raphics is selected in the **V**iew menu.

> *Note:* Although the text in Draft mode appears monospaced, the status bar indicates the actual font and type size of the text at the cursor's location. The document will print in the text's actual font, not the monospaced font.

Draft mode not only simplifies reading the text but also speeds up the screen display. With this faster screen display, you can scroll through the text of your document more quickly when you edit it.

When you have finished entering and editing the text of your document and want to see how it will look when printed, leave Draft mode and return to Page mode by choosing the **V**iew **P**age command or pressing Alt+F5. Note that Draft mode is not saved as part of the document; when you next open a document edited in Draft mode, WordPerfect will display the document in Page mode.

Creating a Business Letter

Typing the Letter

1. Open the File menu and choose New to begin a new document.

2. If you plan to print the text on letterhead, adjust the top margin by pressing ⏎Enter. The Ln indicator in the status bar shows how far down on the page the letterhead will print.

3. To align the date flush right, open the Layout menu, choose **Line, and** then choose **Flush Right**; or press Alt + F7.

4. Type the date.

   or

   Insert a date code by opening the Insert menu, choosing **Date**, and then choosing one of the following options from the **Date** submenu:

   • To insert the text of the current date according to your computer's clock, choose Date **Text**; or press Ctrl + D from the editing screen.

   • To insert a date code that is updated each time you retrieve the letter, choose Date **Code**; or press Ctrl + ⇧Shift + D from the editing screen.

5. Press ⏎Enter several times to move the insertion point down the page to position the first line of the address. Type the address, pressing ⏎Enter at the end of each line. Finally, type the remainder of the letter.

6. To save the letter, open the File menu and choose Save **As**; or press F3. WordPerfect displays the Save As dialog box.

7. Type a name for the letter in the Filename text box, and then choose OK.

Creating an Envelope

Creating an Envelope

1. If you followed the steps in the preceding section for typing a business letter, open the letter now. Open the **File** menu and choose **Open**; or press Ctrl + O. WordPerfect displays the Open File dialog box.

2. Type the file name of a letter in the File**n**ame text box, or select the letter in the list box. Then choose OK.

3. Position the cursor on or above the address in the letter, and then open the **L**ayout menu and choose Envelope.

WordPerfect displays a sample graphic in the bottom left corner of the Envelope dialog box to show you how the printed envelope will look.

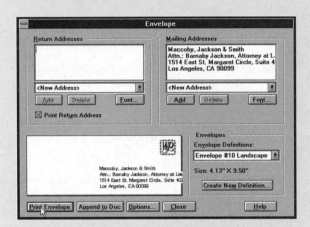

Note: Not all printers have an envelope definition in the PRS printer driver file. If your printer does not have an envelope definition, you will see the Envelope Definition dialog box. To learn how to create an envelope definition, see chapter 7, "Formatting Pages."

4. Choose the **Pr**int Envelope button to print the envelope.

   WordPerfect for Windows can automatically "read" the address from a letter displayed on-screen, and then print the address on an envelope.

   Tip:If the document contains more than one address, WordPerfect for Windows may identify the wrong address. To ensure that it chooses the correct one, move the cursor into the desired address or select the address.

The following options are available in the Envelope dialog box:

- **Ad**d. Choose this option to add the address displayed in the **M**ailing Addresses list to a stored list of addresses you frequently print on envelopes. WordPerfect lists the first line of each address. To choose an address from the list, highlight it and press Enter, or double-click its name.

  You can type an address in the **M**ailing Addresses box, and you can format the address with fonts (choose Fo**nt** to display the Font dialog box).

- **R**eturn Addresses. You can type a return address in this space. WordPerfect shows the position of the return address in the sample envelope. To store this address so that you can use it in the future, choose the **Ad**d button, as described in the preceding section.

- Print Re**tu**rn Address. Select this check box if you want to print the return address; deselect the check box if you want to omit the return address.

- Enve**l**ope Definitions. Choose this option and select a new envelope definition from the drop-down list.

- Create New **D**efinition. This button displays the Create Envelope Definition dialog box, where you can specify a new envelope paper size, type, and location, as well as the envelope printer orientation.

Note: Envelope sizes and definitions are discussed in detail in chapter 7.

- **Print Envelope.** This command button prints the envelope and returns you to the document window.

- **Append to Doc.** This command button moves the insertion point to the end of the current document, inserts a hard page break, and inserts the envelope definition and text. This button is useful when you want to save an envelope definition with a document, or when you want to switch to an envelope printer bin and print the envelope after printing the text of a letter.

- **Options.** This command button displays the Envelope Options dialog box, where you can adjust the position of the mailing and return addresses.

In the Envelope Options dialog box, you also can have WordPerfect automatically read the ZIP code from the address and print a USPS POSTNET bar code on the envelope.

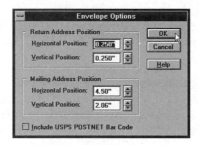

Moving the Cursor

As you create a new document, you will often need to move the cursor (insertion point) to a new place in the text to add or delete characters and words. You can move the cursor to new places in the text with either the mouse or the keyboard. Remember, however, that WordPerfect doesn't allow you to move the cursor to a location where no text yet exists; the cursor moves only through text, spaces, or hidden codes.

Moving the Cursor with the Mouse

The quickest way to reposition the cursor in text that's visible in the active document is with the mouse. Simply position the I-beam pointer so that it is between the characters in the text that need editing, and click the left mouse button.

If, however, the text you need to change is not visible in the document window, you first need to scroll the text into view before you can reposition the cursor with the mouse. If you use the vertical scroll bar to scroll the text, remember that WordPerfect doesn't change the cursor's position. To reposition the cursor, you still need to click the I-beam at the appropriate place in the text after you finish using the scroll bar (see chapter 2 for a discussion of using scroll bars).

Moving the Cursor with the Keyboard

WordPerfect offers a wide array of key combinations, many of which not only move the cursor in the text but also scroll the document. You may find it faster to use key combinations that combine scrolling and moving the cursor than to use the vertical scroll bar and mouse. For example, to scroll to the end of the document by pressing Home and then End is a lot faster than dragging the scroll box to the bottom of the vertical scroll bar and then clicking the I-beam pointer in the text. In many cases when entering text, you may also find it faster to move the cursor with these cursor-movement keys than to use the mouse—you don't have to take your hands away from the keyboard with the cursor-movement keys.

Using the Arrow Keys

Use the keys marked with arrows on either the cursor keypad or, if the Num Lock key is disengaged, the numeric keypad to control the direction of cursor movement. You can use these keys alone and in combination with other keys (see table 3.1).

Table 3.1   Cursor Movement with the Arrow Keys

Keystroke	Movement in Text
PgUp	Moves the cursor up one line.
PgDn	Moves the cursor down one line.
←	Moves the cursor one position to the left.
→	Moves the cursor one position to the right.
Ctrl + →	Moves the cursor to the beginning of the next word to the right.
Ctrl + ←	Moves the cursor to the beginning of the next word to the left.
Ctrl + PgUp	Moves the cursor up one paragraph.
Ctrl + PgDn	Moves the cursor down one paragraph.

Using the PgUp and PgDn Keys

You can use the PgUp and PgDn keys to move the cursor one window-length at a time. PgUp moves the cursor to the top of the active document window. PgDn moves the cursor to the bottom of the active document window.

Note: In WordPerfect for Windows, PgUp and PgDn perform the same functions as the Screen Up key (–) and the Screen Down key (+) on the numeric keypad in WordPerfect for DOS. Pressing – or + on the numeric keypad in WordPerfect for Windows inserts a – or + symbol.

Using the Home and End Keys

You can use the Home and End keys alone and in combination with the Ctrl and Alt keys to move the cursor (see table 3.2). Remember that Home always moves to the beginning of a particular section of text (a line, page, or document), and End moves to the end of it.

Table 3.2   Cursor Movements with the Home and End Keys

Keystroke	Movement in Text
Home	Moves to the beginning of the line.
End	Moves to the end of the line.
Alt + Home	Moves to the beginning of the page.
Alt + End	Moves to the end of the page.
Ctrl + Home	Moves to the beginning of the document.
Ctrl + End	Moves to the end of the document.

Note: To position the cursor before the hidden codes in the text, press the key combination twice. For example, to move the cursor so that it precedes all codes at the beginning of the document, press Ctrl+Home twice.

Using the Go To Key

Using the Go To Key
1. Open the **Edit** menu and choose **Go To**; or press Ctrl + G. WordPerfect displays the Go To dialog box.

2. Choose **Position** and select a position in the Position list box.

   or

continues

85

continued

Choose Page **N**umber. Type a page number or select a page number with the scroll arrows.

or

Choose **B**ookmark and type a bookmark name or select it from the drop-down box.

or

Choose **T**able and type a table name or select it from the drop-down list. To go to a cell or range of cells in the table, choose **C**ell/Range and type a cell/range specification or choose it from the drop-down list.

3. Choose OK.

Use the Go To accelerator key (Ctrl+G) or the **E**dit **G**o To command to move the cursor to a particular page number, to the top or bottom of the current page, or to the cursor's previous position.

When you press Ctrl+G or choose the **E**dit **G**o To command, WordPerfect displays the Go To dialog box.

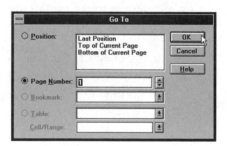

You can choose from the following options in the Go To dialog box:

- To move the cursor to the beginning of a specific page, type the page number in the Page Number text box and choose OK. (When you open the Go To dialog box, the Page Number text box contains the current page number, but typing a new number replaces it.)

- To move the cursor to the beginning of the current page, select the **T**op of Current Page option in the **P**osition list; then choose OK.

- To move the cursor to the bottom of the current page, select the **B**ottom of Current Page option in the **P**osition list; then choose OK.

- To move the cursor to its previous position in the document, select the Last Position option in the **P**osition list; then choose OK.

- To move to a bookmark, choose **B**ookmark, select the bookmark from the drop-down list, and choose OK. To move to a table, choose **T**able, select the table from the drop-down list, highlight or type a table **C**ell/ Range, and then choose OK.

Choosing WordPerfect Commands

WordPerfect commands can be selected directly from the pull-down menus on the menu bar or, in many cases, with function-key equivalents. When you choose some of the more complex WordPerfect commands, the program displays a dialog box that contains more options from which you can choose.

> *Note:* If you use the mouse, you also can choose WordPerfect commands by clicking a particular button on the Button Bar or Power Bar. For complete information on how to customize the Button Bar and Power Bar, and how to create your own Button Bars, see chapter 17, "Creating and Using Button Bars."

Choosing Menu Options

When choosing commands from the pull-down menus, you can use either the mouse or the keyboard. To choose a menu with the mouse, move the pointer to the menu's name and click the left mouse button; the menu opens to display its options. To choose an option from the open menu, click the option. To choose a menu option quickly, drag the pointer down the appropriate menu until you highlight the option; release the mouse button.

To use the keyboard to choose a menu option, press Alt or F10 to select the menu bar; then press the right- or left-arrow key to select the menu you want to open. When the appropriate menu is highlighted, press Enter to open the menu and view its options. To choose an option on the menu, press the down-arrow key until you highlight the option, and then press Enter.

If you highlight an option that has a triangle (➤) next to its name, a *cascading menu* opens to the right of the option. To choose an option from the cascading menu, press right arrow to move to the menu, press down arrow until you highlight the option you want, and then press Enter.

Instead of using the arrow keys to choose menus and menu options, you can type the letter that's underlined in the menu or option name. To open the File menu, for example, press Alt+F. Then, to select the Save option on the File menu, press S. As you learn each command sequence, you can accelerate it by combining the option letters. For example, once you know the File Save command, you can just press Alt+F+S to save your document.

> *Tip:* When accelerating command sequences, keep the Alt key pressed down as you type the menu option letters. Also keep in mind that many of the command sequences used by WordPerfect for Windows are the same in other Windows programs. Commands such as **File Open** (Alt+F+O) and **File Save As** (Alt+F+A), for example, are common to programs such as CorelDRAW! and 1-2-3 for Windows. By learning and using the Alt+*letter* commands in WordPerfect, you sometimes are also learning commands used in other applications.

If a menu option has a keyboard shortcut, its shortcut key is shown next to the option name in the menu. To use a shortcut key to choose a WordPerfect command, press the key combination; the menu does not have to be open. For example, to use a shortcut key to bold some text you have selected, press Ctrl+B. This method is much faster than opening the Font menu and choosing the **B**old option, with either the keyboard or the mouse.

Choosing QuickMenu Options

WordPerfect for Windows' *QuickMenu* feature provides a quick way to choose commands. You click the right mouse button in an area of the screen that pertains to the command you want to choose, and WordPerfect displays a QuickMenu that contains various options.

If you click the right mouse button in the text area of the document window, for example, WordPerfect displays a QuickMenu of commands that affect document text: **P**aste (not available unless text is selected), **F**ont, **Q**uickFormat, **Sp**eller, **C**enter, Flush **R**ight, and **I**ndent. If you click the right mouse button in the header area of the document screen, you see a QuickMenu with options related to headers and footers: **H**eader/Footer and **W**atermark. The header area is located at the top of the document window and is displayed only in Page mode.

QuickMenus are also available from many dialog boxes. For example, clicking the right mouse button in the Filename list in the Save As or Open File dialog box displays the same list of options shown when you choose File **Options**. Clicking the right mouse button on the Directories list displays options for creating and removing directories and for toggling the display between directories, the QuickList, or both.

Wherever you are working in WordPerfect for Windows, click the right mouse button to familiarize yourself with the QuickMenu shortcuts.

Choosing Options in Dialog Boxes

If you choose a menu option that has an ellipsis (...) next to its name, WordPerfect displays a dialog box full of more options. In addition to using dialog boxes to request additional information from you about a menu choice, WordPerfect also uses dialog boxes to display warnings and program messages that inform you of the status of a command or why WordPerfect is unable to carry out the command.

You can reposition a dialog box in the WordPerfect window by dragging its title bar; however, you cannot resize a dialog box.

Dialog boxes often contain different types of boxes and buttons designed to help you make your selections. WordPerfect uses standard Microsoft Windows boxes and buttons, as well as some unique ones.

The standard Windows dialog box includes these items:

- A *text box* provides a data-entry area for you to enter information. To make a new entry, position the cursor (insertion point) in the text box by clicking it with the mouse pointer; then make your edits. Alternatively, you can replace the entry by pressing Tab to highlight the text you want to replace and then typing the new entry.

- A *list box* displays all available choices for an item. If a list box contains more choices than it can display at one time, use the list box's scroll bar to display more choices. To select a different option, click that option with the mouse; or press up arrow or down arrow to highlight the option, and then press Enter.

- A *drop-down list box* displays the default or current selection. This type of box contains a drop-down button to the right of the current choice. To select a different option with the mouse, click the drop-down button to display a list of the available choices; then click the option you want. To select a new option with the keyboard, press up arrow or down arrow until the option you want appears in the list box.

- A *check box* displays a list of options you can toggle on and off. When a check box is selected, an X appears in the box; when a check box is deselected, the box is empty. To select a check box option, click its box with the mouse to put an X in it. You also can select a box by pressing Tab until the item is selected (indicated by a dotted rectangle around the item name), and then press the space bar. To deselect a check box option, click its box with the mouse or press the space bar to remove the X from it.

- An *option button* (also known as a *radio button*) is an option that appears in a group of mutually exclusive options. You can select only one option button from a group of option buttons. When an option button is selected, it contains a black dot. To choose a different option button, simply click it; the previous choice becomes deselected. Alternatively, you can use the arrow keys or type the option button's underlined letter to choose an option button.

- A *command button* (also known as a *pushbutton*) executes a particular action as soon as you choose the button. Command buttons are large rectangular buttons that display the name of the command they initiate. If the name of the command is followed by an ellipsis (...), WordPerfect displays a new dialog box of choices when you click the command button. If the button has a heavy outline, it is the default button; you can select it at any time simply by pressing Enter.

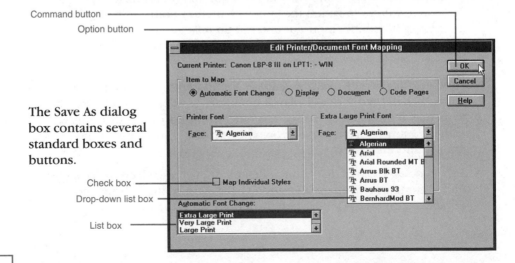

The Save As dialog box contains several standard boxes and buttons.

The Button Bar Editor dialog box uses option buttons.

In addition to the standard Windows boxes and buttons in WordPerfect, you also encounter two buttons that are (so far) unique to WordPerfect for Windows:

- A *pop-up list button* displays the default or current selection, either on a wide button with two triangles at one end (one pointing up and the other down) or in a text box with a separate pop-up list button at one end (one triangle pointing left or down). When you click a pop-up list button and hold down the mouse button, a pop-up list of available choices appears.

  To choose a new option, drag down to the option you want to use and then release the mouse button. To choose a new option with the keyboard, press Tab to select the option that has a pop-up list button, or press the hot key for that item, press the space bar to display a list of options, and press the down arrow until you highlight the option you want to use. Then press Tab to move to the next item in the dialog box, or press Enter to make your choice and exit the dialog box. Note that you cannot use the keyboard to display the pop-up list when the current option is displayed in a text box separate from its pop-up list button. In such a case, you must type the new setting in the text box.

- A *list button* follows text boxes that require a file or directory name. To select a new file or directory from a Select File or Select Directory dialog box, click the list button and then select the desired directory or file in the **Directories** or **Files** list boxes.

The QuickFinder dialog box contains pop-up list buttons for the File Pattern and Search For text boxes. In this example, the Search For pop-up list is open.

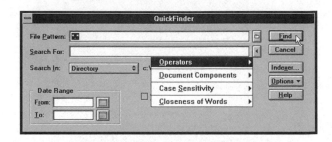

The File Preferences dialog box contains list buttons that enable you to specify directory locations for files of various types.

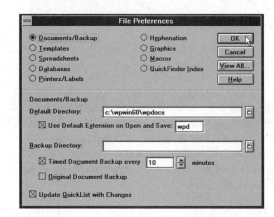

Note: WordPerfect uses more pop-up lists than drop-down lists. You will encounter drop-down list boxes only when there are so many available choices that the choices must be displayed in a list box with a scroll bar.

Many times you need to move around a dialog box to a different item so that you can select a new option for it. If you are using a mouse, click the current selection or the button or box that accompanies the item you want to change. If you are using the keyboard, press Tab to select the next item (from left to right and top to bottom), or press Shift+Tab to move in the opposite direction. WordPerfect shows you which item is currently selected in a dialog box either by placing the cursor in the item's text box or by enclosing the item's description in a dotted rectangle.

To move to a new option for an item that contains a group of options, such as a list of check boxes or option buttons, you can press the arrow keys. You also can quickly select an option in a dialog box by pressing Alt and typing the letter that is underlined in the option name, just as you select menu options.

> *Tip:* In some dialog boxes, WordPerfect automatically selects all the text in the text box of the first item, anticipating that you will most often want to change the setting for this text box. To select a different item in the dialog box by using the item's underlined letter, you must press Alt before pressing the letter key. If you just press the letter key, the program replaces the selected text in the first text box with the letter you type.

If the option you have selected is a text box, you can change its current entry simply by typing in a new one. If only part of the entry requires changing, you can select those characters with the mouse and retype the correct ones. If you need to delete part of the entry, select the characters and then press Del or Backspace.

If you're changing an item that uses a list box, press the up or down arrow to move to the option you want to use. If you're changing an item that uses a check box or an option button, type the underlined letter to select the box or button; if it's a check box that already contains an X, typing its menu letter deselects it.

After you have made all your changes in a dialog box, choose the OK command button. This action records your changes, returns you to your document, and implements the new settings. If you want to leave the menu without Word-Perfect recording any of your changes, choose the Cancel button or press Esc instead.

Canceling Command Selections

To cancel a command selection from a WordPerfect menu you have opened, position the mouse pointer outside the pull-down menu and click the mouse button. You also can press Esc to back out of pull-down menus one level at a time. Keep in mind when using the Esc key that you may need to press it several times before you deactivate the menu bar and return to your document.

If you have opened a dialog box and don't want to change any options, you cannot just click somewhere outside the dialog box's boundary to close it; you must press Esc or choose the Cancel button. You also can close a dialog box by double-clicking its Control menu box or by choosing the Close option from the Control menu. The keyboard shortcut for the Close option is Ctrl+F4.

Saving a Document

Saving a Document the First Time
1. Open the **File** menu, and then choose either the **Save** option or the Save **As** option; or press Ctrl+S or F3.

WordPerfect displays the Save As dialog box, where you specify the name you want to assign to the file.

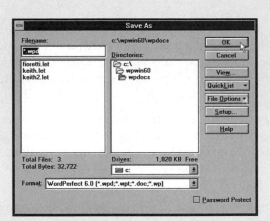

2. Type the file name in the Filename text box. You can use up to eight characters (no spaces), followed by a three-character extension. The extension must be separated from the main file name with a period, such as memoform.wpw.

The Save As dialog box lists the current directory above the Directories list box. If you want to save your file in a different directory, you need to select that directory in the Directories list box. If the directory you want is located on a different drive, select its drive letter (such as b:) from the Drives drop-down list box. If the directory is located in a higher level in the file hierarchy, double-click the next-higher level in the Directories list. If the desired directory is located in a lower level beneath a particular directory, double-click that directory name to open it.

To save the file in a format other than the one used by WordPerfect for DOS, open the Format drop-down list box and scroll through the options. Select the file format in which you want to save the document.

3. Choose OK to save the file.

The document you create on-screen with WordPerfect resides only in the computer's (RAM) memory. Because this memory is erased as soon as you exit WordPerfect, you need to save a copy of the document as a disk file to have a permanent copy of your work.

You can preview the contents of a file listed in the Save As dialog box. To use this feature, highlight a file in the Filename list and then choose the View command button. WordPerfect displays the file in the Viewer window, where you can use the arrow keys or scroll bars to review the contents of the file. To close the Viewer window with the mouse, double-click the upper left corner of the window, or click it once and choose Close; using the keyboard, press Alt+F4.

You can also choose other common file maintenance functions from the Save As dialog box. Choose the File Options command button, and then choose Copy, Move, Rename, Delete, Change Attributes, Print, Print List, Create Directory, or Remove Directory. Each of these options displays a simple dialog box in which you can specify the name of the file or directory to which you want to apply the selected option.

After you have saved a document the first time and you want to save the file with the same name, you can bypass the Save As dialog box. Choose the Save option instead of the Save As option from the File menu, or press Shift+F3. Use this command frequently to save all editing changes made to a document under the same file name.

Note: Make sure that you don't have any text selected when you choose the **File Save As** command; otherwise, WordPerfect will save just the highlighted text under the file name you assign. Of course, selecting text before you choose **File Save As** is fine if you want to save only that text in a separate file only, but highlighting text can be disastrous if you want to save all the text of the document.

Naming Files

When naming your document, the file name must be no longer than eight characters. To the main file name, you can add an extension up to three characters in length. Use a period to separate the main file name from the extension.

When entering the file name and extension, you can use any combination of letters and numbers as well as a few special symbols. You cannot, however, use spaces or any of these symbols:

* ? : ; , \ / &

WordPerfect enables you to use any file name extension you want. Be aware, however, that both WordPerfect for Windows and Microsoft Windows use certain extensions to distinguish different types of program and document files. To prevent confusing your WordPerfect document files with other types of files, avoid using these extensions (see table 3.3).

Table 3.3   Common File Name Extensions Used by WordPerfect and Windows

Extension	Meaning
BK!	WordPerfect backup file
EXE	Program or executable file
HLP	Help file
INI	Windows initial settings file
FON	Windows font file
LEX	WordPerfect spelling dictionary
PIF	Windows program initiation file

Extension	Meaning
THS	WordPerfect thesaurus
WCM	WordPerfect for Windows macro file
WPG	WordPerfect (all versions) graphics file
WPM	WordPerfect macro file
WWB	WordPerfect for Windows Button Bar file
WWK	WordPerfect keyboard file

Associating Files with WordPerfect for Windows

Associating a File Name Extension with WordPerfect

1. In Windows' File Manager, select a WordPerfect document that uses the file name extension you want to associate with WordPerfect for Windows. For example, select a file with the extension WPW. The file icon and name you selected are highlighted in File Manager.

2. Open the File menu from File Manager's menu bar, and then choose the Associate option. The File Manager displays the Associate dialog box.

3. Type the WordPerfect command wpwin.exe in the text box of the Associate dialog box.

4. Choose the OK button.

WordPerfect automatically assigns the file name extension WPD to documents you create. To open a particular WordPerfect document in the File Manager, you need to teach Windows to identify documents with the WPD with the WordPerfect program. You can specify a different WordPerfect default file name extension; for example, you might use WPW (for "WordPerfect for Windows") as the new default extension.

97

Here, WPWIN.EXE is entered in the Associate dialog box to associate the WPW file name extension with WordPerfect for Windows.

From now on, to start WordPerfect and open a particular document at the same time in the File Manager, simply open the file whose name uses in the associated extension. To open the file, you can double-click its icon, or you can select the icon and then either choose the **File O**pen command or press Enter. Continuing with the example, you now can start WordPerfect for Windows by opening any WPW file from the File Manager.

Saving the Document under a New Name

Saving a File under a New Name

1. Open the **F**ile menu and choose Save **A**s, or press `F3`.

2. Select a new directory in the **D**irectories list box and, if necessary, choose a new drive in the **D**rives list box. To save a copy of the document in the same directory but under a new name, edit the file name in the Filename text box.

3. Choose OK when you are done.

After you have saved your document under a file name, you can save a copy of it under a new name by accessing the File menu and choosing the Save **A**s option. This procedure opens the Save As dialog box, where you can edit the file name and change the directory.

Using the Backup Features

Using Backup Features

1. Open the File menu and choose the Preferences option.

2. Choose the Files option.

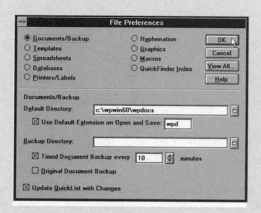

WordPerfect displays the File Preferences dialog box.

3. To turn off the timed backup feature, select the Timed Document Backup option to remove the X from its check box.

   To change the interval between timed backups, turn on the Timed Document Backup option and type the number of minutes in the text box. Instead of typing the minutes in the text box, you can use the mouse; click the button on the right with the upward-pointing triangle to increase the number of minutes, or click the button with the downward-pointing triangle to decrease the number.

   To turn on original backup, place an X in the Original Document Backup check box.

4. To specify a directory where WordPerfect for Windows saves backup files, choose Default Directory and type a new directory name; or click the directory symbol at the right end of the list and specify a directory in the Select Directory dialog box.

continues

continued

5. To tell WordPerfect for Windows to apply a specific file name extension to files that you open and save, choose Use Default Extension on Open and Save; then type the new extension in the text box. (The default extension is WPD.)

6. To have WordPerfect for Windows automatically update any default or user-defined QuickLists with your changes to the Backup and default directories settings, select the Update QuickList with Changes check box.

7. When you have the backup options as you want them, choose OK and then choose Close to return to the document window.

WordPerfect provides two backup features to help you guard against losing work: *original backup* and *timed backup.* Original backup saves an unedited version of your document at the time you save editing changes. Timed backup automatically saves the entire document at the end of a specific time interval—every 10 minutes by default. The original backup feature can protect you against accidentally saving edits to a document that you didn't really want to save; the timed backup feature can help minimize the amount of data lost during a power failure or computer crash.

Note: Neither the original backup nor the timed backup feature replaces frequently using the File Save command to save editing changes. Currently, Windows does not provide as stable an environment as DOS. Unexpected application errors (UAEs) can crash the computer at the most inappropriate times. To fully protect your work, you should leave on timed backup (you might want to reduce the backup interval) and still manually save your work often by choosing File Save or pressing Ctrl+S.

When you install WordPerfect for Windows, original backup is turned off, timed backup is turned on, and the interval between backups is set to 10 minutes.

When the original backup feature is on and you save your editing changes, WordPerfect also saves an unedited copy of the document under the same file name but with the BK! extension. Suppose, for example, that you have just deleted a table from a document called ABCPRO#1.WPW, and you then use the File Save command to save the document under the same name. With original backup on, WordPerfect automatically saves an unedited copy of this document that still contains the table under the file name ABCPRO#1.BK!. Should you need the information in the table you erased from the file, you can retrieve the table by opening the ABCPRO#1.BK1 file (choose **File Open**). You then can save this backup file by renaming it with **File Save As**; or, to save only the information in the table, select the text of the table before you choose **File Save As**.

When the timed backup feature is on, WordPerfect automatically saves all changes made to the active document at the interval you specify. Changes are saved under the file name WP{WP}.BKn, where n corresponds to the number of the document window (between 1 and 9) that contains the active document.

When you exit WordPerfect normally, the program erases these backup files. Should you not exit normally (as with a power failure), WordPerfect preserves these backup files in the directory specified as the backup files directory. When you restart WordPerfect, the program displays the Timed Backup dialog box that prompts you to rename, open, or delete the timed backup files. To open the backup files, each in its own document window, select the **Open** command button. To rename each backup file, select the **Rename** button. To erase all backup files, select the **Delete** button.

> *Note:* To change the directory where WordPerfect saves the original and timed backup files, choose the **File Preferences File** command and enter the path of the new directory, as described in the previous steps.

Closing Document Windows and Exiting WordPerfect

When you are finished using a document, close its document window to clean up the WordPerfect window and free computer memory. WordPerfect provides several methods for closing the active document window:

- Open the **File** menu and choose the **Close** option, or press Ctrl+F4.

- Double-click the Control menu box in the upper left corner of the document window. The Control menu box is visible only when windows are tiled (choose **Window, Tiled**). Alternatively, you can click the Control menu box for the document window and choose the **Close** option from the Control menu. (If the document window is full-size, this box is located on the menu bar, immediately to the left of **File**.)

Note: Don't double-click the Control menu box for the WordPerfect for Windows window, in the extreme upper left corner of the screen. Doing so exits the program.

Tip: You can install a Power Bar button that closes the on-screen file. To find out how to customize the Power Bar, see chapter 17, "Creating and Using Button Bars."

If you have not yet saved the document or have made some changes that are unsaved at the time you close a document window, WordPerfect displays a message box that asks whether you want to save the document.

To save the changes, choose the **Yes** command button.

Under the rare circumstance when you want to close the document window without saving your document, choose the No command button. To avoid closing the document window, choose the Cancel button. Choosing Cancel opens the Save As dialog box, where you can name the file and save it before exiting WordPerfect.

If you have already saved your document, WordPerfect saves the changes under the same file name as soon as you choose the Yes command button. If you haven't saved the document yet, WordPerfect displays the Save As dialog box so that you can give the document a file name.

When you are ready to close all documents in WordPerfect and return to the Windows operating environment, open the File menu and choose the Exit command, or press Alt+F4. WordPerfect displays a message box prompting you to save each document that has not yet been saved (or that contains editing changes you haven't saved) before returning you to Windows.

Using WordPerfect in the Windows Environment

WordPerfect for Windows, unlike its DOS-based predecessors, enables you to run multiple programs and transfer information easily between them. In no time you will find yourself routinely shuttling information to and from WordPerfect for Windows and other Windows programs, even if WordPerfect is the only computer program you ordinarily use. You might copy a table of financial data stored in an Excel worksheet file, for example, into a WordPerfect document or transfer a memo created in WordPerfect for Windows directly into a Word for Windows document.

Returning to Windows without Exiting WordPerfect

To start another program while WordPerfect is still running, you first need to return to the Program Manager in the Windows operating environment. The easiest way to return to the Program Manager is to click the Minimize button in the WordPerfect window. This action reduces the Program Manager to the program icon. You also can return to the Program Manager by pressing Alt+Esc (or by choosing the Switch To option on the Control menu) to display the Task List window. Then choose Program Manager in the list box and click the Switch To command button, or simply double-click Program Manager in the list box.

From the Program Manager, you can start a new program, provided that your computer has sufficient memory. Double-click the appropriate program icon or open the File menu, choose the Run option, and type the correct start-up command, and choose OK.

Switching between WordPerfect and Other Programs

After you have more than one program in memory, you can switch between the programs as often as necessary. To switch to a new program, simply click in that program's window. To make switching back and forth easier, resize and reposition the program windows so that they barely overlap.

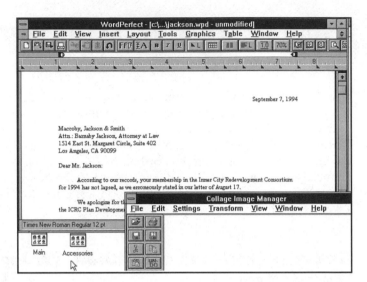

Here, the windows containing WordPerfect and Collage have been positioned one above the other.

If you are running a program in a full-screen window and don't want to move and resize the window or are unable to do this (as is the case if you are running a non-Windows program such as dBASE IV on an 80286 computer, for example), you can switch to a new program via the Task List window. To access this window, press Ctrl+Esc or choose the Switch To option from the Control menu. Locate the program in the list box of this window and double-click its name, or select the program and click the Switch To command button.

Copying and Pasting Text between Programs

Copying and Pasting Text through the Clipboard

1. Start both WordPerfect and the program to which you want to transfer text.

2. Switch to WordPerfect by clicking the WordPerfect window or by using the Task List window (press Ctrl + Esc).

3. Open the WordPerfect document that contains the information you want to transfer to the other program.

4. Use the I-beam pointer to select all the text you want to copy to the other program.

5. Open WordPerfect's Edit menu and choose the Copy option, or press Ctrl + Ins, to copy the selected text to the Clipboard.

6. Switch to the program to which you want to transfer the copied text by clicking its program window or by using the Task List window (press Ctrl + Esc); then open the document in which you want to paste the copied text.

7. In the document, position the cursor where you want the copied text to appear.

8. Open the program's Edit menu and choose the Paste option, or press Ctrl + V.

WordPerfect's Cut, Copy, and Paste commands on the Edit menu simplify moving and copying information. You can move and copy data to new places in the same document or to other open documents. You can even cut and paste data between files created by other programs, such as between a WordPerfect for Windows worksheet and a 1-2-3 for Windows worksheet.

WordPerfect, like all other Windows programs, performs its cut, copy, and paste techniques with the *Clipboard.* The Clipboard is a special reserved area of computer memory that stores any text or graphics you move into it with the Cut or Copy commands. You can retrieve the text or graphics stored in the Clipboard at any time by choosing the Paste command. Because the information stored in the Clipboard stays there until you turn off your computer or replace the Clipboard's contents with other text or graphics, you can copy between any open documents or programs you have running.

Suppose that you have just typed a list of employees—including anniversary dates and telephone extensions—and you want to use this information as the basis for a database table in Microsoft Excel for Windows. Rather than reenter this data in Excel, you can transfer the data to a new worksheet via the Clipboard.

When copying to a spreadsheet program such as Excel, select the first cell you want to contain the copied text. If you copy text to another word processing program, however, you move the cursor or click the insertion point at the place where you want the copied text to appear.

> *Note:* WordPerfect has the capability not only to import data from spreadsheet programs, such as Excel 3.0 or 1-2-3 for Windows, but also to create dynamic links between the spreadsheet and the WordPerfect document. For complete information on how to use these options, see Que's *Using WordPerfect 6 for Windows,* Special Edition.

Summary

In this chapter, you learned how to start WordPerfect from either Program Manager or File Manager in Windows and how to begin a new document. Remember that when you start WordPerfect, the program automatically opens a new, full-size document window where you can begin working on a new document.

Next you learned how to navigate documents. In WordPerfect, you can move the cursor either with the mouse or with a wide variety of key combinations. After learning how to move around and between documents, you then learned how to work with the WordPerfect menus and dialog boxes to choose commands.

Finally, you learned how to name and save the documents you create in WordPerfect and how to quit the program and return to Windows. At the end of the chapter, you were introduced to techniques in Windows that enable you to start other programs while running WordPerfect and to copy and move data between these programs through the Clipboard.

In the next chapter, you will learn the basic editing features of WordPerfect. You will learn how to open existing documents; insert, delete, and undelete text; and cut, copy, and paste text in the same document and between different documents.

4

Editing a Document

Opening documents for editing

Working with multiple documents

Inserting text

Deleting text

Cutting and pasting text

Editing in the Reveal Codes window

Marking changes with Redline or Strikeout

Wordperfect provides a wide array of tools to help you easily revise the documents you create. This chapter concentrates on fundamental editing techniques, including ways to open the document that needs revision; methods for inserting, deleting, and undeleting text; and procedures for opening and working with multiple documents.

After looking at these basic editing techniques, you then can learn about advanced editing features. You can explore techniques for copying and pasting text in the same document, between different documents, and between different programs. Next, you can learn how to use the Reveal Codes command to edit text and, at the same time, edit the hidden codes that format the text. Finally, you can look at WordPerfect's Redline and Strikeout features that enable you to mark suggested editing changes in a manuscript.

Key Terms in This Chapter	
Insert mode	WordPerfect's default editing mode. New text inserts at the cursor's position, and existing text moves to the right and, if necessary, down succeeding lines.
Redline	An attribute indicating text that has been or should be added to a document.
Reveal Codes	The name given to the system of hidden codes that controls the formatting of your document. Hidden codes appear only after you open a special Reveal Codes window.
Strikeout	An attribute indicating text that should be deleted from the document.
Typeover mode	The opposite of Insert mode. New text replaces existing text.

Opening Documents for Editing

Opening a Document: The Basics

1. Open the **F**ile menu and choose the **O**pen command; or press Ctrl + O; or click the Open button on the Power Bar.

2. Type a file name and choose OK.

Before you can edit the contents of a WordPerfect document you have saved on disk, you must open the document in a document window. From the WordPerfect window, open the **F**ile menu and choose the **O**pen command (or press Ctrl+O or click the Open button on the Power Bar).

Opening a Document: A Detailed Look

1. Open the **F**ile menu.

2. Choose the **O**pen command (or press Ctrl + O or click the Open button on the Power Bar).

   WordPerfect displays the Open File dialog box that lists all the files located in the current directory.

3. If the document you want to open is not in the current directory (listed right below the Filename text box), select the correct drive in the Drives drop-down list box, and then specify the correct directory in the Directories list box. You also can display files using the QuickList feature. (You can learn about QuickLists in chapter 9, "Managing Files in WordPerfect.")

   To open a directory, double-click the directory name in the Directories list box (or select the directory name and press ⏎Enter). To view the contents of a directory that is located at a higher level on the directory tree, double-click the next higher directory until you reach the level containing the directory you want.

4. After you have selected the directory that contains your document file, select the file name in the Filename list box.

   If the list box contains more files than can be displayed at one time, use the scroll bar or the cursor keys to bring new files into view.

   Select a file by clicking its file name (or by pressing Tab↹ or Alt + l) and then pressing the down arrow to highlight the file name). To quickly select a document, activate the Name Search feature by clicking a file name at the top of the Filename list box (or selecting this list box with the keyboard), and then begin typing the first few characters of the file name. WordPerfect displays the letters you type in the text box beneath the Filename list box and highlights the first file name that begins with the characters you enter. Stop typing when the name of the file you want to open is listed in the Filename text box.

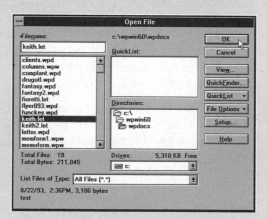

In this example, WordPerfect selected the file name KEITH.LET when the user typed the letters *ke*.

continues

continued

5. Choose the OK button to open the file listed in the Filename text box. (You can open your document and bypass this step entirely if you double-click the file name in the Filename list box.)

    If you know the file name of the document you want to edit, type its name in the Filename text box as soon as you display the Open File dialog box. If the file is not in the current directory, you must include the path name. If C:\DOCS is listed as the current directory, for example, and you want to open ADAMSLTR.592 from a disk in drive A, you must enter the following command in the Filename text box:

        a:\adamsltr.592

    After typing the file name, you can open the document by pressing ⏎Enter (or by clicking the OK button).

Tip: File names of the last four files you opened in WordPerfect for Windows appear at the bottom of the File menu. To open one of these files, click its name (or choose File and press 1, 2, 3, or 4).

To change the default directory, select a directory in the **Directories** list box, then open the Open File dialog box, choose **Setup**, and mark the Change **Default** Directory check box. Then choose OK. The program now uses this directory when performing standard file operations such as saving and retrieving files.

After you open the document file, you can scroll through the text and make all the necessary changes in the document window. If you find you have opened the wrong document, close the file in the document editing window. To close the file, open the **File** menu and choose the **Close** option (or double-click the Control menu box in the document window or press Ctrl+F4). Don't double-click the WordPerfect for Windows Control menu box, which is in the extreme upper left corner of the screen, or you will exit WordPerfect.

If you made any changes to the document before you chose the **File Close** command, WordPerfect displays a dialog box asking whether you want to save your changes. To abandon your changes and close the document window without saving, choose the No option in this dialog box.

Note: If you try to open a document that is already open in a document window, WordPerfect displays a message box informing you that the document is currently in use or is designated as read only. To go ahead and open the document in Read-Only mode, choose the OK button. When you open a document in Read-Only mode, however, the only way you can save editing changes is by opening the **F**ile menu, choosing the Save **As** command, and renaming the document in the Save As dialog box.

Viewing the Contents of Documents

As the list of documents you create in WordPerfect grows, you may not be able to tell what each file contains just by looking at the file name. At times, you even may be unable to locate the file you want to use. File names that seemed so descriptive when you originally named your documents may seem completely cryptic as you now scroll through them.

WordPerfect offers a remedy for such a situation: the File Viewer. When you choose the View command button in the Open File dialog box, the program opens a separate View window. As you select a file in the File**n**ame list box, WordPerfect displays the first part of that file's text in the View window. If you need to see more of the text to identify the document, you can use the scroll bars to move through the text.

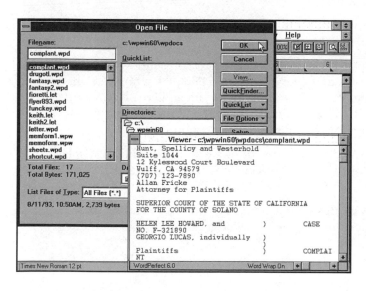

In this example, you see a View window containing a portion of the text of the first document in the Filename list box.

To move down the list of file names in the Filename list box with the View window open, press the down arrow. To move up through the list, press the up arrow. To move to the first file in the list, press Home. To move to the last file in the list, press End.

After you have located the file you want to open, choose the OK button or press Enter. WordPerfect automatically closes the View window when your document opens. To close the View window before you open a document, double-click the Control menu box (or click the Control menu box one time and then choose the Close option, or press Alt+F4).

> *Note:* If the document file you're viewing contains text and graphics, the View window shows only the text. If the file contains only a WordPerfect graphic (WPG file), however, the View window shows the graphic image. If the file contains a graphic image saved in another graphic format, the View window shows only the program codes.

Choosing Open File Options

You can change the way WordPerfect for Windows displays files in the Open File dialog box. Open the Open File dialog box, choose Setup, and then choose from the following options:

- **Show.** Choose Filename Only; Filename, Size, Date, Time; Descriptive Name, Filename; or Custom Columns.

  If you choose Custom Columns, WordPerfect for Windows displays the file name, size, date, and time in the Open File dialog box. You then can rearrange the order of the columns by dragging the column titles with the mouse. However, if you deselect the Show Column Labels check box, you no longer can reorder the columns.

- **Sort By.** To tell WordPerfect for Windows how to sort the file display, choose this option. Then choose Filename, Extension, Size, Date/Time, Descriptive Name, or Descriptive Type.

- **Sort Order.** Choose this option, and then choose Ascending (the default) or Descending to have WordPerfect for Windows sort files accordingly.

- Change **D**efault Directory. Choosing this option makes a directory selected in the Open File dialog box **D**irectories list box the default directory.

- List Files of **T**ype. Choosing this option then choosing a file format from the drop-down list tells WordPerfect for Windows to display all files in the specified format by default. You always can change the format by returning to this dialog box and changing the default.

In the Open File dialog box, WordPerfect for Windows displays a directory tree graphic by default in the **D**irectories list box. WordPerfect for Windows can display a file QuickList in this list box or both a QuickList and a directory tree. For a complete description of QuickList, see the following section, "Using QuickList."

To switch to a display of the QuickList or both the QuickList and directory tree, choose QuickList, and then choose Show **Q**uickList or Show **B**oth.

Notice that unless you choose **Q**uickList or Show **B**oth, the **E**dit QuickList option on the QuickList drop-down box is grayed. With a QuickList displayed, this option becomes available.

You also can choose other common file maintenance functions from the Open File dialog box. Choose File **O**ptions, and then choose **C**opy, **M**ove, **R**ename, **D**elete, Change Attributes, **P**rint, Create Directory, or Remove Directory. Each option displays a simple dialog box where you can specify the name of the file or directory to which you want to apply the selected option.

Using QuickList

Creating or Editing a QuickList

1. From a dialog box that deals with files, such as the Open File dialog box, choose QuickList, and then choose Show **Q**uickList or Show **B**oth.

   WordPerfect for Windows displays the Edit QuickList dialog box.

2. To add or edit a QuickList, highlight an existing list in the **Q**uickList list or choose **A**dd Item.

continues

continued

The Add QuickList Item dialog box enables you to create a QuickList that displays specific files.

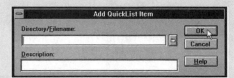

3. In the Directory/Filename box, type a subdirectory and file or file specification, as this example shows:

   C:\WPWIN60\WPDOCS\REPORTS*.RPT

4. In the **D**escription box, type a description for the QuickList item. For example, type Engineering Reports.

5. Choose OK twice to return to the Save As or Open File dialog box.

6. To display the files you just specified, double-click the QuickList item's title in the **Q**uickList. Or choose **Q**uickList, highlight the title, and press ⏎Enter.

   WordPerfect for Windows lists the files in the Filename list.

QuickList lets you display customized file listings quickly. For example, you may want to display all the report files stored in a subdirectory titled C:\WPWIN60\DOCS\REPORTS. QuickList spares you having to type the subdirectory specification every time you want to display the report files.

Working with Multiple Documents

WordPerfect simplifies working with several documents at one time. If your computer has sufficient memory, you can open up to nine documents at one time. Although you may never need to have that many documents open at one time, you probably will work with at least two document windows when cutting and pasting information from one document to another.

Opening a New File

When you start WordPerfect, the program automatically opens a new document
window. If you need to start another document during your work session, open
the File menu and choose the New command (or press Ctrl+N or click the New
Document button on the Power Bar). WordPerfect then opens a new full-size
document window and assigns the next available document number, which
appears in the title bar. For example, if you choose the New command and you
already have one document open named DOCUMENT1, WordPerfect assigns
the name DOCUMENT2 to the new window.

Retrieving One File into Another File

Retrieving a File

1. Position the cursor at the place in the document where you want to
   add the text of the document you are about to retrieve.

   To append the document text onto the end of the active document,
   press Ctrl + End to move the cursor directly to the end of the
   document.

2. Open the Insert menu and choose File.

   WordPerfect displays the Insert File dialog box.

3. If necessary, change the drive and directory as described in an earlier
   section, "Opening a File."

4. Highlight a file name in the Filename list box, and then choose
   Insert.

   WordPerfect
   displays a message
   dialog box asking
   whether you want
   to insert the se-
   lected file into the
   active document.

5. Choose Yes to retrieve the file at the cursor position. Otherwise,
   choose No to cancel the operation.

   If you choose Yes, WordPerfect inserts the entire text of the document into the active document, starting at the cursor position.

Sometimes you may like to incorporate the text of one document into the document in which you're working. WordPerfect enables you to incorporate text from one document into another document with ease.

Opening Multiple Documents in One Step

Opening Several Files in One Step

1. Open the File menu.

2. Choose the Open command.

3. In the Open File dialog box, drag the mouse to highlight sequential files in the Filename list box; or hold down the Ctrl key and click each file you want to open.

4. Choose OK.

Viewing More than One Document Window

As you know, each WordPerfect document you open appears in its own full-size document window, and WordPerfect automatically makes that document window the active window. Only the last open document window, therefore, is visible in the WordPerfect window. To see the other open documents, you must resize and rearrange their document windows.

The easiest way to rearrange document windows is to open the Windows menu and choose the Cascade or Tile option.

Switching between Cascaded or Tiled Windows

To make a new WordPerfect document window active after you have arranged the windows with the Window Cascade or Window Tile command, click the document window with the mouse as follows:

- If the document windows cascade, click the title bar of the document window you want to make active. WordPerfect then places that document window at the front of the stack, highlights its title bar, and displays its scroll bars.

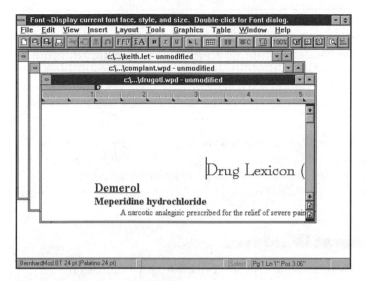

The **Cascade** option arranges the document windows so that they overlap.

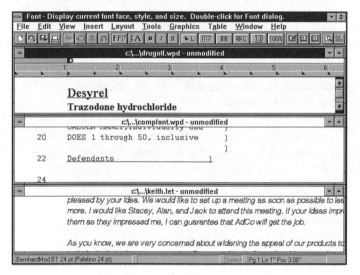

The **Tile** option arranges the document windows one above another.

- If the document windows are tiled, you can click anywhere in any window to make it active. WordPerfect indicates the active document window by highlighting its title bar and displaying its scroll bars.

After clicking the document window you want to use, you can make it full-size. Click the Maximize button in the upper right corner of the document window or click the document window's Control menu and choose the Maximize option.

If you are using full-screen windows or cannot see a particular document window in the WordPerfect window, you can select the document window you want to use from the **W**indow menu. When you open the **W**indow menu, you see a numbered list of all open documents at the bottom. A check mark precedes the active document window. To activate a different document, open the **W**indow menu and select a file name or type the number in front of the file name.

You can select the next open document window by pressing the Next Document key combination, Ctrl+F6. Pressing this key sequence activates in turn each open document window in WordPerfect. To switch to the previous document window, press Alt+Shift+F6.

Closing Document Windows

After you have finished with a document, you can close its window to free computer memory and reduce clutter on the screen. Before you can close a document window, you must make it active. Then you can close the document window by opening the **F**ile menu and choosing the **C**lose option (or by double-clicking the window's Control menu box or by pressing Ctrl+F4).

If you have made changes to the document in the window you're closing, WordPerfect prompts you to confirm your changes. To save changes before closing the window, choose the **Y**es button.

> *Tip:* To clear the active document window of text without closing the active document window, press the Clear key combination, Ctrl+Shift+F4. If you have made changes in the document that aren't saved, WordPerfect displays a message dialog box asking whether you want to discard the current document. To clear the window without saving your changes, choose the **Y**es button. To return to your document where you can save changes with the **F**ile **S**ave command, choose the **N**o button.

Inserting Text

After you have opened a file in a document window, you can begin making all the necessary changes to the file. You can accomplish most edits with the use of three basic techniques: inserting text, replacing text, and deleting text. Before you look at the many ways to delete text in WordPerfect, first learn how you can use the *Typeover* and *Insert* modes to replace or add to existing text.

Adding Text in Insert Mode

By default, WordPerfect is in Insert mode. In Insert mode, WordPerfect inserts any characters you type at the position of the cursor (insertion point) into the text and moves existing text to the right. If the addition of new characters causes existing text to extend beyond the right margin, WordPerfect uses word wrap to reformat the paragraph.

To add new text to a paragraph using the mouse, click the I-beam pointer between the characters where you want to insert the text and begin typing. To add new text using the keyboard, use the cursor keys to move the cursor between the characters and begin typing.

Replacing Text in Typeover Mode

To replace existing text, you can switch to Typeover mode by pressing the Insert key. WordPerfect indicates that you are in Typeover mode by displaying the message Typeover at the left side of the status bar.

After you are in Typeover mode, any characters you type at the cursor's position replace existing characters or spaces to the right. You can use Typeover mode to correct any typing errors you find in the text. After making the corrections, you can return to Insert mode by pressing the Insert key.

Replacing Text in Insert Mode

Instead of toggling between Insert and Typeover modes to replace text, you can replace a section of text by selecting the text you want to replace and then typing the replacement text. As soon as you type your first replacement character, WordPerfect deletes all the selected text.

If you're using the mouse, you can select the text you want to replace by dragging the I-beam pointer over the text (or you can use the mouse selection shortcuts listed in table 2.1 of chapter 2). WordPerfect also enables you to select the various-sized sections of text with the keyboard. Table 4.1 lists these keys and the section of text each shortcut selects.

Table 4.1   Selecting Text with the Keyboard

Key Combination	*Section of Text Selected*
⬆Shift + >	Selects text from cursor to the next character.
⬆Shift + <	Selects text from cursor to the previous character.
Ctrl + ⬆Shift + >	Selects text from cursor to the end of the next word.
Ctrl + ⬆Shift + <	Selects text from cursor to the beginning of the previous word.
⬆Shift + Home	Selects text from cursor to the beginning of the line before codes.
⬆Shift + End	Selects text from cursor to the end of the line.
⬆Shift + ↑	Selects text from cursor up to the previous line.
⬆Shift + ↓	Selects text from cursor down to the next line.
Ctrl + ⬆Shift + ↑	Selects text from cursor to the beginning of the paragraph.
Ctrl + ⬆Shift + ↓	Selects text from cursor to the end of the paragraph.
⬆Shift + PgUp	Selects text from cursor to the top of the document window.
⬆Shift + PgDn	Selects text from cursor to the bottom of the document window.
Alt + ⬆Shift + PgUp	Selects text from cursor to the top of the page.
Alt + ⬆Shift + PgDn	Selects text from cursor to the bottom of the page.
Alt + ⬆Shift + Home	Selects text from cursor to the top of the page.
Alt + ⬆Shift + End	Selects text from cursor to the bottom of the page.

Key Combination	Section of Text Selected
Ctrl + ⇧Shift + Home	Selects text from cursor to the beginning of the document after any codes.
Ctrl + ⇧Shift + Home	Selects text from cursor to the beginning of the document before any codes.
Ctrl + ⇧Shift + End	Selects text from cursor to the end of the document.

Using Abbreviations to Insert Text

Creating and Inserting an Abbreviation

1. Select the text you want to assign to an abbreviation.

2. Open the Insert menu.

3. Choose Abbreviations.

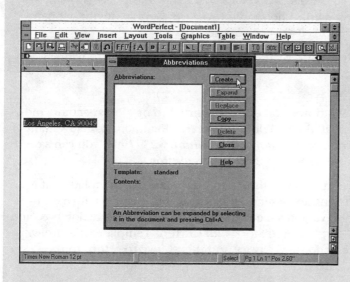

WordPerfect displays the Abbreviations dialog box, which you use to create glossary short-cut keys.

4. Choose Create.

continues

continued

WordPerfect displays the Create Abbreviation dialog box, which enables you to create an abbreviation for the selected text in the current document. In this example, *m23* stands for *on the morning of January 23, 1993.*

5. Choose OK and Close to return to the document screen.

   To expand an abbreviation, type its characters and press Ctrl+A; or open the Insert menu, choose **Abbreviations**, and highlight the name in the **Abbreviations** list. Then choose **Expand**.

   WordPerfect for Windows replaces the typed abbreviation with its expanded text.

With WordPerfect for Windows, you can use shorthand or glossary commands to insert frequently repeated text. For example, if a document contains many occurrences of the phrase *on the morning of January 23, 1993,* you can save time inserting the phrase with a *keystroke abbreviation.*

You can store an abbreviation with the default template or a template that is associated with the current document. To store an abbreviation with a template, highlight the abbreviation's name from the Abbreviations dialog box, and then choose **Create, Template,** and **Store with Current Template** or **Store with Default Template.** Then choose **OK** twice and then **Close** to return to the document screen. To learn more about templates, see chapter 3, "Getting Started."

Notice that in the Abbreviation dialog box you can Re**place,** **C**opy, and **D**elete abbreviations. To use these commands, first highlight an abbreviation in the **Abbreviations** list, and then choose the command.

To replace an abbreviation, first select the new text that you want to assign to the abbreviation. Then open the Insert menu and choose Abbreviations. Highlight the name of the abbreviation in the Abbreviations list, and then choose Replace. WordPerfect prompts you to confirm the replacement. Choose Yes to return to the Abbreviations and assign the selected text to the abbreviation.

Inserting Spaces

To insert spaces between words and phrases, press the space bar. After you press the space bar in Insert mode, WordPerfect inserts the blank space before any existing characters and moves the characters to the right. After you press the space bar in Typeover mode, the program replaces any existing character at the cursor's position with the blank space.

Inserting Tabs

The WordPerfect default Ruler has preset tabs at evenly spaced one-half-inch intervals. To insert a tab at the beginning of a paragraph, press Tab in Insert mode. If you are in Typeover mode, WordPerfect merely moves the cursor to the next tab stop on the Ruler without indenting any text. To see the tab settings in your document, display the Ruler by opening the View menu and choosing the Ruler Bar command or pressing Alt+Shift+F3. (You learn how to change tab settings in chapter 6, "Formatting Paragraphs and Characters.")

Inserting Blank Lines

You use the Enter key to indicate the end of paragraphs and to insert blank lines in the text of your document. When you press the Enter key, WordPerfect inserts a hard return code in the text at the cursor's position and moves the cursor to the beginning of the next line.

To insert blank lines in existing text, position the cursor at the beginning of the line where you want to insert the blank line and press Enter. Inserting a blank line causes existing lines of text to move down the page. Note that unlike inserting spaces or tabs, pressing the Enter key inserts a blank line regardless of whether you are in Insert or Typeover mode.

Deleting Text

In WordPerfect, you normally select (highlight) the text you want to erase before you delete it. You can select text with the mouse or with the keyboard.

To delete text with the mouse, select the characters you want to erase by dragging the I-beam pointer over the characters, or you can use any appropriate selection shortcut (refer to table 4.1). Then press the Backspace or Del key.

Selecting Text with the Keyboard

Instead of selecting text with the mouse, you can select text with the keyboard. To select text with the keyboard, position the cursor immediately in front of the first character you want to erase. Then press the Select key (F8) or hold down the Shift key and use the cursor keys to highlight the rest of the text you want to delete. When you press the Select key (F8), WordPerfect turns on Select mode (shown by the Select indicator on the status bar). After Select mode is on, you can select the text you want to use or delete by using the keys shown in table 4.1. As soon as you have selected all the text to be erased, press Backspace or Del to make the deletion.

> *Tip:* If you're a WordPerfect 5.1 user, you probably are used to marking a block with the Block key combination (Alt+F4). The Select key (F8) works in almost the same way with one significant difference: if you decide you don't want to use the block you have selected, you must press the Select key a second time to deselect the text. You cannot just press the Esc key (the equivalent of the Cancel key in WordPerfect 5.1) to remove the highlighting from the text.

Deleting Text with Keyboard Shortcuts

WordPerfect provides several keyboard shortcuts for deleting various sections of text. When you use these shortcuts summarized in table 4.2, the program not only selects the unit of text but also deletes it at the same time.

Table 4.2   Keyboard Shortcuts for Deleting Text

Key(s)	Section of Text Deleted
Del	Character to the right of cursor (insertion point).
Backspace	Character to the left of cursor (insertion point).
Ctrl + Backspace	Word and trailing space containing cursor.
Ctrl + Del	From the cursor's position to the end of the line.

Undoing a WordPerfect Command

Unlike earlier versions of WordPerfect for DOS, WordPerfect for Windows offers a true undo feature. This feature not only restores deleted text but also gives you a chance to recover when you make other editing mistakes, such as choosing the wrong WordPerfect command. Suppose, for example, that you select some lines of text and center them only to discover that you selected the wrong lines of text. Instead of having to select the text a second time before choosing the appropriate **Layout** menu commands to restore right justification, you now can restore the original justification by using the **Undo** command.

WordPerfect always remembers the last action you made in the document. When you open the **Edit** menu and choose the **Undo** command (or press (Ctrl+Z), WordPerfect restores the document to the state before your last action. You also can press the **Undo** button on the Power Bar.

Keep in mind that you can undo only your last action in WordPerfect. If you choose a new command or begin editing text before you choose **Undo**, WordPerfect changes the **Undo** command so it undoes only the new command you just chose or the edit you just made.

Remember that you cannot undo all WordPerfect commands. Although you can undo most editing commands, for example, you cannot undo most file management commands. If you use the Open File or Save File dialog box to delete a file from your disk, you cannot restore the file with **Undo**; you need to resort to a disk utility or the Undelete command in DOS 6.0 and later versions.

Also, if you accidentally save changes under the wrong file name with the Save option rather than the Save As option on the File menu, you cannot use the Undo command to reverse the action; you must rename the file.

> *Note:* Unlike Edit Undelete, which restores any of your last three deletions at the cursor's position, the Edit Undo command restores the text you last deleted (assuming that was your last action in WordPerfect) at its original position in the document.

Restoring Deleted Text

If you have deleted some text in error, you can restore it by opening the Edit menu and choosing the Undo option (or by pressing Ctrl+Z). To restore deleted text with Edit Undo, you must remember to choose this command before choosing another WordPerfect command.

If you continue editing and then realize that you want to restore some deleted text, you're not too late. You can open the Edit menu and choose the Undelete command (or press Ctrl+Shift+Z) to bring back the text. The Undelete function in WordPerfect for Windows, like Undelete in 5.1, can restore up to the last three deletions you made in the text.

When you choose the Edit Undelete command, WordPerfect displays the highlighted text you last deleted at the cursor's present position. The program also displays the Undelete dialog box.

You can continue to choose the Next or Previous button in the Undelete dialog box to cycle forward or backward through the last three deletions you made. When WordPerfect displays the text you want to restore at the cursor's position, choose the Restore button.

When you choose Restore, the program reinstates the text (and simultaneously deselects it), and the Undelete dialog box disappears. If you don't want to restore any of the last three deletions, choose the Cancel button.

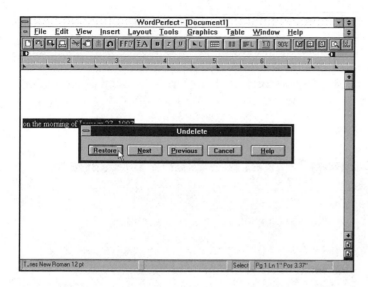

To restore the highlighted text, choose the **Restore** button in the Undelete dialog box. To view the second deletion you made, choose the **Previous** button.

Cutting, Copying, and Pasting Text

Cutting and Pasting Text

1. Select the text you want to cut or copy.

2. Open the **Edit** menu.

3. Choose **Cut** (or press `Ctrl`+`X`).

   or

   Choose **Copy** (or press `Ctrl`+`C`).

4. Move the cursor to the new location, open the **Edit** menu, and choose **Paste** (or press `Ctrl`+`V`).

WordPerfect's **Cut**, **Copy**, and **Paste** commands on the **Edit** menu enable you to easily move or copy blocks of text to new places in the same document or to other documents you have open. You even can cut and paste text between files created by other Windows programs, such as a WordPerfect for Windows file and an Excel worksheet. (See chapter 3, "Getting Started," for more information on transferring information between different programs.)

127

WordPerfect, like all other Windows programs, performs its cut, copy, and paste techniques with the use of the *Clipboard.* You can retrieve whatever text or graphics are stored in the Clipboard at any time by opening the Edit menu and choosing the Paste command. Because the information stored in the Clipboard stays there until you exit Windows or replace the information with other text or graphics, you can copy between any documents you have open or programs you have running.

Copying or Moving Text in the Same Document

Copying or Moving Text

1. Select the text you want to copy or move by using the mouse or the keyboard.

In this example, you select the paragraph you want to move by quadruple-clicking it.

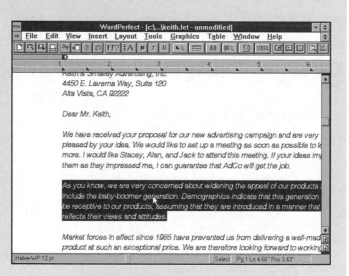

2. Open the Edit menu.

3. To copy the text, choose the Copy option or press [Ctrl]+[Ins] or [Ctrl]+[C]. To move the text, choose the Cut option or press [⇧Shift]+[Del] or [Ctrl]+[X]. Another shortcut technique is to use the Copy and Cut buttons on the Power Bar.

   WordPerfect copies the selected text to the Clipboard. If you choose the Cut option rather than Copy, the program also removes the selected text from the document.

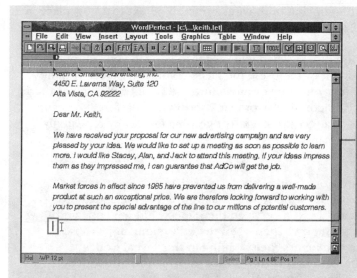

Position the cursor (insertion point) at the place in the document where you want to copy or move the selected text, such as at the beginning of a line.

4. Open the **Edit** menu and choose the **Paste** option (or press `⇧Shift`+`Ins` or `Ctrl`+`V`) to place the copied or cut text in its new spot in the document. You also can choose the Paste button in the Power Bar. WordPerfect reflows the text of the document to accommodate this change.

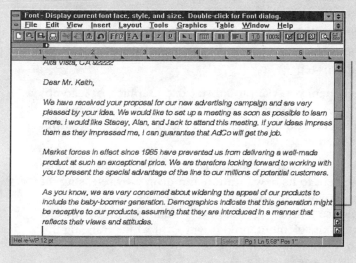

The paragraph you cut and copied to the Clipboard is pasted at the cursor's position when you choose the **Edit Paste** command.

The basic technique for copying or moving a section of text to a new place in your document is the same.

If you ever cut a section of text when you meant to copy it, you can put the text back in the document by choosing the **P**aste command before you move the cursor. Whatever text you copy or move into the Clipboard remains there until you cut or copy something else or exit Windows. Therefore, you can make multiple copies of a section of text (or graphic image) by repeatedly choosing the **P**aste command.

> *Note:* To copy or move hidden codes as well as document text, open the Reveal Codes window and make sure that the codes you want to include are located between the [Select] hidden code and the cursor in this window. Then open the **E**dit menu and choose the **C**opy or Cu**t** command. (See "Editing in the Reveal Codes Window" section later in this chapter for information on hidden codes.)

Using Drag-and-Drop Editing

WordPerfect's *Drag-and-Drop* editing feature enables you to visually relocate text and graphics in a document; this technique is even easier and quicker to use than the Clipboard if you are moving or copying the material only a short distance in the same document.

To use the mouse to pick up and move or copy text or graphics anywhere in a document, follow these steps:

1. Select the element you want to move (text, graphics, or a combination of the two), and then place the mouse pointer anywhere in that selected element. You may notice that the pointer changes from an I-beam to a pointer.

2. Hold down the left mouse button. To *move* the selected element, drag the element to its new location and drop it by releasing the mouse button when the insertion point—which moves with the modified mouse pointer—is where you want to relocate the element. To *copy* the element, hold down Ctrl while dragging the selection to the new location, and then drop the copy in place by releasing the mouse button.

After you press the mouse button to begin dragging your selection, the mouse pointer changes to indicate that the Drag-and-Drop feature is activated, and the insertion point travels with the mouse pointer. The mouse pointer has different icons attached to indicate whether the Drag-and-Drop function is in Move or Copy mode.

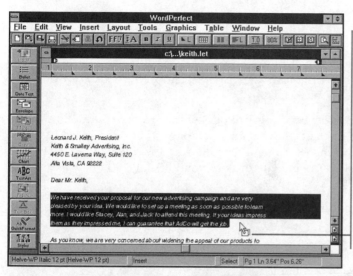

The icon here indicates a Drag-and-Drop procedure in Move mode. Notice the icon appended to the mouse pointer and the insertion point next to the pointer. If you release the mouse button, the highlighted text moves to the insertion point.

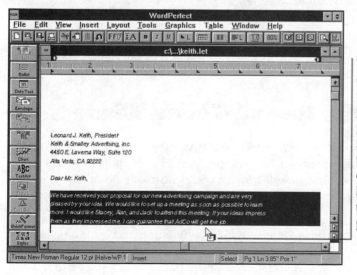

The icon in this example indicates a Drag-and-Drop procedure in progress in Copy mode. If you release the mouse button, a copy of the highlighted text moves to the insertion point.

Copying or Moving Text between WordPerfect Documents

Copying and Moving Text between Documents

1. Select the text you want to copy or move.

2. Open the Edit menu.

3. Choose the Copy option (or press Ctrl + Ins or Ctrl + C) to copy the text, or choose the Cut option (or press Shift + Del or Ctrl + X) to move the text. Alternatively, choose the Copy or Cut button on the Power Bar.

4. Activate the window containing the document where you want to copy or move the text. Activate the document by clicking in its window, by clicking its name in WordPerfect's Window menu, or by pressing the Next Document key combination, Ctrl + F6.

5. Reposition the cursor (insertion point) at the place in the new document window where you want the cut or copied text to appear.

6. Open the Edit menu.

7. Choose the Paste option (or press Shift + Ins or Ctrl + V) to place the cut or copied text in the new document. You also can choose the Power Bar's Paste button.

The technique for copying and moving text between open WordPerfect documents varies only slightly from copying or moving text in the same document.

Editing in the Reveal Codes Window

As you learned in chapter 2, WordPerfect inserts hidden codes into the text of your document as you use various commands. These codes indicate how your document will format when printed. Hidden codes normally do not appear with the text in the document window, thus keeping the document editing window uncluttered.

Some codes, such as the codes for automatic hyphenation and outlining, turn on or off the features. Other codes, such as those for bolding, underlining, and italicizing text, work in pairs. The first code in the pair acts as a toggle that turns on the feature; the second code acts as a toggle that turns off the feature. Still other codes, such as those for selecting a new font or changing the line spacing, turn on the feature until the end of a document or the occurrence of another code that countermands the feature.

Remember that in WordPerfect, you can open the Reveal Codes window by dragging the split box at the top or bottom of the vertical scroll bar to the place in the document window where you want the Reveal Codes window to appear. Or you can open the View menu and choose the Reveal Codes command or press the Reveal Codes key combination, Alt+F3.

Working with Hidden Codes

With the Reveal Codes window open, you can edit the text or codes in the document. When using the cursor keys, notice the cursor (insertion point) moving in the document editing window, as its counterpart (represented by a rectangle) moves through the Reveal Codes window. Because the normal Windows cursor is an insertion point, you notice a discrepancy between the cursor's position in the editing window and its position in the Reveal Codes window. The cursor in the editing window always appears in front of the character; the cursor block in the Reveal Codes window highlights the character.

Each cursor moves with the other until WordPerfect encounters a hidden code in the Reveal Codes window. Then when you press a cursor key, the cursor in the Reveal Codes window jumps across the code and the insertion point in the document editing window appears to remain stationary.

When editing a document with the Reveal Codes window open, you need to be aware of a few special circumstances:

* When you reposition the pointer in the Reveal Codes window and you click the I-beam pointer between two characters in the text, WordPerfect highlights the character that precedes the I-beam.

* To select a hidden code in the Reveal Codes window, click the I-beam pointer anywhere on that code.

* When you select text in the document editing window, WordPerfect inserts a [Select] code in the Reveal Codes window immediately before the first character or code you selected; the cursor highlight is positioned right after the last character or code you selected. If other hidden codes are included between the [Select] code and the cursor in the Reveal Codes window, they too will be affected by the WordPerfect command you choose next.

Here, the insertion point in the document window keeps pace with the cursor block in the Reveal Codes window until WordPerfect encounters a hidden code.

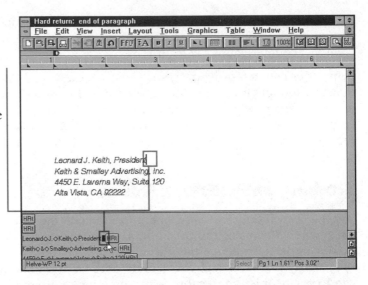

In this Reveal Codes window, WordPerfect inserts a [Select] code in front of the selected text, *Leonard J.*

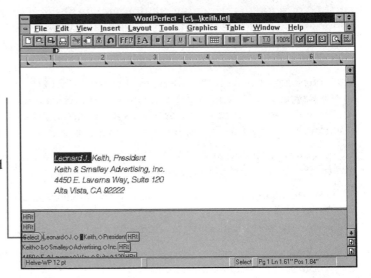

Deleting Hidden Codes

Deleting a Hidden Code

1. Open the Reveal Codes window by dragging the split box to the place in the document window where you want the Reveal Codes window to appear. Or open the View menu and choose the Reveal Codes command or press [Alt]+[F3].

2. Click the code you want to delete in the Reveal Codes window or move the cursor onto the code by using the cursor keys to move the insertion point in the editing window.

3. Press [Del].

You often may want to delete a hidden code in the Reveal Codes window in order to turn off a formatting command such as boldface text or a margin setting, for example. As soon as you delete a hidden code, you immediately notice the effect on the formatting of the document in the editing window.

Note: By default, WordPerfect does not prompt you when you delete a hidden code in the editing window (such as pressing the Backspace key to delete characters to the left of the cursor). However, you can instruct the program to prompt you before it removes a hidden code in the text when the Reveal Codes window is not open. Open the File menu and choose the Preferences Environment command to display the Environment Settings dialog box. Place a check in the Confirm on Code Deletion box. Note that WordPerfect never prompts you when you delete a code in the Reveal Codes window.

Marking Proposed Changes with Redline or Strikeout

Redlining and *strikeout* in WordPerfect enable you to indicate sections in the document that have been edited or require further editing. Redlining indicates where text has been or should be added since the last revision of the document. Strikeout, on the other hand, indicates where text should be or has been deleted from the document. For example, voter pamphlets sometimes use the strikeout technique to indicate which portions of an existing law or ordinance will be repealed if a particular ballot measure passes.

This example shows the pairs of WordPerfect [Redln] and [StkOut] codes in the Reveal Codes window, indicating the extent of redlining and strikeout.

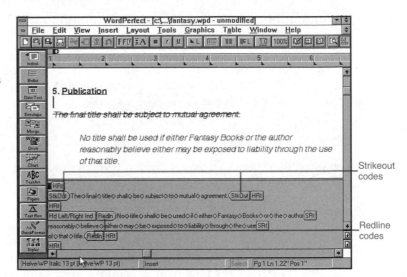

Choosing the Redline Method

Choosing a Redline Method

1. Open the **L**ayout menu.

2. Choose the **D**ocument option. WordPerfect displays a menu of document layout options.

3. Choose the **R**edline Method option.

WordPerfect displays the Document Redline dialog box, in which you specify a Redline method.

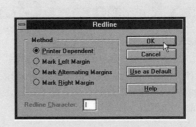

4. Choose one of the four Redline method option buttons.

5. If you chose the Mark Left Margin or Mark Alternating Margins option button in the preceding step, type the character you want to use for redlining (such as ¦) in the Redline Character text box.

6. To make your settings the default for all new documents, choose Use as Default.

7. Choose the OK button to record your changes and return to the document window.

The way WordPerfect displays redlining on-screen does not determine how redlining appears in the printed document. You can choose from the following methods for showing redlining in the printed version:

- **Printer Dependent.** This option marks redlined text according to your printer's definition of redlining. Some printers indicate redlined text by printing a mark in the left margin. Other printers indicate redlined text with shading or highlighting in the printout. Color printers print redlined text in red.

- **Mark Left Margin.** This option indicates redlined text by a vertical bar (or any other character you choose) printed in the left margin.

- **Mark Alternating Margins.** This option indicates redlined text by a vertical bar (or any other character you choose) printed in the outside margin of alternating odd and even pages.

- **Mark Right Margin.** This option indicates redlined text by a vertical bar (or any other character you choose) printed in the right margin.

Marking Text with Redline or Strikeout

Marking Text for Redlining or Strikeout

1. Select with the mouse or keyboard the text to be marked.

2. Open the Layout menu.

3. Choose the Font command or press F9. Then choose the Redline or Strikeout option and choose OK.

If you choose **R**edline, WordPerfect displays all selected text in red on a color monitor. On a monochrome monitor, WordPerfect uses the attribute selected in the Draft Mode Colors dialog box. If you choose Strikeout, the program displays all selected text with a line through it.

Removing Redline and Strikeout Markings

Removing Redline and Strikeout Markings

1. Open the **F**ile menu.

2. Choose the Compare Document option. WordPerfect displays a menu of Document Compare options.

3. Choose the **R**emove Markings option.

WordPerfect opens the Remove Markings dialog box, which enables you to remove all redline markings and strikeout text.

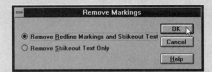

4. Choose Remove **R**edline Markings and Strikeout Text.

   or

   Choose Remove **S**trikeout Text Only.

5. Choose the OK button to return to the document window.

   WordPerfect for Windows removes redline markings and strikeout text in accordance with your choice in step 4.

After you finish editing and the document is in its final form, you can remove all redline markings and strikeout text. When you remove the redline markings, only the special formatting that indicates redlining disappears, not the redlined text itself. When you remove the strikeout markings, however, WordPerfect deletes the actual strikeout text along with the strikeout formatting.

Summary

In this chapter, you learned several basic editing techniques in WordPerfect. These techniques include opening a document for editing, inserting and deleting text, cutting and pasting text, and editing codes in the Reveal Codes window. In addition, you learned how to mark proposed editing changes in a document with the Redline and Strikeout features.

In the next chapter, you look at WordPerfect's more sophisticated editing features. You learn how to use the powerful Search and Replace features to locate and change text or codes in your document. You also learn how to use the Speller to locate misspelled words and the Thesaurus to find alternative terms for overused words in the document.

Proofreading Text

5

WordPerfect for Windows offers many features that help you edit a document quickly. The Find feature enables you to locate sections of text easily. By using the Replace feature, you can make a single edit and then apply it throughout the document; for example, you can change each occurrence of *Boston* to *Cambridge* throughout your entire document.

While the Find and Replace features help you make repetitive editing changes, WordPerfect's Speller, Thesaurus, and Grammatik grammar checker help you put the finishing touches on the contents of your documents. WordPerfect's Speller finds not only misspellings in the text, but also occurrences of double words and questionable capitalization. You can use WordPerfect's Thesaurus to find alternatives for overworked words and to clarify your points.

Grammatik proofreads your document to help you find problems with grammar, writing style, and sentence construction.

Locating text with the Find feature

Using the Replace feature

Correcting errors with the Speller

Using the Thesaurus

Using Grammatik

Key Terms in This Chapter	
Antonym	A word that has the opposite or nearly opposite meaning of another word. WordPerfect's Thesaurus lists antonyms along with synonyms for headwords.
Dictionary	A file called WP{WP}US.LEX, which contains about 115,000 words that WordPerfect uses to check your document for spelling errors. When checking spelling, WordPerfect ignores all words that are spelled correctly in its dictionary.
Headword	A word in the WordPerfect Thesaurus that has a list of synonyms and antonyms.
String	A collection of characters, including codes and spaces, that WordPerfect uses in search and replace operations.
Synonym	A word that has the identical or similar meaning as another word. You can use WordPerfect's Thesaurus to look up synonyms for any headword.

Locating Text with the Find Feature

The Find feature enables you to look for a single character, word, phrase, or hidden code either before or after the cursor's position. The set of characters, or characters and codes, that you want to locate in the document is known as a *string*. You can use WordPerfect's Find feature to quickly locate places in documents that require editing. To locate these places, specify a word or phrase as the search string.

Performing a Search

Searching for Text
1. Move the cursor to the place in the document where you want to begin searching for a word or phrase.

2. Open the Edit menu and choose the Find option, or press the Find key (F2).

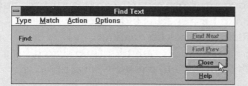

WordPerfect displays the Find Text dialog box, where you specify the string you are searching for and the direction of the search.

3. Type the string in the **F**ind text box of the dialog box.

To locate all occurrences of the string, regardless of the capitalization, type the string in all lowercase letters. For a single word, add a space before and/or after the word as part of the string. For a phrase, be sure to include the spaces between each word.

Note: To find the word *farm* in the text, type farm in the **F**ind text box and then either press the space bar or open the dialog box's **M**atch menu and choose **W**hole Word. If you don't include a space or choose the **W**hole Word option, WordPerfect stops at words that contain the word *farm,* such as *farming, farmed,* and *farmer.*

4. You can tell WordPerfect to search the entire document from the top, or from the cursor forward and then from the top of the document to the insertion point. Open the **O**ptions menu and choose **B**egin Find at Top of Document or **W**rap at Beg./End of Document.

If you select text before opening the Find Text dialog box, you can limit the search to the selected text; open the **O**ptions menu in the Find Text dialog box and choose Limit Find Within Selection.

5. By default, WordPerfect searches an entire document for the search string. To speed up the search, you can tell WordPerfect to exclude headers, footers, footnotes, or endnotes in the search by opening the **O**ptions menu and deselecting the appropriate option, such as Include Headers in Find.

6. Specify the direction of the search by choosing the **F**ind Next or Find **P**rev command button to initiate the search. WordPerfect locates the first occurrence of the search string.

The following search options also are available from the Find Text dialog box:

- **Type Specific Codes.** By default, WordPerfect searches for text, but this option enables you to search for a specific hidden code. A hidden code, such as Soft Hyphen or Right Tab, has no qualifiers; however, a specific hidden code has qualifiers such as a 12-point font. To search for a specific code, open the **Type** menu and choose **Specific Codes.**

WordPerfect displays the Specific Codes dialog box. Select the code you want to search for; then choose OK to return to the Find Text dialog box.

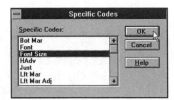

Type any additional keystrokes that may be required for the specific hidden code—for example, type 2" to locate a left margin of 2 inches.

- **Match Case.** WordPerfect can locate words or phrases that exactly match the case of the search string; for example, you might want to find *dBASE* but not *dBase* or *DBASE.* To specify an exact-case match, open the **Match** menu and choose **Case.**

- **Match Font.** WordPerfect can locate search text typed in a specific font and font size. To specify a font match, open the **Match** menu and choose **Font.**

WordPerfect displays the Match Font dialog box, where you can specify the font, style, point size, and attributes.

If, after choosing Match Case or Match Font, you change your mind and decide to search only for text, open the **Match** menu and choose **Font** again. Select the Text Only and then choose OK and choose **Find** Next or Find **Prev** to restart the search.

- **Match Codes.** WordPerfect can locate codes that you include in the search string. To include a code in the search string, open the **Match** menu and choose **Codes.**

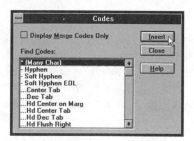

WordPerfect displays the Codes dialog box. In the Find **Codes** list box, select the code you want to insert in your search string.

To search for merge codes, you can choose the Display **Merge** Codes Only check box to limit the Find Codes list to merge codes. Choose **Insert** to add the selected code to the search string.

Tip: Keep in mind that in cases of paired codes, such as [Bold On] and [Bold Off], you need to select one or the other. If, for example, you are searching for an occurrence of a bold code followed by boldfaced text, insert the [Bold On] code and then type the word in the Find **For** text box. If you are searching for a non-boldfaced word preceded by the [Bold Off] code, insert the [Bold Off] code, add a blank space, and then type the word in the text box.

Tip: If you highlight a word or phrase before initiating a search with the Edit **Find** command or by pressing F2, WordPerfect inserts the selected text in the Find text box of the Find Text dialog box, together with any attribute codes included in the text. (To search the selected text for a search string, open the **Options** menu from the Find Text dialog box and choose Limit Find Within Selection.)

- **Action Select Match.** WordPerfect can automatically select (highlight) the search string when it finds it in the document text. To choose this option, which is the default, open the **A**ction menu and choose **S**elect Match. After finding the search string, WordPerfect selects it.

- **Action Position Before and Action Position After.** WordPerfect automatically selects (highlights) a search string when it finds it in the document text. If you prefer, you can tell WordPerfect to position the cursor before or after the located text. Open the **A**ction menu, choose Position **B**efore or **A**ction, and then choose Position **A**fter.

- **Action Extend Selection.** If you select text before initiating a search, WordPerfect can extend the selection up to and including the search text. To choose this option, open the **A**ction menu and choose **E**xtend Selection. When you choose Find **N**ext or Find **P**rev, WordPerfect selects all text from the current insertion point up to and including the search text.

When WordPerfect locates the first occurrence of the search string, it selects the search string in the document text and pauses.

> *Tip:* While the Find Text dialog box is displayed, you can click in the document window and edit the text; click in the Find Text dialog box to resume the search. With the keyboard, press Esc to move to the document window, edit the text, and then press F2 (or choose **E**dit **F**ind) to redisplay the Find Text dialog box and resume the search.

To locate the next occurrence of the string, choose the Find **N**ext button in the Find Text dialog box. To locate the previous occurrence of the string, choose Find **P**rev. When WordPerfect cannot locate any more occurrences of the search string in the direction you have specified, the program displays a Not Found dialog box. Choose OK to return to the Find Text dialog box; then choose **C**lose to cancel the search and return to the document window.

> *Tip:* To return the cursor to its original position in the document prior to the search, choose the **E**dit **G**o To command or press Ctrl+G; then select Last Position in the **P**osition list box and choose OK.

Using Wild-Card Characters

Searching for Unknown Characters

1. Move the cursor to the place in the document where you want to begin searching for a word or phrase.

2. Open the **Edit** menu and choose the **Find** option, or press the Find key (F2). WordPerfect displays the Find Text dialog box.

3. Type only the characters you are certain of; then add the wild-card code.

4. Open the **Match** menu, and choose **Codes** to display the Codes dialog box.

5. Select [*(Many Char)] in the Find Codes list box.

6. Choose the **Insert** command button to insert the code into the **Find** text box.

7. Type the rest of the string you are sure of; then choose **Find Next** or **Find Prev**.

WordPerfect includes two *wild-card codes* in the Codes dialog box: [*(Many Char)] to replace many characters, and [?(One Char)] to replace a single character. You can use the wild cards in a string when you are uncertain of how a particular word or phrase was spelled in the text.

You can substitute the [?(One Char)] code for a single occurrence of any character in a string, including the first character or a space. If you want to locate the last name of a client, for example, but you aren't sure whether it's spelled *Smith* or *Smyth* in the text, you can insert the [?(One Char)] code between *Sm* and *th* to locate either spelling in the document. You might use the [*(Many Char)] code, for example, to find the words *Johnson*, *Johnson's*, and *Johnsons*. In the Find text box, type Johnson followed by a [*(Many Char)] code.

Replacing Text and Codes with the Replace Feature

Using Replace

1. Open the Edit menu and choose **Replace**; or press Ctrl + F2. WordPerfect displays the Find and Replace Text dialog box.

2. In Find text box, type the text you want WordPerfect to find in the document.

3. In the Replace With text box, type the text that WordPerfect should use to replace the text you typed in the Find text box.

4. Choose one of the following command buttons: **Find**, **Replace**, or **Replace All**.

WordPerfect's Replace feature works much like the Find feature. When you use Replace, however, you enter a replacement string as well as a search string. You can use the Replace feature to replace a string of text or codes with different text or codes, or you can use it to remove the string completely from the document. To remove unwanted text or codes, you simply leave the Replace With text box blank.

Replacing a String

Replacing Characters, Words, and Other Strings

1. Position the cursor in the document where you want the search and replace operation to begin.

2. Open the Edit menu and choose the **Replace** option, or press the Replace key combination (Ctrl + F2).

   WordPerfect displays the Find and Replace Text dialog box where you enter the search and replace strings.

3. Enter the search string in the Find text box.

   You can use the same options described earlier in the sections "Performing a Search" and "Using Wild-Card Characters." For example, you can search and replace hidden codes.

4. Choose Replace **With**, and enter the replacement string.

   Enter text for the replacement string exactly as you want it to appear in the document. Be sure to include capitalization and punctuation in the string. If you are replacing codes, select the codes from the Codes dialog box, as described in the previous sections "Performing a Search" and "Using Wild-Card Characters."

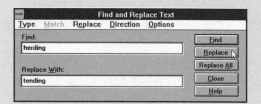

In this example, *herding* is the search string and *tending* is the replacement string.

   Tip: To delete the search string from the document, leave the Replace **With** text box blank.

5. To search and replace on a case-by-case basis, choose the **Replace** command button to start the search operation.

   WordPerfect highlights the first occurrence of the search string in the specified direction. To replace the highlighted string with the replacement string, choose the **Replace** command button. To skip the replacement and find the next occurrence of the search string, choose the **Find** button. To replace all occurrences automatically, choose Replace **All**. (For more details, see "Performing a Global Find and Replace.") WordPerfect does not pause to let you confirm each replacement.

6. Repeat step 5 until you have replaced all the desired occurrences; then choose the **Close** button in the Find and Replace Text dialog box.

   After WordPerfect has located the last occurrence of the search string, the program displays the Next Not Found message box. Choose the **Close** command button to close the Find and Replace Text dialog box.

   To return the cursor to its original position in the document, choose the **Edit Go** To command (or press Ctrl+G), select Last Position from the **Position** list box, and choose OK.

Performing a Global Find and Replace

Using Global Find and Replace

1. Position the cursor at the beginning of the document by pressing
   Ctrl + PgUp.

2. Open the **Edit** menu and choose the **R**eplace option, or press
   Ctrl + F2.

3. Enter the string you want to replace in the Find text box; then enter
   the new string in the Replace With text box.

   You can use the same options described earlier in the sections
   "Locating Text with the Find Feature" and "Using Wild-Card
   Characters."

4. Choose the Replace **A**ll command button.

Instead of using the Replace feature to perform the search-and-replace operation on a case-by-case basis, you can perform the operation globally throughout
a document. Use this method when you are sure that you want all occurrences
of the search string changed. You need to be careful when performing a global
search and replace because you cannot undo the damage if you make a mistake
(the Undo feature restores only the last replacement in the document).

When performing a global search and replace, make certain that the search
string you are about to replace throughout the document does not occur inside
another word or phrase you don't want changed. If you are globally replacing
the word *exam* with *test,* for example, make sure that you enter a space after
exam in the Find **F**or text box so that WordPerfect replaces only the word
exam. Otherwise, if you used the word *examination* in the document,
WordPerfect will change it to *testination* when you perform the global search
and replace.

Tip: Before beginning a global replace, save the document. This precaution ensures that if your global search and replace goes awry, you can return to the original document. To return to your original, use the **File Close** command to close the document, and then use the **File Open** command to retrieve the version just saved.

Correcting Errors with the Speller

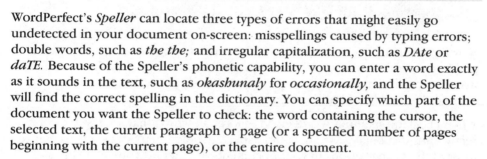

Using the Speller: The Basics

1. Open the **Tools** menu and choose **Speller**. Or click the Speller button on the Power Bar.

2. Choose **Start**.

WordPerfect's *Speller* can locate three types of errors that might easily go undetected in your document on-screen: misspellings caused by typing errors; double words, such as *the the;* and irregular capitalization, such as *DAte* or *daTE.* Because of the Speller's phonetic capability, you can enter a word exactly as it sounds in the text, such as *okashunaly* for *occasionally,* and the Speller will find the correct spelling in the dictionary. You can specify which part of the document you want the Speller to check: the word containing the cursor, the selected text, the current paragraph or page (or a specified number of pages beginning with the current page), or the entire document.

The Speller uses a dictionary that contains about 115,000 words. This dictionary is contained in a file called WP{WP}US.LEX. The dictionary is divided into two parts: a list of common, frequently used words, and a list of main words most often found in a dictionary. As you add words to the dictionary, they are placed in a supplementary dictionary file called WP{WP}US.SUP. You can edit the WP{WP}US.SUP dictionary file as you would any other WordPerfect document.

Tip: Save your document before beginning a spell-check if you think you may need to return to the previous version of the document.

Checking a Word, Page, Document, or Selection

Using the Speller: A Detailed Look

1. To check the spelling of a word, paragraph, or page, position the cursor anywhere in that word, paragraph, or page.

2. Open the **T**ools menu and choose the **S**peller option, or press Ctrl + F1. WordPerfect opens the Speller window. Alternatively, click the Speller button on the Power Bar.

3. Open the Check menu and specify how much of the document you want WordPerfect to check. By default, unless a block of text has been selected, the program chooses the **D**ocument option and checks the entire document. The Check menu options are discussed in detail further in this section.

4. Choose the **S**tart command button. WordPerfect starts checking the spelling of each word in the specified section of text.

WordPerfect can check the spelling of the current word, selected text, paragraph, page, or document. WordPerfect also can check spelling from the insertion point to the end of the page or document, or for a specified number of pages beginning with the current page.

When checking spelling, WordPerfect ignores all words that are spelled correctly in its dictionary. As you would expect, the dictionary does not recognize most of the proper nouns in your documents. If you find yourself using a particular proper noun routinely, you can add the noun to the supplementary dictionary; the Speller will no longer stop at that term.

When selecting the amount of text to check, choose from the following options:

- **W**ord checks the spelling of the word containing the cursor.

- **S**entence checks the sentence that contains the cursor.

- **P**aragraph checks the paragraph that contains the cursor.

- **P**age checks the page that contains the cursor.

- **D**ocument checks the spelling of the entire document. This option is the default menu choice. If you choose **D**ocument, the Speller checks the text in headers, footers, footnotes, and endnotes as well as the body text of the document.

Note: When you spell-check an entire document, you can place the cursor anywhere. When WordPerfect reaches the end of the document, it starts checking from the top of the document and stops at the point where you began the spelling check.

- To End of Document checks the spelling from the cursor's position to the end of the document.

- Selected Text checks the spelling of the currently highlighted text.

- Text Entry Box checks the spelling of text that you enter in a text box in a WordPerfect dialog box. For example, if you start the Speller by pressing Ctrl+F1 when typing an entry in the Subject: field of the Document Summary dialog box, WordPerfect opens the Speller window and automatically chooses the Text Entry Box option on the Check menu. At other times, this option is grayed (unavailable).

- Number of Pages displays the Number of Pages text entry box, where you can specify the number of pages to check, beginning with the current page.

Tip: To check the spelling of a block of text, select that block of text with the I-beam pointer before opening the Speller window. You also can select the text while the Speller window is displayed: open the Speller's Check menu, choose Selected, and choose the Start command button. WordPerfect checks the selected text and then deselects it.

Selecting an Alternative Spelling

If the Speller finds a word not included in any of the dictionary lists, WordPerfect highlights the word in the text and offers alternative spellings in the Suggestions list box. Near the top of the Speller window is the message Not found, followed by the unknown word selected in the text. The program also places in the Replace With text box the first alternative word listed in the Suggestions list box.

The Suggestions list box displays two types of alternative spellings: typographic suggestions and phonetic suggestions. To replace the unknown word highlighted in the text with the first alternative spelling in the Replace With text box, choose the Replace command button.

To select one of the other alternative spellings shown in the Suggestions list box, select the term by clicking it with the mouse or by pressing the arrow keys until the term is highlighted; then choose the **R**eplace command button to replace the unknown word in the text with the alternative you selected. If the unknown word you are replacing is capitalized, WordPerfect will capitalize the replacement.

In this example, the suggested spelling listed in the **W**ord text box, *livestock,* will replace the highlighted, un-known word, *livestack.*

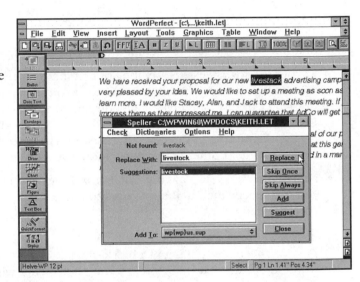

> *Tip:* If you use the mouse, you can replace the unknown word by double-clicking the alternative word in the Suggestions list box.

After WordPerfect replaces the unknown word with an alternative word, the program automatically continues to check the rest of the selected text for more unknown words.

Using the Other Speller Options

Many correctly spelled words do not appear in the WordPerfect dictionary, especially proper names and specialized terms. If the Speller window does not display the correct spelling, you can use one of the following options:

- To guess the correct spelling, type your guess in the Replace **W**ith text box and choose the S**u**ggest command button. If your guess is found in the dictionary and you want to replace the unknown word in the text with it, choose the **R**eplace command button. When attempting to enter an approximation of the spelling, you can enter the ? wild-card character to represent a single unknown character or the * wild-card character to stand for multiple unknown characters.

- Choose the Skip **O**nce command button to have the Speller ignore this particular occurrence of the unknown word. The Speller stops at any subsequent occurrences in the text.

- Choose the Skip A**l**ways command button to have the Speller ignore the current and all subsequent occurrences of the unknown word in the document. Use this option when you know that the word is spelled correctly but don't want to add it to the supplementary dictionary.

- Choose the **Ad**d command button to add the unknown word to the supplementary dictionary. The Speller ignores all further occurrences of the word in the text and adds the word to the supplementary dictionary file when the spelling check is completed.

- Choose the **C**lose command button to close the Speller window and cancel the spelling check.

You do not have to choose a suggested alternative spelling. You can type your editing changes into the Replace **W**ith text box of the Speller window. When you finish entering the correct word, choose the **R**eplace button; the Speller replaces the highlighted word in the text with the word you typed. WordPerfect then checks the spelling of this replacement. If the spelling is not found in one of the dictionaries, the program selects the replacement word in the text and suggests another replacement for it in the Replace **W**ith text box.

If you see something you want to edit while spell-checking your document, you can interrupt the process. While the Speller is paused at an unknown word, click the I-beam pointer in the text you want to edit. After making your changes, you can resume the spell-check from the insertion point by activating the Speller window choosing the **R**esume button.

Ignoring Words with Numbers

If your document contains words with numbers, such as *B52* or *RX7,* the Speller stops at each occurrence unless you deselect the Words with **N**umbers option on the Speller's **O**ptions menu. After you disable this option, WordPerfect ignores all words that contain both letters and numbers in the document.

Eliminating Double Words

WordPerfect's Speller searches for double words, such as *and and*. When the Speller finds double words, the Speller window displays the message `Duplicate words` and highlights the duplicate words in the document.

To delete one of the duplicates in the text, choose **R**eplace in the Speller window. To ignore the particular pair of double words that the program has highlighted and continue this type of checking, choose the Skip **O**nce or Skip **A**lways button.

If you want WordPerfect to ignore all occurrences of double words when spell-checking your document, open the Speller's **O**ptions menu and deselect the **D**uplicate Words option before you choose the **S**tart command button.

Correcting Irregular Case

The Speller also can check for common capitalization errors. If the program locates a word with questionable capitalization, it displays the message `Capitalization`, followed by the word in question.

Here, the Speller finds a word that has irregular capitalization: *CAlifornia*.

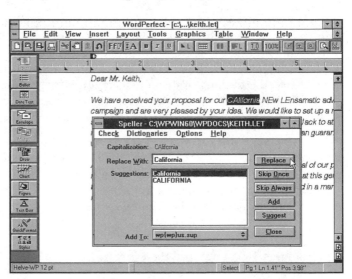

To change the capitalization of a word, choose the **R**eplace command button in the Speller window. To ignore a particular word with irregular case that the program has highlighted and continue this type of checking, choose Skip **O**nce or Skip **A**lways.

If you want WordPerfect to ignore all occurrences of irregular capitalization when spell-checking a document, open the Speller's Options menu and deselect the Irregular Capitalization option before choosing the Start command button.

Replacing Misspelled Words Automatically

WordPerfect for Windows can replace misspelled words in a document automatically, without asking for verification of each replacement. To turn on this option, open the Speller's Options menu and choose Auto Replace before you choose Start.

> *Note:* Before relying on the Auto Replace feature, you should use the Speller for a time in "manual" mode to ensure that the Speller doesn't make undesired corrections.

Using a Document Dictionary

You can create specialized dictionaries that the Speller uses to check specific documents. When you choose this option, WordPerfect automatically creates a new dictionary and links it to the current document. This option is useful when you need to spell-check documents that contain many technical terms that aren't used in other documents. To create a document-specific dictionary, open the Speller's Options menu and choose Document Dictionary before choosing Start.

Finding the Right Word with the Thesaurus

Using the Thesaurus
1. Positon the cursor within the word you want to look up in the Thesaurus.

2. Open the Tools menu and choose Thesaurus; or press Alt + F1 ; or click the Thesaurus button on the Power Bar.

WordPerfect's *Thesaurus* can improve your writing by helping you find alternative choices for many common words in your document. The Thesaurus is similar to the Speller except that the Thesaurus lists alternative word choices instead of alternative spellings.

The Thesaurus program uses a file named WP{WP}US.THS that consists of approximately 10,000 *headwords.* Headwords are words associated with lists of alternative word choices. The Thesaurus contains about 140,000 alternative words.

If the word you are looking up is a headword in the Thesaurus, WordPerfect displays a list of *synonyms* (words with identical or similar meanings) and *antonyms* (words with opposite or nearly opposite meanings). You can choose one of these alternative words and substitute it for the selected word in the text, or the Thesaurus can provide you with more choices.

Displaying Synonyms and Antonyms

Using the Thesaurus to Replace a Word

1. Move the cursor to the word you want to look up in the Thesaurus.

   You can place the cursor immediately before the first letter, immediately after the last letter, or anywhere within the word.

2. Open the **Tools** menu and choose **T**hesaurus, or press the Thesaurus key combination (Alt + F1). Alternatively, click the Thesaurus button on the Power Bar.

WordPerfect opens the Thesaurus window.

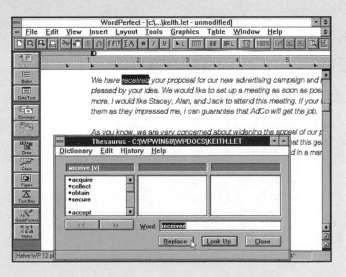

3. Select the alternative word you want to use. WordPerfect places that word in the **W**ord text box.

   If the list box contains many words, WordPerfect displays a scroll bar you can use to scroll new choices into view.

4. Choose the **R**eplace command button to replace the selected word in your text with the alternative word choice shown in the **W**ord text box.

   Tip: When substituting an alternative word in the text, WordPerfect does not try to match the tense of the word it is replacing. If you look up *worked* (past tense) in the Thesaurus, for example, the program will show synonyms and antonyms for the singular noun form and the present tense of the verb form (*work*). If you select *labor* (the first synonym for the verb form of *work*) as the replacement for *worked,* you must add *-ed* to the substitution to match the original past tense.

If the word you are looking up is a headword in the Thesaurus, the Thesaurus window displays a word list of synonyms and antonyms (*ant*) arranged in a list box with a scroll bar. Synonyms precede antonyms and are divided into groups by parts of speech, such as adjectives (*a*), nouns (*n*), or verbs (*v*). The word you are looking up appears at the top of the list box.

Looking Up More Alternative Words

If none of the synonyms or antonyms listed in the Thesaurus window are appropriate, you can look up alternative synonyms or antonyms. To look up more words, double-click any of the words preceded by a bullet—headwords— in the list, or select the word and press Enter.

When you double-click a headword, WordPerfect expands the list of alternatives by displaying synonyms and antonyms for that word in a subsequent list box. The program also traces your path with the hand icon from one list to another, pointing from the selected headword to the next box of alternatives.

The Thesaurus window can display no more than three list boxes at a time; however, you are not limited to looking up only three list boxes. The Thesaurus will automatically scroll the list boxes to the right within the Thesaurus window as needed. When using more than the three list boxes, you can move between the lists by clicking the left- and right-arrow buttons in the lower left corner of the Thesaurus window.

In this example, the Thesaurus displays *acquire* as the synonym for the highlighted word *received,* and headwords *gain* and *increase* are selected to show other alternatives.

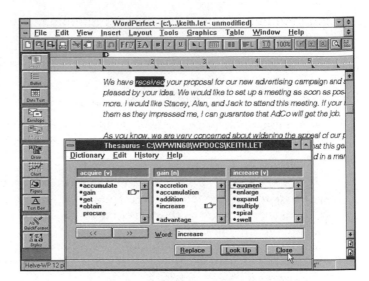

To clear the list boxes to scroll through one list of alternatives, you can use the Thesaurus' History menu to select the headword synonyms. The History pull-down menu shows all the headwords you have looked up, in order from last to first. When you select one of these headwords, WordPerfect clears the list boxes and places the alternative terms you have selected for the headword in the first list box. To bring back any of the other lists, select its headword in the History pull-down menu.

To clear the list boxes and review only the alternatives for the headword *increase,* choose increase from the History pull-down menu.

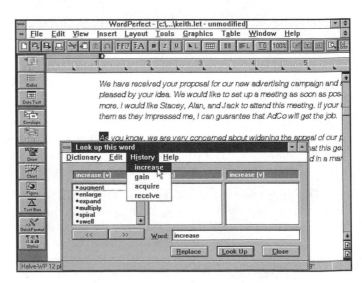

Using the Look Up Option

If the word you are looking for is not a headword in the Thesaurus, the Thesaurus window will be empty. You will see the message Word not found in the lower left corner of the status bar.

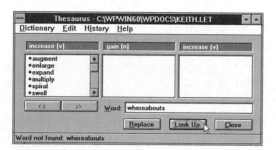

In this example, the Thesaurus shows no alternatives for *whereabouts,* which isn't a headword. Notice the Word not found message in the status bar.

To look up alternative terms, you must enter a synonym of your own, such as *locale,* in the Word text box; then choose the Look Up command button.

If the word you looked up is a headword, WordPerfect displays a list of synonyms and antonyms for it in the Thesaurus window. You can substitute any of these new word choices by selecting one and choosing the Replace command button.

When you are ready to exit the Thesaurus, choose the Close command button. To return to editing without closing the Thesaurus window, reduce the window to an icon by clicking the Minimize button or choosing the Minimize option on the Control menu.

Using the Grammar Checker

Using Grammatik

1. Open the Tools menu and choose Grammatik; or press
   Alt + Shift + F1 ; or click the Grammatik button on the Power Bar.

2. Choose the Start command button.

WordPerfect for Windows includes a powerful grammar checker, Grammatik, that can help you identify and correct errors in writing style, grammar, and sentence construction. During a grammar-checking session, Grammatik can also check spelling. Grammatik can adapt its rules to ten writing styles, depending on the type of document you want to check—informal, business, and so on. You can customize Grammatik so that it identifies the errors you make most frequently and overlooks errors you seldom make, thus speeding the grammar-checking operation.

Starting Grammatik

Checking Writing Style with Grammatik

1. Open the **Tools** menu and choose **Grammatik**; or press
   Alt + ⇧Shift + F1 ; or click the Grammatik button on the Power Bar.

WordPerfect for
Windows dis-
plays the
Grammatik
dialog box.

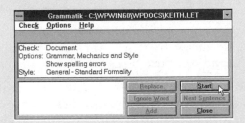

2. Open Grammatik's **Check** menu and choose one of the following options to grammar-check the indicated portion of the document: **Sentence**, **Paragraph**, **Document** (the default), To End of Document, or Selected **Text**.

3. Choose the **Start** command button to begin checking grammar immediately, with default options for writing style, grammar, sentence mechanics, and so on.

4. Choose the Next Sentence command button to continue checking.

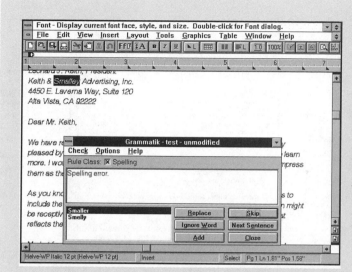

Grammatik begins checking the document and stops at the first error—in this case, a questionable spelling. You can choose **Replace**, Ignore **Word**, or **Add**, as described in the previous section "Correcting Errors with the Speller."

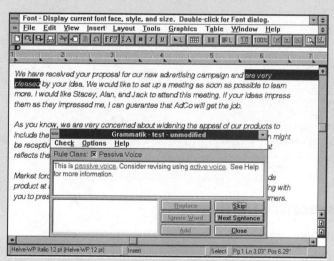

In this example, Grammatik stops at a questionable use of passive voice.

5. Click in the document and make any necessary corrections to the sentence.

   or

   Click **Skip** to skip this error and continue checking.

continues

continued

To display infor-
mation about the
specific error,
open Gram-
matik's **Help**
menu and
choose **Rule
Class**. Grammatik
displays the
Grammatik 5
window, with
specific informa-
tion about the
error—in this
case, passive
voice.

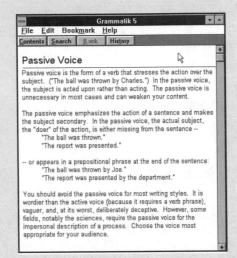

6. In the Grammatik 5 window, open the **File** menu and choose **Exit**; or click in the document and make any needed corrections; or click in the Grammatik dialog box to return to the dialog box.

7. Choose **Resume** to continue checking.

8. When you reach the end of the document, WordPerfect displays a dialog box asking whether you want to close Grammatik. Choose **Yes** or **No**.

Choosing Grammatik Options

The following useful options are available from the Grammatik dialog box:

- **Options**, **Writing Style**. When you choose this option, Grammatik displays the Writing Style dialog box, where you can choose one of the ten supplied writing styles. Grammatik uses appropriate rules to check General, Advertising, Business Letter, and other documents. In the Writing Style dialog box, choose **Writing Style**, highlight a style, and choose **OK**. From the Writing Style dialog box, you also can choose a "Formality Level" for grammar checking. Choose **Standard**, **Formal**, or **Informal**, depending on the degree of formality you want to convey.

You can customize any of the supplied writing styles, and you can customize the Custom 1, Custom 2, or Custom 3 writing styles to tailor a writing style to your own needs. Highlight a style in the **Writing Style** list box; then choose **Edit**.

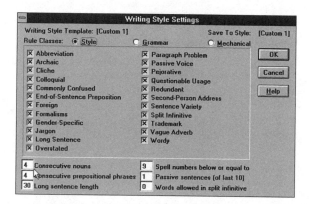

WordPerfect displays the Writing Style Settings dialog box, where you can customize a writing style.

Choose the **Style** radio button, and choose the options you want by selecting the desired check boxes. Enter numbers for Consecutive nouns and so on at the bottom of the Writing Style Settings dialog box. Then choose the **Grammar** or **Mechanical** radio button to display their corresponding options. When you finish selecting the options you want, then choose Save and OK to return to the Grammatik dialog box.

- **Options, Checking Options.** Choose this option to display the Options dialog box.

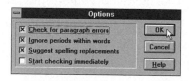

Mark the options you want in the Options dialog box and choose OK to return to the Grammatik dialog box.

- Choose **Options**, then choose **Grammar, Mechanics and Style.** Choosing this option causes Grammatik to check for grammar errors specifically related to mechanics and style.

- **Options, Grammar and Mechanics.** When you choose this option, Grammatik checks for these types of errors and doesn't check for errors in style.

- **Options, Statistics.** When you choose this option and choose **S**tart from the Grammatik dialog box, Grammatik displays the Document Statistics dialog box, without pausing to let you correct spelling and grammar errors.

The Document Statistics infor-mation box shows a list of grammar-related statistics for the document.

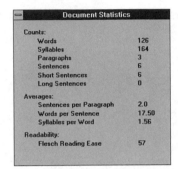

Document statistics help you determine whether you are using overly long and complex sentences and words. To close the Document Statistics box and return to Grammatik, double-click the control box or press Alt+F4.

Summary

In this chapter, you learned how to search and replace text in a document, check your document for spelling errors, and look up synonyms and antonyms for particular terms. These proofreading techniques can help you eliminate errors from your documents and make them more interesting to read.

In the next chapter, you will learn how to format your documents at the paragraph and character levels. As part of this process, you will learn how to change margins, tabs, line spacing, justification, fonts, and text attributes.

Formatting Paragraphs and Characters

Formatting refers to the appearance of text in a finished document. As a WYSIWYG word processing program, WordPerfect can display on-screen almost all the formatting you assign to your document.

Formatting occurs on three levels in a WordPerfect document: the document level, where formatting affects the layout of the pages; the paragraph level, where formatting affects the layout of each paragraph of text; and the character level, where formatting affects the font, size, and type styles assigned to individual characters and words.

This chapter examines the WordPerfect features you use to format your document at the paragraph and character levels. The next chapter looks at formatting on the document level. In the Windows version of WordPerfect, you can perform most paragraph and character formatting in the document editing window using the Ruler and the Power Bar.

WordPerfect for Windows makes extensive use of styles to perform formatting chores. In some cases, you can choose to format paragraphs and characters—centering text on a line, for example—using styles or individual formatting commands. This chapter introduces you to working with styles.

Changing the units of measurement

Understanding the Ruler

Indenting paragraphs

Changing justification

Aligning text

Understanding fonts

Changing line spacing

Using special characters

Controlling line breaks

Key Terms in This Chapter

Auto code placement	System that places certain formatting codes that affect an entire paragraph or page at the beginning of the paragraph or page. The codes then replace any other like codes. This feature prevents the build-up of codes that cancel one other in a document.
Font	A particular type style in a specific point size, such as 10-point Helvetica. In WordPerfect, you can assign fonts from the Ruler, the Font menu, or the Font dialog box.
Line height	The amount of space that WordPerfect assigns between lines, measured from the bottom of one line to the bottom of the next.
Ruler	An on-screen bar you can use to control paragraph and character formatting, such as tab settings, margin settings, line spacing, justification, fonts, and styles.
Style	A group of formatting commands that you can apply with a few mouse clicks or keystrokes. When you edit a style, WordPerfect for Windows reformats your document automatically.

Changing the Units of Measurement

Changing Units of Measure

1. Open the File menu and choose Preferences.

2. Choose Display from the Preferences dialog box.

3. In the Display Preferences dialog box, choose Document.

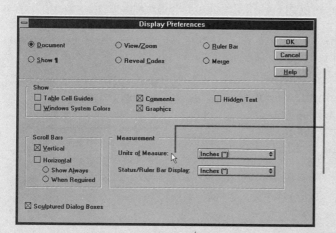

WordPerfect displays the Document preference settings, including Units of Measure and Status/Ruler Bar Display.

4. To change the units for dialog boxes, choose Units of Measure and choose Inches ("), the default; Inches (i); Centimeters (c); Millimeters (m); Points (p); or 1200ths of an inch (w).

   WordPerfect uses the character in parentheses to indicate the current unit of measure: 5" or 5i for five inches, for example.

5. Choose Status/Ruler Bar Display to change the unit of measure that WordPerfect uses in the Status Bar and Ruler.

6. Choose OK, Close to record your changes to the units of measurement and return to the document.

Now, in any dialog box that requires you to specify a measurement, such as for margins in the Margins dialog box, the default settings display using the new units you have chosen.

WordPerfect enables you to specify one unit of measurement for the display and entry of numbers in dialog boxes and another for the display on the status bar. The unit of measurement you choose for the display and entry of numbers appears in the dialog box when you change settings. Most of the time, however, you will want to maintain the same unit for the settings you enter in dialog boxes and those displayed in the status bar.

You can, however, specify the measurement in any other units by adding an abbreviation that indicates the type of units you're using. WordPerfect then converts your entry into the default units of measurement. If, for example, you have changed the units of measurement for the Display and Entry of Numbers option to centimeters but want to enter the line height measurement in points, you can append *p* to the number of points you enter, as in 24p (which the program converts to 0.85c).

You can use the following abbreviations to change settings that have a nondefault unit of measurement:

Code	Unit of Measurement
i or "	Inches
p	Points
c	Centimeters
m	Millimeters
w	1200ths of an inch

Tip: Keep in mind that WordPerfect converts any fractions you enter in dialog boxes to decimal equivalents. If you enter a measurement as 2/3, for example, WordPerfect converts the fraction to 0.666 when you move to the next text box.

Understanding the Ruler

The Ruler is one of the most powerful and easy-to-use features in WordPerfect. The Ruler is composed of two parts: the first line displays the current left and right margin settings, and the second line contains a *tab ruler* showing all the current tab settings. Notice that the Power Bar and Button Bar contain buttons for formatting tasks: adding tabs, setting line spacing, choosing a font, using styles, and using the QuickFormat feature.

To display the Ruler in the active document editing window, choose the View menu and choose **R**uler Bar (or press Alt+Shift+F3).

The command to display the Ruler acts like a toggle switch: to hide the Ruler to maximize the amount of text in the document window, choose the **V**iew **R**uler Bar command again, or press Alt+Shift+F3 a second time.

> *Tip:* To keep the screen from becoming too cluttered when you have the Ruler, Power Bar, and Button Bar displayed, move the Button Bar to the bottom or side of the screen. Move the mouse pointer onto the Button Bar until it becomes a hand; then drag the Button Bar to the desired location. To learn more about using the Button Bar and Power Bar, see chapter 2, "Getting Acquainted with WordPerfect for Windows."

Adjusting the Left and Right Margins

The first line of the Ruler indicates the document margins. In the bar are two triangles facing one another, icons representing the left and right margin settings. The shaded areas on the left and right side of the bar graphically depict the actual margins—that is, the distance between the left and the right edge of the paper and these margin settings.

By default, WordPerfect sets a one-inch left and right margin for your document. On an 8 1/2-inch wide page, WordPerfect places the left margin setting at the one-inch mark and the right margin setting at the 7 1/2-inch mark on the Ruler.

The easiest way to change the left or right margin is to drag the icon representing the margin you want to change to the desired ruler setting. When you click a margin icon, WordPerfect displays a dotted line that runs down the edge of the document. As you drag the margin icon left or right, this dotted line moves, helping you determine how the margin adjustment will affect the text. As soon as you reset a margin, WordPerfect immediately reflows the text of your document to conform to the new setting.

Left margin

Left margin setting

Right margin setting

Right margin

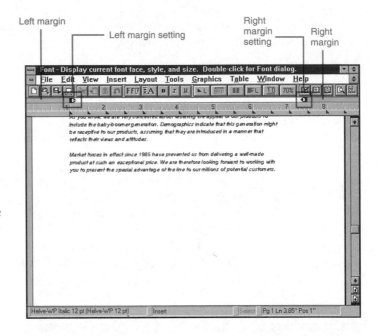

In this document, you can see the current left and right margins, represented by the gray areas. The margin settings are represented by the triangular icons.

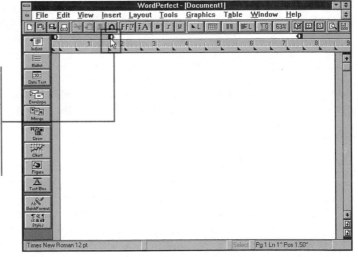

In this example, the left margin icon has been dragged to the 1 1/2-inch mark on the Ruler, increasing the left margin to 1 1/2 inches.

You also can change the left and right margin settings by typing new values in the **Left** and **Right** text boxes in the Margins dialog box. When the Ruler is displayed in the document window, you can display the Margins dialog box by double-clicking anywhere in the margin area (the gray portion) of the Ruler or by double-clicking the margin icon.

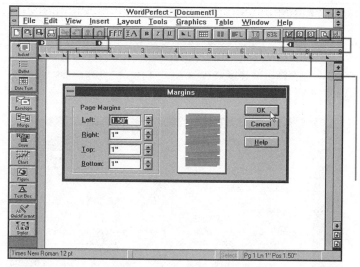

To display the Margins dialog box, double-click one of the margin areas or margin icons.

To display the Margins dialog box with a QuickMenu, click the right mouse button in the margin area of the Ruler or above the units line on the tab ruler; then choose **Margins**.

You also can display the Margins dialog box by opening the **Layout** menu and choosing **Margins**, or you can press Ctrl+F8.

When the Margins dialog box is displayed, you can change the left and right margins by entering new values in the **Left** and **Right** text boxes before choosing OK. (For information on using the Margins dialog box to set new top and bottom margins, see chapter 7, "Formatting Pages.")

When you change the left or right margin setting in the document, WordPerfect inserts a [Lft Mar:] or [Rgt Mar:] code at the beginning of the paragraph that contains the cursor (insertion point). If you increase the left margin to two inches, for example, WordPerfect inserts the code [Lft Mar:2"] at the beginning of the paragraph that contains the cursor. This code controls the left margin setting for the rest of the document until another margin code is encountered.

If you change your mind about the new margin settings, place the cursor somewhere in the paragraph where the margins change; then reset the margins by moving the margin icons on the Ruler or by entering new values in the Margins dialog box. You also can return to the default one-inch margins by opening the Reveal Codes window and deleting the margin code at the beginning of the paragraph.

Auto Code Placement

The system that WordPerfect uses to place codes at the beginning of a paragraph, regardless of where the insertion point is located in that paragraph, is called *auto code placement*. Auto code placement also replaces any code of the same type with the new settings you choose.

In this example, even though the cursor is located in the middle of the first paragraph, when the left margin is increased to 1.2 inches, WordPerfect inserts a [Lft Mar: 1.20"] code at the beginning of that paragraph.

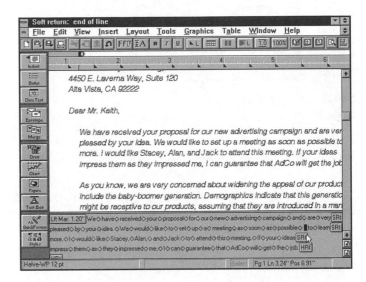

When you then increase the left and right margins to two inches without moving the cursor, WordPerfect replaces just the margin settings in the original left/right margin code.

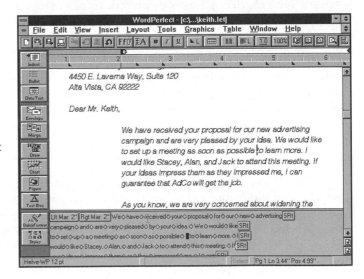

Not all formatting codes use auto code placement. The following list indicates the features for which WordPerfect uses auto code placement. Note that WordPerfect automatically places a few codes at the beginning of the current *page* rather than the current *paragraph*.

Codes Moved to Beginning of Paragraph

Columns

Hyphenation zone

Word and letter spacing

Justification

Line spacing

Line numbering

Line height

Left and right margins

Paragraph numbering

Tab set

Word spacing justification limits

Codes Moved to Beginning of Page

Center page

Footer

Header

Top and bottom margins

Page numbering

Page size

Suppress page numbering

Tab Settings in WordPerfect

WordPerfect's default tab ruler sets uniform left-justified tab stops positioned at 1/2-inch intervals. The program supports four types of tab settings: left, center, right, and decimal (see table 6.1).

Table 6.1   Types of Tab Settings Available in WordPerfect

Type	Effect on Text
Left	Left-justifies text at the tab stop. In Insert mode, WordPerfect indents existing text to the tab stop. This type of tab is the default.
Center	Centers text at the tab stop. This type of tab is commonly used to center column headings in tables.
Right	Right-justifies text at the tab stop.
Decimal	Justifies text on the alignment character (by default, the period) at the tab stop so that any text typed before the period is right-justified, and any text typed after the period is left-justified. This type of tab is commonly used to align columns of numbers on the decimal point.

Each type of tab has its own marker in the Ruler. In this example, a left tab is set at 3.5 inches, a center tab at 3.75 inches, a right tab at 4.25 inches, and a decimal tab at 4.75 inches.

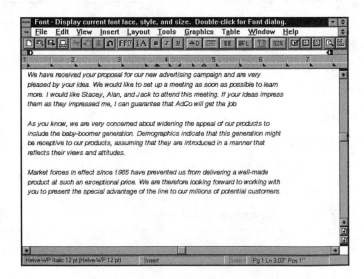

Left Tab	Center Tab	Right Tab	Decimal.Tab
			$3.45
			$45.67
			$234.56
		Gloria	
		John	
		Cynthia	
	Gloria		
	John		
	Cynthia		
Gloria			
John			
Cynthia			

In this example, you see text formatted with the four different types of tabs supported by WordPerfect.

Each type of tab setting can have a *dot leader*—a series of periods preceding the tab. To add dot leaders to the four types of tab icons on the Ruler, click the dot leader button at the beginning of the line that contains the tab icons. This procedure adds periods to the basic triangular shape of the tab icons. Click the dot leader icon a second time to remove dot leaders from the tabs and return the tab icons to their original shape.

The Tab Ruler

The easiest way to change individual tab settings for your document is to change the tab ruler directly. On the tab ruler, you can reposition a tab stop or delete it entirely. You also can use the dot leader button and tab icons beneath the tab ruler to change the type of tab on the Ruler or to add new tab stops to it.

To space any of your tabs at unequal intervals on the Ruler, use the mouse to drag the tab icons to new locations. Click the tab icon you want to move and drag it until it is aligned with the desired tick mark on the tab ruler.

Deleting Tabs

To remove an existing tab stop, click and drag the tab icon you want to remove off the tab ruler before you release the left mouse button. To delete several tabs at one time, position the mouse pointer in the space (gray area) to the left of the first tab in the group you want to delete. Then drag the pointer to the left or right. As you drag, WordPerfect selects each tab. When you have highlighted all the tabs you want to remove, drag the group off the Ruler before releasing the mouse button.

By default, tabs "snap" to the nearest increment displayed on the tab ruler. To set tabs more precisely using the tab ruler, you can disable this feature. Choose File, Preferences, Display, Ruler Bar. Under Ruler Bar Options, remove the X from the Tabs Snap to Ruler Bar Grid check box.

While you are viewing the Ruler Bar preferences, you can also set two other options. To have WordPerfect show a dotted line on the Ruler Bar indicating the current location of the cursor in document text, be sure the Show Ruler Bar Guides check box is marked. To display a sculptured Ruler Bar—one with beveled edges—choose Sculptured Ruler Bar.

Changing the Type of Tab

Changing Tab Types

1. Drag the tab you want to replace off the tab ruler.

2. Click the right mouse button in the tab ruler to display the QuickMenu, or click the Tab Set button on the Power Bar to display a drop-down menu of tab types.

3. From either menu, choose the type of tab you want to create. You can choose any of the four tab types, with or without dot leaders.

4. Click in the tab ruler beneath the numbered ruler bar to insert a tab of the type you chose in step 2.

   As soon as you release the mouse button, the new tab marker appears on the ruler.

By default, all tabs on the tab ruler are left-aligned. You can change any tab to another type by following the same steps.

Adding Tabs

Creating a Tab

1. Click the right mouse button in the tab ruler to display the QuickMenu, or click the Tab Set button on the Power Bar to display a drop-down menu of tab types.

2. From either menu, choose the type of tab you want to create.

3. Click the tab ruler beneath the numbered ruler bar to insert a tab of the type you chose in step 2.

   As soon as you release the mouse button, the new tab marker appears on the ruler.

   An icon for the new tab stop appears beneath the tick mark on the Ruler. If you find that you have positioned the tab icon on the wrong tick mark, move the tab by dragging it to the correct place on the Ruler.

The Tab Set Dialog Box

When you need to modify only a few individual tab settings in your document, make your changes on the tab ruler as discussed earlier. To set tabs very precisely, set a series of uniformly spaced tabs across the ruler, or use the Tab Set dialog box to delete all existing tabs before setting new ones.

> *Tip:* The easiest way to delete all tab settings is to open the Tab QuickMenu by clicking the right mouse button on the tab ruler, and then select Clear All Tabs.

To display the Tab Set dialog box when the Ruler is displayed, double-click a tab stop on the tab ruler or one of the tab icons on the bar beneath the tab ruler. Or click the right mouse button anywhere on the tab ruler; then choose Tab Set from the QuickMenu.

You also can display the Tab Set dialog box by choosing the Layout, Line, Tab Set.

Deleting All Tabs

To delete all existing tabs, click the Clear All command button in the Tab Set dialog box. If you ever delete tabs by mistake with this button, you can restore the original tab settings by clicking the Default command button. WordPerfect deletes the tabs from the Ruler.

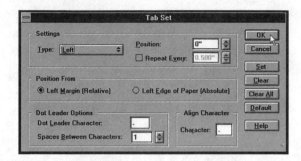

This is the Tab Set
dialog box.

Any tabs you set with the options on the Tab Set dialog box are added to the
tabs already on the tab ruler. Many times, especially when setting uniform tabs,
you will want to delete all existing tabs first.

Setting Uniform Tabs

Setting Uniform Tabs

1. Open the Layout menu, choose Line, and then choose Tab Set.
   WordPerfect displays the Tab Set dialog box.

2. In the Tab Set dialog box, place an X in the Repeat Every check box.

3. Enter the first tab position in the Position text box.

4. In the Repeat Every text box, enter the amount of space you want
   between each tab in the Ruler.

5. By default, the Left Align option button beneath Tabs is selected. To
   set uniform tabs of another type, select the appropriate type from the
   Type drop-down list: Center, Right, Decimal, Dot Left, Dot Center,
   Dot Right, or Dot Decimal.

6. By default, WordPerfect positions the tabs relative to the current left
   margin. To set tabs absolutely from the left edge of the page, choose
   the Left Edge of Paper (Absolute) option button.

7. To check the spacing of your uniform tabs in a Position list box
   before you put them into effect, click the Set command button. You
   can skip this step and go on to step 7 if you don't want to review the
   tab settings in this list box.

8. Choose OK to set the tabs, format your text according to the tabs,
   and return to your document.

By default, WordPerfect sets uniform left-aligned tabs spaced at one-half inch increments across the entire ruler, starting at the zero inch mark.

Remember, if you don't delete all existing tab stops before you follow these steps, WordPerfect adds the new uniform tabs you have just defined to the existing tabs.

Setting Nonuniform Tabs

Setting Nonuniform Tabs

1. Choose **L**ayout, **L**ine, **T**ab Set, and in the **P**osition text box, enter the Ruler measurement for the new tab you want to add.

2. Choose the **S**et command button.

   WordPerfect displays the tab in the tab ruler.

3. If you don't want to add additional tabs to the Ruler (uniform or varying), choose OK to add the tab to the Ruler and format your text.

4. To add more tabs, repeat steps 1 and 2.

Changing Dot Leader and Align Characters

Changing the Dot Leader and Align Characters

1. Choose **L**ayout, **L**ine, **T**ab Set, and in the Tab Set dialog box, choose Dot **L**eader Character.

2. Press `◆Backspace` to delete the default character (a dot); then type the new dot leader character.

3. To adjust the spacing between dot leader characters, choose Spaces **B**etween Characters and type a new spacing; or use the scroll arrows to change the number.

4. To change the align character for decimal-aligned tabs, choose **C**haracter, press `◆Backspace` to delete the default character (a dot), and type the new character.

5. Choose OK to return to the document screen.

Indenting Paragraphs

When you use one of WordPerfect's Tab or Indent features, the settings in your document control how the text of a paragraph is indented. Never use the space bar to indent text in a document. WordPerfect cannot properly indent or align your text when you use a proportionally spaced font and you indent with the space bar. When you press the space bar, WordPerfect inserts individual spaces in the text. When you press the Tab or Indent keys, WordPerfect inserts a hidden code that indents the text to the next available tab setting.

Indenting the First Line of a Paragraph

Press Tab to indent only the first line of a paragraph from the left margin. Each time you press Tab, the cursor moves to the next tab stop on the Ruler.

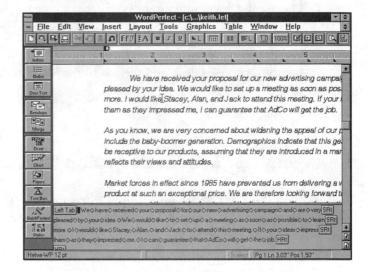

Remember that you must be in Insert mode to indent existing text with Tab. If the program is in Typeover mode when you press Tab, WordPerfect moves the cursor to the next tab stop without indenting the text.

Indenting a Paragraph on the Left

To indent a paragraph at the left margin, open the **L**ayout menu and choose **P**aragraph, **I**ndent; or press F7. The cursor moves to the next tab stop to the right, temporarily resetting the left margin. Everything you type until you press Enter is indented to this tab stop.

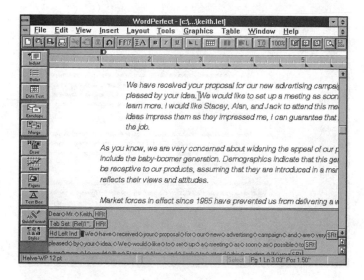

Press F7 to indent an entire paragraph from the left margin.

To indent a paragraph more than one tab stop, open the **L**ayout menu and choose **P**aragraph Indent; or press F7 until the cursor is located at the tab stop on which you want to align the left margin of your paragraph.

You can indent an existing paragraph by opening the **L**ayout menu and choosing **P**aragraph Indent or by pressing F7. Make sure that the cursor is located at the start of the paragraph and the program is in Insert mode at the time you choose the command.

Indenting a Paragraph on the Left and Right

To indent a paragraph from the left and right margins, open the **L**ayout menu and choose **P**aragraph, **D**ouble Indent; or press the key combination Ctrl+Shift+F7. The cursor moves to the next tab stop to the right, and the left and right margins are reset temporarily. Everything you type until you press Enter is indented one tab stop on the left and right.

To indent a paragraph more than one tab stop on the left and right, open the **L**ayout menu and choose **P**aragraph **D**ouble Indent; or press Ctrl+Shift+F7 until the cursor is located at the tab stop on which you want to align the left margin of your paragraph.

You can indent an existing paragraph on both sides using this command or the key combination. Make sure that the cursor is located at the start of the paragraph and the program is in Insert mode.

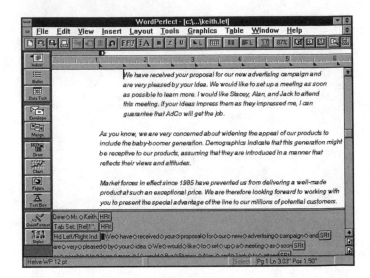

Press the Double Indent key combination, Ctrl+Shift+F7, to indent an entire paragraph from both the left and right margins.

Creating a Hanging Indent

Creating a Hanging Indent

To create a hanging indent for a new paragraph, follow these steps:

1. Position the cursor at the beginning of a new line.

2. Open the Layout menu; then choose Paragraph, Hanging Indent (or press Ctrl + F7).

3. Type the text of your paragraph.

To format an existing paragraph with a hanging indent, follow these steps:

1. Position the cursor at the beginning of the first line of the paragraph.

   If the paragraph has been indented with a tab, press +Backspace to remove the tab from the first line. Then make sure that the program is in Insert mode.

2. Open the Layout menu and choose Paragraph, Hanging Indent; or press Ctrl + F7 .

   WordPerfect indents all the lines of the paragraph except for the first line.

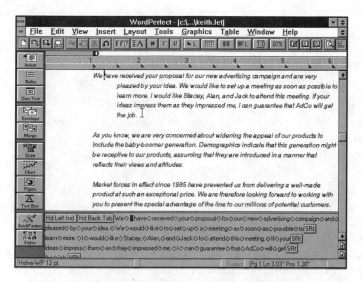

Press the Hanging Indent key combination, Ctrl+F7, to indent every line of a paragraph except the first one.

WordPerfect enables you to create a hanging indent by choosing **Layout**, **Paragraph**, **Hanging** Indent or by pressing the Hanging Indent key combination, Ctrl+F7. With a hanging indent, the first line of the paragraph is flush with the left margin and the rest of the paragraph is indented to the first tab stop.

When word wrap moves the first word to the second line of the paragraph, WordPerfect moves the word to the first tab stop to indent the line. The program continues to indent every line (except the first one) until you press Enter to end the paragraph. You also can add a hanging indent to an existing paragraph.

Changing the Type of Justification

Changing Justification

1. Move the cursor into the paragraph for which you want to change justification.

continues

continued

2. Open the Layout menu, choose Justification, and then choose **Left** (the default), **Right**, **Center**, **Full**, or **All**. Alternatively, click the Justification button on the Power Bar and select the justification option you want.

   If you prefer to use the keyboard, you also can choose left justification by pressing `Ctrl`+`L`, right justification with `Ctrl`+`R`, center justification with `Ctrl`+`E`, and full justification with `Ctrl`+`J`.

Tip: With full justification turned on, WordPerfect for Windows ordinarily doesn't justify the last line of a paragraph to avoid inserting too much space between words. If you open the Layout menu and then choose Justification All, WordPerfect forces justification of the last line of each paragraph. You can apply this setting to logos and headings, forcing wide letterspacing for a special "designed" effect.

Justification determines the way the lines of text in each paragraph are aligned. Table 6.2 describes the five types of justification that WordPerfect supports.

Table 6.2   Types of Justification Available in WordPerfect

Option	Effect on Text
Left	Justifies text on the left margin, leaving a ragged right margin. This is the default justification for all new documents.
Right	Justifies text on the right margin, leaving a ragged left margin.
Center	Centers all lines of text.
Full	Justifies text on the left and right margins, except the last line of the paragraph.
All	Justifies text on the left and right margins, including the last line of the paragraph.

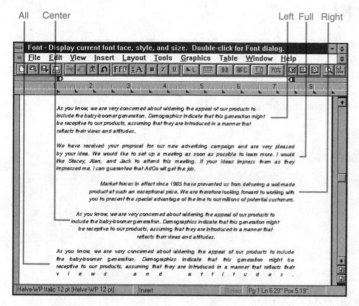

This document shows five paragraphs, each formatted with a different type of justification.

WordPerfect makes changing the type of justification in your document very easy. Just position the mouse pointer on the Justification button on the Power Bar and hold down the left mouse button until a pop-up list containing the five justification options appears. Drag down the list until you highlight the justification option you want to use. Release the mouse button to choose the option.

As soon as you choose a new type of justification, WordPerfect realigns the text of the paragraph that contains the cursor, or for the selected text, or until it encounters another justification code.

Sometimes you may need to apply a particular justification to just one section of the document. To set off a paragraph of quoted material, for example, you may want to use full justification. To apply a particular justification to one section, first select the text. Then choose the new type of justification from the pop-up list on the Justification button on the Power Bar; alternatively, open the Layout menu, choose Justification, and then choose the type of justification you want.

Aligning Text

Instead of changing the alignment for several or even all paragraphs in your document, you may simply need to modify the alignment of a single short line, when entering a report title or heading, for example. You can choose to center a line of text between the margins, center text on a specific point in a line, or align a line flush with the right margin.

Centering a Line between Margins

Centering a Line

To center a line of text between the left and right margins before you have typed the line, follow these steps:

1. Position the cursor at the beginning of the new line you want to center.

2. Open the **Layout** menu, choose **Line**, and then choose **Center**; or press ⬆Shift + F7.

   or

   Click the right mouse button in the text area of the document window to display the QuickMenu; then choose Center.

   or

   Click the Justification button on the Power Bar and choose the Center option from the pop-up list.

   When you choose this command, the cursor moves so that it is centered between the left and right margins.

3. Type the line of text you want to center. As you type, the text adjusts to the left and right, remaining centered.

4. Press ⏎Enter to end centering.

To center a line of text after you have typed it, follow these steps:

1. Position the cursor at the beginning of the line, before the first character. To center several lines of text, select those lines with the I-beam pointer.

2. Open the **Layout** menu, choose **Line**, and then choose **Center**; or press ⟨⇧Shift⟩ + ⟨F7⟩.

   or

   Click the right mouse button in the text area of the document window to display the QuickMenu; then choose **Center**.

   or

   Click the Justification button on the Power Bar and choose the Center option from the pop-up list.

   WordPerfect centers the line between the left and right margins.

Centering Text on a Specific Point

Centering Text on a Specific Point

1. Position the cursor at the beginning of the blank line where you want the centered text to appear.

2. Press ⟨Tab⟩ or press the space bar until the cursor is positioned at the point on which you want the text centered.

3. Open the **Layout** menu, choose **Line**, and then choose **Center**; or press ⟨⇧Shift⟩ + ⟨F7⟩.

   or

   Click the right mouse button in the text area of the document window to display the QuickMenu; then choose **Center**.

   or

   Click the Justification button on the Power Bar and choose the Center option from the pop-up list.

4. Type the text.

   WordPerfect centers the text on the cursor's original position as you type.

5. Press ⟨Tab⟩ or the space bar to move the cursor to a new position on the same line, or press ⟨↵Enter⟩ to advance to the next line.

Aligning Flush Right

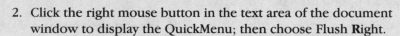

Aligning Text Flush Right

To align a line of text flush right as you type it, follow these steps:

1. Position the cursor at the beginning of a blank line.

2. Open the **Layout** menu, choose **Line**, and then choose **Flush Right**; or press (Alt)+(F7).

   or

2. Click the right mouse button in the text area of the document window to display the QuickMenu; then choose Flush **Right**.

   When you choose this command or press (Alt)+(F7), the cursor aligns with the right margin.

3. Type the text of the line you want aligned with the right margin.

   WordPerfect inserts the text from right to left as you type.

4. Press (┛Enter) when you have finished entering the right-aligned text.

   WordPerfect inserts a hard return at the end of the line and moves the cursor back to the left margin of the next line.

To align a single line of existing text with the right margin, follow these steps:

1. Position the cursor at the beginning of the line.

2. Choose the **Layout**, **Line**, **Flush Right**; or press (Alt)+(F7).

   or

3. Click the right mouse button in the text area of the document window to display the QuickMenu; then choose Flush **Right**.

   When you choose this command or press the Flush Right key combination, the cursor aligns with the right margin.

4. If the line is not terminated by a hard return, press (End); then press (┛Enter).

WordPerfect makes aligning individual lines of text with the right margin easy. This technique is most useful when you enter the inside address flush right in a business letter.

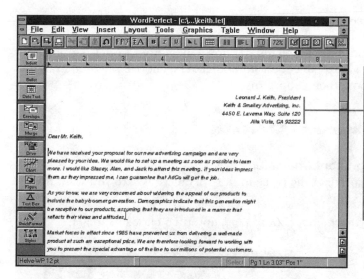

You can open the **Layout** menu, choose **Line**, and then choose **Flush Right** to align individual lines of text with the right margin, as in the inside address of this letter.

Aligning Text on a Decimal or Other Characters

Aligning numbers is the most common use for aligning text using the decimal align feature. Numbers often look best when they are aligned along the decimals, especially if they do not have the same number of digits. In some instances, you also may want to align text along another character, such as a dollar sign or space. The next two sections explain how to use decimal align and change the alignment character.

Using the Decimal Align Key Combination, Alt+Shift+F7

Using Decimal Align

1. Position the cursor at the beginning of a blank line.

2. Press `Tab ⇥` to move the cursor to a position where you have set a decimal tab stop.

3. Type the text that precedes the alignment character.

   All text moves to the left of the tab stop until you type the alignment character.

4. Type the alignment character (such as the period) followed by any text that comes after it.

   All text typed after the alignment character moves to the right of the tab stop.

191

You can use a hard decimal tab to align numbers in columns even when the tab stop you are using is not a decimal tab. To insert a hard tab code, open the Layout menu and choose the following options: Line, Other Codes, Decimal, and Insert. To insert a hard tab code with dot leaders, choose Decimal from the Other Codes dialog box; then choose Insert.

Changing the Alignment Character

Changing the Alignment Character

1. Position the cursor at the place in the document where you want the setting to take effect.

2. Open the Layout menu, choose Line, and then choose Tab Set.

WordPerfect displays the Tab Set dialog box, where you can specify a new decimal align character.

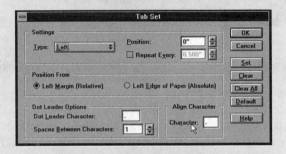

You also can display the Tab Set dialog box by clicking the right mouse button anywhere in the tab ruler and then choosing Tab Set from the QuickMenu, or by double-clicking a tab marker in the tab ruler.

4. Choose Character and enter the new alignment character, such as : or $, in the text box. To make a space the alignment character, press the space bar.

5. Choose OK to return to the document window.

Tip: You also can use decimal tabs to align names and addresses on a colon (:) or to align monetary amounts around the dollar sign ($). To align text with colons or dollar signs, you first must change the alignment character from a period to a colon or dollar sign before you use the Tab Align feature.

Note: When you change the decimal align character and choose OK, WordPerfect inserts at the cursor location. If you change your mind and want to return to the original decimal align character without opening the Tab Set dialog box, open the Reveal Codes window and delete the [Dec/Align Char:] code.

Understanding Fonts

The individual character represents the most basic unit of text in your document. In WordPerfect, you can adjust a character's font (typeface), size, and appearance (or attribute). You can choose from among *proportionally spaced* or *monospaced* fonts.

In a proportionally spaced font, different letters take up different amounts of horizontal space. An *m*, for example, takes up about three times the space of a *t* in a proportionally spaced font. Helvetica and Times Roman are examples of two popular proportionally spaced fonts.

In a monospaced font, different letters take up the same amount of horizontal space. Most typewriter fonts are monospaced. Courier, the most popular monospaced font for word processing, is often used as the initial font for most printers in WordPerfect because, as a monospaced font, it is easy to read on-screen.

```
Courier is one of the most popu-
lar monospaced fonts. It main-
tains a standard character width,
yet is easy to read.
```

Times Roman represents an old standard in typesetting. It is easy to read in any point size.

In this example, you see text set in Courier, a monospaced font, followed by text set in Times Roman, a proportionally spaced font.

Fonts are also characterized as *serif* or *sans-serif*. Serif fonts, such as the old standard Times Roman, use small angular strokes (called *serifs*) to finish most letters. Serif fonts are most often used to set long passages of text because they are generally considered easy to read. Sans-serif fonts, such as the ever-popular Helvetica, use few, if any, serifs and are usually reserved for headings or shorter lines of text.

In this example, you see text set in Helvetica, a sans-serif font, followed by text set in New Century School-book, a serif font.

Without a doubt, Helvetica is the most popular and most used sans serif font on microcomputer systems.

New Century Schoolbook is a most distinctive serif font. This font was developed for children's reading primers.

Font size in WordPerfect is always measured in *points* (a point is approximately 1/72 inch). This vertical measurement extends from the top of the ascender to the bottom of the descender.

This line is set in 8-point Palatino.

This line is set in 10-point Palatino.

This line is set in 12-point Palatino.

This line is set in 14-point Palatino.

This line is set in 18-point Palatino.

This line is set in 24-point Palatino.

This line is set in 36-point Palatino.

This line is set in 48-point Palatino.

In this example, you see text set in the Palatino font in a wide array of point sizes.

The appearance attributes you can add to a font include a wide array of effects. The most common of these attributes are bold, underline, and italics. In addition, some printers can produce effects such as outline, shadow, or small caps.

In this example, you see text set in ITC Avant Garde Gothic Book, using a number of different attributes.

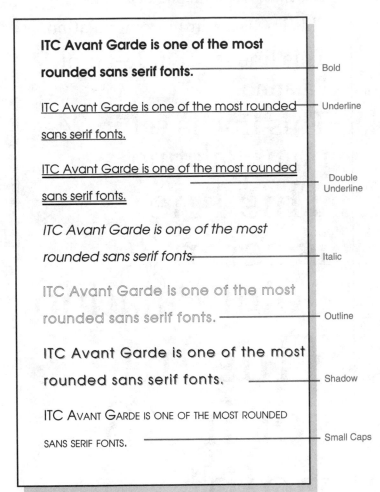

ITC Avant Garde is one of the most rounded sans serif fonts. — Bold

<u>ITC Avant Garde is one of the most rounded sans serif fonts.</u> — Underline

<u>ITC Avant Garde is one of the most rounded sans serif fonts.</u> — Double Underline

ITC Avant Garde is one of the most rounded sans serif fonts. — Italic

ITC Avant Garde is one of the most rounded sans serif fonts. — Outline

ITC Avant Garde is one of the most rounded sans serif fonts. — Shadow

ITC AVANT GARDE IS ONE OF THE MOST ROUNDED SANS SERIF FONTS. — Small Caps

Note: In traditional printing, a font refers to a particular typeface in a single size and style, such as 12-point Helvetica italic or 14-point Times Roman bold. In WordPerfect and other Windows word processing programs, the term *font* is sometimes used as a synonym for typeface because the point size and style (appearance) of a font are selected independently of the font itself.

Choosing a Font

Changing the Font

1. Position the cursor at the place in the document where you want the font to change.

2. Open the Layout menu and choose Font; or press F9.

   or

   Click the right mouse button in the text area of the document window to display the QuickMenu; then choose Font.

   or

   Click the Font button on the Power Bar to display a drop-down list of available fonts; then click the desired font on the list.

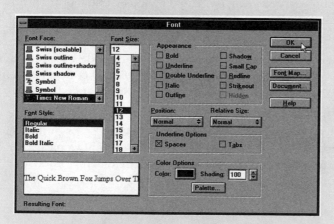

Unless you use the Font button on the Power Bar, WordPerfect displays the Font dialog box, where you specify the typeface, point size, and appearance of the new font.

continues

continued

3. Choose the font you want to use in the Font Face list box.

   When you choose a new font, WordPerfect previews how this font will look in your document by setting the sample text The Quick Brown Fox Jumps... in the box. The sample text also reflects any modifications you make to the font's point size or appearance.

4. To change the size of your new font, select or type the number of points in the Font Size list box.

5. To add attributes to the font, choose the desired options from the Appearance, Position, or Relative Size boxes.

   WordPerfect shows you how your selections will appear in the document before you put them into effect.

6. After the sample text in the Font dialog box appears the way you want it, choose OK to apply your font, size, and appearance choices to the text of your document.

The type of printer you use determines to a large extent the number of fonts available in WordPerfect. If you are using a laser printer such as the HP LaserJet III or Apple LaserWriter, you can choose from literally hundreds of different fonts in a wide variety of sizes and appearances.

When you start a new document, WordPerfect uses the font designated as the initial font for the printer you are using (when you choose a new printer, this initial font usually changes). You can, however, change the font for all or just a portion of your document.

When you choose a new font, WordPerfect inserts a [Font:] code with the name of the font at the cursor position in the document. The [Font:] code affects all text that follows until the end of the document or until you change to a new font and the program encounters a new [Font:] code.

You can apply a new font to new or existing text by using the steps outlined in this section. If you find that you want to apply a new font to only a particular section of the document, select the text you want to change before choosing the new font in the Font dialog box.

Applying Attributes to Text

Many times, you need to enhance only a part of your text with an attribute such as bold or underlining. You may, for example, want to enhance a heading with boldface type or indicate the title of a periodical or book in italics.

You can apply an attribute to your text as you enter the text or after you enter it. The procedure for applying an attribute before you enter the text is slightly different from that for applying an attribute to existing text.

Using Bold, Italics, and Underlining in the Text

Adding Bold, Italic, or Underlining

1. Open the Layout menu and then choose Font, **Bold**, and OK; or press `Ctrl`+`B`; or click the Bold Font button on the Power Bar.

   The font name in the status bar is displayed in bold to indicate that bold is on.

2. Type the text to appear in boldface type.

   The text you type appears in boldface in the currently selected font.

3. To turn off bold, repeat step 1.

   The font name on the status bar returns to the normal font to indicate that bold is off.

   To italicize or underline new text, use the same steps, but choose **Italic** or **Underline** instead of **Bold**; press `Ctrl`+`I` or `Ctrl`+`U`); or click the Italic Font or Underline Font button on the Power Bar.

   To boldface existing text, select the text you want to make bold by using the I-beam pointer; then repeat steps 1 and 2 above.

Because the bold, italics, and underline attributes are so common in documents, WordPerfect provides different ways to apply these attributes. You can use the **Bold**, **Italic**, and **Underline** options on the Font dialog box; you can use the respective shortcut key combinations Ctrl+B, Ctrl+I, and Ctrl+U to add these three attributes; or you can click the Font Size, Bold Font, Italic Font, or Underline Font button on the Power Bar.

Note: Remember that you can remove an attribute you have applied to your text. Select the enhanced text with the I-beam pointer; then choose the same attribute. To remove bold from a section of text, for example, select the text; then press Ctrl+B. WordPerfect returns the text to normal.

The quickest way to boldface, italicize, or underline text in your document is by using the shortcut key combinations. Notice that these key combinations also act as toggle switches, enabling you to remove the same attribute you added by pressing the keys a second time.

Superscripting and Subscripting Text

Applying Superscript and Subscript

1. Open the Layout menu and choose Font; or press F9. Choose Position and Superscript (or Subscript); then choose OK.

   This step turns on the superscript or subscript attribute.

2. Type the character or characters you want to appear as superscripts or subscripts.

   WordPerfect shows the characters you type above or below the baseline of the regular text.

3. To turn off super- or subscripting, press the → to move past the closing super- or subscript code; or repeat step 1 above.

   This step turns off the super- or subscripting and returns the font to normal size.

   If you need to super- or subscript characters after they have been typed, select the characters with the I-beam pointer; then repeat step 1. WordPerfect surrounds the selected text with opening and closing superscript or subscript codes.

Superscript and subscript are other font attributes that are available from the Font dialog box. A *superscript* is a character that is printed above the normal line of text in a smaller point size (if supported by your printer), as in $E=mc^2$. A *subscript* is a character that is printed below the normal line of text and, if possible, in a smaller point size, as in H_2SO_4.

Converting Text to a Different Case

Converting Case

1. Select the text you want to convert.

2. Choose Edit, Convert Case. WordPerfect displays the following options: Uppercase, Lowercase, and Initial Capitals.

3. To convert all the letters in the selected text to uppercase (capital) letters, choose Uppercase. To convert all the letters in the selected text to lowercase letters, choose Lowercase. To format each word with an initial capital letter, choose Initial Capitals.

The Convert Case option on the Edit menu makes converting text to all uppercase or all lowercase easy.

When using the Convert Case feature to change text to all lowercase letters, keep these two exceptions in mind:

- WordPerfect does not lowercase *I* or words starting with *I*, followed by an apostrophe (such as *I'm* or *I'll*).

- WordPerfect does not lowercase the first letter of the first word that follows a period in the selected text. (The program assumes that a capital letter following a period marks the beginning of a new sentence.) To have WordPerfect lowercase a capital letter that follows a period, make sure that the selected text does not include the preceding punctuation.

Changing the Line Spacing

By default, WordPerfect uses single-spacing in each new document you create. When necessary, you can increase or decrease the line spacing in half-line increments. When you change the line spacing, WordPerfect places a [Ln Spacing:] code in the document, indicating the number of lines. This code is placed at the beginning of the current paragraph and affects all text from that point to the end of the document or until the program encounters another [Ln Spacing:] code.

The simplest way to change the line spacing is with the Line Spacing button on the Power Bar. You can use this button to set the following line spacing in your document: 1.0, 1.5, 2.0, or Other. If you choose Other, WordPerfect displays the Line Spacing dialog box, where you can set line spacing to precise values in increments as small as one thousandths of an inch.

To change the line spacing with the Power Bar, click the Line Spacing button on the Power Bar and hold down the left mouse button until the pop-up menu of line spacing options appears. Then drag down the pop-up list until the line spacing option you want to use is highlighted. Release the mouse button to put the line spacing into effect.

Using the Line Spacing Dialog Box

1. Open the Layout menu, choose Line, and then choose Spacing.

   or

   Click the Line Spacing button on the Power Bar and choose Other from the pop-up menu.

WordPerfect displays the Line Spacing dialog box.

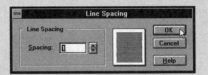

2. To increase the line spacing in 1/10-line increments, click the up arrow after the Spacing text box until the text box contains the line spacing you want to use. To decrease the line spacing in 1/10-line increments, click the down arrow until you reach the desired line spacing.

   You also can type the desired line spacing, such as 3.5 or 4, in the Spacing text box. You can specify line spacing in fractions or decimals. If you type a fraction, WordPerfect translates it; for example, 1 1/8 inch becomes 1.12 inch.

3. After you have set the desired line spacing, choose OK.

To use a line spacing other than 1 (single-space), 1 1/2, or 2 (double-space), you must set the line spacing from the Line Spacing dialog box.

Adjusting the Line Height

Adjusting Line Height

1. Open the Layout menu, choose Line, and then choose Height.

WordPerfect displays the Line Height dialog box.

2. Choose the Fixed option button; then enter the number of points you want for the line height in the Fixed text box.

3. Choose OK.

   When you want the program to determine the line height again, return to the Line Height dialog box and choose the Auto option button.

Note: Typographers measure line height in points. (A point is 1/72 inch.) To specify line height in points, in the Fixed text box, type the number of points by the letter p. When you choose OK, WordPerfect translates the measurement in points to a decimal figure; for example, 12p becomes 0.167 inch.

Line height refers to the vertical distance between the baseline (the invisible line on which the text rests) of one line and the baseline of the next line. WordPerfect calculates the line height for you. This measurement is determined by the size of the fonts used in the text.

In most situations, automatic line height works just fine. Sometimes, however, you may need to limit the line height in a section of text. When creating a newsletter, for example, you may need to decrease the line height for a particular story to make the text fit on one page.

Note: Don't confuse line height with line spacing. The line height calculated by WordPerfect is always multiplied by the line spacing in effect. Thus, if you choose double spacing for your text, the line height is increased to twice the distance from when single spacing was in effect.

Formatting Text with QuickFormat

You use WordPerfect's *QuickFormat* feature to copy formatting from one paragraph to another paragraph, to multiple selected paragraph styles, or to both. This useful feature lets you format text quickly with the mouse instead of choosing commands from the Layout menu.

Using QuickFormat

1. Move the cursor into a paragraph that has the format you want to copy; or select text whose formatting you want to copy.

2. Open the Layout menu and choose **QuickFormat**; or click the QuickFormat button on the Button Bar; or click the right mouse button in the document text window and choose **QuickFormat** from the QuickMenu.

3. Choose **F**onts and Attributes to copy only the fonts and attributes

WordPerfect displays the QuickFormat dialog box.

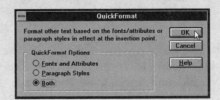

of the paragraph that contains the cursor; choose **Paragraph Styles** to copy only the paragraph styles; or choose **B**oth to copy fonts, attributes, and styles.

4. Choose OK. The cursor becomes a paint roller.

5. Drag the paint roller over the text you want to reformat.

6. Open the **L**ayout menu and choose **Q**uickFormat to reformat the selected text; click the QuickFormat button on the Button Bar; or click the right mouse button in the document text window and choose **Q**uickFormat from the QuickMenu.

Formatting Text with Bullets and Numbers

Bullets are special characters that are very useful for formatting lists. WordPerfect can automate the task of formatting paragraphs with bullets or numbers. You can insert a single bullet, or WordPerfect can automatically insert a new bullet each time you press Enter to start a new paragraph. If you specify paragraph numbering, WordPerfect for Windows can automatically increment the paragraph number and insert a new number when you press Enter.

Inserting Bullets and Numbers

1. Open the **I**nsert menu and choose **B**ullets & **N**umbers; or click the Bullet button on the Button Bar.

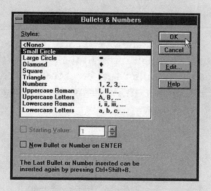

WordPerfect displays the Bullets & Numbers dialog box.

2. In the **S**tyles list, highlight one of the ten bullet and number types.

3. To have WordPerfect automatically insert a new bullet or another incremented number whenever you press ⏎Enter to begin a new paragraph, choose the **N**ew Bullet or Number on Enter check box.

continues

continued

4. If you selected a number, choose Starting Value and type or use the scroll bars to insert a new starting number.

5. Choose OK to return to the document window.

   If you choose New Bullet or Number on Enter in step 3, WordPerfect inserts a new bullet or number when you press Enter to begin a new paragraph. You also can insert a new bullet or number of the same type as the last bullet or number entered anywhere in the document by pressing Ctrl + ⇧Shift + B.

Using Special Characters

Using Special Characters

1. Open the Insert menu and choose Character; or press Ctrl + W.

   WordPerfect displays the WordPerfect Characters dialog box.

2. Choose Character Set and choose the new set from the pop-up list.

3. To insert a character from the Characters box, click the character with the mouse or, if you know the number in the set, enter the number of the character in the Number text box. You can choose a character in a set that isn't displayed by entering the set and character number in the Number text box.

The WordPerfect Character feature includes many useful and decorative characters that can be printed graphically.

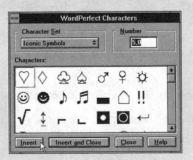

4. To insert the character you have selected in the Characters box and leave the dialog box displayed, choose the **Insert** button. To insert the character and close the dialog box, choose Insert and Close.

Note: You can select and insert a character at the same time without closing the WordPerfect Characters dialog box by double-clicking that character with the mouse.

Tip: Special characters called *bullets* are useful for formatting lists. A bullet is a solid or empty symbol, usually a circle, square, asterisk, or triangle. You can create bullets with the WordPerfect Characters command, or you can use the Bullets & Numbers command, described in the preceding section. To enter a bullet in your document, select the bullet in the Typographic Symbols set of the WordPerfect Characters dialog box and then double-click the symbol or choose Insert (or Insert and Close).

Many special characters, such as math symbols and foreign language characters, are not directly available from the keyboard. To use these special characters in your documents, select them from WordPerfect's character sets in the WordPerfect Characters dialog box. When you are composing text that uses several foreign characters, you can keep this dialog box displayed. With the dialog box displayed, you can continue to select characters without opening the dialog box each time.

WordPerfect includes 15 predefined sets of special characters, offering you almost any special symbol or foreign language character you may need. Each set is numbered from 1 to 15, and each character within the set is also numbered. For example, 4 is the number of the Typographic Symbols set, and 5 is the number of the paragraph symbol (¶) in that set. The program refers to this symbol as 4,5.

If a particular character in one of the sets is not available as part of the font you are using, WordPerfect still can print the character—provided that your printer can print graphics—by treating the character as a graphic.

Tip: To view more of the characters in a set, in the WordPerfect Characters dialog box, click the Control Menu box in the upper left corner of the dialog box, choose Size, and use the mouse to resize the box by dragging the sides or corners.

Controlling Line Breaks

WordPerfect offers several features to help you control how and when a line breaks in a paragraph. Perhaps the most commonly used method for controlling line breaks is the Hyphenation feature. You can use this feature to hyphenate words and reduce the raggedness of the right margin when your document is left-justified or reduce the amount of white space between words when using full justification.

In addition to Hyphenation, WordPerfect also gives you a host of typesetting controls that enable you to determine how lines break by increasing or decreasing the amount of space between the letters and words on the line. These typesetting controls are essential if you are using WordPerfect to perform desktop publishing applications. For complete information on their use, see Que's *Using WordPerfect 6 for Windows,* Special Edition.

Keeping Text Together with Hard Spaces

Normally, WordPerfect splits a pair of words at the space separating the words when the second word extends beyond the right margin. Sometimes, however, you may want to prevent word wrap from separating two or more words on different lines. You may enter a date such as January 11, 1991, for example, and not want the month, day, or year split on different lines by word wrap.

To prevent words from separating on different lines, you must enter a hard space between each word to bind the words together. To enter a hard space in WordPerfect, press Ctrl+space bar.

In the regular document window, a hard space appears no different from a regular space. If, however, you open the Reveal Codes window, you see a [HSpace] code. To convert a hard (nonbreaking) space to the normal (breaking) space, delete the [HSpace] code in the Reveal Codes window; then replace it by pressing the space bar alone.

Note: You also can insert a hard space into the document by choosing Layout, Line, Other Codes. Choose the Hard Space [HSpace] option button; then choose Insert.

Hyphenating Text Manually

You can manually hyphenate words by entering any of the following types of hyphens supported by WordPerfect:

- *Hard hyphen.* Press - (the hyphen key) to separate compound words that always require hyphenation, such as *self-defense* and *mother-in-law.* Use this hyphen when you don't care whether the words are separated on different lines by word wrap. Hard hyphens are always visible in the document and are always printed.

- *Dash character.* Press Ctrl+- to bind together hyphenated words into one unit so that if the words fall at the end of a line and extend beyond the right margin, WordPerfect wraps the entire hyphenated word to the next line. Use dash characters in hyphenated terms whose parts should always stay together on a line, such as dates (07-31-92) or products (Lotus 1-2-3).

- *Soft hyphen.* Press Ctrl+Shift+- to indicate where a word should be hyphenated when that word extends beyond the right margin. When the word does not extend beyond the margin, the hyphen is not visible in the document and is not printed. WordPerfect inserts this type of hyphen when you use the automatic Hyphenation feature.

Using the Hyphenation Feature

Using Hyphenation

1. If necessary, press Ctrl + Home to move the cursor to the beginning of the document you want to hyphenate.

2. Open the the Layout menu and choose Line to display the Line options.

continues

209

continued

3. Choose Hyphenation.

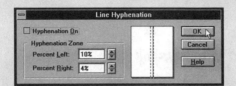

WordPerfect
displays the Line
Hyphenation
dialog box.

4. Turn on hyphenation by choosing the Hyphenation **On** check box so that an X appears in it.

5. Choose OK to return to the document.

Manual hyphenation is reserved for terms that require a hyphen to be correct. When you want to hyphenate your text to control line spacing problems, use WordPerfect's automatic Hyphenation feature.

By default, WordPerfect's Hyphenation feature is turned off. When you turn it on, the program uses a hyphenation dictionary to decide how to hyphenate words at the end of lines that would otherwise wrap to new lines. The hyphenation dictionary is contained in the WP{WP}US.LEX file.

By using the Hyphenation feature, you can reduce the raggedness in the right margin when the justification is set to Left, or you can reduce the white space between words when the justification is set to Full.

You can use the Hyphenation feature in two ways. You can turn on the Hyphenation feature and make hyphenation decisions as you type the text of the document, or you can enter all the text and then go to the beginning of the document, turn on Hyphenation, and scroll through the document to hyphenate it.

Note: The Hyphenation Zone percentages in the Line Hyphenation dialog box determine when a word is hyphenated. Increasing the size of the zone decreases the number of words that are hyphenated. Decreasing the size of the zone increases the number of words that are hyphenated. For more information on changing the Hyphenation Zone, see Que's *Using WordPerfect 6 for Windows,* Special Edition.

The Hyphenation Prompt setting in the Environment Preferences dialog box determines how WordPerfect behaves when you turn on hyphenation.

To change the Hyphenation Prompt setting, open the Environment Preferences dialog box by choosing **F**ile, **P**references, **E**nvironment; then choose from the following options:

- **N**ever prevents WordPerfect from automatically making hyphenation decisions in the document.

- **W**hen Required enables WordPerfect to prompt you about hyphenation. You decide where to hyphenate the word only when the word is not found in the hyphenation dictionary.

- **A**lways enables WordPerfect to prompt you about hyphenation. You decide where to hyphenate a word each time a word needs to be hyphenated.

If you choose **W**hen Required or **A**lways for the Hyphenation **P**rompt setting, WordPerfect displays the Position Hyphen dialog box when it encounters a word that requires hyphenation. The Position Hyphen dialog box contains a text box that shows the word requiring hyphenation and WordPerfect's suggestion about where to position the hyphen. To change the way the word is hyphenated, click in the word or use the left or right arrow to reposition the hyphen. When you have made your hyphenation decision, choose the Insert **H**yphen button to hyphenate the word.

If you decide that you don't want the word hyphenated, choose the **I**gnore Word button. The program wraps the entire word to the next line in the document. When you choose this option, WordPerfect changes the space before the word to a soft return code [SRt], and the program adds an Ignore Word code [HyphIgnWrd] in front of the word. This code prevents WordPerfect from prompting you to hyphenate the word again while the Hyphenation feature is turned on.

In addition to the Insert **H**yphen and **I**gnore Word command buttons, the Position Hyphen dialog box also contains three other buttons you can use as follows:

- Choose the Hyphenation **S**Rt command button to insert a hyphenation soft return instead of a hyphen at the cursor's position in the word. WordPerfect inserts a [HyphSRt] code that breaks the word at the selected position without adding a hyphen. You can use this option to indicate where to hyphenate words separated by slashes, such as *either/or,* when these words extend beyond the right margin.

- Choose the Insert **S**pace command button to insert a space instead of a hyphen at the cursor's position in the word.

- Choose the **S**top Hyphenation button to suspend automatic hyphenation temporarily. This feature enables you to scroll to a new part of the document or check the spelling of a section of the document without being interrupted by the Position Hyphen dialog box.

> *Note:* You can manually insert a hyphenation soft return or a hyphenation Ignore Word code in a word by choosing the codes in the Insert Special Codes dialog box. To access this dialog box, choose the **L**ayout **L**ine **O**ther Codes command.

Summary

In this chapter, you learned how to make formatting changes on the paragraph and character levels. You learned how you can use the Ruler to change the left and right margins; set tabs; and change the font, point size, justification, and line spacing. You also learned how to control where lines break using manual and automatic hyphenation.

In the next chapter, you learn about formatting at the next level, document formatting. You learn how to change the top and bottom margins, add headers and footers, and control how pages break in a document.

Formatting Pages

7

Choosing the paper size

Changing the top and bottom margins

Centering top to bottom

Using Advance

Using headers and footers

Numbering pages

Suppressing page formats

Controlling page breaks

Formatting with styles

The preceding chapter examined formatting at the paragraph and character levels. This chapter examines formatting at the document level. In document formatting, you are primarily concerned with the overall layout of the page and any reoccurring elements in the design.

This chapter covers choosing the paper size and type; changing the top and bottom margins; adding headers, footers, and page numbers; and controlling page breaks in the document. In addition, the chapter looks at techniques for vertically centering text between the top and bottom margins, adding watermarks to a page, keeping sections of text together on a page, and accurately positioning text on a page.

Finally, this chapter shows you how to format your document with styles. With WordPerfect styles, you can rest assured that repeated elements in a document (such as section headings and titles) are formatted uniformly. You can universally modify the elements' formatting by editing the assigned style.

Key Terms in This Chapter

Footer
Text that is automatically printed at the bottom margin of every page of the document.

Hard page break
A page break that you manually insert in the document. A hard page break appears as a double line across the document window.

Header
Text that is automatically printed at the top margin of every page of the document.

Orphan
In WordPerfect, the first line of a paragraph that appears alone at the very bottom of a page.

Soft page break
A page break that WordPerfect automatically inserts in the document. A soft page break appears as a single line across the document window.

Styles
A named collection of all codes and standard text used to format a particular element in the document, such as a heading. A style ensures formatting consistency and lets you easily modify the look or contents of an element throughout the entire document.

Watermark
Text printed over other text on the page, usually in a lighter shade of gray. Watermarks are typically used to print company logos and other graphic symbols on letterhead, flyers, etc.

Widow
In WordPerfect, the last line of a paragraph that appears alone at the very top of a page.

Choosing the Paper Size

Choosing a Paper Size

1. Position the cursor at the top of the page where you want the new paper size to take effect.

   To change the page size for the entire document, position the cursor at the beginning by pressing Ctrl + Home.

2. Open the Layout menu, choose Page, and then choose Paper Size.

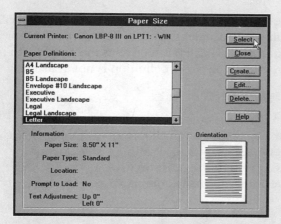

WordPerfect displays the Paper Size dialog box with a list that contains the paper definitions. This dialog box also shows you the name of the current printer.

3. Select a paper definition in the Paper Definitions list box by clicking it or by using the arrow keys.

4. Choose the Select command button (or press ↵Enter) to put your new paper size into effect and return to your document.

By default, WordPerfect assumes that you will print your document on 8 1/2-by-11-inch paper in *Portrait mode* (where text runs parallel to the short side of the paper). If you want to use a different paper size or intend to change the orientation to *Landscape mode* (where text runs parallel to the long side of the paper), choose a different paper definition for your document.

A paper definition includes information on the size of the paper, paper type (the name assigned to the paper definition), the location of the paper in the printer (continuous, bin, or manual feed), and the orientation of the printing on the page (portrait or landscape). For most printers, WordPerfect comes with several predefined forms, including Standard, Labels, and Envelopes.

Paper definitions are directly related to the printer you are using and are therefore limited to the printer's capabilities.

The default paper type is Standard, which uses 8 1/2-by-11-inch paper continuously fed in the portrait orientation. When you choose a new paper definition, WordPerfect inserts a [Paper Sz/Type:] code into the document at the top of the current page. If necessary, the program will also adjust and repaginate the text to suit the new paper size and orientation you selected. To return to the Standard paper size and type, open the Reveal Codes window (open the View menu and choose Reveal Codes or press Alt+F3), locate the [Paper Sz/Type:] code, and delete the code.

If your printer doesn't have a paper definition that matches the one specified by the [Paper Sz/Type:] code in your document, WordPerfect uses the Letter paper definition to print the document. This definition enables the program to print a document with any printer, even if the paper definition is not available.

> *Note:* If you select the Windows printer driver from the Printers list in the Select Printer dialog box, you can choose only one paper size for the entire document (see chapter 8, "Printing a Document," for details on changing the printer driver). If you use the WordPerfect printer driver, however, you can change the paper size for different sections.

Using Envelopes

Creating an Envelope Paper Definition

1. Open the Layout menu and choose Envelope.

    WordPerfect displays the Envelope dialog box. WordPerfect can automatically read an address into the Mailing Address text box in the Envelope dialog box.

2. Choose Create New Definition.

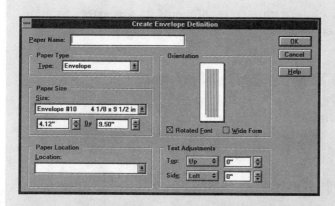

WordPerfect displays the Create Envelope Definition box, which you can use to customize an existing envelope definition or create a new one.

3. Choose the options you want as described in the following list. Then choose OK to return to the Envelope dialog box.

The Create Envelope Definitions dialog box contains the following options:

- **Paper Name.** Type a name for the new envelope definition in this text box.

- **Type.** Choose this option and select a paper type from the drop-down list: Envelope, Letterhead, Labels, etc.

- **Size.** Choose this option and select a standard size from the drop-down list. Then type or use the scroll arrows to specify the dimensions of the new definition in the **By** boxes.

- **Rotated Font.** Marking this box specifies Landscape mode printing (where the text runs parallel to the long edge of the paper). When you select this option, the example graphic reflects your changes.

- **Wide Form.** Marking this box tells WordPerfect to print the paper inserted in the printer along its long edge. When you choose this option, the example graphic reflects your changes.

- **Top and Side.** These options tell WordPerfect where to position text on the envelope. Choose **Up** or **Down** from the Top drop-down list, and then choose **Left** or **Right** from the Side drop-down list. Then use scroll arrows or type Text Adjustment specifications in the text boxes.

If you need to print envelopes in sizes that aren't supported by WordPerfect, you can create your own, customized envelope definitions. You can also customize an existing envelope definition by adjusting its size, paper location, landscape or portrait orientation, and text printing position.

Creating a New Paper Definition

Creating a Paper Definition

1. Open the **L**ayout menu, choose **P**age, and then choose Paper **S**ize.

   WordPerfect displays the Paper Size dialog box.

2. Choose the C**r**eate command button.

WordPerfect displays the Create Paper Size dialog box.

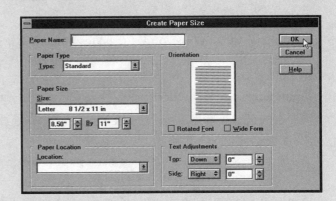

3. Choose one of the predefined paper types from the **T**ype drop-down list. The Paper Type specifies the name of the paper definition. Regardless of which name you use, you still must specify the other settings the print definition uses.

4. Type a name for the new paper type in the **P**aper Name text box.

5. To change the paper size, choose one of the predefined sizes in the **S**ize pop-up list.

6. If you choose the User Defined Size option, enter a customized paper size by typing a width and length in the **B**y text boxes.

7. You can use one of the options under Text Adjustments to change where the printing begins. To adjust where the printing starts in relation to the top edge of the paper, choose either the **U**p or **D**own option in the T**o**p pop-up list and then enter the distance in its text box on the right. To adjust where the printing begins in relation to

the left side of the paper, choose either the **Left** or **Right** option in the **Side** pop-up list and then enter the distance in its text box.

8. By default, the **Rotated Font** and **Wide Form** options are not selected. If you're using a printer that can rotate the fonts on the page (such as a laser printer) and want to print in Landscape mode, choose Rotated Font to print in Landscape mode with vertical paper orientation. (Notice that as you choose options in this dialog box, the Orientation sample graphic reflects your changes.) To print in Landscape mode in the landscape (wide) paper orientation, choose **Wide Form**. The sample graphic again reflects your changes.

9. To change the paper location, choose **Location** and an option from the pop-up list.

10. Choose the OK button to add your new paper definition and return to the Paper Size dialog box.

    WordPerfect adds the new paper definition to the list of paper definitions in the **P**aper Definitions dialog box.

11. After you are back in the Paper Size dialog box, you can use the new paper definition you just created. Choose it in the list box before you choose the **S**elect command button. Otherwise, just choose the **C**lose button to return to your document without choosing a new definition.

Note: For specific information on creating a custom paper definition for mailing labels, see chapter 11, "Using Merge for Mass Mailings."

When you create your own paper definitions, WordPerfect has several paper types that you must choose from in the Type list. These are: Standard, Bond, Letterhead, Labels, Envelope, Transparency, Cardstock, Glossy Film, Clay Based, or Other.

You can base your paper definition on one of the predefined sizes in the **S**ize list (see the following list) or create your own size by using the User Defined Size option.

Option	Size
Letter	8 1/2 inches by 11 inches
Legal	8 1/2 inches by 14 inches
Executive	7 1/4 inches by 10 1/2 inches
A4	210 mm by 297 mm
B5	182 mm by 257 mm
Envelope #10	4 1/8 inches by 9 1/2 inches
User Defined Size	(Enter the size you want.)

Specifying Binding Offset

Specifying a Binding Offset

1. Open the Layout menu, choose Page, and then choose Binding.

WordPerfect
displays the Binding
Options dialog box.

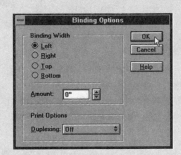

2. Choose a Binding Width: Left, Right, Top, or Bottom. Then enter the amount of binding offset in the Amount text box.

3. If your printer can offset collated copies in its output bin, choose Duplexing from the Binding Options dialog box; then choose From Short Edge or From Long Edge.

4. Choose OK to return to the document window.

If you plan to bind the document and want to specify a binding offset, you can indicate whether this offset should apply to the left, right, top, or bottom edge of the paper. By default, the Left Binding option is chosen.

Changing the Top and Bottom Margins

Changing Top and Bottom Page Margins

1. Position the cursor on the page where you want the new margins to take effect. To change margins for the entire document, be sure to move the cursor to the beginning of the document by pressing Ctrl + Home.

2. If the Ruler is displayed, you can double-click either the left or right margin icon on the Ruler to display the Margins dialog box, or you can click the right mouse button anywhere on the Ruler to display a QuickMenu and then choose Margins. Otherwise, open the Layout menu and then choose Margins (or press Ctrl + F8).

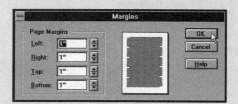

WordPerfect displays the Margins dialog box where you can modify all four margins for your document.

3. To change the top margin, choose the Top text box; then enter the new value.

   As you adjust the top and bottom margins, the sample graphic reflects your changes.

4. To change the bottom margin, choose the Bottom text box; then enter the new value.

5. Click the OK button in the Page Format dialog box to put your new margins into effect and return to the document.

By default, WordPerfect sets all four page margins at one inch (1"). As you learned in chapter 6, "Formatting Paragraphs and Characters," you can use the

Ruler to change the left and right margins. To change the top and bottom margins, however, you must use the Margins dialog box.

Whenever you change the margins, WordPerfect inserts [Top Mar:] and [Bot Mar:] codes in the document at the top of the current page. When you move the insertion point to the left of one of these codes in the Reveal Codes screen, the codes change to indicate the size of the margin, as in

[Top Mar: 1.10"]

To return to the default 1-inch margin settings, open the Reveal Codes window (Alt+F3) and delete the codes.

If you are using a laser printer, WordPerfect will not accept top or bottom margins smaller than a certain minimum (0.250 inches on some, 0.300 inches on others). If you try to set smaller margins, the program will display a message dialog box when you choose OK. When you choose OK in this message box, the program returns you to the Margins dialog box. Enter the minimum for your printer in the offending text box.

Centering Top to Bottom

Centering a Page Vertically

1. Position the cursor somewhere on the page that contains the text you want to center vertically.

2. Open the **Layout** menu, choose **Page**, and choose **Center**.

WordPerfect displays the Center Page(s) dialog box.

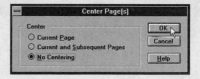

3. Choose Current **P**age to center just the page that contains the cursor, or choose Current and **S**ubsequent Pages to center all pages from the current page forward, or choose **N**o Centering to turn off page centering.

4. Choose OK to put the centering into effect and return to the document window.

WordPerfect makes centering text between the top and bottom of the page a snap. This technique comes in handy when you create a title page that vertically centers the title, byline, and a few lines of explanatory text.

Positioning Text on the Page with Advance

Using Advance

1. Position the cursor at the place in the document where you want to advance your text.

2. Open the **Layout** menu, choose **Typesetting**, and then choose **Advance**.

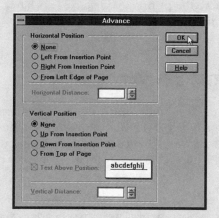

WordPerfect displays the Advance dialog box, where you indicate how much and in what direction the text should advance.

3. To advance the printer up, down, left, or right relative to the cursor's vertical position in the document, choose **Up From Insertion Point**, **Down From Insertion Point**, **Left From Insertion Point**, or **Right From Insertion Point**; then enter the amount of the advance in the Horizontal Distance or Vertical Distance text box.

4. To advance the printer an absolute distance down or right from the top or left edge of the page, choose **From Top of Page** or **From Left Edge of Page**; then enter the amount to advance in the Vertical Distance or Horizontal Distance text box.

continues

223

continued

5. To advance text above the current position by an absolute distance, choose From **T**op of Page; then choose Text Above **P**osition and enter an amount in the Vertical Distance text box.

6. Choose the OK button to return to the document.

   WordPerfect inserts the corresponding Advance code(s) into the document at the cursor's position and advances the cursor to the position specified in the Advance dialog box.

WordPerfect's Advance feature enables you to advance the printer to a specific position on the page before it prints. You can use this feature to position text quickly and accurately on the page without the use of spaces or hard returns. Advance enables you to move the printer up, down, left, or right, relative to the cursor's current position in the document. You also can use Advance to indicate a specific location on the page where the printing will start. This latter option is most useful when you are filling in preprinted forms.

Using Headers and Footers

A *header* is information (text or graphics) that prints just above the top margin. A *footer* is information that prints just below the bottom margin of the page. WordPerfect inserts one blank line between the text on the page and the header or footer. Typical header and footer information may include chapter or section titles, page numbers, and revision dates and times.

You can define two different headers (Header A and B) and two different footers (Footer A and B) in the same document. These two headers and two footers can appear on every page as long as you format them so that their text does not overlap each other. If you plan to copy the document on both sides of the paper and bind it, however, define one header and footer (Header A and Footer A) for odd pages and the other header and footer (Header B and Footer B) for even pages.

Birkie, The Sheltie Movie Star

Shetland Sheepdogs have a long history of performing, although admittedly most of that history is fulfilling such tasks as herding livestock. Well, meet Birkie, the star performer in the Walt Disney production television movie *The Little Shepard Dog of Catalina!*

This is the story of a champion Shetland Sheepdog who becomes lost on Catalina Island, off the coast of California. Luckily for him, the dog finds his way to a farm that offers him a new home. Here, the dog's natural herding instinct is recognized by Bud Parker, a farm hand. Bud trains Birkie in herding and the two soon become inseparable.

In the mean time, the dog's real owner on the mainland of California discovers Birkie's whereabouts. When he comes upon Birkie, the heroic little dog is busy trying to prevent an Arabian stallion from falling off a cliff to his death. After witnessing this encounter, the dog's real owner decides to let Birkie stay in his new home.

Birkie, whose real is Gaywyn Sandstorm (Shane for short) is a registered Shetland Sheepdog who is owned by Carol Snip in St. Louis, Missouri. He is the grandson of two Sheltie greats, Ch. Malpsh Great Scot on his sire's side, and Ch. Kawartha's Matchmaker on his dam's side.

Draft: September 2, 1991

In this example, you see a document page that uses both a header and a footer.

The headers or footers you define for your document are not displayed in Draft View, but they are displayed in Page View. To see how headers and footers will look when printed, look at the page in Page View by choosing the **View** menu and the **Page** option or by pressing Alt+F5.

Creating a Header or Footer

Creating a Header or Footer

1. Position the cursor somewhere on the page where you want the header or footer to appear. If you want the header or footer to appear on all pages, move the cursor to the beginning of the document by pressing Ctrl + Home.

2. Open the Layout menu, and then choose Header/Footer.

WordPerfect displays the Headers/Footers dialog box.

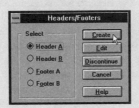

Another way to open the Headers/Footers dialog box is to click the right mouse button in the header or footer area of the document window in Page View and then choose Header/Footer from the QuickMenu.

3. Indicate whether you are creating your first header (Header **A**), second header (Header **B**), first footer (Footer A), or second footer (Footer B) by choosing the appropriate option button under Select.

WordPerfect displays the header/footer editing window.

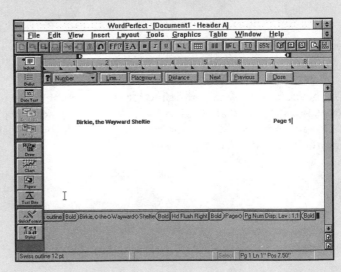

WordPerfect displays the Placement dialog box.

4. Choose **C**reate, and then choose Placement.

5. Type the text and place any graphics you want to appear in your header or footer.

6. Choose **C**lose to return to the document window.

Header or footer text can consist of several lines, because WordPerfect subtracts lines from the body text to make room for the header and footer. Format this text as you would regular document text. For information on placing graphics, see chapter 16, "Using Columns and Graphics."

When you define a header or footer in your document, WordPerfect inserts a code that identifies the header or footer by showing its letter. For example, with Reveal Codes turned on in the header editing screen, WordPerfect displays the following code for Header A: [Open Style: HeaderA]. With Reveal Codes turned on in the document window and the insertion point placed immediately to the left of the header code, WordPerfect displays the expanded header code: [HeaderA: Every Page, [Open Style]. With the insertion point anywhere else, WordPerfect abbreviates the code: [HeaderA]. To delete the header or footer, you must locate this header or footer code in the Reveal Codes window and remove the code.

Inserting a Page Number in a Header or Footer

WordPerfect can print the current page number in a header or footer. To insert a page number code, from the header or footer editing screen, choose Number, **P**age Number. WordPerfect inserts a [Pg Num Disp] code in Reveal Codes. With the insertion point to the immediate left of the code, WordPerfect expands the code. For example: [Pg Num Disp: Lev: 1;1].

Placing Headers and Footers on Odd or Even Pages

You can create different headers or footers, each of which prints only on odd or even pages. This is useful when you want to print a header with left-aligned text on right-facing pages and right-aligned text on left-facing pages. To specify on which pages WordPerfect should print the current header or footer, from the header or footer editing screen, choose Placement and choose Odd Pages, Even Pages, or Every Page, and then choose OK.

Inserting the File Name in a Header or Footer

You may find it useful to identify documents by a file name printed in a header or footer. To insert the file name, choose Insert, Other, Filename; or choose Insert, Other, Path and Filename from the Header or Footer editing screen. WordPerfect inserts the corresponding code in the document. You will not see the file name or path and file name in Page View or Draft View, but the file name or path and file name will print at the location of the code.

Editing a Header or Footer

Editing Headers and Footers

1. Open the Layout menu, and then choose **Header/Footer**.

   WordPerfect displays the Headers/Footers dialog box.

2. Choose the header or footer you want to edit; then choose the **Edit** command button.

   Tip: You can quickly display a header or footer in the header/footer editing screen by displaying Reveal Codes (Alt + F3) and double-clicking the header or footer's hidden code.

   WordPerfect opens the document window containing your header or footer.

3. Make your editing changes to the header or footer, as described in a previous section, "Creating a Header or Footer."

4. Choose **Close** to record your changes and close the window.

Tip: In Page View, you can edit the text of a header or footer directly. Just click in the header or footer and make any changes. However, you cannot insert page number codes and perform other functions that are available only in the header/footer editor.

Discontinuing a Header or Footer

Discontinuing a Header or Footer

1. Position the cursor somewhere on the first page you want to print without the header or footer.

2. Open the Layout menu, and then choose Header/Footer.

   WordPerfect displays the Headers/Footers dialog box.

3. Choose **Discontinue**.

In some documents, you may want to discontinue the printing of a particular header or footer at some point in the document by following the steps above. WordPerfect inserts a code, such as [End Header A], that discontinues the header or footer on that page and all succeeding pages in the document. If you choose **Discontinue** on the page where the header or footer is located, WordPerfect deletes the header/footer code.

Adding a Watermark to a Document

Creating a Watermark

1. With the cursor anywhere on the page where you want to print a watermark, open the Layout menu and choose the **Watermark** option.

The Watermark dialog box appears.

continues

continued

2. You can print one or two watermarks on a page. Choose Watermark
   A to create the first watermark and Watermark **B** to create a second
   watermark.

3. Choose Create.

The Watermark
editing screen.

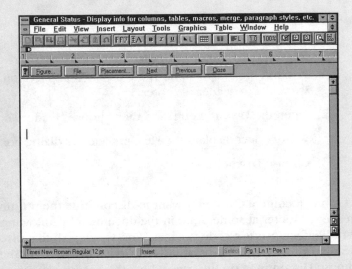

4. Choose watermark editing screen options as described in the accompanying text; then choose the **Close** command button on the Watermark feature bar to insert the watermark and return to the document screen.

WordPerfect can help you format and print watermarks. A watermark consists of text or a graphic image printed over the contents of a page. Watermarks are usually, but not always, printed in a lighter shade of black or color than the regular text.

Tip: You can create page borders from the **L**ayout menu with the **P**age, **B**order/Fill command or with the Watermark feature. Watermark borders can be formatted and edited as graphic images, so you can change their size, position, and the like, independent of other page format settings. The supplied watermark page borders are decorative and could not be duplicated with the Border/Fill feature. To insert a page border as a watermark, from the watermark editor, choose **F**igure and in the Insert Image dialog box look for the file names that begin with *bord* and contain the letter *p* indicating a page border; for example, bord01p.wpg.

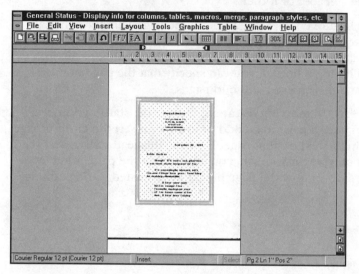

WordPerfect document in Full Page view, showing a page border created with a watermark graphic image.

Tip: WordPerfect for Windows comes with 30 preformatted watermarks that you can retrieve into the watermark editor with the **F**igure command. In the Insert Image dialog box, look for file names water01.wpg through water30.wpg in the Filename list box.

> *Tip:* To quickly display an existing watermark in the watermark
> editor, turn on Reveal Codes (Alt+F3) and double-click the
> watermark's hidden code.

Numbering Pages

Inserting a page code in a header or footer with the Numbering command is
not the only way to number your pages in WordPerfect. You also can use the
program's Page Numbering feature to number the pages automatically even
when you aren't using a header or footer.

The Page Numbering feature enables you to place the page number either at
the top or bottom margin so that the page number is flush with the left or right
margin or centered between them. If you are copying the document on both
sides of the page and having it bound, you can specify that the page number
alternate left and right between even and odd pages.

You also can use the Page Numbering feature to change the starting number,
change the page type, force a page to be odd or even, or insert the current page
number somewhere in the text on that page. By using this feature to insert the
page number instead of typing it yourself, you ensure that the page number
remains correct regardless of how the page breaks are adjusted during editing.

Formatting Page Numbers

Formatting Page Numbers
1. Position the cursor somewhere on the page where you want page
   numbering to begin. To number the entire document, move the
   cursor to the beginning by pressing Ctrl + Home.

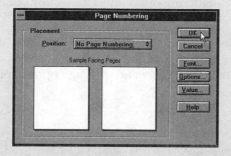

WordPerfect displays the Page Numbering dialog box where you indicate the type of numbering, starting page number, and the position of the page number.

2. Open the **Layout** menu, choose **Page**, and then choose **Numbering**.

3. By default, **No** Page Numbering is chosen in the **Position** pop-up list. To start page numbering, choose the appropriate option in the **Position** pop-up list: Top **Left**, Top **Center**, Top **Right**, **Alternating** Top, **Bottom** Left, **Bottom** Center, **Bottom** Right, **Alternating** Bottom.

   As soon as you choose an option, WordPerfect illustrates the page number position in the Sample Facing Pages area in the dialog box.

   To set a new number for a page, choose the **Value** command button. In the Numbering Value dialog box, choose New **Page** Number in the area for Page, Chapter, Secondary, and/or Volume settings; then enter or scroll to a new page number in the text box. Choose OK to return to the Page Numbering dialog box.

   To change the numbering style, such as from Arabic to Roman numerals, choose the **Options** command button. In the Page Numbering Options dialog box, choose a numbering style from the pop-up list for **Page**, **Secondary**, **Chapter**, and/or Volume. Choose OK to return to the Page Numbering dialog box.

4. Choose OK to return to the document window.

When you use the Page Numbering feature, WordPerfect inserts at the beginning of the page a [Pg Num Pos:] code that indicates the position of the page number. If you modified the starting number in the Numbering Value dialog box as described above, the program inserts the appropriate code showing the new page value (for example, [Pg Num Disp: Lev: 7;7] or [Pg Num Set]).

To delete page numbering from the entire document, you must locate the [Pg Num Pos:] code in the Reveal Codes window and delete it. To stop page numbering at a certain page in the document, position the cursor on the page where the numbering should stop; then return to the Page Numbering dialog box and choose the **No** Page Numbering option under **P**osition. Choose the OK button.

Page Numbers, like headers and footers, are not displayed in Draft View but are displayed in Page View. To see how page numbers will look when printed, switch to Page View. Choose the **V**iew menu and the **P**age option, or press Alt+F5.

> *Note:* The Pg indicator on the status bar always shows the current page number in Arabic numerals even when you have specified Roman numerals for the new page number. This means that the indicator will display the current page as Pg 3 even when the program prints the page number as iii.

Suppressing Page Formats

Suppressing Page Formatting

1. Position the cursor somewhere on the page where you want to suppress the page number, header, or footer.

2. Open the **L**ayout menu, choose **P**age, and then choose **S**uppress.

WordPerfect displays the Suppress dialog box.

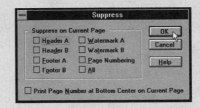

3. Under Suppress on Current Page, put an × in all the check boxes whose page formatting features you don't want to print on the page.

4. If you want the page number centered at the bottom margin, place an × in the Print Page **N**umber at Bottom Center on Current Page check box.

Note that this feature works only when you are numbering pages with the Page Numbering feature, not when you place a page number code in a header or footer.

5. Choose the OK button to return to the document.

   WordPerfect inserts a [Suppress:] code at the beginning of the current page, indicating the type of page formatting that is suppressed for that page. To restore formatting you have suppressed, locate this [Suppress:] code in the Reveal Codes window and delete it.

WordPerfect enables you to turn off page numbering or suppress the printing of a header or footer for a single page so that no number, header, or footer appears on that page. The number, header, or footer will appear as usual on all following pages.

Controlling Page Breaks

WordPerfect indicates page breaks on the screen as single or double lines in the document window. The program differentiates between a *soft page break*, which it automatically inserts when you have typed enough lines to fill a page, and a *hard page break*, which you insert manually whenever you want to begin a new page. The program uses a single line to represent a soft page break and a double line for a hard page break.

The program uses the current paper size and top and bottom margins to determine where a soft page break should occur. It also calculates the space required for any headers, footers, page numbers, or footnotes when determining the placement of a soft page break.

Here, you see a line across the document editing screen. The line indicates a soft page break. (In Draft View, WordPerfect displays a soft page break as a single line.)

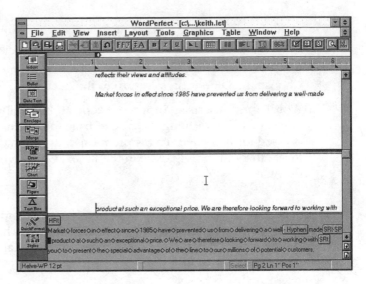

The format code for a soft page break is [SRt-SP]. When you add or delete text from a page, WordPerfect adjusts the placement of the soft page break.

Inserting Hard Page Breaks

To insert a hard page break, position the cursor at the place in the document where you want the new page to start and then press Ctrl+Enter.

To force a page break at a certain place in the document (for example, at the beginning of a new section or after a title page), insert a hard page break.

When you insert a hard page break, WordPerfect displays the same double line across the document editing screen as it displays for a soft page break. In Draft View, WordPerfect displays a hard page break as a double line.

At the place in the text where you press Ctrl+Enter, WordPerfect inserts the code [HPg] in the document. To remove a hard page break, open the Reveal Codes window, locate the [HPg] code, and delete it.

Keeping Text Together on a Page

Sometimes when WordPerfect inserts a soft page break, it divides text that should remain together on a single page. For example, a soft page break might split a table between two pages so that some of the rows of data end up alone at the top of a new page without the table title and the column headings (which appear at the bottom of the previous page).

WordPerfect provides several methods for keeping text together on a page. These methods enable you to protect certain text from unwanted page breaks at the time you enter the text. The text then stays together regardless of how the page breaks are adjusted as you edit the document.

Using Block Protect

Using Block Protect

1. Select with the I-beam pointer the text that should appear on the same page.

2. Open the **L**ayout menu, choose **P**age, and then choose **K**eep Text Together.

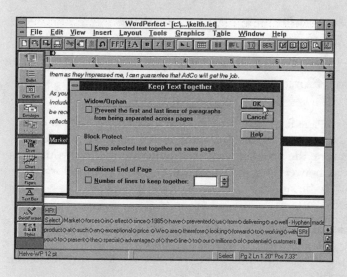

WordPerfect displays the Keep Text Together dialog box.

3. Choose **K**eep selected text together on same page; then choose OK to return to the document screen.

   Now the selected block of text will always appear on the same page.

When you select a block of text and then choose Layout, Page, Keep Text Together, WordPerfect places a [Block Pro] code at the beginning of the block and a [Block Pro] code at the end of the block.

To remove block protection, open the Reveal Codes window and delete either of the [Block Pro] codes that WordPerfect places around the text you selected.

Using Conditional End of Page

Using Conditional End of Page

1. Count the number of lines that should remain together on the same page.

2. Move the cursor to the line immediately above the lines you want to keep together.

3. Open the Layout menu, choose Page, and then choose Keep Text Together.

   WordPerfect displays the Keep Text Together dialog box.

4. Choose Number of lines to keep together; then enter the number of lines that should always stay together on a page in the text box.

5. Choose OK to return to the document window.

The Conditional End of Page feature is similar to Block Protect. Instead of selecting the text, however, you specify the number of lines to keep together. When you use this feature, the program groups the number of lines you specify so that they don't break between pages. This feature is quite useful, for example, when you want to be sure that a heading is always followed by a certain number of lines of text.

When you use this feature, WordPerfect inserts a [Condl EOP:] code that indicates the number of lines to keep together. If you ever want WordPerfect to split the text with a page break, open the Reveal Codes window and delete the [Condl EOP:] hidden code.

Using Widow/Orphan Protection

Turning on Widow/Orphan Protect

1. Position the cursor at the place in the document where you want to prevent widows and orphans. To prevent them in the entire document, move the cursor to the beginning by pressing Ctrl + Home.

2. Open the Layout menu, choose Page, and then choose Keep Text Together.

   WordPerfect displays the Keep Text Together dialog box.

3. Choose Prevent the first and last lines of paragraphs from being separated across pages; then choose OK to return to your document.

WordPerfect's Widow/Orphan Protection can prevent single lines from being "stranded" at the top or bottom of a page. In WordPerfect, a paragraph's first line alone at the bottom of a page is an *orphan;* a paragraph's last line alone at the top of a page is a *widow.*

When you choose this option, WordPerfect inserts a [Wid/Orph: On] hidden code in the document at the top of the current page. To turn off Widow/Orphan protection at a certain place in the document, repeat the preceding steps 1-4. WordPerfect inserts a [Wid/Orph: Off] code in the document at the cursor's position. This code turns off the Widow/Orphan feature.

Forcing a Page to Be Odd or Even

Forcing a Page to Be Odd or Even

1. Open the Layout menu, choose Page, and then choose Force Page.

   WordPerfect displays the Force Page dialog box.

2. Choose Current Page Odd or Current Page Even.

   continues

continued

WordPerfect inserts a hard page code before the current page, if necessary, to force the page to print with an odd or even page number.

3. To force a new page, regardless of odd or even page number, choose New **Page**.

4. Choose OK to return to the document screen.

The Force Page feature is particularly useful when you want the first page of a chapter or section to print on an odd or even page. WordPerfect inserts a hard page code, if needed, to ensure that the page prints as you specified, with an odd or even page number.

Using Subdivide Page

Subdividing Pages

1. Open the **Layout** menu, choose **Page**, and then choose Subdivide Page.

WordPerfect displays the Subdivide Page dialog box.

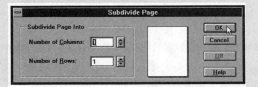

2. In the Number of **Columns** text box, type the number of columns or use the scroll arrows to enter the number.

3. In the Number of **Rows** text box, type the number of rows or use the scroll arrows to enter the number.

As you change the settings, your choices are reflected in the sample graphic.

4. Choose OK to return to the document window.

5. Insert the text and graphics for the first section of the subdivided page.

6. To insert the next section of the page, press Ctrl + Enter.

7. When you finish inserting text and graphics in the last section of the page, pressing Ctrl + Enter creates a new subdivided page. To turn off Subdivide Page for the new page, before or after you press Ctrl + Enter to insert the new page, choose the **L**ayout menu; then choose the **P**age, Subdivide Page, and **Off** options.

   WordPerfect turns off Subdivide Page and returns you to the document window.

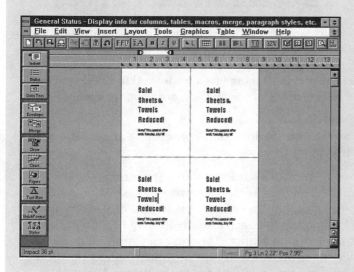

The figure shows a four-part subdivided page in Full Page Zoom mode.

WordPerfect can automatically subdivide a page for you. This feature greatly simplifies placing two or more equal-sized sections of text on the same page. For example, with Subdivide Page you can print four invitations on a single 8 1/2-by-11-inch sheet of paper and then cut the paper afterwards.

Note: The Subdivide Page feature can only divide a page into equal-sized sections. To divide a page into unequal-sized sections, use graphics boxes and/or columns. To learn how to use graphics boxes and columns, see chapter 16, "Using Columns and Graphics."

Tip: To insert the same text in each panel of a subdivided page, create the text in the first panel; then select the text and press Ctrl+C to copy the text onto the Clipboard. Press Ctrl+Enter to move into the next panel and press Ctrl+V to insert the text. Repeat these steps for each of the remaining panels.

Formatting a Document with Styles

WordPerfect's Styles feature provides a powerful tool for formatting documents that use a similar or identical layout. A *style* consists of the WordPerfect codes that control the appearance of your document. When you choose a style that you have created, the format codes it contains are inserted in the document. These codes control the formatting of the text you are about to enter or have already entered.

Using styles (instead of individual WordPerfect commands) to format a document offers several advantages.

- *Faster formatting.* Using a style greatly reduces the number of keystrokes required to accomplish complex formatting tasks. For example, you can create a style that chooses a new font and point size, changes the justification from left to full, increases the leading by a point, and chooses Bold as the font appearance. Then you can apply all these formatting changes to any heading in your document simply by selecting the heading, clicking the Styles button on the Button Bar, and choosing the name of the style from the list box that appears.

- *Consistent formatting.* Using a style assures you that the same format codes are applied to the text whenever the style is used in the document. For instance, when you use a style to format your headings in a document, you can be sure that they all share the same formatting.

- *Easier formatting changes.* By changing the codes in a style, you can apply those format changes immediately to all text to which that style is applied. For example, if you have used a style to format headings in a document and then decide you want the headings in a larger font size, you have to change only the point size in the style to have all headings in the document appear in the new size.

WordPerfect supports two kinds of styles: open and paired. An *open* style is one whose formatting remains in effect from the cursor's position in the document to the end of the document. A style that enters and formats a standard header for your document is an example of an open style. A *paired* style is one whose formatting is turned on and off throughout the document and affects only a specific portion of the text. A style that formats each first-level heading in a report is an example of a paired style. You would turn on the style before you enter each heading and then turn it off right after.

Defining a Style Using Quick Create

Using the Style Quick Create Command

1. The easiest way to create a style is to enter a paragraph of text and then use the Quick Create style command to copy its formatting into a style. After the example paragraph has the appearance you want your style to create, follow the remaining steps.

2. Select all the paragraph text with the I-beam pointer. Make sure that you select text that includes all the codes used in formatting the paragraph. To make sure of this, open the Reveal Codes window ([Alt]+[F3]).

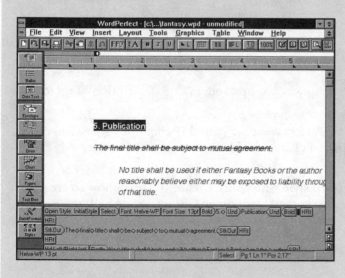

In this example, you select this sample title along with the codes that change the font and bold the text.

3. Open the Layout menu, and then choose Styles; press [Alt]+[F8]; or click the Styles button on the Button Bar.

continues

243

continued

WordPerfect
displays the Style
List dialog box that
shows the styles
currently available
in the active docu-
ment.

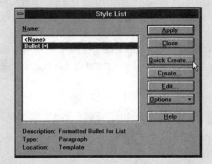

4. Choose **Q**uick Create.

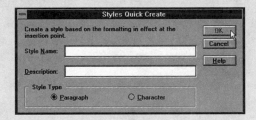

WordPerfect
displays the
Styles Quick
Create dialog
box.

5. Enter the name for your new style in the Style **N**ame text box.

6. Choose the **D**escription text box and enter a description of up to 54 characters.

7. By default, WordPerfect creates a paired (**Paragraph**) style. You can also create a paired character style by choosing **Character**.

You cannot create an open style with Quick Create. To learn how to create open styles, see the next section, "Creating or Editing a Style with the Styles Editor."

Creating or Editing a Style with the Styles Editor

Creating or Editing a Style with the Styles Editor

1. From the document window, open the **L**ayout menu and choose **S**tyles; or press [Alt]+[F8]; or click the Styles button on the Button Bar.

2. To create a style, choose **C**reate in the Style List dialog box.

   or

   To edit an existing style, highlight its name in the **N**ames list and choose **E**dit.

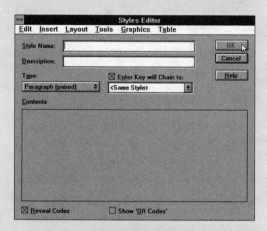

WordPerfect displays the Styles Editor dialog box.

Tip: To display the Styles Editor dialog box for an existing style, open the Reveal Codes window ([Alt]+[F3]) and double-click the style's hidden code.

3. In the Styles Editor, type a name for the new style in the **S**tyle Name text box.

4. Choose **D**escription and type a description for the new style.

5. Choose **T**ype and select a type from the pop-up list: **P**aragraph (paired) (the default), **C**haracter (paired), or **D**ocument (open).

   When creating a paired style, the Enter key can insert a hard return as usual, it can turn off the paired style, it can turn the style off and then back on again, or it can link the style to another style.

continues

245

continued

6. To assign an action to the Enter key, choose Enter Key will Chain to; then choose an option from the pop-up box: <Same Style> (the default) or <None> or choose the name of an existing style from the pop-up list.

7. Choose Contents.

   In the Contents text box, WordPerfect displays the text at the cursor location in your document.

8. To display formatting codes only in the Contents box, mark the Reveal Codes button.

9. To display style on and off codes in the Contents box with the Reveal Codes check box selected, choose Show 'Off Codes'.

10. In the Contents box, type any text and formatting codes for the style.

11. Choose OK to return to the Style List dialog box.

    WordPerfect inserts the name of the new style in the Name list.

12. Choose Close to return to the document screen, or choose Apply to return to the document screen and apply the style immediately.

You can create a style with Quick Create, as described in the preceding section, or you can use the Styles Editor to create a new style. The process is essentially the same, except that when you use the Styles Editor, WordPerfect does not automatically copy the formatting of the current paragraph or selected text into the new style. Instead, you must enter the formatting codes in the Styles Editor.

Managing Styles

Using Style Options

1. From the document window, open the Layout menu and choose Styles; press Alt + F8; or click the Styles button on the Button Bar.

   WordPerfect displays the Style List dialog box.

2. Choose Options and choose an option from the pop-up list.

3. Choose Close from the Style List dialog box to return to your document.

From the Style List dialog box, you can perform a number of essential style management tasks; for example, you can display WordPerfect's supplied styles or just styles that you've created. You can copy or delete styles, and you can reset a system style to its default state after you've edited it. You can retrieve styles for use with a new document. And you can save styles in a separate file so that you can use them with new documents.

For details about the options in the Option dialog box, refer to Que's *Using WordPerfect 6 for Windows,* Special Edition.

Applying a Style

Applying a Style as You Type Text

1. With the cursor at the place where you want the formatting to begin, open the Layout menu and choose Styles; or press Alt+F8.

2. Choose the name of the style you want to use in the Names list box.

3. Choose Apply.

   WordPerfect returns you to your document and inserts the style code. If you're using an open style, enter the rest of the text for your document. If you're using a paired style, enter only the text you want to format with the style before you turn off the style.

4. To turn off the style, press ↵Enter and open the Reveal Codes window (Alt+F3); then press ↑ and Del to remove the opening [Para Style:] or [Char Style:] code from the beginning of the new paragraph.

Applying a Style to Existing Text

1. Select the text you want to format with the style.

2. Open the Layout menu and choose Styles; or press Alt+F8.

3. Choose the name of the style you want to use in the Names list box.

4. Choose the Apply command button to apply the formatting contained in the style to the selected paragraph or paragraphs of text.

   WordPerfect formats the text with the paired style and continues to apply the style in accordance with your instructions for the action of the Enter key when you created the style.

continues

247

continued

5. To turn off the style, press `↵Enter` and open the Reveal Codes
    window (`Alt`+`F3`); then press `↑` and `Del` to remove the opening
    [Para Style:] or [Char Style:] code from the beginning of the new
    paragraph.

When you apply a paired style to selected text, WordPerfect turns off the style at
the end of the text.

After you have created styles, you can begin applying them to the text in documents. When using an open style, turn on the style at the appropriate place in
the document. When using a paired style, you must first select existing text and
then apply the style, or turn on the style and enter the text it formats, and
finally turn the style off again.

Summary

In this chapter, you learned about WordPerfect's document formatting features,
including how to change the paper size, create a new paper definition, change
the top and bottom margins, center text vertically on a page, use headers and
footers, number pages, control page breaks, and format the document with
styles.

In the chapter ahead, you will learn how to print the documents you create
with WordPerfect. You also will learn how to preview your printouts before
printing.

8

Printing a Document

W ith WordPerfect, you can easily print all or part of any document you create. You can print just the text you have selected, a range of pages, or the entire document. When you print multiple pages or the entire document, you can print the document in the active document window or a document file on disk.

In WordPerfect, you can print with one of WordPerfect Corporation's printer drivers or a printer driver supplied with the Microsoft Windows program. If you use WordPerfect 6.0 for DOS in the office, you can maintain complete printing compatibility between WordPerfect for Windows and WordPerfect for DOS by using the WordPerfect printer driver designed for your printer. This printer driver ensures that all the fonts you routinely use are available when you use the DOS or Windows version of WordPerfect. If you use other Windows programs such as Excel or PageMaker, you can maintain complete printing compatibility between WordPerfect for Windows and your other Windows applications by using the Windows printer driver designed by Microsoft for your printer. This printer driver ensures that all the fonts you routinely use in other Windows programs are available in WordPerfect for Windows.

Regardless of the type of printer driver you choose, WordPerfect uses the Windows Print Manager to manage the print job. You can therefore continue to edit documents in WordPerfect as soon as WordPerfect sends the print job to the Print Manager.

In this chapter, you learn all the basic printing techniques, including selecting a printer (when multiple printers are installed). The material covered in this chapter assumes, however, that you have already installed your printers with the Windows Setup program or the WordPerfect for Windows installation program.

Key Terms in This Chapter	
Windows printer driver	Special Windows printing resource file developed by Microsoft Corporation for a type of printer that tells all Windows programs how to communicate with the Windows Print Manager. Windows printer drivers are installed with the Printers program icon in the Control Panel of the Windows desktop.
WordPerfect printer driver	Special printing resource file developed by WordPerfect Corporation for a type of printer that tells the program how to communicate with the Windows Print Manager. WordPerfect printer drivers are installed with the WordPerfect installation program.

Selecting a Printer

Selecting a Printer
1. Open the File menu and choose Select Printer. WordPerfect displays the Select Printer dialog box.

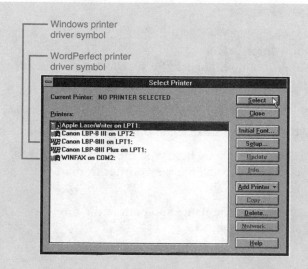

Windows printer
driver symbol

WordPerfect printer
driver symbol

The dialog box
shows the current
printer and a list of
available printers.

The names of the printers listed in the **Printers** list box change when you choose a new printer driver. If you have installed printers for Windows that haven't been installed in WordPerfect, these printers appear in the list box. Notice that WordPerfect printer drivers are listed with the "WP" symbol and Windows printer drivers are identified by a Windows symbol.

2. Select the name of the printer you want to use in the **Printers** list box, and then choose the **S**elect command button.

WordPerfect uses the printer you choose to print all documents until you return to the Select Printer dialog box and choose another one.

You must have your printer properly installed and selected before you can print with it in WordPerfect. If you have more than one printer, you must install each one. Then, to use a new printer, select the one you want to use before using the **File Print** command.

Installing a Printer Driver

Installing a WordPerfect Printer Driver

1. From the WPWIN6.0 group, double-click the WPWIN6.0 installation icon.

2. From the Installation Type dialog box, choose **Options**.

3. Choose **P**rinter from the Additional Installation Options dialog box.

4. In the Select Printer Directory dialog box, type the name and path of the directory that you want to install the new printer from in the Install From text box.

5. In the Install To text box, type the name and path of the directory that you want to install the printer to.

6. Choose OK.

7. When WordPerfect prompts you to insert the Install 1 disk, insert the disk, and in the **D**iskette Location text box type the name of the drive where you inserted the disk.

8. In the WordPerfect Printer Drivers dialog box, double-click a printer name in the Printers list, or select the printer name of the drive where you inserted the disk.

9. Repeat step 8 for any other printers you want to install. Then choose OK.

10. Insert the required disks as prompted.

    After installing the new printer drivers, you are returned to the Additional Installation Options dialog box.

11. Choose **C**lose, **E**xit to return to the Windows Program Manager.

    Note: The installation program does not run while WordPerfect is running. To install a new printer, you need to save your document and exit WordPerfect before running Install.

Adding a Printer

Adding a Printer

1. Open the File menu and choose Select Printer. WordPerfect displays the Select Printer dialog box.

2. Choose Add Printer. WordPerfect displays the Add Printer dialog box.

3. Choose WordPerfect or Windows from the pop-up list to add the corresponding type of printer driver.

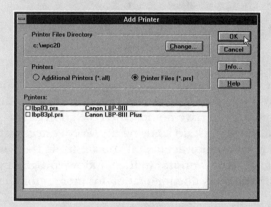

If you choose WordPerfect, a list of the installed WordPerfect printer drivers appears in the Printers list box.

If you choose Windows, the Windows Printers dialog box appears. To learn how to use the Windows Printers dialog box, consult the *Windows User's Guide*.

4. Select the name of the printer you want to add.

5. To display the names of other printer drivers from the currently installed *.ALL file, choose Additional Printers and then select the name of the printer you want to add.

   When you install WordPerfect for Windows, it creates the printer *.ALL file, which includes drivers for other printers similar to the ones you have installed.

6. To switch to a different directory that contains other printer drivers, choose Change and use the Select Directory dialog box to switch to the new directory.

continues

253

continued

7. To display specific information about a printer driver, select the driver in the Printers list box; then choose Info, review the information in the text window, and choose Close to return to the Add Printer dialog box.

    WordPerfect displays the Printer Information text box with information about the printer. If the printer includes a sheet feeder, you can choose Sheet Feeder from the Printer Information dialog box to display information about the sheet feeder.

8. Choose OK to add the printer and return to the Select Printer dialog box.

If you don't see the printer you want in the Select Printer dialog box, you can add the printer to the list if you have installed the printer file that contains information about the printer. If you have not installed the appropriate printer resource file for your printer, you must do so using the WordPerfect installation program. (See the preceding section for details.) If you are using the Windows printer drivers, you must add the new printer in the Windows program with the Control Panel (consult your Windows documentation for more information).

Choosing a Printer Initial Font

Choosing a Printer Initial Font

1. Open the File menu and choose Select Printer. WordPerfect displays the Select Printer dialog box.

2. Choose Initial Font.

3. Choose a font in the Font Face list box.

    As you make selections, the sample graphic at the bottom of the dialog box reflects your changes.

4. Select a font size in the Font Size list box. If your printer has scalable fonts, you can type a size in the text box at the top of the list box.

5. Select a font style in the Font Style list box.

WordPerfect
displays the
Printer Initial
Font dialog box.

Using WordPerfect Printer Setup Options

Choosing Printer Setup Options

1. Open the File menu and choose Select Printer. WordPerfect displays the Select Printer dialog box.

2. Choose a WordPerfect printer driver in the **Printers** list box, and then choose Setup.

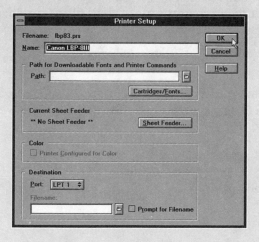

WordPerfect
displays the Printer
Setup dialog box.

continues

255

continued

3. Type a new printer driver name in the **N**ame text box, if desired.

4. Choose the **P**ath text box and type the path where downloadable fonts and printer command files are located.

   To display the Select Directory dialog box, click the icon at the right end of the **P**ath text box.

   If your printer uses cartridges or downloadable fonts, you can choose the Cartridges/**F**onts button to display the Select Fonts dialog box. For more information on selecting fonts, consult Que's *Using WordPerfect 6 for Windows,* Special Edition.

5. If your printer has a sheet feeder, choose **S**heet Feeder and select a sheet feeder from the Select Sheet Feeder dialog; then choose OK to return to the Printer Setup dialog box.

6. If your printer supports color printing, choose Printer **C**onfigured for Color to enable color printing.

7. Choose **P**ort to change the printer port if needed, and choose one of the LPT or COM port options from the pop-up list.

8. To print documents to a file by default, choose **F**ile from the pop-up list, choose Fi**l**ename, and type the name of the file that you want WordPerfect to write all documents to; or choose **P**rompt for Filename. WordPerfect then prompts you to type a file name whenever you print a document to a file.

9. Choose OK to return to the Select Printer dialog box.

If you select a WordPerfect printer driver in the Select Printer dialog box and then choose S**e**tup, WordPerfect displays the Printer Setup dialog box, where you can customize printer options.

Note: To learn how to set up a Windows printer driver, consult the *Windows User's Guide*.

Updating Printer Drivers

If you obtain an updated *.PRS printer driver file, you can update the driver from the Select Printer dialog box. Highlight a printer driver name in the **Printers** list box and then choose **U**pdate. WordPerfect updates the printer driver from the new driver file.

Copying or Deleting a Printer Driver

From the Select Printer dialog box, you can copy or delete a printer driver. You may want to copy a file, for example, in order to use printer driver customization options to print certain documents. Highlight the printer in the **Printers** list box and then choose **C**opy or **D**elete. WordPerfect prompts you for confirmation before deleting the file or asks you to type a new file name before copying the file.

Testing Your Printer

Printing the PRINTER.TST Document

1. Open the File menu and choose **O**pen; press Ctrl + O; or click the Open button on the Power Bar.

2. In the Open File dialog box, select wpwin60 in the **D**irectories list box, select PRINTER.TST in the File**n**ame list box, and then choose OK.

3. Open the File menu and choose **P**rint; press F5; or click the Print button on the Power Bar.

4. In the Print dialog box, choose **P**rint to print the document.

continues

continued

Here, you see a copy of the PRINTER.TST document printed by an Apple LaserWriter IINT.

WordPerfect includes a single-page document called PRINTER.TST that you print to test the capabilities of the printer you have selected. To print this test document, follow the preceding steps.

Printing Your Documents

After you have selected the printer you want to use, printing your documents with WordPerfect is simple. You just open the document you want to print choose the **File Print** command; press F5; or click the Print button on the Power Bar. Then you specify how much of the document you want to print along with any other print settings, such as the number of copies, binding width, and print quality of the text and graphics. The section that follows describes options for printing.

Printing the Current Page or Entire Document

Printing the Current Page or Document

1. Open the document you want to print by opening the **File** menu and choosing **Open**. The Open File dialog box appears.

   If the document is already open, make its document window active by selecting the document in the **Window** menu.

2. Open the **File** menu and choose **Print**; press F5; or click the Print button on the Power Bar.

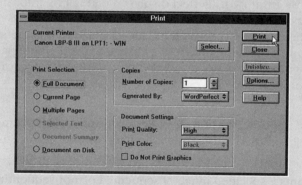

WordPerfect displays the Print dialog box, where you specify the print options you want to use before sending all or part of the document to the Print Manager.

3. At the top of the Print dialog box, WordPerfect shows the name of the current printer. To use a different printer, choose the **Select** button. Then, in the Select Printer dialog box, specify the name of the printer as described earlier in the section "Selecting a Printer."

continues

259

continued

4. By default, WordPerfect selects the Full Document button under Print Selection. To print the current page only, choose the Current Page button.

5. By default, WordPerfect prints a single copy of the current page or document. To print multiple copies, enter the new value in the Number of Copies text box or use the up- or down-arrow icons to select the number of copies.

6. WordPerfect can generate multiple copies of a document with the pages of each copy collated during printing. If your printer is capable of controlling this function, the printer can generate multiple copies, reducing the printing time; the copies, however, are collated. To do this, change the WordPerfect setting in the Generated By pop-up list to Printer.

7. If necessary, change any of the Print dialog box settings.

8. Choose Options to display the Print Output Options dialog box, and set Formatting Options and Output Bin Options.

9. Choose the Print command button.

   When you choose Print, WordPerfect displays a dialog box informing you of the page or pages being sent to the Windows Print Manager. To cancel printing, you must select the Cancel button in this message dialog box before WordPerfect has had a chance to send all the pages to the Print Monitor. As soon as this dialog box disappears, you can return to work in WordPerfect.

You have a great deal of control over how WordPerfect prints your documents. You control the printing features by using the following options in the Print dialog box:

- **Multiple Pages** prints a specified range of sequential or nonsequential pages.

Choosing **Multiple Pages** displays the Multiple Pages dialog box, where you can specify the pages to print by choosing **Page**(s), **Secondary Page**(s), **Chapter**(s), and **Volume**(s). Choose the **Print** command button to return to the Print dialog box.

The following list indicates sample print ranges you can enter in the Multiple Pages dialog box.

Print Range	Pages Printed
3	Only page 3
3 7 or 3,7	Pages 3 and 7
3-7	Pages 3 through 7, inclusive
3-	All pages from page 3 forward
-7	All pages up to and including page 7
iii-vii	Roman numeral pages iii through vii, inclusive

Note: If you are printing labels using a paper definition that prints multiple labels on the same physical page, WordPerfect automatically prints all the labels for the number of pages you specify. Unlike Version 5.2 and previous versions of WordPerfect for Windows, WordPerfect 6.0 no longer considers each label a separate page.

• Selected Text prints text selected in the document. This option is available only when text is selected.

- Document Summary prints the document summary along with the full document or a range of pages. If the on-screen document does not include a document summary, this option is grayed.

- **Document on Disk** prints a document stored on disk. Except for the Filename text box, the Document on Disk dialog box contains the same options as the Multiple Pages dialog box, described earlier with the **Multiple Pages** option. If you choose **Document on Disk** and then choose the **Print** command button, WordPerfect displays the Document on Disk dialog box.

You can type a
document name or
click the icon at the
right end of the
Filename text box
to use the Select
File dialog box.

- **Number of Copies** prints more than one copy of the current document. Enter the number of copies in the text box or click the up and down arrows to change the settings.

- **Generated By** (for a description of this option, see step 6 earlier in this section).

- **Print Quality** sets print quality to **High**, **Medium**, or **Draft**. Experiment with this setting to see whether the WordPerfect or Microsoft Windows printer drivers for your printer enable you to print fast-, low-, or medium-resolution documents for proofing.

- **Print Color** enables color printing if your printer supports color. Choose this option and then choose **Black** (for black-and-white printing) or **Color** from the pop-up list.

- Do Not Print **Graphics** greatly speeds up printing by omitting graphic images from the printed text. WordPerfect prints box borders but omits the graphic images.

When you choose the **O**ptions command button in the Print dialog box, WordPerfect displays the Print Output Options dialog box, as explained in step 8 of the preceding steps.

Here you see the Print Output Options dialog box.

The following paragraphs describe the options in the Print Output Options dialog box:

- Print **D**ocument Summary prints only the document summary. (To print the document summary in addition to a range of pages, choose Document Summary from the Print dialog box as described earlier.

- **B**ooklet Printing prints the pages in "signature" order so that you can more easily bind the pages in the correct page order for reproduction as a booklet.

- Print in **R**everse Order (Back to Front) prints a document beginning with the last page. This option is useful if your printer stacks pages by default in reverse order, requiring that you manually collate each printed document.

- Print **O**dd/Even Pages prints only the odd-numbered or even-numbered pages. Choose this option and then choose **B**oth (the default), **O**dd, or **E**ven to print the corresponding pages in the document.

- **S**ort, **G**roup, and **J**ogger allow you to specify options available with printers that have multiple output bins or a page jogger feature. For specific information, refer to your printer documentation.

Previewing a Document Before Printing

Nothing is quite as disappointing as printing a long document only to discover that it is not quite right and that you must reprint the entire document. To avoid wasting paper and valuable time, you can preview the effects of your formatting commands in Page View by choosing View, **Page**; or by pressing Alt+F5.

Summary

In this chapter, you learned how to print the documents you create in WordPerfect for Windows. As part of this process, you learned how to select the printer you want to use and print all or part of the document in the active document window. You also learned how to print a document saved on disk.

The next chapter covers managing the files you create in WordPerfect. In the chapter, you will learn how to password-protect your documents, create lists for quickly locating your documents, and perform basic file housekeeping chores.

Managing Files in WordPerfect

9

Y ou have already learned some basic file management tasks such as naming, saving, and opening files. This chapter covers some of the other valuable procedures for managing and securing your documents. You will learn how to protect files with passwords so that unauthorized users cannot access your documents, how to add document summaries to files, how to find files quickly with QuickFinder, how to use QuickList to help you quickly identify and retrieve documents, and how to back up your documents.

Saving a document with a password

Creating a document summary

Using QuickList to identify directories

Using file management options

Using QuickFinder to locate files

Key Terms in This Chapter

Document summary	Synopsis of the contents and vital statistics about a document that can help you quickly identify and locate the document at a later date.
QuickFinder	The WordPerfect file-indexing and retrieval utility.
QuickList	Descriptive alias you can assign to a directory to help you quickly locate its contents.

Saving a Document with a Password

When you protect your files with WordPerfect's password-protection system, you prevent access to the files by unauthorized users. The only people who can open a protected document are those who know the password. This feature is particularly useful for documents that contain confidential information.

Note: WordPerfect will not allow you to view the contents of a password-protected document in a File Viewer window until you can enter the password correctly.

Assigning a Password

Assigning a Password

1. Open the file that contains the document you want to assign a password to (open the **File** menu and choose **Open**, or press `Ctrl`+`O`). If the document is already open but its document window is not active, make the window active by choosing the document's name in the **Window** menu.

2. If you opened an existing document, open the File menu and choose the Save **As** option; or press `F3`.

   or

   If you are saving a document for the first time, choose **Save**; press `Ctrl`+`S`; or click the Save button on the Power Bar.

   WordPerfect displays the Save As dialog box.

3. Select the **Password Protect** check box in the lower right corner of the Save As dialog box.

4. Choose OK.

   If you saved the file previously, WordPerfect prompts you to confirm that you want to replace the file.

5. Choose **Yes**.

WordPerfect displays the Password dialog box, where you can enter a password for the document you are saving.

continues

267

continued

6. Type a password in the Type Password for Document text box.

   As you type, WordPerfect displays an asterisk for each character of the password.

7. Choose OK.

   WordPerfect displays the Password dialog box and prompts you to retype the password to ensure that you enter the password without typing errors.

8. Type the password a second time.

   WordPerfect again enters an asterisk for each character you type.

9. Choose OK. WordPerfect assigns the password to the document and returns you to the document window.

Note: Be very careful with passwords: You cannot open a document and remove or change the password unless you know the password.

Opening a Password-Protected File

Opening a Password-Protected File

1. Open the File menu and choose Open; press Ctrl + O; or click the Open button on the Power Bar.

   WordPerfect displays the Open File dialog box.

2. Enter the file name in the Filename text box, or choose the file name in the Files list box. Then choose the Open command button.

WordPerfect displays the Password dialog box.

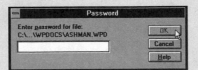

3. Type the password in the Enter Password for File text box.

   WordPerfect again inserts an asterisk for each character you type.

4. Choose OK.

   If you enter the password correctly, WordPerfect opens the file.

   If you enter the wrong password, however, WordPerfect displays an `Incorrect password entered` message.

5. Choose OK and try opening the file again.

Deleting or Changing a Password

The only way to delete a password is to open the locked document with the File Open command (which requires you to successfully reproduce the password); choose the File Save As command; and remove the mark from the Password Protect check box. Then choose OK, and choose Yes to replace the previous version of the file. The password is removed, and you can open the file without typing the password.

To change a password, you must first open the locked file by accurately reproducing the password. Then choose the File Save As command again and assign a new password.

Creating a Document Summary

With WordPerfect, you can add a document summary to any document you create. The summary will help you identify the contents at a glance and find the document quickly. A document summary can include a descriptive or long file name (up to 68 characters long), a descriptive file type, the original creation date, the date of last revision, and the name of the author and typist, along with other distinctive information about the file, such as the account, the keywords, and an abstract of the file's contents.

You also can print the contents of the document summary, either by itself or as part of the print job when you print the document. And you can save the document summary in a separate file.

Entering Document Summary Information

Creating a Document Summary

1. If necessary, open the document you want to add the document summary to (open the **File** menu and choose **Open**, or press [Ctrl]+[O]). If the document is already open but its document window is not active, make the window active by choosing the **Window** menu and then the document's name.

2. Open the **File** menu and choose Document Summary.

WordPerfect displays the Document Summary dialog box where you enter the reference and descriptive information that identifies the document.

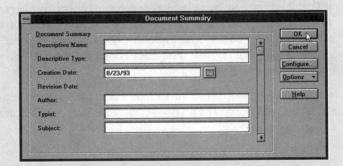

3. Enter all the reference and descriptive information in the appropriate text boxes. (These text boxes are described shortly.)

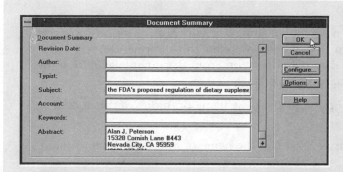

WordPerfect can extract information from your document and insert it in the corresponding document summary fields.

4. Choose OK to save the document summary information and return to the editing screen.

5. Open the File menu and choose Save or Save As to save the document summary as part of the file.

Use any of the following options when entering information in the Document Summary dialog box.

- *Descriptive Name.* Use this option to enter a descriptive file name up to 68 characters long. You can display this long file name in the Open File and Insert File dialog boxes. If the file is password-protected, Word-Perfect does not show the summary information in the Open File or Insert File dialog box, but displays a [Password Locked] message instead.

- *Descriptive Type.* Use this option to enter a descriptive file type up to 68 characters long. For example, you could use Contracts as the descriptive type for all the contracts you create in WordPerfect. The descriptive type information also can be displayed in the Open File and Insert File dialog boxes.

- *Creation Date.* Use this option to enter a new creation date. The current date and time is automatically entered into this text box when you create the document summary. To revise this date and time, enter the date and time following the pattern of the current date and time (dashes between the parts of the date, colon between the hours and minutes, and *a* for A.M. and *p* for P.M.).

- *Revision Date.* WordPerfect automatically inserts the date and time when you create a document summary and choose **Options**, **Extract Information From Document**. To update this information, you must choose **Options**, **Extract Information From Document** again from the Document Summary dialog box.

- *Author.* Use this option to enter the name or initials of the document's author.

- *Typist.* Use this option to enter the name or initials of the document's typist.

- *Subject.* Use this option to enter the subject of the document. If the document already contains this information following the heading RE: in the document, you can copy this text by choosing the **S**ubject text box and then choosing **Options**, **Extract Information From Document**. If this information changes in the document, you must update it in the Document Summary by again choosing **Options**, **Extract Information From Document**.

To view the following document summary fields, press Tab or use the scroll bar to bring the fields onto the screen.

- *Account.* Use this option to enter an account name or number assigned to the document.

- *Keywords.* Use this option to enter keywords that can be used to locate the document quickly, using QuickFinder in the Open File or Insert File dialog box.

- *Abstract.* Use this option to enter a synopsis of the document's content. You can have WordPerfect copy the first 400 characters of the document into the Abstract text box by choosing **Options**, **Extract Information From Document**.

Printing and Saving a Document Summary

Printing Only a Document Summary

1. Open the **F**ile menu and choose Document Summary.

   WordPerfect displays the Document Summary dialog box

2. Choose **O**ptions, and then choose **P**rint Summary from the drop-down list.

> Descriptive Name:
> Descriptive Type:
> Creation Date: 8/22/93 2:47:47 PM
> Revision Date: 8/22/93 2:47PM
> Author:
> Typist:
> Subject: The FDA's proposed regulation of dietary supplements
> Account:
> Keywords:
> Abstract: Alan J. Peterson15328 Cornish Lane #443Nevada City, CA 95959(916) 277-774August
> 22, 1993The Hon. Steven FiorettiU.S. SenateWashington, DC 20510Dear Sen. Fioretti:Re: The
> FDA's proposed regulation of dietary supplementsA recent issue of the New England Journal of
> Medicine reported that as many as one third of the U.S. adult population have used or presently
> use alternative healing methods.Do we really want to create an enormous new "criminal" class?
> And do we really want to give the FDA an enormous new enforcement mission?The FDA's
> proposed regulation of health foods smacks of extreme hypocrisy. To apply these guidelines
> consistently, they would have to enforce prescription-only use of alcohol and tobacco. Which, of
> course, they will never do, thanks to the financial power of the tobacco and alcohol
> lobbies.Obviously, there are dangerous food supplements that should be labeled as such.

WordPerfect prints the summary on the currently selected printer.

Note: You can also print just a file's document summary by choosing the File menu and the Print option and then choosing Document Summary and OK.

Printing a Document Summary and a File

Printing a File and a Summary

1. Open the File menu and choose Print; press F5; or click the Print button on the Power Bar.

   WordPerfect displays the Print dialog box.

2. Choose Options.

3. Select the Print Document Summary check box.

4. Choose OK and Print to begin printing the document along with its summary.

   WordPerfect prints the document summary before it prints the remainder of the host document.

Saving a Document Summary in a File

Saving a Summary in a File

1. Open the File menu and choose Document Summary.

   WordPerfect displays the Document Summary dialog box.

2. Choose Options, and then choose Save Summary As New Document from the drop-down list.

WordPerfect
displays the Save
Document
Summary dialog
box.

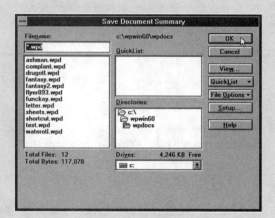

3. Type a file name for the document summary.

   or

   To save the document summary for another file, choose the file in the Filename list box, and then type a name for its summary.

4. Choose OK.

   WordPerfect saves the document summary file in WordPerfect for Windows 6.0 format and returns you to the Document Summary dialog box.

Setting the Document Summary Preferences

Setting Document Summary Preferences

1. Open the File menu, and then choose Preferences and Summary.

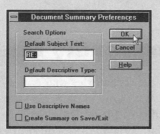

WordPerfect displays the Document Summary Preferences dialog box.

2. To change the heading used to identify the Subject text for the document summary, replace RE: in the **Default Subject Text** text box.

   If, for example, you routinely create subject summaries for memos, you could change RE: to SUBJECT:. WordPerfect automatically copies the subject of the memo into the Subject text box when you choose **Options, Extract Information From Document** in the Document Summary dialog box.

3. To have WordPerfect add a default descriptive type for you in the Descriptive Type text box in the Document Summary dialog box, enter the text for your type in the **Default Descriptive Type** text box.

4. Choose the **Use Descriptive Names** check box to turn on the display of descriptive file names in the Open File and Insert File dialog boxes.

5. To have the program display the Document Summary dialog box whenever you save a document with the **File, Save** or **File, Save As** command or when you try to close the document window before saving the file, select the **Create Summary on Save/Exit** check box.

6. Choose OK and then Close to return to the document window.

If you want, you can set the Document Summary Preferences so that Word-Perfect displays the Document Summary dialog box when you save a new document or try to close its document window. You then can create document summaries for all your documents without remembering to choose the Layout,

Document, Summary command. You also can change the heading used to identify subject text in your documents and specify a default descriptive type as part of the Document Summary Preference settings. And you can turn on display of descriptive file names in the Open File and Insert File dialog boxes using the Document Summary Preferences dialog box.

Using QuickLists to Identify Directories

With QuickList, you can easily identify the directories that contain the document files you regularly need and use. With QuickList, you assign a descriptive title to any directory, single file, or wild-card file specification. You can then choose that directory, file, or group of files by its title. You don't have to remember the directory path or take the time to choose it by typing a subdirectory path and file name specification. For example, assume that you store letters and memos in a directory called c:\wpwin\letters. With the QuickList feature, you can assign the name *Letters* to this directory and then choose this directory and its contents simply by choosing the Letters QuickList. You can use QuickLists in any dialog box that uses directories and file lists, including the Open File, Save As, or Insert File dialog boxes.

With the QuickList, you are not limited to a maximum of eight characters when assigning a title to a directory, as you are when creating and naming directories in DOS. You can make the names in the QuickList as descriptive as you like; for example, assume Sarah and Alan share the same computer in an office but each one uses a separate directory for storing letters. Their directories are named c:\wpwin\sarah\letters and c:\wpwin\alan\letters. In the QuickList, these directories could be named *Sarah's Letters* and *Alan's Letters*.

Editing or Creating a QuickList

Creating or Editing a QuickList

1. Choose a WordPerfect command that uses a Filename list box, such as the File Open command.

2. Choose QuickList and choose one of the following options:

- Show **QuickList**. This replaces the **Directories** list box with a **QuickList** list box that shows any QuickLists you've defined.

- Show **Directories**. This default setting displays a directory tree in the **Directories** list box.

- Show **Both**. This reduces the default **Directories** list box to a smaller size and adds a **QuickList** list box above it.

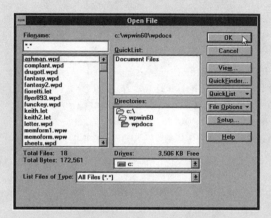

When you choose **Both**, WordPerfect displays list boxes for **QuickList** and **Directories**.

3. To create a new QuickList or edit an existing one, choose **QuickList** and choose **Edit** QuickList from the pop-up menu.

WordPerfect displays the Edit QuickList dialog box, showing you the descriptive names for the Document Files, Graphics Files, Macros, and Styles libraries in the **QuickList** list box.

continues

277

continued

WordPerfect
displays the Add
QuickList Item
dialog box where
you specify the
path name.

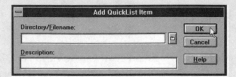

4. Type the path name of the directory, or use the list button to choose
   the directory for the **Directory/Filename** text box.

   You also can specify a particular file as part of the path name to
   create a QuickList item just for that document. For example, if
   you often need to work with a file called stdcontr in the
   c:\wpwin\contracts directory, you can enter
   c:\wpwin\contract\stdcontr in the **Directory/Filename** text box.

5. Choose the **Description** text box. When you do, WordPerfect copies
   the directory name you just entered in the Directory/**Filename** text
   box to this text box. If you want, replace this text with the descriptive
   name you want to appear in the **QuickList** list box.

   For example, you can enter Standard Contract in the **Description** text
   box. This is the QuickList title that will now appear in the QuickList
   list box.

6. Choose OK to return to the Edit QuickList dialog box.

7. To edit an existing QuickList, choose it in the **QuickList** list box in the
   Edit QuickList dialog box; then choose **Edit**.

   WordPerfect returns you to the Edit QuickList Item dialog box, which
   is exactly the same as the Create QuickList dialog box. To edit the
   item, repeat steps 5 through 7.

8. From the Edit QuickList dialog box, choose OK to return to the Open
   File, Save As, or Insert File dialog box.

Displaying Files with QuickList

Displaying Files with QuickList

1. Choose a WordPerfect command that uses a directories and files dialog box, such as **File Save As, File Open,** or **Insert File.**

2. Make sure that the QuickList list box is displayed. If not, choose **QuickList** and choose Show **QuickList** or Show **Both.**

3. In the **QuickList** list box, click the descriptive name of the directory or file you want to list in the **Filename** list box. Or choose the name with the arrow keys.

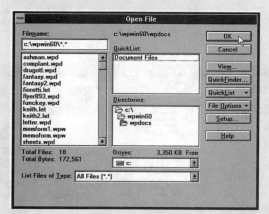

WordPerfect displays the entire directory path after Filename and all the files in that directory in the Filename list box.

If appropriate, choose the file you want to use in the **Filename** list box, or enter the new file name in the **Filename** text box.

4. Choose the appropriate command button, such as **Open.**

Note: Remember that you can always display the **Directories** list box once again in a dialog box by choosing **QuickList** and then choosing Show **Directories** or Show **Both.**

Using File Management Options

WordPerfect simplifies common file housekeeping chores such as copying, moving, renaming, or deleting files. In addition, the program enables you to search for files on a disk by specifying a pattern followed by the file name or words contained in the file.

You can perform any of these tasks with the File **O**ptions pop-up menu located on the Open File, Insert File, and Save As dialog boxes. When you display a dialog box that uses file name and directory list boxes, choosing File **O**ptions displays a pop-up list with the following options for performing file management operations.

- **C**opy. To copy a file, choose it in the File**n**ame list box and then choose File **O**ptions and **C**opy.

You can perform many file management functions with the File Options pop-up list.

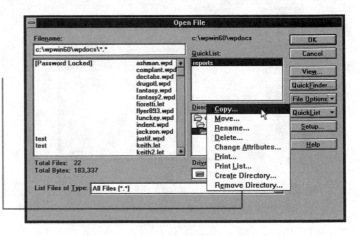

Type a name for the new file in the **T**o text box. If you select the **D**on't Replace Files with the Same Size, Date, and Time check box, WordPerfect assigns the current date, time, and file size to the new copy. Choose **C**opy to copy the file and return to the previous dialog box.

- **M**ove. To move a file, choose it in the File**n**ame list box and then choose File **O**ptions and **M**ove.

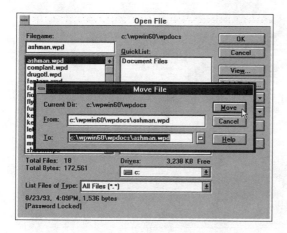

WordPerfect displays the Move File dialog box.

Choose **To** and type the new location for the file, and then choose **Move** to move the file and return to the previous dialog box.

- **Rename.** To rename a file, choose it in the **File**name list box and then choose File **Options** and **Rename**.

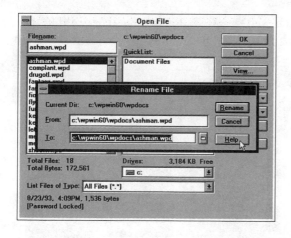

WordPerfect displays the Rename File dialog box.

Choose **To** and type a new name for the file; then choose **Rename** to rename the file and return to the previous dialog box.

- **Delete.** To delete a file, choose it in the **File**name list box and then choose File **Options** and **Delete**.

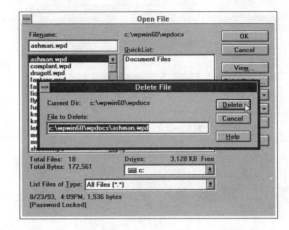

WordPerfect
displays the Delete
File dialog box.

Choose **D**elete to delete the file and return to the previous dialog box.

Note: Be careful when using the Delete command, because Word-Perfect does not prompt you before deleting the file.

- Change **A**ttributes. To change the attributes of a file, choose it in the File**n**ame list box and then choose File **O**ptions and Change **A**ttributes.

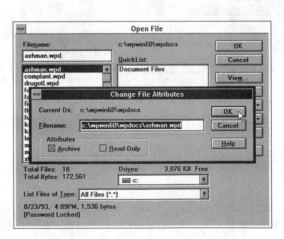

WordPerfect
displays the Change
Attributes dialog
box.

Choose **A**rchive (the default) to save the file as an archive file. You can edit and save archived files normally. Or you can choose **R**ead-Only to save the file and prevent yourself or other users from making changes to the file and saving the edited versions.

Note: Anyone who edits the file in WordPerfect can change the attribute to **Archive**. To protect files securely, see the section "Saving a Document with a Password" earlier in this chapter.

- **Print.** To print a file, choose it in the **Filename** list box and then choose File **Options** and **Print**.

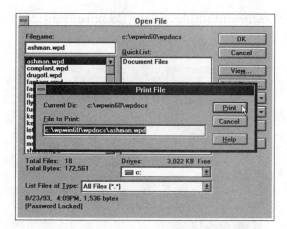

WordPerfect displays the Print File dialog box.

In the **File to Print** text box, type the name of the file you want to print or accept the name of the selected file; then choose **Print** to print the file and return to the previous dialog box.

- **Print List.** To print a list of files, choose the files in the **Filename** list box and then choose File **Options** and **Print List**.

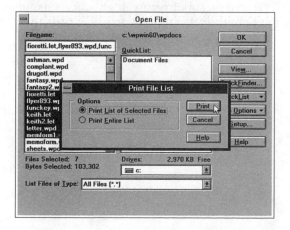

WordPerfect displays the Print File List dialog box.

If you chose more than one file in the Filename list box, WordPerfect chooses the Print List of Selected Files button. To begin printing the file list, choose **Print**.

If you didn't choose any files in the Filename list box, or if you chose just one file, WordPerfect chooses the Print Entire List button. To begin printing the entire list of files in the Filename list box, choose **Print**.

• Create Directory. To create a new subdirectory, choose File **Options**, Create Directory.

WordPerfect displays the Create Directory dialog box.

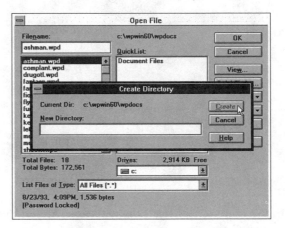

Type the name and path for the new directory in the **New Directory** text box; then choose **Create**. WordPerfect creates the new directory and returns you to the previous dialog box.

• **Remove Directory.** To remove a subdirectory, highlight its name in the **Directories** list and then choose File **Options**, Remove Directory.

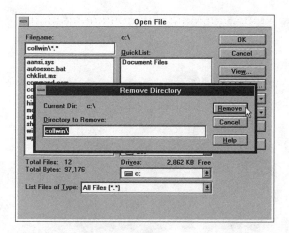

WordPerfect
displays the Remove
Directory dialog
box.

Choose **Remove** to remove the directory, or type the name of a different directory in the **Directory** text box and then choose **Remove**. If the directory contains files, WordPerfect displays a message box with the prompt: WARNING! Directory [directory name] contains files. Remove directory anyway? If the directory contains subdirectories, the prompt reads: WARNING! Directory [directory name] contains files and subdirectories. Remove directory anyway? Choose **Yes** to remove the directory and its files and subdirectories, or choose **No** to cancel the process.

Tip: You can apply the following commands to more than one file at a time: **Move**, **Delete**, Change **Attributes**, and Print **List**. Before choosing the command, drag the mouse to highlight sequential files in the Filename list box, or select the first file in the group, hold down Shift, and select the last file. To choose nonsequential files, hold down Ctrl while you choose each file.

Using QuickFinder to Locate Files

WordPerfect's QuickFinder helps you locate files quickly. To search for files, you index the files you want to find. Then, you search the indexed files, using sophisticated search logic. For example, you could locate all the files that contain the term *Smith & Bornstein, Inc.,* but that do not contain the term *contract termination date.*

285

Indexing Files with QuickFinder

Indexing Files with QuickFinder

1. Open the File menu and choose QuickFinder.

   WordPerfect displays the QuickFinder dialog box.

2. Choose Indexer, and in the Default Directory For Saving Indexes
   dialog box, choose OK to accept the Default Index Path.

   WordPerfect displays the QuickFinder File Indexer dialog box.

3. Choose Create.

WordPerfect
displays the
Create Index
Name dialog box.

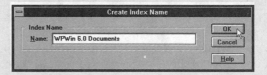

4. Type a name for the new index in the Name text box, and then
   choose OK.

WordPerfect
displays the
Create Index
dialog box.

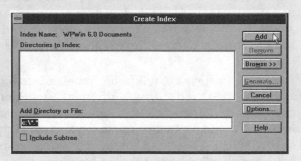

5. Choose Add Directory or File and type the subdirectory and file name
   specification for the files you want WordPerfect to index, and then
   choose Add.

   WordPerfect grays the Add command button.

6. To include subdirectories under the specified subdirectory, select the
   Include Subtree check box.

7. To view a list of files and directories so that you can choose files
   visually, choose Browse.

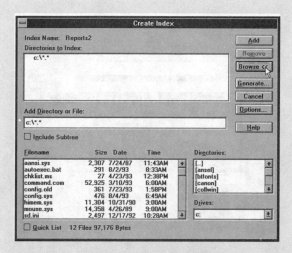

WordPerfect expands the Create Index dialog box, adding **Filename**, **Directories**, and **Drives** list boxes.

8. To replace the **Filename** list box with a **QuickList** list box, select the **QuickList** check box.

9. To choose multiple directories in the **Directories** list box, drag the mouse to choose sequential directories, or hold down ⌖Shift and click the first directory and the last directory in the series. To choose nonsequential directories, hold down Ctrl while you choose each directory.

   WordPerfect displays all the files in the selected directories in the **Filename** list box.

   Note: You cannot choose groups of files in the **Filename** list box. You must choose files individually and choose **Add** to add each file to the **Directories to Index** list box.

10. Choose **Add** to add the selected directories to the **Directories to Index** list box.

11. To remove a directory or file from the index, select it and choose **Remove**.

12. To begin indexing the selected directories and files, choose **Generate**.

continues

continued

While it indexes files, WordPerfect displays a message box that indicates its progress. When the work is complete, it displays the Index Completed dialog box.

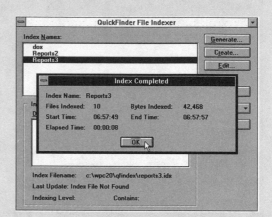

13. Choose OK, and then close the other dialog boxes to return to the document window.

To learn more about customizing QuickFinder's indexing options, see Que's *Using WordPerfect 6 for Windows,* Special Edition.

Editing an Existing Index

To edit an existing index, choose the **F**ile menu and then choose **Q**uickFinder; then choose an existing index in the Index **N**ames list box and choose **E**dit. The steps to edit an existing index are essentially the same as for creating a new index. To change indexing options, follow the directions given previously in this chapter under "Indexing Files with QuickFinder."

Managing QuickFinder Indexes

Managing QuickFinder Indexes

1. Open the **F**ile menu and choose **Q**uickFinder. In the QuickFinder dialog box, choose Indexer.

   WordPerfect displays the QuickFinder File Indexer dialog box.

2. Choose Options, and then choose an option from the pop-up box.

   To learn more about QuickFinder indexing options, see Que's *Using WordPerfect 6 for Windows,* Special Edition.

3. Choose Close to return to the document screen.

Searching with QuickFinder

Searching with QuickFinder

1. Open the File menu and choose QuickFinder.

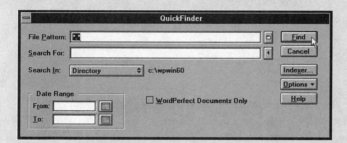

WordPerfect displays the QuickFinder dialog box.

2. Choose Search In and tell QuickFinder where you want to search:

   Directory (the default). When you choose this option, QuickFinder searches the current subdirectory.

   Disk. When you choose this option, QuickFinder searches an entire disk. QuickFinder displays a disk list box where you can use scroll arrows to identify the disk you want to search.

   Subtree. When you choose this option, QuickFinder searches the entire subdirectory tree under and including the current directory.

   QuickFinder Index. When you choose this option, QuickFinder displays a list box where you can use scroll arrows to choose the QuickFinder index you want to use to conduct the current search.

3. Choose WordPerfect Documents Only to have QuickFinder limit the search to documents saved in WordPerfect format.

continues

continued

4. To search for files saved on a specific date, or during a range of dates, choose From and type the starting date; then choose To and type the ending date. You can also specify dates by clicking the calendar icons to the right of the From and To text boxes.

QuickFinder can display calendars where you can visually choose starting and ending dates for a search.

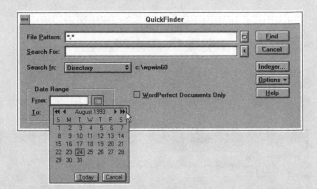

5. If you clicked the Calendar button, click a starting or ending date. Use the scroll arrows at the top of the calendar to scroll forward or backward a month or year at a time.

6. To search only files saved with today's date, choose Today from the calendar graphic.

7. To insert a date in the From or To text box, click the date in the calendar graphic. WordPerfect closes the calendar and inserts the date in the text box.

8. Choose File Pattern and type the file pattern you want to search. To choose a subdirectory pattern visually, click the Select Directory icon at the right side of the text box.

9. Choose Search for and type the pattern of the text you want to search for. Type text patterns without quotes (for example: Terminator).

   Note: Although you must type search patterns without quotes, quotes are used for clarity in identifying search patterns in the discussion that follows.

10. To use search operators, click the button at the right side of the text box; then choose one of the options (see table 9.1 later in this chapter).

11. After you've entered search patterns and specified the location and date range of files to search, choose **Find**.

    QuickFinder locates files that contain the search patterns you specified.

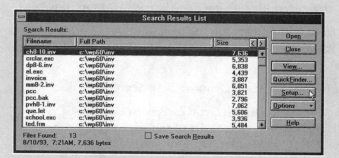

When it finishes searching, QuickFinder displays the Search Results List dialog box.

12. To view the contents of a file, highlight its name in the **Search Results** list box and choose **View**. WordPerfect displays the file's text in the File Viewer.

13. To sort the files in the Search Results list box, choose **Setup**.

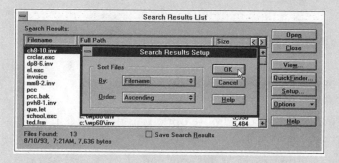

WordPerfect displays the Search Results Setup dialog box.

14. Choose **By**, and then choose a sort criterion: Filename (the default), **Extension**, **Size**, **Date/Time**, Descriptive **Name**, Descriptive **Type**, or Full **Path**.

continues

291

continued

15. Choose **Order**, and then choose a sort order: **Ascending** (the default) or **Descending**.

16. Choose OK to return to the Search Results List dialog box.

17. Choose **Options** to copy, move, rename, delete, print, or print a list of files from the Search Results list box. These options are discussed earlier in this chapter, under "Using File Management Options."

18. To open one or more files listed in the Search Results list box, choose it (or them) and choose Ope**n**. WordPerfect opens the selected file(s).

19. To save the results of the search, choose Save Search **R**esults.

    If you choose Save Search Results, you can redisplay the Search Results List dialog box with the results of the your most recent search. Choose File, QuickFinder, **O**ptions, and Last Search **R**esults.

20. Choose **C**lose to exit the Search Results List dialog box and return to the document window.

If you've already indexed files with QuickFinder as described in the preceding sections of this chapter, you can search for text very quickly. QuickFinder can also search un-indexed files, but the search process takes longer.

Using Search Operations

Searching with QuickFinder's Search Operations

1. Open the **F**ile menu and choose QuickFinder.

2. In the QuickFinder dialog box, choose options as described in the preceding section, "Searching with QuickFinder."

3. Choose the left-pointing arrow at the right end of the Search For text box, and then choose Options from the pop-up menu.

4. After you finish choosing options from the QuickFinder dialog box, choose Find to complete the search, as described in the preceding section, "Searching with QuickFinder.

With QuickFinder, you can use sophisticated search logic. Table 9.1 lists the basic search operations you can choose in the QuickFinder dialog box. In addition to these simple search operations, QuickFinder offers advanced commands for very complex searches. To learn more about advanced options, see Que's *Using WordPerfect 6 for Windows,* Special Edition.

Note: The operators in table 9.1 must be preceded and followed by a space.

Table 9.1   QuickFinder's Search Operations

Operator	Sample Word Pattern	Finds
AND - &	exciting&new	Files that contain the words *exciting* and *new*
OR - ¦	exciting ¦ new	Files that contain the words *exciting* or *new* or both words
NOT - !	exciting !	Files that contain the word *exciting* but not *new*
Followed By - ..	exciting...new	Files that contain both words, with *exciting* before *new* anywhere in the document
Group - ()	(/Firstpage (/Line new exciting))	Files that contain the words *new* and *exciting* on the same line on the first page
Any Single Character - ?	new?	Files that contain the word *new* plus a single character (for example, *news*)
Zero or More Characters - *	new*	Files that contain all variations of words that begin with *new,* with or without other charac ters (for example, *new, news, and newness*)

Summary

In this chapter, you learned how to perform basic file management tasks in WordPerfect for Windows, including how to save a file with a password, add a document summary to a file, and create QuickLists to help you identify the directories that contain your files.

In the next chapter, you will learn how to record and play back macros. As you will soon discover, you can record any sequence of tasks that you routinely perform in WordPerfect and then play back this sequence. After you learn the general procedure for recording and playing macros, you will learn how to create a library of macros that you can use in your work.

Creating Macros

10

Understanding macros

Recording macros

Playing macros

Editing macros

Creating a macro library

Macros enable you to record a series of commands and keystrokes in WordPerfect and then play them back exactly as you entered them. You can use macros to automate any task or series of tasks you routinely perform. Macros can automate simple tasks such as typing the closing for a letter or entering the name of your company.

After you create a macro, you can play back its keystrokes and commands by selecting the macro in the Play Macro dialog box. If the macro is one you use all the time, you can assign it to a button on a Button Bar or a key combination on the keyboard. These techniques make playing the macro even faster and easier than usual.

This chapter shows you how to create and edit simple macros. At the end of the chapter, you will find step-by-step instructions for creating macros you can include in your own macro library.

Caution: Macros created in WordPerfect 5.1 or 5.2 for Windows may not be compatible with WordPerfect 6.0 for Windows. If you run an incompatible macro, WordPerfect 6.0 for Windows recompiles the macro in the 6.0 macro file format. When this happens, the program asks whether you want to overwrite the original macro file or save the new 6.0 macro file under a new file name. To retain a copy of the original macro so that you can run it with earlier versions of Word-Perfect for Windows, save the recompiled 6.0 macro with a new file name.

Key Terms in This Chapter

Compile Refers to the process by which WordPerfect for Windows translates macro commands recorded as text in a macro file into commands that the program can execute when you play the macro. Each time you save a macro in a macro file, WordPerfect for Windows automatically compiles the macro as it saves it. Should the macro contain a command with errors that would prevent the macro from running successfully, the program will generate an error message allowing you to cancel the compilation. All such errors must be corrected before you can run the macro.

Document macro Macros created for the current or new document whose keystrokes and commands are recorded as text only. You cannot play a document macro unless you save it as a macro file with the **S**ave & Compile button on the Macro Feature Bar.

Macro A prerecorded log of WordPerfect commands and keystrokes saved in a file. The log plays back the commands when the file is selected. WordPerfect enables you to assign a macro to a button on a Button Bar or a key combination on the keyboard.

Quick macro A temporary (unnamed) macro that you can play only until you exit WordPerfect for Windows. To create a quick macro, you do not give it a name prior to choosing the **R**ecord button in the Record Macro dialog box to start recording your keystrokes and commands. To play a quick macro, you do not enter a name prior to choosing the **P**lay button in the Play Macro dialog box.

Understanding Macros

The general procedure for creating simple macros is very straightforward:

1. Turn on the macro recorder.

2. Select a location for the new macro (you can save it as part of the current template, a separate file in the current directory, or in text-only format as part of the current or a new document).

3. Assign a name (up to eight characters long) and a description to your macro. (The description tells what the macro does.)

4. Type the text you want the macro to type, and choose the WordPerfect commands you want the macro to perform.

5. Turn off the macro recorder.

After you have defined a macro, you can run the macro by opening the **Tools** menu, choosing **Macro**, and then selecting the macro name (or its number) at the bottom of the menu. You can also run the macro by pressing Alt+F10 or choosing **Macro** on the **Tools** menu, and then choosing the **Play** command and then selecting the macro in the Play Macro dialog box.

Recording a Macro

Recording a New Macro

1. Open a new document. Or, if you want the macro to open a new document for you, start recording when no documents are open.

2. Open the **Tools** menu, choose **Macro**, and then choose **Record**; or press [Ctrl]+[F10].

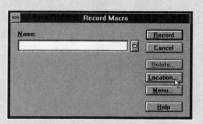

The Record Macro dialog box appears.

continues

continued

3. By default, WordPerfect for Windows saves each new macro in a file in the directory containing the WordPerfect for Windows program files (normally \WPWIN60). To change the location, choose the Location button.

WordPerfect displays the Macro Location dialog box so that you can specify where you want the macro recorded.

In the Record To area of this dialog box, choose the radio button that indicates the location you want to use: Current Template, Default Template, Current Document, or New Document. If you don't want your newly selected location to become the new program default for saving all future macros you create, choose the Use as Default option to remove the X from its check box. Then choose OK or press ⏎Enter to close the Macro Location dialog box.

4. When saving the macro as part of the current or default template or in a file, enter a file name of up to eight characters for your macro in the Name text box of the Record Macro dialog box. Alternatively, you can name a macro CTRL*x* or CTRLSFT*x,* where *x* represents a character such as *p*. You can use any keyboard character from A to Z or 0 to 9 after CTRL or CTRLSFT to name your macro. WordPerfect saves your macro under this file name with the WCM extension when you finish recording the macro.

If you're recording a quick macro that you don't want saved because you're only going to use it during the current work session in Word-Perfect for Windows, omit this step and leave the Name text box empty.

5. Select the Record button or press ⏎Enter to begin recording the macro.

WordPerfect closes the Record Macro dialog box, changes the mouse pointer to the international "Don't" symbol, and displays the Macro Record message in the status bar to remind you that all your actions in WordPerfect are being recorded. If the file name you specified for the macro already exists, WordPerfect displays a message dialog box asking whether you want to replace the existing macro. Choose the **Yes** button to replace the existing macro with the one you are about to create. Choose the **No** button to save the macro under a different name.

6. Enter the text and select the commands you want to include in your macro, in the sequence you want them recorded. If you need to move the insertion point or select text, you must use the keyboard (you can only use the mouse to choose menu commands and make dialog box selections when recording a macro).

7. When you have finished choosing the WordPerfect commands and entering the text for the macro, open the **Tools** menu, choose **Macro**, and then choose the **Record** command again (or just press Ctrl + F10 again).

   WordPerfect immediately turns off the macro recorder, and the Macro Record message disappears from the status bar.

When you record a macro, you are creating a log of all the actions you perform while the recorder is on. This log, therefore, contains all the WordPerfect commands you select as well as any text you enter. Besides recording your commands, WordPerfect also modifies the current document as you record the macro. For this reason, you may want to open a new document before you begin recording a macro.

Pausing the Recording of a Macro

When recording a macro, all your actions (except for certain actions performed with the mouse—see "Using the Mouse When Recording a Macro," next) are included in the macro unless you temporarily pause the recording. To pause the recording, open the **Tools** menu, choose **Macro**, and then choose **Pause**.

After choosing the Pause command, the message Record Pause appears on the status bar. During the pause, all commands or keystrokes you make are *not* recorded as part of the macro. When you are ready to resume recording your macro, open the **Tools** menu, choose **Macro**, and then choose Pause again to deselect this option. As soon as you do this, the Record Pause message is replaced by the Macro Record message in the status bar and all commands and keystrokes are once again recorded in the macro. When you have finished recording and are ready to save the macro, open the **Tools** menu, choose **Macro**, and then choose the **Record** command as you normally do.

Using the Mouse When Recording a Macro

When recording a macro, be careful how you use the mouse. You can use the mouse to select WordPerfect menu commands and dialog box options, size a document window, cycle through open document windows, or close a document window. WordPerfect will record all these actions in your macro.

You cannot, however, use the mouse to scroll the text of a document with the scroll bars, move the insertion point through the text, or select text—WordPerfect cannot record these actions. To move the insertion point in a document while recording a macro, use the arrow keys alone or in combination with the Ctrl key. To scroll the text of a document when recording a macro, use PgUp and PgDn. To select text when recording a macro, click the insertion point immediately before the first character you want to select, and then press F8, the Select key, or hold down the Shift key as you press the appropriate arrow key.

Playing a Macro

Playing a Macro Saved on Disk or in a Template

1. Open the **Tools** menu, choose **Macro**, and then choose **Play**; or press `Alt` + `F10`.

WordPerfect displays the Play Macro dialog box, where you specify the macro you want to play.

2. If need be, change the location of the macro by choosing the Location button and then selecting the appropriate radio button (File on Disk, Current Template, or Default Template) in the Macro Location dialog box.

3. Type the name of the macro (you don't have to include the WCM extension), and then choose the **Play** button or press `↵Enter`.

   If you're playing a macro file saved on disk, you can click the File-list button and select the macro file in the Select File dialog box.

> If you're playing a macro file saved as part of the current or default template, you can select the macro by double-clicking the macro's name in the **Macros In Template** list box beneath the **Name** text box.
>
> If you're playing a quick macro, choose the **Play** button or press ⏎Enter without entering a macro name in the **Name** text box.

You can play the macros you create in any active document window. WordPerfect saves all macros saved as files in the directory containing your program files. (normally \WPWIN60). If you named your macro CTRL*x*.WCM or CTRLSFT*x*.WCM, where *x* represents a character such as *k*, you can play it back by pressing Ctrl+K or Ctrl+Shift+K. WordPerfect plays back the commands and keystrokes in the macro you selected exactly as you recorded them.

Using Other Ways to Play Macros

You may use some macros saved in files so frequently that you need a faster method for playing the macro than opening the Play Macro dialog box and selecting the macro to play. To speed up the selection and playback of such macros, WordPerfect for Windows offers three choices: you can assign the macro to the **Macro** menu; you can create a button for the macro and add it to a Button Bar; or you can assign the macro to a key combination on the current keyboard.

Assigning a Macro to the Macro Cascading Menu

Assigning a Macro to the Macro Cascading Menu

1. Open the **Tools** menu, choose **Macro**, and then choose **Play**; or press Alt + F10.

   WordPerfect displays the Play Macro dialog box.

2. If the macro wasn't recorded as a file on disk, choose the **Location** button to open the Macro Location dialog box. Choose the radio button of the location of the macro you want to assign to the cascading menu (**Current Template** or **Default Template**), and then choose OK or press ⏎Enter.

continues

continued

3. Choose the **M**enu button in the Play Macro dialog box.

WordPerfect
displays the
Assign Macro
to Menu
dialog box.

4. Choose the **I**nsert button.

The Select Macro
dialog box
appears, where
you indicate the
macro you want
to add to the
menu.

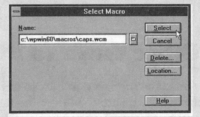

5. Enter the macro's full path name in the **N**ame text box, and choose OK or press ⏎Enter. Or use the File-list button to open the Select File dialog box, and then choose the macro file by double-clicking it.

6. Choose the **S**elect button in the Select Macro dialog box or press ⏎Enter.

   WordPerfect closes the Select Macro dialog box and returns to the Assign Macro to Menu dialog box. The name of the macro file you just chose appears selected in the Available Macros list box.

7. Repeat steps 4 through 6 for each macro you want to assign to the cascading menu.

8. When you're finished adding macros to the Macro menu, choose the OK button to add the macros listed in the Available Macros list box to the menu.

   WordPerfect closes the Assign Macro to Menu dialog box and returns to the Select Macro dialog box.

9. Choose the Cancel button to close the Play Macro dialog box and return to the current document window.

The next time you choose **Macro** on the **Tools** menu to open the Macro cascading menu, you will see your macro(s) listed at the bottom, with a number between 1 and 9 preceding each one.

You can assign up to nine different macros to the **Macro** cascading menu that appears when you choose **Macro** on the **Tools** pull-down menu. Each macro you assign to this cascading menu is given a number between 1 and 9, followed by the macro's name. The macros appear as menu options in numerical order at the bottom of the menu.

To play a macro that has been assigned to the **Macro** cascading menu, choose **Macro** on the **Tools** menu and then choose the macro name or number on the **Macro** cascading menu. You can do this quickly with the mouse or with the keyboard by pressing the Alt key, and then typing TM plus the number (between 1 and 9) of the macro you want to play. For example, to play the first macro listed on the cascading menu, you press Alt and then type TM1.

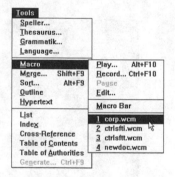

Here you see how the Macro cascading menu appears after adding four macros to this menu.

Tip: If you find that you no longer want a particular macro to appear on the **Macro** cascading menu (for example, you may have nine macros assigned and want to make room for a tenth macro), you can remove the macro from the menu by accessing the Play Macro dialog box, choosing the **Menu** button, selecting the macro to remove, and then choosing the **Delete** button. When you delete a macro from the Macro cascading menu, WordPerfect for Windows renumbers the remaining macros on the menu.

Assigning a Macro to the Button Bar

Adding a Macro to the Button Bar

1. If no Button Bar is currently displayed, click the View Button Bar button on the Power Bar; or open the View menu and choose **Button Bar**.

2. If the Button Bar displayed is not the one to which you want to add the macro, click the Button Bar with the secondary mouse button, and then select the name of the Button Bar you want to modify on the Button Bar QuickMenu.

3. Click the Button Bar with the secondary mouse button, and then choose **Edit** on the Button Bar QuickMenu.

   WordPerfect displays the Button Bar Editor for the currently displayed Button Bar.

4. Choose the Play a **Macro** radio button.

In the Button Bar Editor dialog box, WordPerfect displays the **Add** Macro button, which allows you to indicate the macro for which you want to add a button.

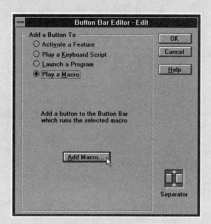

5. Choose the **Add** Macro button to open the Select Macro dialog box. In the **Name** text box, enter the file name (including path) of the macro you want to add to the Button Bar; or click the File-list button and select the macro file in the Select File dialog box. Then choose the **Select** button or press ⏎Enter.

   WordPerfect adds a button for the macro at the end of the current Button Bar. At the top of the button, WP appears; below the button, the name of the macro appears.

6. Repeat step 5 until you have added buttons for all the macros you want to appear on the current Button Bar.

7. To relocate a macro button on the Button Bar, drag it to its new position.

8. When you have the Button Bar the way you want it, choose the OK button to close the Button Bar Editor dialog box and return to the current document window.

If you use the mouse, you can add commonly used macros to one of the Button Bars supplied with WordPerfect for Windows or one of the custom Button Bars you create yourself. To play a macro assigned to a button on a Button Bar, you simply display the Button Bar and then click the macro button.

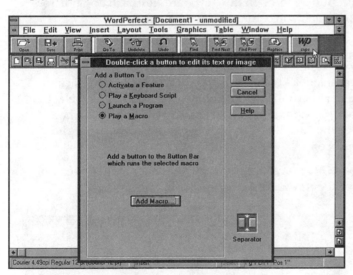

In this example, the program adds the WP Caps button at the end of the Edit Button Bar. Now you can click the Bullet button whenever you want to play the CAPS.WCM macro to capitalize every character in a word.

Tip: For more information on creating and using Button Bars in WordPerfect, see chapter 17, "Creating and Using Button Bars." You will find ideas for creating custom Button Bars by using WordPerfect commands and macros.

Assigning a Macro to the Keyboard

Assigning a Macro to a Custom Keyboard

1. Open the File menu and choose Preferences to open the Preferences dialog box.

2. Double-click the Keyboard icon, or choose Preferences, followed by Keyboard to open the Keyboard Preferences dialog box.

3. Select the name of the custom keyboard to which you want to assign your macros in the Keyboards list box. Note that you cannot modify the keyboard layouts WordPerfect for Windows supplies; these layouts are enclosed in a pair of angle brackets, as in <WPWin 6.0 Keyboard> or <WPDOS Compatible>.

4. Choose the Edit button to open the Keyboard Editor dialog box for the keyboard to which you want to assign macros.

5. Choose the key combination you want to use to play your macro in the Choose a Key To Assign or Unassign list box.

   You can quickly select a key combination in this list box by clicking the keys in the keyboard dialog box below. For example, to select H+Ctrl+Shift in the Choose a Key To Assign or Unassign list box, you simply click the Ctrl, Shift, and H keys in the keyboard at the bottom of the screen.

6. Choose the Play a Macro radio button in the Assign Key To area on the right side of the Keyboard Editor dialog box.

WordPerfect displays the Assign Macro button below the Assign Key To radio buttons.

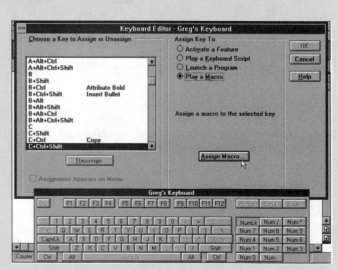

7. Choose the Assign Macro button to open the Select Macro dialog box, where you enter the file name (including the path) of the macro you want to add to the keyboard; or click the File-list button, select the macro file in the Select File dialog box, and choose the Select button or press ⏎Enter.

   The macro name now appears to the right of the currently selected keys in the Choose a Key To Assign or Unassign list box.

8. Repeat steps 5 through 7 until you have assigned all the macros you want to have access to when using this custom keyboard.

9. Choose the OK button to close the Keyboard Editor dialog box and return to the Keyboard Preferences dialog box.

10. Choose the Select button or press ⏎Enter to select the custom keyboard to which you just assigned the macros, and then choose the Close button in the Preferences dialog. Otherwise, to close this dialog box without selecting the modified keyboard, choose the Close button in the Keyboard Preferences dialog box, followed by the Close button in the Preferences dialog box.

    Now, whenever you select the custom keyboard to which you added the macro(s), you can play your macro(s) by pressing the keys you assigned to each one.

If you prefer using the keyboard, you can add commonly used macros to a custom keyboard that you create (see Que's *Using WordPerfect 6 for Windows, Special Edition* for details) and then play the macros by pressing the key combinations assigned to the macros. When assigning keys to macros, you assign combinations to any key combinations, including function keys and the Ctrl key plus a letter or number key, such as Ctrl+K, or Ctrl+Shift plus a letter or number key, such as Ctrl+Shift+V.

Tip: The keys you assign to a macro work only while the keyboard you just created is current. If your macro no longer works when you press the assigned key combination, chances are that WordPerfect is using a different keyboard from the one containing your macro keystroke assignment. To see if this is so, open the Keyboard Preferences dialog box (by opening the File menu, choosing Preferences, and then selecting Keyboard). If the keyboard you created is not listed as the current keyboard, select this keyboard in the Keyboards list box, and then choose the Select button or press Enter in the Keyboard Preferences dialog box.

Editing a Macro

Steps for Editing a Macro

1. Open the Tools menu, choose Macro, and then choose Edit to open the Edit Macro dialog box.

2. If necessary, change the location of the macro by choosing the Location button and then selecting the appropriate radio button (File on Disk, Current Template, or Default Template) in the Macro Location dialog box.

3. Type the name of the macro you want to edit (you don't have to include the WCM extension); then choose the Edit button or press ↵Enter.

   If you're editing a macro file saved on disk, you can click the File-list button and select the macro file in the Select File dialog box.

   If you're playing a macro file saved as part of the current or default template, you can select the macro by double-clicking the macro's name in the Macros In Template list box beneath the Name text box.

   If you're editing a quick macro, choose the Edit button or press ↵Enter without entering a macro name in the Name text box.

   WordPerfect for Windows inserts the complete text of the macro you selected into a new document window and displays the Macro Feature Bar.

4. Make your changes to the macro commands by editing the existing commands or adding new macro commands to the document.

   | Command Inserter... |

   You can edit the text of this macro document as you would any normal document text. To insert a new WordPerfect for Windows macro command in the text, choose the Command Inserter button on the Macro Feature Bar and select the macro command to insert at the insertion point.

   | Save & Compile |

   | Save As... |

5. When you have finished editing the macro, choose the Save & Compile button to save the changes to the macro with the same file name. To save your changes under a new file name, choose the Save As button instead (make sure that you don't alter the WCM file extension when changing the file name).

To run successfully, some macros depend upon the conditions that existed when you recorded the macros. If these original conditions are not present, the macro may try to perform an action that is no longer possible, and an error will occur when you try to play the macro. An error will occur, for example, if you play a macro that opens a document in a particular directory and you have moved or deleted that document from the directory.

When WordPerfect encounters an error during playback, a message dialog box appears describing the error. After you clear the message box by selecting the OK button and if the program is unable to run the macro, the WordPerfect Macro Facility will display a new message box indicating that WordPerfect is canceling the execution of the macro. If this happens, WordPerfect stops playing the macro as soon as you clear the message box .

When the WordPerfect Macro Facility encounters an error in a macro, an error message box similar to this one appears.

If WordPerfect cancels the execution of the macro, you will have to edit the contents of the macro to play the macro again successfully. Editing a macro is easy to do in WordPerfect for Windows; you simply select the macro file to edit, edit its contents, and save and compile the macro file with the Save and Compile button on the Macro Feature Bar (you can also open macro files and make changes to them exactly the same way as document files).

> *Caution:* All macros you create in WordPerfect for Windows begin with the macro command Application (A1;"WordPerfect";Default;"US"). This command indicates that WordPerfect is the recipient of the following macro commands (as opposed to some other WordPerfect Corporation Windows application). For the macro to run successfully, this command must remain intact at the top of the file.

After you have edited your macro, you can save and compile the macro by choosing the Save and Compile button on the Macro Feature Bar. If you have introduced any syntax errors into the commands in the macro, a WordPerfect Macro Facility Syntax Error dialog box appears, indicating the location of the first macro command that the interpreter can't process. At that point, you can select the Continue Compilation button to check for any other syntax errors in the macro; or you can select the Cancel Compilation button to immediately terminate the compilation of the macro. After you select Cancel Compilation, the WordPerfect Macro Facility finishes compiling the rest of the macro, and the Syntax Error dialog box disappears.

This WordPerfect Macro Facility Syntax Error dialog box indicates the number of the line and character in the macro that contains the first instruction the macro can't understand.

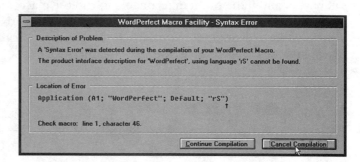

You must then edit the macro again, correcting the syntax errors located during compilation. After correcting these errors and saving your changes with the Save and Compile button, you are ready to play the macro again. This time, assuming that you have taken care of all the syntax errors, the program will then successfully play back all of its commands.

> *Tip:* WordPerfect for Windows offers a complete on-line macro command help facility to which you can refer when adding and editing macro commands. To get help with macro commands, open the Help menu and choose Macros. Also, refer to Que's *Using WordPerfect 6 for Windows,* Special Edition for more information on using the Macro Command language.

Creating a Library of Useful Macros

This section provides you with several practice macros you can create for your own macro library. Here, you will find step-by-step instructions for creating the following macros:

- A macro that types your company's name and address

- A macro that capitalizes the first word in a line of text such as a title

- A macro that transposes two characters

- A macro that opens a new document, changes the top and bottom margins to suit your letterhead, and then chooses a new font

A Macro for Entering the Company Name and Address

Creating the Company Name Macro

1. Open the **Tools** menu, choose **Macro**, and then choose **Record**; or press Ctrl + F10. This step opens the Record Macro dialog box.

2. Type corp in the **Name** text box, and then choose the **Record** button or press ↵Enter.

   The mouse pointer changes to the international "Don't" symbol, and the Macro Record message appears in the status bar.

3. Type your company name and address on three lines. To format the text, choose the appropriate commands on the pull-down menus or use the keystroke shortcuts.

4. Open the **Tools** menu, choose **Macro**, and then choose **Record**; or press Ctrl + F10 again.

   WordPerfect saves the macro, and the Macro Record message disappears from the status bar.

Test your name and address macro. To test the macro, open a new document by choosing **New** on the **File** menu, and then choose **Macro** on the **Tools** menu followed by **Play**, or press Alt+F10. Type corp in the **Name** text box and press Enter. The macro should immediately type the company name and address on three lines.

A Macro for Capitalizing Each Word in a Line

Creating the Initial Caps Macro

1. If necessary, open a new document by opening the File menu and choosing New, and then type this sentence (in all lowercase letters): the queen of hearts made some tarts.

2. Open the Tools menu, choose Macro, and then choose Record; or press Ctrl + F10. This step opens the Record Macro dialog box.

3. Type ctrlsfti in the Name text box, and then choose the Record button or press Enter.

   The mouse pointer changes to the international "Don't" symbol, and the Macro Record message appears in the status bar.

4. Press Home to move the insertion point to the beginning of the line of text. Then press F8 (Select) and press End to select all the text to the end of the line.

5. Open the Edit menu, choose Convert Case, and then choose Initial Capitals.

6. Open the Tools menu, choose Macro, and then choose Record; or press Ctrl + F10 again.

   WordPerfect saves the macro, and the Macro Record message disappears from the status bar.

To test your macro that converts initial lowercase letters to capital letters, press Enter and type (all in lowercase) **the knave of hearts stole those tarts**, and then press Ctrl+Shift+I to capitalize each word in the sentence.

A Macro for Transposing Two Characters

Creating the Character Transposition Macro

1. If necessary, open a new document by opening the File menu and choosing New, and then type ht (lowercase letters).

2. Open the Tools menu, choose Macro, and then choose Record; or press Ctrl + F10. This step opens the Record Macro dialog box.

3. Type ctrlsftt in the **Name** text box, and then choose the Record button or press ⏎Enter.

   The mouse pointer changes to the international "Don't" symbol, and the Macro Record message appears in the status bar.

4. Press F8 (Select) and press ← to select the letter *t*.

5. Press Ctrl+X to cut the selected character and copy it onto the Clipboard. Then press ← and press Ctrl+V to insert the character in its proper position.

6. Press → to move the insertion point one character to the right.

7. Open the **Tools** menu, choose **Macro**, and then choose **Record**; or press Ctrl+F10 again.

   WordPerfect saves the macro, and the Macro Record message disappears from the status bar.

To test your transposition macro, type **ie** after *th*, and then press Ctrl+Shift+T to change the order of the letters to *ei*. Finish by typing an **r** to create the word *their*.

A Macro for Starting a New Letter

Creating the New Letter Macro

1. Open the **Tools** menu, choose **Macro**, and then choose **Record**; or press Ctrl+F10. This step opens the Record Macro dialog box.

2. Type newdoc in the **Name** text box, and then choose the **Record** button or press ⏎Enter.

   The mouse pointer changes to the international "Don't" symbol, and the Macro Record message appears in the status bar.

3. Open the **File** menu, and choose **New** to open a new document.

4. Open the **Layout** menu and choose **Margins**; or press Ctrl+F8. This step opens the Margins dialog box.

5. Choose the **Top** option, and then enter 2.5 as the new top margin. Press Tab, and then enter 1.5 as the new **Bottom** margin. Press Tab and press ⏎Enter to close the Margins dialog box.

continues

313

continued

6. Open the **Layout** menu and choose **Font**; or press F9. This step opens the Font dialog box.

7. Choose Arial as the new font in the Font Face list box, and then choose 10 as the new point size in the Font Size list box. Choose the OK button to close the Font dialog box.

8. Open the **Tools** menu, choose **Macro**, and then choose **Record**; or press Ctrl + F10 again.

   WordPerfect saves the macro, and the Macro Record message disappears from the status bar.

This macro opens a new document, increases the top and bottom margin settings for printing the first page of a letter on letterhead, and then selects 10-point Arial as the new font. You can use the macro when you need to start a new business letter. When you create this macro, you should adapt it to suit the stationery your company uses. If you use a particular paper definition (such as Letterhead) for the first page of business letters, you will want the macro to select this paper definition for you.

Test your new document macro. To do this, open the **Tools** menu, choose **Macro**, and then choose **Play**; or press Alt+F10. In the Play Macro dialog box, type newdoc in the Name text box and press Enter.

WordPerfect should open a new document window and make the changes to the margins and the font. Open the Reveal Codes window and check to see that your macro has inserted the correct codes for changing the top and bottom margins and selecting 10-point Arial as the new font.

Summary

In this chapter, you learned how to use macros to automate routine tasks. In addition to learning how to record and play back simple macros, you also learned how to assign macros to the Macro cascading menu, assign macros to buttons on custom Button Bars, and assign macros to keys as part of custom keyboard layouts. Finally, you learned how to edit the contents of macros when you need to rectify simple errors to get them to run once again.

In the next chapter, you will learn how to use the Merge feature to insert variable information in a standard format. The Merge feature will help you create personalized form letters, address envelopes, create mailing labels from an address list, and so forth.

11

Using Merge for Mass Mailings

Understanding the merge operation

Creating a data file

Creating a form file

Performing the merge

Addressing envelopes

Printing mailing labels

The Merge feature, often referred to as *mail merge,* represents one of WordPerfect's most versatile tools for increasing office productivity. Use the Merge feature any time you need to insert variable information in a standard format. For example, use merge to create personalized form letters, to address envelopes, to create mailing labels from an address list, to assemble a phone directory from an employee list, or even to fill in invoice forms from a sales history.

Key Terms in This Chapter	
Data file	A file containing the variable data or individual data items that are merged into the primary merge file. These data items are organized into a rigid format of fields and records.
Field	The basic unit of information that makes up a record in a secondary merge file. Each field contains the same type of information, such as the company name, address, city, state, and ZIP code.
Form file	A skeleton document containing the fixed format into which particular data items are merged.
Merge	To assemble a document by inserting variable data into a fixed format.
Record	A collection of fields containing related information pertaining to a single entity such as the record for IBM Corp., for example.

Understanding the Merge Operation

A typical merge operation involves two files: a *form file* (previously known as the *primary file*), or skeleton document, that contains the standard information into which data items are merged, and a *data file* (previously known as the *secondary file*) that contains these data items.

The form file contains merge codes and the text that is to remain the same in each copy of the document produced by the merge operation. You place the merge codes wherever you want to insert variable data into the fixed text of the form file. When the merge operation is completed, the merge codes are replaced with data items from a data file or entries made from the keyboard.

The data file contains related variable data organized into fields and records. All the information related to a single entity in the data file, such as a company or an employee, makes up a *record*. Within each record, each individual data item, such as the company name, telephone number, street address, and so on, is known as a *field*.

During the merge, WordPerfect determines which fields in the data file to use and where to insert their data in the form file by matching the merge codes you have placed in both merge files. When the program performs the merge, it creates a copy of the form file with the variable data from the appropriate fields for *every* record in the data file. For example, when you merge a form letter with a data file containing 20 records of variable information, you end up with 20 personalized letters.

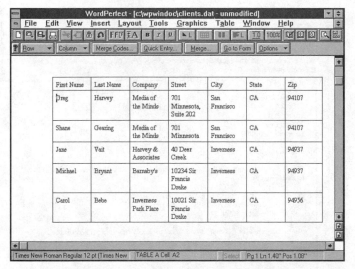

This is a sample form file used in a merge.

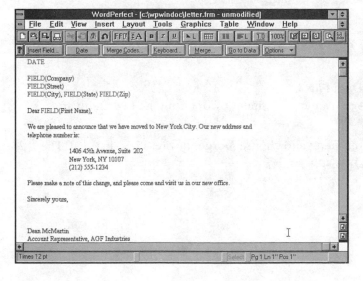

This is a sample data file used in a merge.

These letters
resulted from
merging the
sample data file
and form file.

August 17, 1993

Media of the Minds
701 Minnesota, Suite 202
San Francisco, CA 94107

Dear Greg,

We are pleased to announce that we have moved to New York City. Our new address and
telephone number is:

August 17, 1993

Media of the Minds
701 Minnesota
San Francisco, CA 94107

Dear Shane,

We are pleased to announce that we have moved to New York City. Our new address and
telephone number is:

August 17, 1993

Harvey & Assocates
40 Deer Creek
Inverness, CA 94937

Dear Jane,

We are pleased to announce that we have moved to New York City. Our new address and
telephone number is:

> 1406 45th Avenue, Suite 202
> New York, NY 10107
> (212) 555-1234

Please make a note of this change, and please come and visit us in our new office.

Sincerely yours,

Dean McMartin

Creating a Table Data File

Creating a Table Data File

1. If necessary, open a new document by opening the **File** menu and
   choosing **New**.

2. Open the **T**ools menu and choose **M**erge, or press ⇧Shift + F9. The
   Merge dialog box appears.

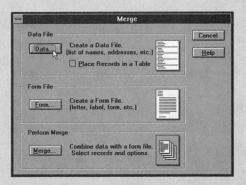

You can use the options in the Merge dialog box to create a new data or form file or to perform a merge.

3. To put the records in a table, select the **Place Records in a Table** check box.

4. Choose the **Data** button to open the Create Data File dialog box.

You can use the options in the Create Data File dialog box to name the fields you want to use.

5. Type the name for the first field in the **Name a Field** text box, and then select the **Add** button or press ⏎Enter.

   WordPerfect for Windows inserts the name in the **Field Name List** box below.

6. Type the name for the next field, and then select the **Add** button or press ⏎Enter.

7. Repeat step 6 until you have added field names for all the fields you will need in the data file.

continues

continued

8. If you find that you need to rename a field, click the field name (or choose **Field Name List** and use ⬆ or ⬇ to select the name) and choose the **Replace** button to return the field name to the **Name a Field** text box where you can replace or edit the field name. When finished editing, press ↵Enter to insert the revised field name in **Field Name List** box.

9. If you need to remove a field name from the list, select the name and choose the **Delete** button.

10. If you need to reposition a field name in the list, select the name and choose the Move Up or Move Down button until the field name is in the proper order in the list.

11. Choose the OK button to close the Create Dialog box.

    WordPerfect for Windows automatically displays the Quick Entry dialog box that you can use to enter the records for your new data file.

12. If you want, enter the information for the first set of records (see "Entering Information in a Data File" later in this chapter for details). When you finish your data entry, or if you decide that you would like to enter records later, choose the **Close** button.

    WordPerfect for Windows then displays a dialog box asking whether you want to save your changes.

13. Choose the **Yes** button, and then enter a file name for your data file in the Save Data File As dialog box (the program automatically suggests DAT as the file name extension). When you have finished, choose the OK button.

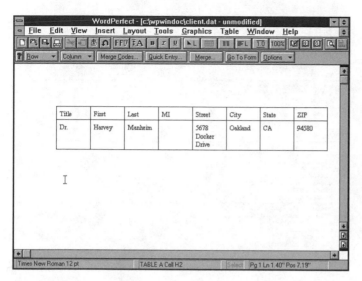

When you create a table data file, the program inserts the field names in the first row of the table; you enter the records in the new rows below.

When creating the data file, you need to make sure that its structure is uniform; otherwise, the merge will not work properly. Every record in the file must have the same number of fields, and the fields must remain in the same order in all records. If you do not have information for a particular field in a record, you must still save the field's place in the record even though it is currently blank. If you skip a field in a record because you don't have any information for it or you mix up your entries and place them in the wrong fields, WordPerfect will merge the wrong information into the form file.

The easiest way to ensure that your data file has a uniform structure is to create it as a WordPerfect table. When you use the table structure, each row of the table contains a record, while each column contains a field. You enter the information that you have for each field of a particular record in the appropriate table cell (see chapter 15, "Creating Tables," for more on working with tables).

Creating a Text Data File

In addition to creating a data file as a WordPerfect table, you can also create the data file as a text file. When you create a text data file, you must indicate the separations between the fields in a record and the records in the file with special merge codes.

In a text data file, ENDFIELD codes indicate each field and ENDRECORD codes indicate each record.

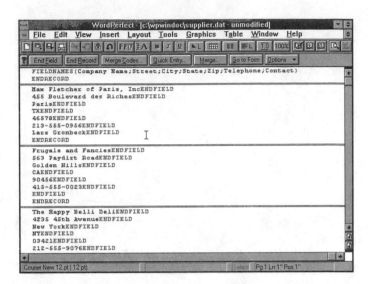

To create a text data file, you follow the same steps for creating a table data file (see "Creating a Data File" earlier in this chapter), except that you don't select the Place Records in a Table check box in the Merge dialog box before you select the Data button.

When you create a new text data file, the program inserts a FIELDNAMES merge code that lists the fields in the data file followed by an ENDRECORD code.

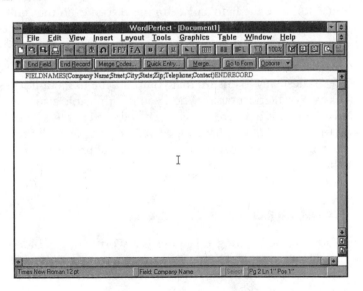

Entering Information in a Data File

When you create a new data file, WordPerfect for Windows automatically opens the Quick Data Entry dialog box that you can use to enter all the records you need in the data file. (You can also open this dialog box on your own by pressing Alt+Shift+Q or by clicking the Quick Entry button on the Merge Feature bar.)

To enter data for your records in the Quick Data Entry dialog box, you simply type the information for each field in its text box, and then press Tab or choose the Next Field button to advance the insertion point to the next field. If you see that you have made a mistake in an entry in an earlier field, press Shift+Tab or choose the Previous Field button until you have located the insertion point in the field's text box.

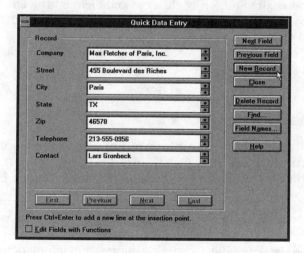

The Quick Data Entry dialog box contains text boxes for all the fields you defined for the data file.

When you have finished entering all the information you have for the fields in the record, choose the New Record button to clear the text boxes in the Quick Data Entry dialog box so that you can make the entries for the next record. When you have finished entering all the information for the new records in the data file, choose the Close button. WordPerfect for Windows will then ask you whether you want to save your changes to disk. Choose the Yes button to save the new records right then. If you choose No, you can still use the Save command on the File menu to save the changes prior to closing the data file.

Tip: You can also enter records directly into a table or text data file. To enter records in a table, open the table data file, position the insertion point in the first cell of the row, and enter the information. Press Tab to advance to the next field. When you reach the last field in the record, press Tab to add a blank row to the table for the next record. (See chapter 15, "Creating Tables," for more information.)

To enter records in a text data file, position the insertion point at the bottom of the data file (Ctrl+End) and type the information for the first field. When you finish, press Alt+Shift+F or click the End Field button in the Merge Feature bar to insert an ENDFIELD code and a hard return, and then enter the information for the next field. Continue in this manner until you enter the information for the last field (be sure to press Alt+Shift+F or click the End Field button after each field entry even when you don't have information for the field). Press Alt+Shift+R or click the End Record button to insert an ENDRECORD code and a hard page break in the data file so that you can begin entering the next record.

Editing Records in the Data File

Quick Entry...

Not only can you use the Quick Data Entry dialog box to enter new records but also to edit existing records. To open the Quick Entry dialog box in a data file, press Alt+Shift+Q or click the Quick Entry button on the Merge Feature bar.

After opening the Quick Data Entry dialog box, you can use the Next, Previous, First, and Last buttons to move through the records in the data file until you come upon the one you need to edit. You can also use the Find button to locate a particular record by searching for specific information in one of its fields. When you choose the Find button, the Find Text dialog box appears. In the text box, enter the text for which you want to search, and then choose the Find Next button. The program displays the first record containing text that matches the search text. To find another record with the search text, choose the Find Next button again. To return to a matching record that was displayed earlier, choose the Find Prev button. When you locate the record you need to edit, choose the Close button to close the Find Text dialog box.

After displaying the record you want to edit, you can then change the information by positioning the insertion point in the field and making your modifications to the text just as you would document text. If you need to delete the current record entirely instead of editing some of its information, you select the **Delete Record** button.

Caution: Be very careful when using this button. WordPerfect for Windows does *not* ask you for confirmation before removing the record, and you can't use the Undo button to restore the record (you would have to reenter the field information from scratch).

When you're finished editing the records in your data file, choose the **Close** button in the Quick Entry dialog box. WordPerfect for Windows records your changes in the table or text of the data file, and displays the message dialog box asking whether you want to save your changes to disk. After you select the **Yes** button, the program displays the Save As dialog box where you can choose the OK button or press Enter to save your edits with the same file name. WordPerfect then displays another dialog box, warning you that you are about to replace an existing data file with the modified data file. Choose the **Yes** button again and complete the procedure.

Creating a Form File

Creating a Letter Form File

1. If necessary, open a new document by opening the **File** menu and choosing **New**.

2. Open the **Tools** menu and choose **Merge**, or press ⟨Shift⟩+⟨F9⟩. The Merge dialog box appears.

3. Choose the **Form** button.

The Create Form File dialog box appears.

4. In the **Associate** a Data File text box, enter the file name of the data file that you will be using with the form file you're about to create, or click the File-list button, select the file to use in the Select File dialog box, and choose OK or press ⟨Enter⟩.

continues

327

continued

If you don't know which data file you're going to use and therefore don't want to set up an association, choose the **None** radio button, and then choose OK or press ⏎Enter.

5. Type the text of your letter. To insert the current date (as a code) in the text of the form letter, press Alt + ⇧Shift + D or click the **Date** button on the Merge Feature Bar to insert the DATE merge code into the text.

6. At the places in the text of the form letter where you want to insert information for a particular field in the associated data file when you perform the merge, press Alt + ⇧Shift + I or click the **Insert Field** button on the Merge Feature Bar to open the Insert Field Name or Number dialog box; then double-click the field name or select it, and choose the **Insert** button or press ⏎Enter.

If you need to use field information in a data file other than the one you associated with the form file (or you didn't associate a data file with the form file), choose the **Data File** button, select the data file to use in the Select Data File to Associate dialog box, and choose OK or press ⏎Enter. Then, choose the field to use in the Insert Field Name or Number dialog box before you choose the Insert button. If you need to refer to the data file while creating the form letter to check on some aspect of the data file, press Alt + ⇧Shift + G or click the **Go To Data** button. When you are ready to return to the form letter, press Alt + ⇧Shift + G again or click the **Go To Form** button (Go To Data changes to Go To Form as soon as you select the button).

When you choose the Insert button, WordPerfect for Windows then inserts a FIELD merge code containing the name of the field. For example, if you choose the First Name field, the program inserts FIELD(First Name) at the insertion point's present position in the form file.

7. When you finish typing the standard text and inserting the field codes that indicate where the information from the records of the data file is to be placed during the merge, open the File menu and choose the **Save** command or click the Save Document button on the Power bar. In the Save As dialog box, enter the file name for the new form file (the program suggests the file extension FRM for the form file) and choose OK or press ⏎Enter.

The form file consists of all standard text plus FIELD merge codes that indicate what data items are to be used from the data file. In addition to the FIELD codes, you will often want to insert the DATE merge code in the form file. When you perform the merge, WordPerfect replaces the DATE code with the current date.

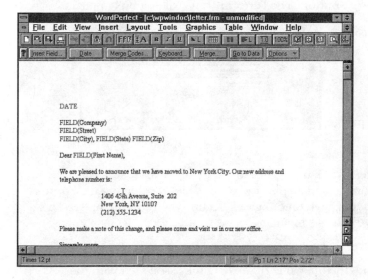

Here you see the final form file for a standard form letter, complete with the FIELD merge codes needed to substitute the right information in the data file.

Before you perform the merge, check over your form file to make sure that you have entered all the field names correctly. Remember that each field name listed in the FIELD merge code will be replaced by information from that field in each record in the data file when you perform the merge.

Merging the Form and Data Files

Performing a Typical Merge

1. Open the File menu and choose Open (or click the Open Document button on the Power Bar). When the Open File dialog box appears, enter the file name of the form file you want to use in the merge operation and choose OK or press ↵Enter.

continues

continued

2. Press [Alt]+[⇧Shift]+[M], click the **Merge** button on the Merge Feature Bar, or open the **Tools** menu and choose **Merge**. The Merge dialog box appears.

3. Select the **Merge** button. The Perform Merge dialog box appears.

In the Perform Merge dialog box, you indicate the files you want to merge, as well as choose the merge options.

4. Check the files listed in the Files to Merge text boxes. If necessary, change the form file, data file, and output file by selecting the appropriate option and then entering or selecting the right file name. The Files to Merge options include:

   - **Form File:** <Current Document>

   - **Data File:** the file name of the data file associated with the current form file

   - **Output File:** <New Document>

   To send the merged documents directly to the printer rather than a new document window, be sure to choose the **Output File** option and then select the **Printer** setting in the pop-up list.

5. By default, WordPerfect for Windows merges all the records in the data file with the form file to create a letter for each record in the data file. To use only some of the records in the merge, choose the **Select Records** button and then mark the records or specify the range or condition under which they should be selected in the Select Records dialog box (see "Selecting the Records To Merge" later in this chapter for details), and then choose OK or press [↵Enter].

6. If you want WordPerfect for Windows to print envelopes for each document created during the merge, choose the **Envelopes** button, and then fill out the return address in the Return Addresses text box and insert the FIELD codes for the mailing address in the Mailing Addresses text box (see "Addressing Envelopes" later in this chapter for details).

7. By default, the program separates each merged document with a hard page return, prints one copy of each merged document, and leaves a blank line in the merged document when it encounters an empty field in a particular record in the data file. To change any of these default settings, choose Options to open the Perform Merge Options dialog box, change the appropriate settings, and then choose OK or press ⏎Enter.

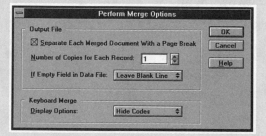

Here you see the Perform Merge Options dialog box, where you can specify a number of variations for your merge.

- To have the program print each merged document as part of one long document without hard returns between each record (as when creating a phone log using names and telephone numbers in the data files), select the Separate Each Merged Document With a Page Break check box to remove the x.

- To print multiple copies of each merged document, choose the Number of Copies for Each Record option, and then enter the number of copies to be printed or select the number with the up- and down-arrow buttons.

- To eliminate a blank line from the merged document when the program encounters an empty field in the data file, choose the If Empty Field in Data File option and change the setting from Leave Blank Line to Remove Blank Line.

8. When you have finished selecting the files to merge, records to merge, and merge options, choose the OK button to close the Perform Merge dialog box and perform the merge.

WordPerfect displays a Please Wait dialog box indicating which records are being merged. When you select New Document as the Output File option and the program finishes the merge, you are placed at the end of the last merged document (or envelope, if you used the Envelopes option) in the current or new document window.

continues

continued

When you choose Printer, the program begins printing each merged document (and attached envelope when you use the Envelopes option).

9. Check over the merged documents in the new document window. If everything looks all right, you can print the merged documents by opening the File menu and choosing the Print command or by clicking the Print button on the Power Bar.

10. To save the merged documents in the new document window in a disk file, open the File menu and choose the Save command or click the Save Document button on the Power Bar. To abandon the file with the merged documents, open the File menu and choose the Close command (Ctrl+F4), and then choose the No button in the Save Changes to Document dialog box.

After you have created the form and data files you want to use, you are ready to perform the merge. WordPerfect enables you to merge the files to the current document or a new document window, directly to the printer, or to an existing disk file (which you can print later on). If you open the form file before you start the merge (as described in the preceding steps), you will want to use the New Document Output File option. When, however, you start the merge from an empty document window, you can use the Current Document Output File option (of course, you must then specify the file name of the form file in the Form File text box).

If you merge to the current or a new document window, you can then preview the letters, sort them, or make any last-minute editing changes before you print them. When you are using a very large data file and your computer does not have sufficient memory to hold all the merged documents, you may, however, have no choice but to merge directly to the printer.

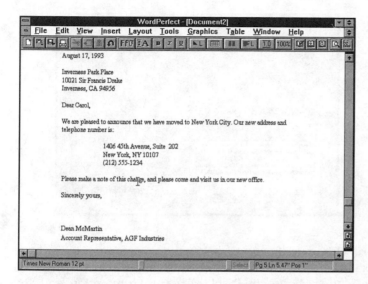

Here you see the last letter created by the merge that was output to a new document window.

If you scroll toward the beginning of the document, you see each completed letter (there is a letter for each record in the data file). As you scroll through the letters, you will notice that WordPerfect has replaced all the merge codes with the appropriate data from the data file and has separated each one with a hard page break. The letters are now ready to print, and each letter will be printed on a separate page.

Selecting the Records to Merge

With WordPerfect for Windows, you can select just some of the records in the data file to use in the merge. When selecting records, you can either individually mark the records to use, designate the range of records to use, or specify a selection condition that must be met before WordPerfect for Windows will use the record.

To select records by any of these methods, you open the Perform Merge dialog box and choose the Select Records button to open the Select Records dialog box. To mark the records individually in the data file, you need to choose the Mark Records radio button in this dialog box. When you do this, the Select Records dialog box changes so that it displays the part of the first set of records in the Record List.

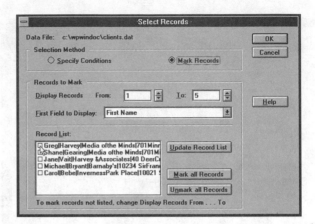

When you choose the **Mark Records** radio button, the Select Records dialog box changes to show the first set of records in the Record List box.

To select a record for inclusion in the merge, select the record in the Record List box to place an x in its check box. To control which records are displayed when making your selections, choose the **Display Records From** option, and then enter the starting record number in its text box and the ending number in the **To** text box. To change the first field to be displayed in the Record List box, choose the **First Field to Display** option, and then select the field name in the drop-down list box. After making these changes, you need to choose the **Update Record List** button to show the range of records and the first field displayed. After marking all the records to be included, choose the OK button or press Enter.

To select a range of record numbers in the Select Records dialog box, choose the **Record Number Range** option, and then enter the first record number to include in the **From** text box and the last record number to include in the **To** text box (record numbers are counted sequentially in the data file: in a table data file, down the rows; in a text data file, down the document at each ENDRECORD code).

To enter a selection condition, use the text boxes in the columns with the field names over them in the Select Records dialog box to specify the criteria for selecting a record to merge. It is here that you specify the field to use in the different Field text boxes and then enter the value, list of values, or range of values that are to be matched during the merge in the various Cond text boxes.

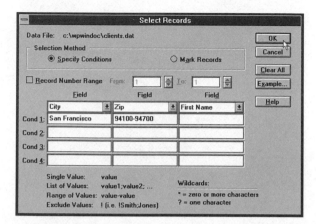

Here you see the selection condition city is San Francisco, and the ZIP code is between 94100 and 94700 inclusive.

To help you set up the selection condition, you can use the Example button to display sample criteria in the condition table.

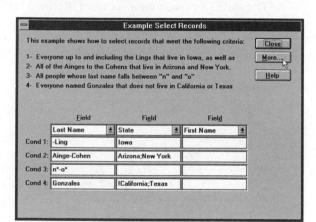

Here you see the sample conditions that appear when you choose the Example button.

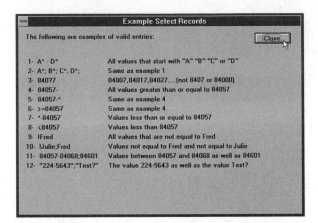

Here you see the examples of valid entries that appear when you choose the **M**ore button.

When developing selection conditions, keep in mind that the values entered under various fields in the same row (that is, for the same condition; Cond **1**, Cond **2**, and so on) form an AND condition, meaning that all of the field criteria must be met before WordPerfect will select the record for merging. When you enter more multiple selection conditions (by entering values for Cond **1**, Cond **2**, and so on), they form an OR condition, meaning that the program will select a record when either of their criteria are met in a particular record.

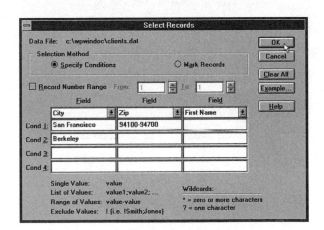

Here you see the selection condition city is San Francisco and the ZIP code is between 94100 and 94700, or the city is Berkeley (and the ZIP code is any-thing).

Addressing Envelopes

WordPerfect 6.0 for Windows makes it a snap to address envelopes for each of the merged letters you create. When you use the Envelope feature with a merge, the program attaches an envelope to each merged letter that is generated. To create an envelope, you choose the Envelopes button in the Perform Merge dialog box.

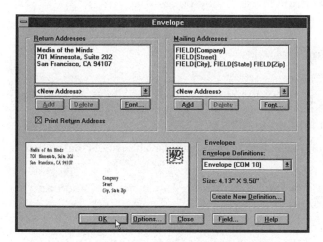

When you choose the Envelopes button, WordPerfect opens the Envelope dialog box where you enter the return address and the FIELD merge codes to create the mailing address.

To enter the return address, choose **R**eturn Addresses, and then either type in a new return address in the text box or select one that you have previously added in the drop-down list box. After entering a new return address, you can add it to the list of return addresses by choosing the **A**dd button. To select a new font for the return address, choose the Fo**n**t button. When the Address Font dialog box appears, select the font face, size, appearance, and color, and then choose OK or press Enter. If you intend to use envelopes that have the return address preprinted, you need to select New Address in the drop-down list box to clear any address in the **R**eturn Addresses text box, or select the Print Ret**u**rn Address check box to remove the x so that the address displayed in the text box is not used in the merged envelopes.

To enter the mailing address, you need to choose **M**ailing Addresses, and then use the F**i**eld button to insert the FIELD codes needed to generate the mailing addresses from the records in the data file. When setting up the mailing address with the FIELD codes, be sure to include any standard text or punctuation (like the comma between the city and state) between the codes that you insert. To select a new font for the mailing address, choose the **F**ont button. When the Mailing Address Font dialog box appears, select the font face, size, appearance, and color, and then choose OK or press Enter.

337

After entering the return and mailing address for the envelope, check the size and type of envelope listed in the Envelopes Definitions text box. Make sure that the envelope size is the one that you intend to use when printing the merged envelopes. If not, you can select a new definition in the drop-down list or you can create a new definition with the Create New Definition button. When you have finished filling out the addresses and selecting the envelope definition, choose the OK button or press Enter to close the Envelope dialog box and return to the Perform Merge dialog box.

Printing Mailing Labels

1. If necessary, open a new document for the label form file by opening the File menu and choosing New (or click the New Document button on the Power Bar).

2. Open the Layout menu and choose Labels. The Labels dialog box appears.

3. Select the label definition to use in the Labels list box, and then choose Select or press ⏎Enter.

4. Open the Tools menu and choose Merge (or press ⬆Shift + F9) to open the Merge dialog box, and then choose the Form button.

5. If the Create Merge File dialog box appears, choose OK or press ⏎Enter to use the label form in the current document window.

6. In the Associate a Data File text box, type the name of the data file you will use when generating the labels during the merge; or choose the File-list button and select the file name in the Select File dialog box. Then choose OK or press ⏎Enter.

7. Create the mailing address by inserting the FIELD codes. Choose the Insert Field button on the Merge Feature bar that appears, and then select the appropriate fields from the associated data file in the Insert Field Name or Number dialog box. When the Insert Field Name or Number dialog box appears, select the field you want to insert in the Field Names list box, and choose the Insert button or press ⏎Enter.

    When inserting the FIELD codes for the fields you need in generating the mailing address, don't forget to type in any standard text or punctuation (such as the comma between the city and state).

`Insert Field...`

8. When you're finished inserting the FIELD codes for the labels, choose the **C**lose button in the Insert Field Name or Number dialog box.

9. Save the label form by opening the File menu and choosing **S**ave (Ctrl + S); or click the Save Document button on the Power Bar (the program will suggest FRM as the file name extension when entering the new file name).

10. When you're ready to merge the label form with its associated data file, press Alt + ⇧Shift + M or click the **M**erge button on the Merge Feature Bar, and then choose the **M**erge button to open the Perform Merge dialog box.

Merge...

11. Check over the Files to Merge settings in the Perform Merge dialog box. Choose the **O**ptions button if you want to change any of the merge settings. Choose the **S**elect Records button if you want to mark the records to use or set up a condition for selecting records. When you have got the settings the way you want them, choose OK or press ↵Enter to start the merge.

The process for printing mailing labels with the Merge feature merely requires that you create a merge form file using a label form and then insert the appropriate FIELD codes in the label form. After that, it's a simple matter of merging the label form containing the merge codes with the data file and then printing the results.

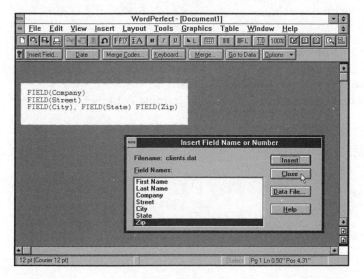

Here you see a label form containing the FIELD codes needed to generate the mailing addresses during the merge.

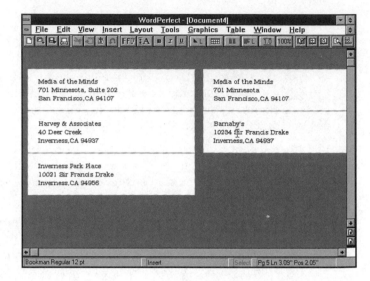

Here you see the final labels generated during the merge.

Summary

In this chapter, you learned how to use the powerful Merge feature of WordPerfect 6.0 for Windows. You learned how to prepare a data file that contains all the information you want to merge. You then learned how to prepare form files for generating and mailing labels. Remember that the form file indicates where each piece of information in the data file should be substituted during the merge. You then learned how to merge information either to the current or a new document window, where you can preview the results, or directly to the printer.

In the next chapter, you will learn how to sort and select information in your documents. As you will see, WordPerfect for Windows enables you to sort text at two levels: lines and paragraphs. You also will learn how to sort rows of a table, records in your text data files, and records in parallel columns.

12

Sorting and Selecting Data

Understanding sorting

Performing different types of sorts

Selecting the records to sort

W ordPerfect provides you with a powerful Sort feature that you can use to arrange data in your document or to select only the information you want to use. Examples of two simple applications for the Sort feature include sorting lines that contain employees' names, addresses, and telephone numbers to create an alphabetical phone list, and sorting a client secondary merge file by ZIP code to conform to the postal service rules for bulk mailing. When sorting the client secondary file by ZIP code, you could also use WordPerfect's Select feature to restrict the records to only those clients whose companies are located in California and have ZIP codes between 94600 and 94950.

Key Terms in This Chapter

Field	The basic component of a record. Each field in a record contains the same type of information, such as a company's city, state, and ZIP code. When sorting lines or paragraphs, each field is separated by tabs or indents. When sorting merge records in a text data file, each field is defined by an ENDFIELD code. When sorting columns, each column within the parallel column is a field. When sorting rows of a table, each cell in the table corresponds to a field.
Key	The words that determine how the records in a document are sorted or which records are selected. WordPerfect enables you to define up to nine (9) keys for sorting and selecting.
Record	A collection of related information in a file: a line of text when sorting lines, a paragraph when sorting paragraphs, a record in a text data file when sorting merge records, an entire parallel column when sorting columns, or a row when sorting table rows.
Select	To extract some of the records in a document based on selection conditions that you specify.

Understanding Sorting

The Sort feature in WordPerfect helps you alphabetize lines, paragraphs, and records in a text merge data file (discussed in chapter 11, "Using Merge for Mass Mailings"), parallel columns (discussed in chapter 16, "Using Columns and Graphics"), or rows of a table (discussed in chapter 15, "Creating Tables"). When sorting lines, paragraphs, parallel columns, or records in a merge data file, WordPerfect sorts all the information in the active document unless you restrict the sorting to specific lines, paragraphs, or records by selecting them before you open the Tools menu and choose Sort. When sorting a table created with the Table feature, the program sorts all the rows in the entire table (except for the first row when it contains headings or field names) unless you restrict the rows to be sorted by selecting them before performing the sort.

WordPerfect performs the sorting right on the screen in the active document window. To save the results, save the document under the same file name by opening the File menu and choosing Save, or save the sorted document under a new name by opening the File menu and choosing Save As.

Choosing the Kind of Sorting

The kind of sorting you choose depends on the way the information is organized. The section of text that is rearranged when you perform the sort is called the *record.* Each record contains individual data items called *fields,* which are made up of one or more words. Each record is sorted according to a key word in a particular field.

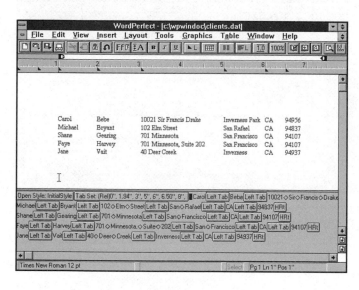

A Line sort is for sorting lines of text when the individual data items are separated into columns by tabs or indents and for records separated by a single hard return.

A Paragraph sort is for sorting paragraphs when individual data items are separated into columns by tabs or indents and records are designated by at least two consecutive hard returns.

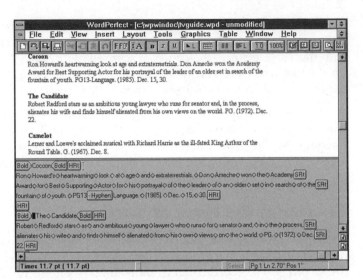

A Merge Record sort is for sorting records in a text data file when individual fields are separated by ENDFIELD merge codes and records are dcsignated by ENDRECORD merge codes.

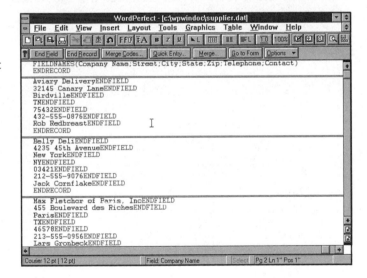

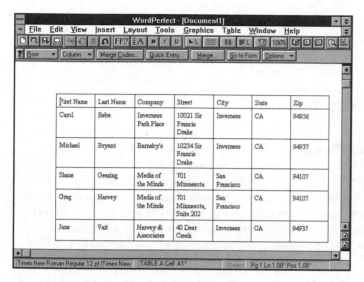

A Table Row sort is for sorting tables created with the program's Table feature when individual fields correspond to the cells in the table and records correspond to the rows.

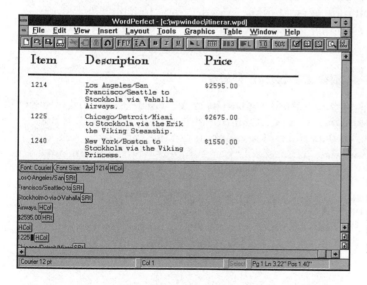

Choose a Column sort when sorting parallel columns in which individual fields correspond to the columns in the parallel column separated by hard returns, and when records correspond to the entire parallel column separated by hard page breaks.

Selecting the Sort Order

When sorting, you can choose between two sort orders: *ascending* (the default), which places text in alphabetical (A to Z) order and numbers from negative to positive order, or *descending*, which places text in Z-to-A order and numbers from positive to negative. When you use the ascending sort order, WordPerfect places any numeric entries before words. When you select descending order, the program reverses this system.

Defining the Sort Keys

As mentioned earlier, WordPerfect uses sort keys to reorder or select the records you are sorting. To arrange a list of names in alphabetical order, for example, the word of the field that contains the last name is the first sort key. In performing sort operations, you often need to define more than one sort key to obtain the desired order. If, for example, your list of names contains several Smiths or Browns, sorting on the last name key alone is not sufficient. To indicate how to order the duplicate Smiths and Browns in the list, you have to define the word of the field containing the first name as a second sort key as well.

WordPerfect enables you to define up to nine different sort keys. You seldom, if ever, need to define all nine keys. Multiple keys do come in handy, however, when you are sorting data that contains several more encompassing categories.

Selecting the Type of Sort Key

When defining a sort key, you must designate its type. WordPerfect enables you to choose between two types of keys: *Alpha* (for alphanumeric), which is the default type that treats all data (including numbers) in the sort key as text, or *Numeric,* which treats all data in the sort key as numbers (thus ignoring any text).

Choose Alpha as the type when the sort key contains both text and numbers or the key contains numbers of the same length that don't need to be evaluated numerically, such as ZIP codes or telephone numbers. Suppose, for example, that you want to sort the following lines of text in ZIP code order:

ABC Printing	101 E. 10th St.	Oakland	CA	94602
Easy Auto	34 Oak Street	Belair	MA	01234
Blair, Inc.	4565 5th Avenue	New York	NY	10012

To do this, you would designate the ZIP field as an Alpha key (all the ZIP codes have five digits).

Choose the Numeric type when the sort key contains numbers that should be evaluated numerically, such as those containing sales figures or salaries. When the numbers in the key are not all the same length, you must select Numeric as the sort key type to have them sorted correctly. Suppose, for example, that you want to sort the following lines of text in ascending order of the number of units:

Units	Code	Description
63	BU100	Tongs
2	BG100	Barbecue grill
16	OV110	Oven mitts
1	BC300	Barbecue cover

If you sort these items with the units field as an Alpha sort key, WordPerfect sorts the lines into this order:

Units	Code	Description
1	BC300	Barbecue cover
16	OV110	Oven mitts
2	BG100	Barbecue grill
63	BU100	Tongs

Notice that the 16 oven mitts are incorrectly placed in front of the 2 barbecue grills. This is because with an Alpha key, WordPerfect treats each digit in the field like a letter, so 16 gets precedence over 2 and is placed before it.

If, however, you sort these items with the units field as a Numeric sort key, WordPerfect correctly sorts the lines according to the value in ascending order as follows:

Units	Code	Description
1	BC300	Barbecue cover
2	BG100	Barbecue grill
16	OV110	Oven mitts
63	BU100	Tongs

This time, WordPerfect sorts the units according to their value rather than their digits and correctly places the 2 barbecue grills before the 16 oven mitts.

> *Tip:* When sorting numbers, don't confuse the sort order (ascending versus descending) with the type of sort key. The type of sort key determines whether WordPerfect ranks the records according to the value of numeric entries. The sort order determines whether these records are then ordered from lowest to highest values or from highest to lowest values.

Performing the Sort

General Steps for Sorting Records

1. Open the document that contains the records you want to sort by opening the **File** menu and choosing **Open**, or use the Open Document button on the Power Bar.

2. To sort records in only a section of the document, select the lines, paragraphs, merge records, or parallel columns you want to sort. If you are performing a table sort, place the insertion point somewhere in the table. To sort only particular rows, select those rows.

3. Open the **Tools** menu and choose **Sort**, or press [Alt]+[F9].

WordPerfect displays the Sort dialog box in which you define the kind of records to sort and the keys to use.

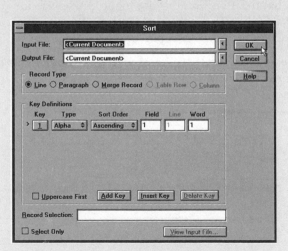

4. By default, WordPerfect for Windows assumes that you want to sort the records in the current document window and place the sorted results in the same window. If this is not the case and you want to sort the records in a file on disk, choose the Input File option and the name of the disk file you want to sort in the text box. You can specify the file to sort by choosing Select File option in the pop-up list, and then selecting the file in the Select Input File dialog box.

   If you want the sorted results to be saved in a file rather than appear in the current document window, choose the Output File option, and then enter the name of the file in which you want the sorted records saved. You can also specify the file in which to save the sorted records by choosing Select File option in the pop-up list, and then selecting the file in the Select Output File dialog box. Note that when sorting tables or parallel columns, you can output the results only to the current document window.

5. Designate the kinds of records you are sorting by choosing the Line, Paragraph, or Merge Record radio button under Record Type.

   By default, the Line radio button is selected as the record type and the Table Row and Column radio buttons are dimmed unless you positioned the insertion point in the cell of a table or a parallel column before you opened the Tools menu and chose Sort. In that case, the Table Row or Column radio button automatically is selected.

6. Define all the keys (up to nine) required to sort your records correctly in the Key Definitions area of the Sort dialog box. If the first key contains duplicates (such as last names), you can add a second key (such as first name) that tells WordPerfect how to sort the duplicates. To add a new key, select the Add Key button.

   In defining each key, choose between the Alpha and Numeric Type option in the pop-up list, the Ascending and Descending Sort Order option, and designate the number of the field, line, and word (or cell, line, and word in the case of a table sort) to be used—see the following sections for details on specifying keys for different types of records.

7. By default, WordPerfect for Windows places lowercase letters before uppercase letters when text is sorted in an Alpha sort. If you want uppercase letters to appear first, choose the Uppercase First option to place an X in its check box.

continues

continued

8. When you have finished specifying the sorting criteria, choose OK or press ⏎Enter to perform the sort.

   WordPerfect briefly displays a message box that informs you of the progress of the sort and the number of records that are being rearranged.

Tip: If your document has never been saved or contains unsaved text, save a copy of the unsorted document by opening the **File** menu and choosing **Save**, or choosing the Save button on the Power Bar. Saving a copy of the document in its unsorted state gives you a backup copy of the information should you make a mistake in defining the sort keys and get unwelcome results when you perform the sort.

The procedure for sorting information in WordPerfect is the same regardless of what kind of sorting you are performing. In each sort, you must open the document to be sorted, designate the kind of records you are sorting, and define the sort keys before you perform the sort. When the sort is completed, the box disappears and you return to your document, which contains the records in the new order.

To sort the list of names and addresses in ascending ZIP code and last name order, use Field 4 and Word 1 for Key 1 and Field 1 and Word –1 for Key 2. Use the negative number in Key 2 to have WordPerfect use the last word (in this case, the last name).

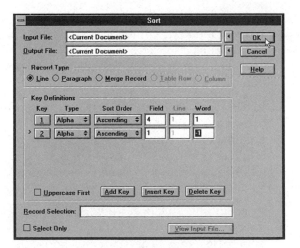

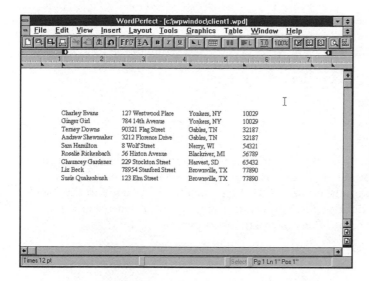

In this figure, you see the list of names and addresses after they have been sorted in ascending ZIP code and last name order.

If you are satisfied with the sorted results and want to retain them, you can save the file. If you didn't get the results you expected, open the Edit menu and choose Undo or press Ctrl+Z right away to restore the records to their previous order.

Specifying Keys for Sorting Lines

Use the Line sort when you need to sort simple lists in which each entry is on its own line in the document. You also can use the Line sort to sort tables created with tabs, provided that each column (or field) is separated by the same number of tabs and each row (or record) consists of a single line terminated by a hard return.

For purposes of the Line sort, a new field begins with a tab and a new word with a space, hyphen (-), or slash (/). When sorting a tabbed table, each column is a field and should be separated by the same number of tabs; otherwise, WordPerfect will not sort the data as you intend.

In determining the field number for the sort key, count each column separated by tabs from left to right in the table. In determining the number of the word in a field, you normally count each word from left to right in the field. If, however, each field doesn't contain the same number of words, you may have to count the words in the opposite direction to obtain the correct sort. When you count from right to left in the field, enter the number of the word as a negative number. If, for example, you want to sort on the last name in the following list of names

Jay Schnyder

Allan C. Grill

Shane W. Gearing

you cannot use 3 (when counting words from left to right) as the Word number of the sort key because the first entry in the list consists of only two words. Notice, however, that the last name is the first word in every name in the list when counting from right to left. You can therefore sort this list correctly by entering −1 in the Word number for the first sort key.

If, however, you want to sort on the last name in the following list of names

Jay Schnyder

Allan C. Grill

John B. Anderson III

Shane W. Gearing

you cannot use −1 as the Word number because WordPerfect counts III as the first word on the right instead of *Anderson* and sorts the list as follows:

Shane W. Gearing

Allan C. Grill

John B. Anderson III

Jay Schnyder

The only way to have WordPerfect sort this list of names correctly is to join the last name *Anderson* and the title III with a hard space (entered by pressing Ctrl+space bar) before you specify −1 as the Word number. When the person's last name and title are joined with a hard space, the program treats the two words as a single word and correctly sorts the names into the following order:

John B. Anderson III

Shane W. Gearing

Allan C. Grill

Jay Schnyder

This technique can be used with any other suffix, such as *Jr.* or *Dr.*

Specifying Keys for Sorting Paragraphs

Use Paragraph sorting when you are sorting text that consists of more than one line. For purposes of paragraph sorting, WordPerfect considers a record to be any text that is separated by two hard returns in a row (one to terminate the paragraph and the other to enter a blank line). You can, therefore, use this type of sorting to sort a heading along with its associated paragraph as long as the heading and the paragraph text are separated by only one hard return.

When you select **P**aragraph Record Type in the Sort dialog box, all three options in the Keys Definitions area (Line, Field, and Word) become available. In paragraph sorting, records are separated by two or more hard returns, lines are separated by single hard or soft returns, and fields are separated by tabs or indents.

When specifying the Line number for each sort key, you generally count the lines from top to bottom in the paragraph. You can, however, count the line numbers from bottom to top, in which case you enter a negative number for the line (just as you can when counting words from left to right).

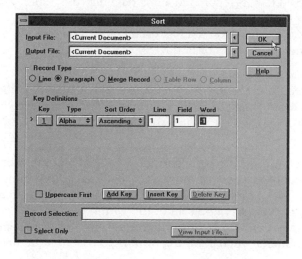

To sort these movie descriptions in ascending alpha-betical order by title (in the first line of each paragraph), you define Key 1 as Line 1, Field 1, and Word –1. Use a negative number in Word to have WordPerfect ignore *The* in the movie titles and sort the C's correctly.

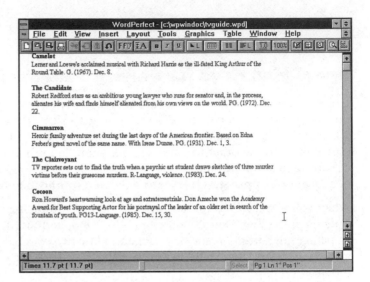

In this figure, you see the paragraphs after they were sorted alphabetically by title. Notice that the C's are in correct alphabetical order.

Specifying Keys for Sorting Merge Records in Text Data Files

Merge Record sorting is used to sort records in a text data file (use Table Row sorting to sort a table data file—see chapter 11 for information on creating a data file for merge operations). In a text data file, each field is separated by an ENDFIELD merge code and each record by an ENDRECORD merge code and a hard page break.

When you select **Merge Record** as the Record Type in the Sort dialog box, the options under Key Definitions change to Field, Line, and Word. In a merge sort, fields are separated by ENDFIELD merge codes, and lines are separated by single hard returns.

When specifying each sort key for this type of sort, determine the number of the field by counting fields from top to bottom in the record. When determining the line number, enter a positive number when counting from top to bottom or a negative number when counting from bottom to top within the field. When determining the word number, enter a positive number when counting from left to right or a negative number when counting from right to left in the field.

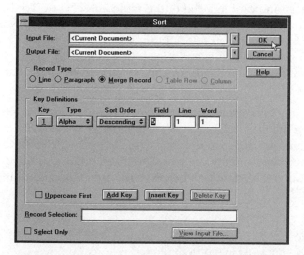

To sort these merge records in descending ZIP code order, define Key 1 as Field 5, Line 1, and Word 1.

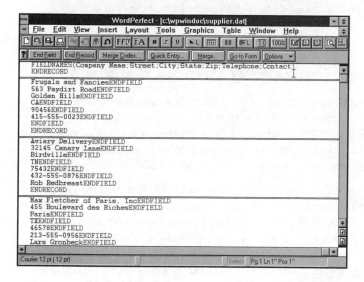

In this figure, you see the merge records after they were sorted in descending ZIP code order.

Specifying Keys for Sorting Table Rows

Table sorting is used to sort rows of a table created with the WordPerfect Table feature (see chapter 15 for information on creating tables with this feature). In such tables, records correspond to the rows of the table, and each row is divided into cells (which correspond to fields).

355

When you position the insertion point in a cell of the table and choose **Tools Sort** (Alt+F9), the **T**able Row radio button under Record Type automatically is selected in the Sort dialog box. When you select **T**able Row option, the options under Key Definitions change to Cell, Line, and Word. In a table sort, cells correspond to each column of the table, and lines are separated by single hard returns.

When specifying each sort key for sorting table rows, count each cell from left to right. When determining the line number, enter a positive number when counting from top to bottom or a negative number when counting from bottom to top within the field. When determining the word number, enter a positive number when counting from left to right or a negative number when counting from right to left in the field.

> *Tip:* When WordPerfect sorts rows of a table, it moves the cells' borders along with the data. To avoid unexpected results, remove the lines before you sort the data, and then put the lines back after sorting.

Specifying Keys for Sorting Parallel Columns

Column sorting is used to sort text set in parallel columns (sometimes called side-by-side columns) created with the Columns feature (see chapter 16 for information on creating parallel columns). For purposes of sorting parallel columns, records correspond to the entire parallel column and the columns within each parallel column correspond to a separate field.

When you place the insertion point within your parallel columns and choose **Tools Sort** (Alt+F9), the **C**olumn radio button under Record Type automatically is selected in the Sort dialog box. When the Column option is selected, the options under Key Definitions change to Column, Line, and Word. In a table sort, columns correspond to each column from left to right in a parallel column separated by [HCol] codes, and lines are separated by single hard returns.

When specifying each sort key for sorting table rows, count each column from left to right. When determining the line number, enter a positive number when counting from top to bottom or a negative number when counting from bottom to top within the column. When determining the word number, enter a positive number when counting from left to right or a negative number when counting from right to left in the line.

Selecting Records

WordPerfect's Select feature enables you to extract only those records in a file with which you want to work. To do this, set up a selection statement in the Record Selection text box of the Sort dialog box. When you select the OK button, WordPerfect sorts only those records that meet the condition in the selection statement (if you only want to select records without reordering, you must choose the Select Only option to put an X in its check box).

You can use the Select feature whenever you need to work with just a particular set of records. You could use the Select feature, for example, in a text data file, to target a mailing to a particular area of New York City, by restricting the records in the file to only those in which the city is New York and the ZIP code is between 10005 and 10110.

> *Caution:* When selecting records, be aware that WordPerfect will eliminate all records from the file that don't match your selection criteria (whether you sort the records or not). For that reason, you should take the precaution of outputting the selected records to a new file. If this is not possible (as is the case when working with tables or parallel columns), you need to remember to open the File menu and choose Save As and give the file containing just the selected records in the current document window a new file name (so that you can retain a copy of the file with all the records under the original file name).

Specifying the Selection Statement

When specifying the selection statement by which records are selected, you need to include the following items:

* A defined key in the form *key#*, where # is the number of the key you are referring to, such as *key1* or *key2*.

* A comparison operator that indicates the relationship between the key and the condition that must be met. Table 12.1 shows the operators that you can use.

- A condition that indicates the criteria each record must meet in order to be selected. When entering the condition part of the selection statement, keep in mind that WordPerfect doesn't differentiate between upper- and lowercase letters.

Suppose, for example, that you want to select only the records in a table in which the state is New York and state is defined as the first key in the Key Definitions. You would enter key1=New York in the **R**ecord Selection text box. In this example, *key1* is the key number, = (equal to) is the operator, and *New York* is the condition that must be met in order for the record to be selected.

To sort and extract only the records in which the department is Administration, enter key1=Administration as the selection statement.

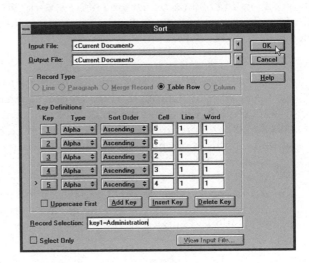

Table 12.1   Operators Used in Selection Criteria

Symbol	Meaning	Example
¦	Or	key1=Boston ¦ key1=Cambridge
&	And	key2>=945001 & key2<=94600
=	Equal to	key3=Smith
<>	Not equal to	key4<>TX

Symbol	Meaning	Example
>	Greater than	key5>$45,000
<	Less than	key6<12
>=	Greater than or equal to	key7>=a * key7<=f
<=	Less than or equal to	key8<=115
()	Parentheses are used to group keys that should be evaluated together.	(key9=CA + key9=AZ) * (key1>$95,000 * key1<$200,000)

When specifying the selection statement, you can create compound criteria by using the symbol & (And) or ¦ (Or) between conditions. When entering a compound selection statement, you must repeat the key number before each condition in the statement. In other words, to restrict the records to those in which the state is either Indiana or Illinois, you cannot enter key1=IN + IL. Instead, you must repeat the key reference and the comparison operator, as in key1=IN + key1=IL.

Creating a Global Selection Statement

When you select records, WordPerfect enables you to create a global selection statement that selects records as long as an entry in any part of the record meets the condition(s). When you set up a global select statement, you don't identify a particular key. To find all records that contain the name *Davis*, for example, regardless of whether this name is located in the first name, last name, address, or city field of a record, you would enter keyg=Davis in the **R**ecord Selection text box. When you create a global selection statement with *keyg* and aren't sorting the records (that is, you select the **S**elect Only option), you don't have to define any sort keys before you choose the OK button to extract the records.

Summary

In this chapter, you learned about WordPerfect's sorting and selecting capabilities. You learned how to perform a Line, Paragraph, Merge Record, Table Row, and Column sort. You also learned how to extract only those records in a document that meet the conditions you specify.

In the next chapter, you learn about many of the annotating features in WordPerfect 6.0 for Windows. You learn how to number lines in a document, add text and sound comments, work with bookmarks, and use hypertext to make jumps between particular locations in a document. In addition, you learn how to add footnotes or endnotes to the text.

Outlining

13

Understanding
outlining in
WordPerfect 6.0
for Windows

Creating an outline

Editing an outline

Collapsing and
expanding the outline

Moving outline
headings

Outlining in WordPerfect 6.0 enables you not only to organize your thoughts in a logical manner but also to determine how this information is viewed. In this chapter, you learn how to set up formal outlines, select the type of outlining to use, and how to collapse and expand the outline so that only the outline levels with the information you need to see at the time are displayed in the current document window.

Key Terms in This Chapter	
Body text	Any text in the outline that is not part of a particular outline level heading. Body text is not formatted according to any of the outline styles and can be hidden while all or part of the outline level headings are displayed.
Demote	To change the level of an outline heading by moving it to the previous level.
Outline family	The current outline level heading plus all text and levels below it until you reach the next outline heading at the same level.
Outline level	One of eight different levels possible in an outline. The outline level determines the appearance and formatting of the numbering (if the outline style selected uses numbers) and outline text.
Outline style	Determines the kind of numbering and formatting assigned to each outline level in your outline.
Outline text	Any text that you add to the outline heading for each level in the outline. WordPerfect for Windows automatically numbers (if your outline style uses numbers) and formats the outline text according the style assigned to its outline level.
Promote	To change the level of an outline heading by advancing it to the next level.

Understanding Outlining in WordPerfect 6.0 for Windows

WordPerfect 6.0 for Windows' outline feature makes it easy to create formal outlines that use a system of various numbers and letters to mark the different outline levels. In addition, you can use this feature to create nontraditional outlines that format each outline heading in a slightly different manner without resorting to the use of any system of numbers and letters.

In a formal outline, each outline level is numbered consecutively and uses the same style of numbering, such as I, II, III,... for first-level heads; A, B, C,... for second-level heads; 1, 2, 3,... for third-level heads; and so forth. In addition to a different style of numbering (or letters), each outline style is usually indented the same amount from the left margin.

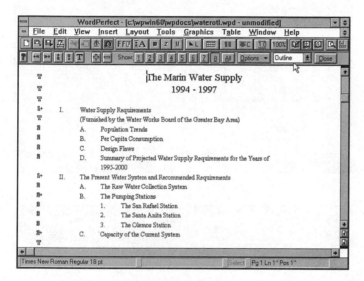

This formal outline uses the I, A, 1 outline style to mark the different outline levels.

In a nontraditional outline, each outline level is formatted in the same way without relying on any system of numbers or letters to mark the particular level. You can use this type of outline in any document that uses a system of different level headings that all need to be formatted in the same way. You could, for example, have your level one headings appear underlined and bold in a very large type size, second-level headings in bold in a large type size, and third-level headings in bold in a normal text size.

When you create such an outline, the paragraphs of text that appear beneath each report heading are not actually part of the outline structure (this text is considered to be *body text* in contrast to the headings, which are considered to be *outline text*). Because WordPerfect for Windows enables you to hide the body text under all or particular outline levels, you can hide everything but your headings should you need to see only them. You also can determine what information in the outline is displayed by collapsing and expanding particular levels of the outline. This capability to hide what you don't need to see in the outline lets you concentrate on only the text and outline headings that you need to work with or print.

363

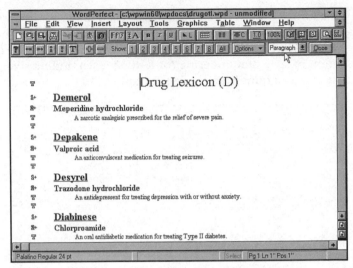

This nontraditional outline doesn't use numbers and letters to mark the outline levels.

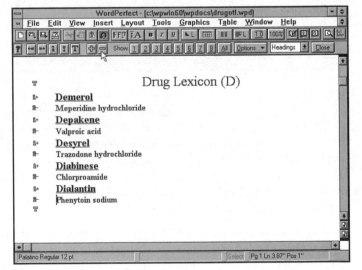

This example shows an outline after hiding all the body text so that only the headings are displayed.

Tip: If all you need to do is create a numbered list in your document, you don't need to go to the trouble of creating a formal outline. Instead, you can do this more simply with the new Bullets and Numbers feature. See "Formatting Text with Bullets and Numbers" in chapter 6 for details.

Creating an Outline

Creating a Formal Outline

1. Position the insertion point at the place in the document where you want the outline to appear.

2. Open the **T**ools menu and choose **O**utline.

   WordPerfect for Windows turns on outlining, displays the Outline Feature Bar, inserts 1. for the first level of the outline (using the Paragraph outline style), and indents the line so that you can enter the text of the initial first-level heading in the outline. The program indicates that this is a first-level heading by inserting 1 in the left margin.

3. Type the text for the initial first outline heading, and then press `↵Enter`.

   WordPerfect for Windows inserts 2. and indents the line so that you can enter the text of the second first-level heading in the outline. The program indicates that this is a first-level heading by inserting another 1 in the left margin.

4. If your outline has no subheads under the initial first-level heading, type the text of the second first-level heading, and press `↵Enter`.

   If you need to promote the outline level so that you can enter the initial second-level head, press `Tab⇄` or click the Next Level button (right arrow) on the Outline Feature Bar to change 1. to a., and then type this heading.

   If you need to enter body text under an outline heading that shouldn't have a number or letter indicating the outline level, press `⬅Backspace` to delete the number or letter indicating the outline level, and then type body text. WordPerfect for Windows indicates that this is body text by replacing the outline-level number in the left margin with a T.

5. Continue in this manner, entering the outline headings as required by your particular outline. To advance the heading to the next lower outline level (WordPerfect for Windows uses the same level until you change it), press `Tab⇄` or `Alt`+`⇧Shift`+`N`, or click the Previous Level (left arrow) button on the Outline Feature Bar before you type the heading.

continues

continued

If you advance the heading's outline level too much, you can move to a previous level by pressing ⌧Shift + Tab⌧ or Alt + ⌧Shift + P, or by clicking the Previous Level (left arrow) button on the Outline Feature Bar.

To convert the outline level to body text, use ⌧Backspace to remove the outline number or letter. If you convert an outline level that you shouldn't have, press Alt + ⌧Shift + T or click the Body Text button on the Outline Feature Bar to convert the text from body text to part of the outline.

6. To use a style of numbering other than Paragraph style—which uses 1, a, (1), (a), and so on—click the drop-down list button to the right of the Outline Definitions list box in the Outline Feature Bar and select the name of the new style.

You can also select a new outline style by pressing Alt + ⌧Shift + O or clicking the **Options** button on the Outline Feature Bar, and then choosing **Define Outline** to open the Define Outline dialog box. Double-click the style you want to use in the **Name** list box or select its name, and then choose OK.

7. When you have finished entering all the headings and body text and modifying the outline levels, turn off outlining and remove the last outline number or letter by pressing Alt + ⌧Shift + O or clicking the **Options** button on the Outline Feature Bar, and then choosing **Mark End**.

8. Remove the display of the outline-level numbers and the Outline Feature Bar from the window by pressing Alt + ⌧Shift + C or by clicking the **Close** button on the Outline Feature Bar.

When you create a formal outline in WordPerfect 6.0 for Windows, the program automatically numbers and formats each outline level you add, according to the outline style you use. The program offers the following outline styles from which to choose:

- *Bullets.* Marks the different outline levels with various types of bullets/symbols and successive indentations.

- *Headings.* Marks the different outline levels with various types of formatting; no outline numbers, letters, symbols, or system of sequential indentations are used.

- *Legal.* Marks the different outline levels with legal numbering—1, 1.1, 1.1.1, and so on—and successive indentations.

- *Legal2.* Marks the different outline levels with legal numbering—1, 1.01, 1.01.01, and so on—and successive indentations.

- *Numbers.* Marks the different outline levels with the same combination of numbers and letters as the Paragraph style—1., a., i., (1), and so on—but without using successive indentations.

- *Outline.* Marks the different outline levels with the combination of Roman and Arabic numerals and letters used in traditional outlining—I., A., 1., a., and so on—and successive indentations.

- *Paragraph.* Marks the different outline levels with a combination of numbers and letters—1., a., i., (1), and so on—and successive indentations.

> *Tip:* If none of the predefined outline styles suit your needs, you can, of course, customize one of the existing styles or create a custom style of your own. For details on how to create outline styles, refer to Que Corporation's *Using WordPerfect 6 for Windows,* Special Edition.

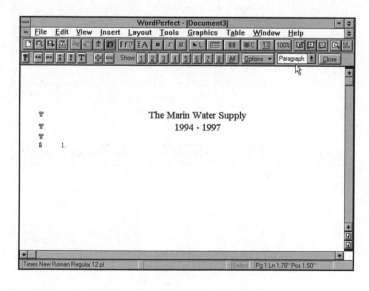

When you start a new outline in a document, the program automatically selects the Paragraph outline style for you and numbers the initial heading for the first outline.

367

After you enter the
initial first-level
heading and press
Enter, the program
automatically
inserts the next
number for your
next first-level
outline heading.

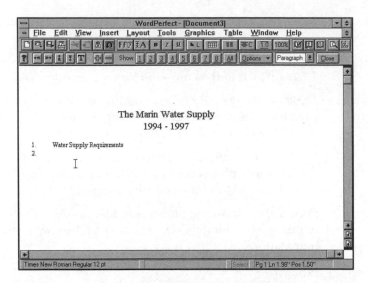

To enter the initial
second-level
heading, press Tab
to promote the
outline level, and
then enter the
heading text.

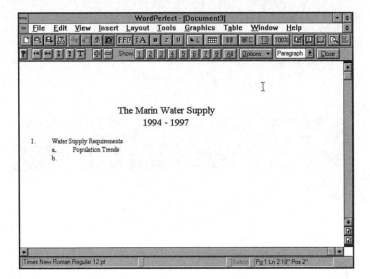

Editing an Outline

After you create an outline, if you add a new heading at a certain outline level or promote or demote an existing heading to that outline level, WordPerfect for Windows automatically renumbers the headings at that level in the outline to reflect this modification. The program also automatically renumbers the headings at the same level when you delete a particular outline heading, change its outline level, or convert outline text to regular body text.

Remember that you can use Tab and Shift+Tab (Back Tab) to change the level of a particular heading in the outline. To promote the heading to the next outline level of a heading, place the insertion point after the outline numbers (or symbol) and press Tab. To demote the heading to the previous outline level, place the insertion point after the outline numbers (or symbol) and press Shift+Tab.

To convert an outline heading to body text (so that it is no longer formatted or renumbered as part of the outline), place the insertion point somewhere in the text of the heading and then press Alt+Shift+T or click the Body Text (T) button on the Outline Feature Bar. Note that you use the same keystrokes to convert a paragraph of body text to an outline heading. After you have converted the paragraph of body text to an outline heading, you can promote or demote its level in the outline with Tab and Shift+Tab just as you would any other outline heading.

> *Caution:* Before you can promote or demote outline headings or convert them to body text (and body text to outline text), WordPerfect for Windows must be in Outline view. You can tell when the program is in Outline view because the Outline Feature Bar is displayed at the top of the window and the outline level numbers and T's (indicating body text in the outline) are displayed in the left margin. To switch to Outline view, open the **T**ools menu and choose **O**utline. To switch back to normal Page view, press Alt+Shift+C or click the **C**lose button on the Outline Feature Bar.

Understanding the Outline Feature Bar

The Outline Feature Bar contains buttons you use to create and edit your outline and control which outline levels are displayed. The Outline Feature Bar is displayed when you open the **T**ools menu and choose the **O**utline command to switch to Outline view. To remove the Outline Feature Bar from the Word-Perfect program window, press Alt+Shift+C or click the **C**lose button on this bar, which switches you back to Normal view.

The Outline Feature Bar contains buttons that make it easy to modify your outline or control which outline levels are displayed.

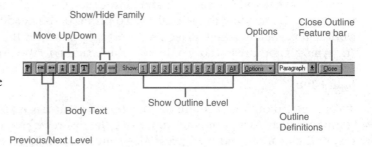

Collapsing and Expanding the Outline

WordPerfect for Windows enables you to control exactly which outline levels are displayed in the document. The easiest way to do this is to switch to Outline view and click the Show Family button on the Outline Feature Bar; or press Alt+Shift and the number of the outline level (**1** through **8**) representing the highest outline level you want to see.

If you select the Show **1** button, the outline shows only the first-level headings.

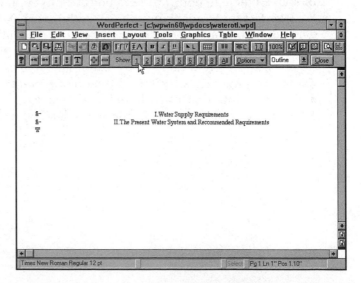

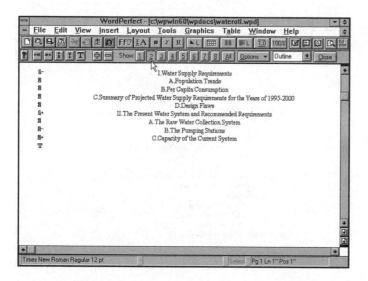

If you select the Show **2** button, the outline shows up to the second level of headings.

In addition to selecting which outline levels are displayed in the outline, you also can show more or less detail in particular areas by expanding and collapsing individual outline families. In WordPerfect for Windows, an *outline family* consists of the current outline heading plus all subordinate headings and text up to the next heading at the same level. To collapse a particular outline family, place the insertion point somewhere in the heading that's at the beginning of the family and press Alt+Shift+H or click the Hide Family button (–) on the Outline Feature Bar. To expand a particular outline family, place the insertion point in the heading at the beginning of the family and press Alt+Shift+S or click the Show Family button (+) on the Outline Feature Bar.

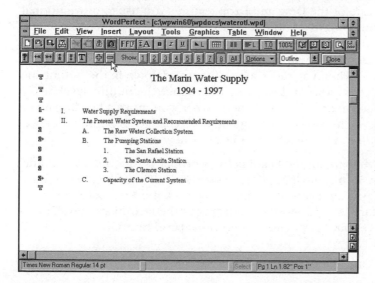

Click the Hide Family button (–) to collapse the outline family that begins with the initial first-level heading.

371

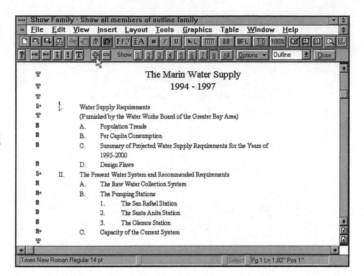

Click the Show
Family button (+)
to expand the initial
first-level outline
family.

After collapsing certain levels of the outline—whether universally with the
Show **1** through **8** buttons or individually with the Hide Family button—you
can redisplay all the outline levels, including all the outline headings and body
text, by pressing Alt+Shift+A or clicking the **All** button on the Outline Feature
Bar.

Moving Outline Headings

When working with an outline, you can rearrange the outline headings without
using the Cut and Paste or the Drag and Drop features you use to move normal
text. To move a heading up in an outline, place the insertion point somewhere
in the heading, and then press Alt+Shift+U or click the Move Up button (up
arrow). To move a heading down, press Alt+Shift+W or click the Move Down
button (down arrow). When you move a heading up or down in the outline in
this manner, WordPerfect for Windows does not change the outline level but
moves the heading above or below the others. When you move a heading up or
down in the same level, however, the program does change its outline number
or letter (if your outline style uses them) to suit its new position.

Of course, after moving an outline heading to its proper position in the outline,
you can then modify its outline level, if necessary. To move the heading to the
next lower level, press Tab, press Alt+Shift+N, or click the Next Level button
on the Outline Feature Bar. To move the heading to the next higher level, press
Shift+Tab, press Alt+Shift+P, or click the Previous Level button.

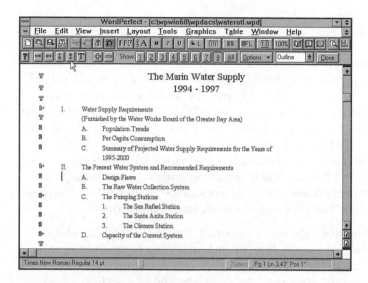

This sample shows an outline after moving the *Design Flaws* heading from the D position under major point I to the A position under major point II.

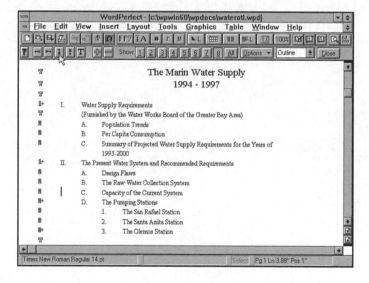

This sample shows the same outline after moving the *Capacity of Current System* heading from the D position under major point II to the C position.

Summary

In this chapter, you learned how to harness the power of the WordPerfect for Windows outline feature to create formal outlines. Remember that to create an outline in the default Paragraph style, you open the **T**ools menu, choose the **O**utline command, and type the text for the initial first-level heading. When you press Enter, the program inserts new outline numbers at the same outline level. To change levels, press Tab or click the Next Level button on the Outline Feature Bar. If you need to move a heading to a previous level, press Shift+Tab or click the Previous Level button. When you finish entering the headings for your outline, you can turn off the outline by pressing Alt+Shift+O or choosing the **O**ptions button, and then choosing the **M**ark End command.

In the next chapter, you learn the many ways that WordPerfect for Windows enables you to annotate your document, including adding nonprinting comments; creating bookmarks for finding your place in a document; and creating footnotes or endnotes at the bottom of the page, the end of a section, or the end of the document.

Annotating a Document

WordPerfect 6.0 for Windows offers a wide variety of tools for annotating specific elements in your document. You will find that the program provides the appropriate tool for everything from numbering the lines on each page to letting you cite references in the form of footnotes or endnotes.

This chapter introduces the basic reference tools included in WordPerfect. You learn how to number lines automatically as well as to annotate the document with comments and bookmarks. In addition, you learn how to add footnotes and endnotes either on the page or at the end of a section or chapter.

Adding line numbers to a document

Adding comments to a document

Adding sound clips to a document

Creating bookmarks

Using Hypertext to jump to a bookmark

Adding footnotes and endnotes

Using WordPerfect's other reference features

Key Terms in This Chapter

Bookmark	An invisible marker added to the text that you can use to quickly find that place in the document.
Comment	A nonprinting note that you can add anywhere in the text of your document. WordPerfect enables you to search for comments and convert them to regular text if you want to print them.
Endnote	A numbered comment or reference that appears at the end of a section or document. When you add endnotes, WordPerfect automatically numbers the notes and formats them at the place you specify in the document.
Footnote	A numbered comment or reference that appears at the bottom of the page. When you add footnotes, WordPerfect automatically numbers the notes and formats them in the footer of the appropriate page.
Hypertext	Creates link between specific text in a document and a particular document, bookmark, or macro. When you select a hypertext link to another document, the program opens that document. When you select a link to a macro, the program plays that macro (see chapter 10, "Creating Macros"). When you select a link to a bookmark, the program moves the insertion point directly to that bookmark.

Numbering Lines

Adding Numbers to the Lines of a Document

1. Place the insertion point in the line in which you want the line numbering to begin.

2. Open the Layout menu, choose Line, and then choose Numbering.

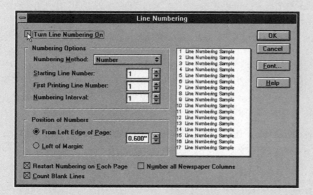

The Line Numbering dialog box appears.

3. Select Turn Line Numbering **O**n.

4. To change the numbering from Arabic numerals to letters or Roman numerals, choose Number **M**ethod and select the new method in the drop-down list box: **L**owercase Letter, **U**ppercase Letter, **L**owercase Roman, or **U**ppercase Roman.

5. To start the line numbering with a number after 1, choose **S**tarting Line Number, and then enter the new number or select it with the up- and down-arrow buttons.

6. If you want the printing of the line numbers to start after line number 1, choose **F**irst Printing Line Number, and then enter the new number or select it with the up- and down-arrow buttons.

continues

continued

7. If you want the line numbers to increase at an interval other than 1 (as in 1, 2, 3, and so on), choose Numbering Interval, and then enter the new number or select it with the up- and down-arrow buttons.

8. By default, WordPerfect positions the line numbers 0.600 inches in from the left edge of the paper. To change the amount of space between the left edge of the page and the line number, enter a new value in the From Left Edge of Page text box. To position the number this distance from the left margin rather than the left edge of the page, choose the Left of Margin radio button.

9. By default, WordPerfect for Windows restarts the line numbering on each new page of the document. To make the numbering continuous throughout the document, choose the Restart Numbering on Each Page option to remove the × from its check box.

10. To number only nonblank lines in the document, choose the Count Blank Lines option to remove the × from its check box.

11. If your document uses newspaper columns (see chapter 16) and you want the lines in each column numbered, choose the Number all Newspaper Columns option to put an × in its check box.

12. If the line numbering in the sample box appears the way you want it in the document, select the OK button or press ⏎Enter to put line numbering into effect in the document.

WordPerfect makes it easy to number the lines in your document. Line numbering is very useful in legal briefs and contracts; it makes referring to a specific clause easier.

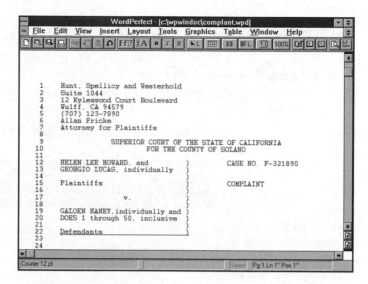

When you number the lines in a WordPerfect document, the program numbers the body text, footnotes, and endnotes, but not the headers and footers.

Line numbers appear in the document editing window as long as the program is not in Draft mode. If you can't see the line numbers on the displayed page after defining them, you need to switch to Page or Two Page mode by opening the **View** menu and choosing the **Page** or **Two Page** command.

> *Tip:* When auto code placement is on, WordPerfect for Windows places the [Ln Num:On] code—which turns on line numbering—at the beginning of the current paragraph, regardless of where the insertion point is located in that paragraph. Chapter 6 explains auto code placement in more detail.

If you reach a place in the document where you don't want to number the lines, you can turn off line numbering by opening the **Layout** menu, choosing **Line**, and then choosing **Numbering**. When the Line Numbering dialog box appears, choose the Turn Line Numbering **On** option to remove the x from its check box. This step inserts a [Ln Num:Off] code at the beginning of the current paragraph. If you find that you need to remove line numbering from a document, locate the [Ln Num:On] code in the Reveal Codes window and delete it.

Adding Comments to a Document

Inserting a Comment in the Text

1. Place the insertion point in the document where you want the comment to appear.

2. Open the Insert menu, choose Comment, and then choose Create.

WordPerfect displays the Comment Feature Bar and places the insertion point in a special Create Comment window in which you enter the text of your comment.

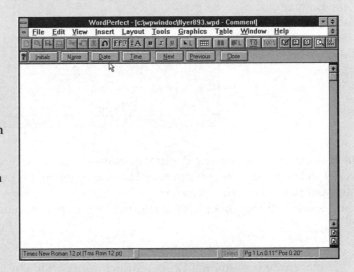

3. Type the text of your comment in the Create Comment window. To insert your name in the comment (as entered in the User Info for Comments and Summary area of the Environment Preferences dialog box), choose the Name button on the Comment Feature Bar. To insert the current date or time in the comment, choose the Date or Time button on this bar. If you want your initials (as entered in the User Info for Comments and Summary area of the Environment Preferences dialog box) to appear in the Comment icon, choose the Initials button on the Comment Feature Bar.

4. Apply any new fonts, font sizes, or attributes you want applied to the comment text.

5. When the text of your comment is the way you want it to look, press Alt + ⇧Shift + C or select the Close button to hide the Comment Feature Bar and insert either the Comment icon (if you're in Page or

Two Page mode) or the text of your comment in your document at the position of the insertion point (if you're in Draft mode).

When the program is in Page mode, WordPerfect for Windows displays a Comment icon in the left margin of the line containing the comment you're creating.

You can add notes (referred to as *comments*) to any WordPerfect document. You can use comments to clarify points made in the text or to remind yourself of changes that you still need to make. Suppose, for example, that you need to create a table in your document with data from a 1-2-3 for Windows worksheet, but the worksheet is not yet ready to import. At the place where you want the table to appear, you can insert a document comment reminding yourself to import the 1-2-3 worksheet (see chapter 15, "Creating Tables," for information on how to create a table). When the worksheet is ready to import, you can use the Search feature to locate the comment in the text and to create your table by importing the worksheet data there.

When WordPerfect is in normal Page mode, the program places in the left margin a Comment icon that you must click to display the comment text in a balloon. When WordPerfect is in Draft mode, the comment appears in a shaded box at the insertion point's position (splitting the line of text if the comment is placed somewhere in its midst).

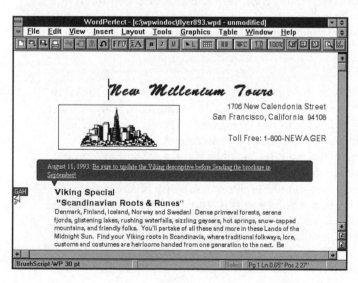

In Page mode, you click the Comment icon to display the comment text in a balloon.

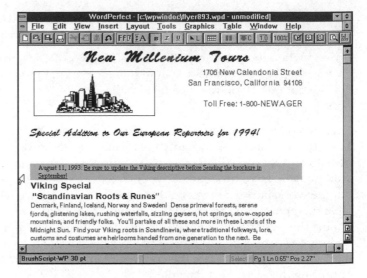

In Draft mode, the comment appears in a shaded box.

Keep in mind that even when WordPerfect displays the comment in the document in Draft mode, the program does not print the comment with the rest of the text. To print a comment, you must first convert it to text.

When you create a comment, WordPerfect inserts a [Comment] code into the document at the position of the insertion point. To locate a comment quickly, use the Find feature to search for the [Comment] code (see chapter 5, "Proofreading Text"). To remove the comment from the document, delete the [Comment] code.

Tip: Before you can have WordPerfect for Windows insert your name in a comment or use your initials in the Comment icon, you must add your name and initials in the Environment Preferences dialog box. Open the **F**ile menu and choose P**r**eferences to display the Preferences dialog box. Then double-click the **E**nvironment icon or choose the **E**nvironment command from the **P**references pull-down menu to open the Environment Preferences dialog box. Choose **N**ame to enter your name in its text box, **I**nitials to enter your initials in its text box, and User Co**l**or to select a color that WordPerfect will apply to both the Comment icon and in the comment balloon when the program is in Page mode. Then choose OK or press Enter to close the Environment Preferences dialog box, and choose **C**lose to close the Preferences dialog box.

If you put multiple comments on the same line, WordPerfect for Windows displays a special Comment icon in Page View. Click this icon to show balloons at the exact location of your comments (to display the comment text, you then click the desired balloon).

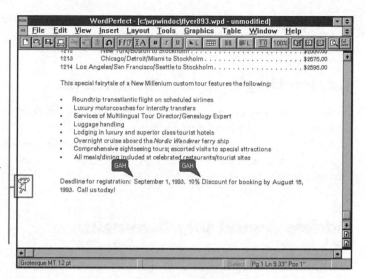

Editing a Comment

You can edit a comment at any time after inserting it into your document. The easiest way to open the Comment editing window with the text of your comment and display the Comment Feature Bar is to double-click its Comment icon in the left margin when the program is in Page mode.

If you have added more than one comment to the same line, you can't double-click the Comment icon (because it represents more than one comment). To edit a comment in this case, you must position the insertion point after the [Comment] code for the comment you want to edit, and then open the Insert menu and choose Comment. Then choose Edit to open the Comment editing window.

After you finish making changes to your comments in the Comment editing window, choose the Close button to hide the Comment Feature Bar and return to your document.

Converting a Comment to Text

To print a comment in your document, you first must convert the comment to text. To change a comment to text, place the insertion point after the [Comment] code for the comment you want to edit, and then open the Insert menu, choose Comment, and choose Convert to Text. WordPerfect for Windows inserts the comment text in the line at the insertion point.

Converting Text to a Comment

You also can convert normal text to a comment in your document. Select the text and open the Insert menu, choose Comment, and then choose Create. After you convert selected text into a comment in this manner, the text disappears from the normal document and appears only in the comment balloon (in Page mode) or the shaded box (in Draft mode).

Adding Sound Clip Comments

Inserting a Sound Clip Comment into the Document

1. Position the insertion point in the document where you want the comment with the sound clip to appear.

2. Open the Insert menu and choose Sound. The Sound Clips dialog box appears.

3. Choose the Insert button to open the Insert Sound Clip into Document dialog box.

4. To give the sound clip a descriptive name, choose the Name option, replace the temporary name (Clip #1, Clip #2, and so on) with your own name, and press Tab⇥.

5. Type the name of the file or use the file list button to select the file containing the sound effects, music, or dictation you want to add to the sound clip comment in the File list box.

6. By default, WordPerfect for Windows links the sound file to the current document rather than storing it in the document (sound files are notoriously large). If you would prefer to store the sound file in the WordPerfect document, choose the Store in Document radio button.

7. Choose OK twice to close the Insert Sound Clip into Document and Sound Clips dialog boxes and to insert the Sound icon (an eighth note in a bubble) for the sound clip comment in the left margin of the current line.

If you have a sound card in your computer, you can insert sound files that contain dictation, sound effects, or even musical selections. These sound clip files can be in one of two formats: MIDI (Music Instrument Digital Interface) files that use the MID extension or Windows sound files using the WAV file extension.

When you insert a sound file in your WordPerfect document, the program inserts a Sound icon in the left margin of the current line along with a [Sound] hidden code that appears at the end of the current line. If you need to delete the sound clip, open the Reveal Codes window, and then drag the [Sound] code out of the Reveal Codes window or place the Reveal Codes cursor after this code and press Backspace.

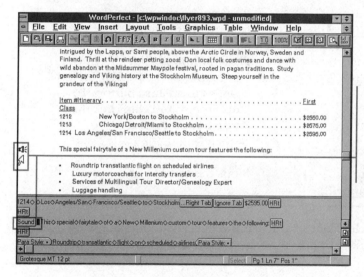

The Sound Clip icon in the normal document window with its [Sound] hidden code in the Reveal Codes window below.

Playing a Sound Clip

You can play a sound clip by double-clicking the Sound icon. If the comment contains dictation or some other voice note that you might have to pause and replay, you can play the sound clip with the buttons on the Sound Feature Bar.

To display the Sound Feature Bar, click the Sound icon with the secondary mouse button, and then choose **T**ranscribe from the QuickMenu that appears. Choose from the following Sound Feature Bar options:

Sound Feature Button Bar or Keystroke	Action
Click the **R**ew button or press [Alt] + [⇧Shift] + [R]	Rewinds the sound clip.
Click the **FF** button or press [Alt] + [⇧Shift] + [F]	Forwards the sound clip.
Click the **R**eplay button or press [Alt] + [⇧Shift] + [A]	Restarts the sound clip from the beginning.
Click the **P**lay button or press [Alt] + [⇧Shift] + [P]	Plays the sound clip. During playback, the **P**lay button changes to a **P**ause button. To pause the sound clip, click the **P**ause button or press [Alt] + [⇧Shift] + [P].
Click the **S**top button or press [Alt] + [⇧Shift] + [S]	Stops the sound clip.

To replay the sound clip from a particular place, you can drag the scroll box in the scroll bar to the place where you want to start, and then choose the Play button.

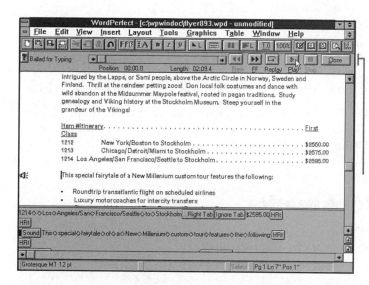

The Sound Feature Bar lets you control how you listen to the sound clip.

Recording Sound Clips

If you have a microphone for your sound card, you can record voice messages and insert them into your documents as sound clip comments. You might, for example, record a message reminding yourself (or whoever works on the document) that some missing information should be inserted into the document before it's distributed in the office, or you might record some dictation that another typist will later enter as document text.

To record a sound clip, open the Insert menu and choose Sound. Then choose the Record button to open the Windows Sound Recorder utility in its own dialog box. To begin recording your message, click the Microphone button (the Microphone icon is at the bottom right of the Sound Recorder dialog box). When you have finished recording, click the Stop button (the button with the square to the left of the Microphone button). To replay the voice message, click the Play button (the button with one triangle pointing right).

If, after listening to the sound clip, you need to increase the volume, open the Effects menu and choose Increase Volume (by 25%). To decrease the volume, choose Decrease Volume. To re-record your message from a particular point, drag the knob on the slider bar until it's where you want to start re-recording (you can see the number of seconds in the Position box above on the left). Then click the Microphone button and start talking.

When you have the voice message the way you want it, you need to save it in its own file by opening the File menu and choosing Save. After selecting the directory, assigning a file name in the File Name text box, and choosing OK in the Save As dialog box, you can then exit the Sound Recorder by double-clicking the Control menu button or opening the File menu and choosing Exit.

After recording a sound clip and saving it in its own file in this manner, you can then insert it in your document following the procedure already outlined (see "Adding Sound Clip Comments" earlier in this chapter for details).

Creating Bookmarks

Inserting a Bookmark into the Document

1. Place the insertion point at the place in the text where you want the bookmark to appear. If you want to be able to select the text when you go to the bookmark, highlight the text with the insertion point.

2. Open the Insert menu and choose Bookmark to open the Bookmark dialog box.

3. Choose the Create button to open the Create Bookmark dialog box.

4. WordPerfect for Windows displays the first 20 or so characters after the insertion point as the default name in the Bookmark Name text box. To accept the default name as the bookmark name, choose the OK button. To give the bookmark another name, replace the highlighted default name by entering your new bookmark name, and then choose OK or press ⏎Enter.

WordPerfect for Windows lets you mark your place in the text of the document with an electronic bookmark, which you can then use to go directly to that place at any time during editing. Using a bookmark is somewhat like marking the section where you're working in a document by inserting a special character in the text and then using the Find feature to locate that character whenever you need to move the insertion point to that section of the document again. The big difference between using a bookmark to mark your place and a special character is that the bookmark isn't visible in the text as a character would be (WordPerfect for Windows inserts a hidden [Bookmark] code), and you don't have to use the Find feature to locate the bookmark; you simply open the

Bookmark dialog box, select the bookmark's name, and then choose the **Go** To button to find it.

With the Bookmark feature, you can create bookmarks that the program can locate and select. Suppose, for example, that you need to copy a title. To make it easy to copy the title into the Clipboard so that you can paste it other places, you can create a bookmark that selects this text when you go to the bookmark, which you can then copy into the Clipboard.

To create a bookmark that selects the text when you go to it, you need only to have the text selected at the time you create the bookmark. Then, when you want WordPerfect to select the bookmark's text, you open the Bookmark dialog box and choose the Go To & **S**elect button. Of course, if you only want to locate the bookmark text without selecting it, you can do this by choosing the **G**o To button rather than the Go To & **S**elect button in the Bookmark dialog box.

When you create a standard bookmark, WordPerfect for Windows inserts a [Bookmark] code that displays the name of the bookmark at the insertion point. When you create a bookmark that selects the text, the program inserts a pair of [Bookmark] codes: one in front of the first selected character and another after the last selected character.

When you're finished with a bookmark, you can remove it from the document either by opening the Bookmark dialog box, selecting the bookmark's name in the **B**ookmark List, and choosing the **D**elete button or by locating the [Bookmark] hidden code in the Reveal Codes window and deleting it.

Using the QuickMark Feature

WordPerfect for Windows offers you a special bookmark called a *QuickMark* that you can set on the fly. To create a QuickMark at the insertion point, press Ctrl+Shift+Q (you also can create the QuickMark by opening the Bookmark dialog box and choosing the **S**et QuickMark button). After you create the QuickMark bookmark, you can move the insertion point directly to it by pressing Ctrl+Q (or you can use the **F**ind QuickMark button in the Bookmark dialog box).

> *Tip:* When you know you will have to return to a place in a document to do more work later, use the QuickMark to mark your place before you save and quit WordPerfect for Windows. Then, when you reopen the document, all you have to do is press Ctrl+Q to move the insertion point to where you left off.

Using Hypertext to Jump from Bookmark to Bookmark

Creating a Hypertext Link to a Bookmark

1. Create the bookmark for which you want to create a hypertext link (see the steps "Inserting a Bookmark into the Document").

2. Make current the document that contains the text you want to use as the hypertext link, and then select the text.

3. Open the **T**ools menu and choose **H**ypertext to display the Hypertext Feature Bar.

4. Press Alt + ⇧Shift + T or click the Create button on the Hypertext Feature Bar to open the Create Hypertext Link dialog box.

   Create...

5. To create a hypertext link to a bookmark in the current document, choose the Go to **B**ookmark radio button, and then select the bookmark name in the drop-down list box.

   To create a hypertext link to a bookmark in another document, choose the Go to Other **D**ocument radio button. Select the document by entering the file name or using the File list button. Then choose **B**ookmark and select the bookmark name in the drop-down list.

   To create a hypertext link that simply opens another document, choose the Go to Other **D**ocument radio button. Select the document by entering the file name or select it without selecting a bookmark in the **B**ookmark text box below.

6. To change the appearance of the document text containing the hypertext link from underlined text in a different color to a button, choose the **B**utton radio button under Appearance.

7. When you finish defining the action and appearance of the hypertext link, choose the OK button or press ⏎Enter to close the Create Hypertext Link dialog box.

You can use the new Hypertext feature to create direct links to the bookmarks that you insert in your documents. By setting up a link to a bookmark, you can jump directly from the hypertext link to the bookmark's location in a single command and return to your starting point just as easily.

Not only can you link to bookmarks in the same document containing the hypertext links, but you can build links to other documents or to bookmarks in other documents as well. When you jump from a hypertext link to another document or a bookmark in another document, WordPerfect for Windows opens the document (if it's not already open) and makes its document window current. If you have linked to a bookmark, the program also moves the insertion point to that bookmark in the other document. If you then jump back to your starting point, the program automatically closes the document (if it had to open the document to make the jump to the bookmark).

When you create a hypertext link, WordPerfect for Windows indicates which text constitutes the hypertext link by making the text underlined and bold and displaying it in another color (green) or, if you prefer, inside a shaded button.

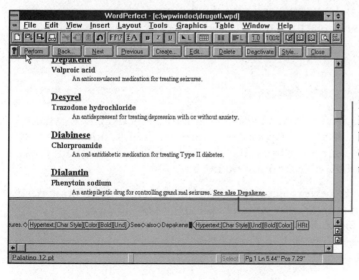

Here you see a hypertext link to a bookmark in the default underlined text style.

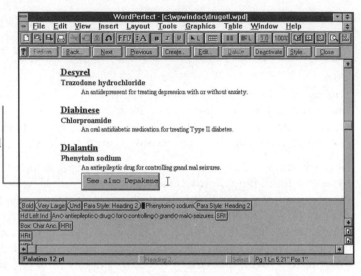

Here you see a hypertext link to a bookmark displayed in a button.

> *Tip:* In addition to creating hypertext links that take you to book-marks in a document, you also can create links that play macros when you select them. To create a hypertext link that plays a macro you have created, open the Create Hypertext Link dialog box, choose the **R**un Macro radio button, and type the file name of the macro to link to or select the macro in the drop-down list. (See chapter 10, "Creating Macros," for more information about macros.)

Making Hypertext Jumps

Before you can make a jump from a hypertext link to the bookmark to which it's linked, you must activate the Hypertext feature. To do this, open the **T**ools menu and choose **H**ypertext to display the Hypertext Feature Bar. Then, press Alt+Shift+A or click the **A**ctivate button on the bar.

After you activate the Hypertext feature, you can jump to the linked bookmark by placing the I-beam pointer somewhere in the hypertext link, and then clicking the primary mouse button. If the link is displayed as text rather than as a button, you also can make the jump to the linked bookmark by placing the insertion point somewhere in the link text, and then pressing Enter. Note that you also can make a jump when the insertion point is not on the hypertext link by choosing the Next button on the Hypertext Feature Bar (or pressing Alt+Shift+N) until the insertion point is on the hypertext link, and then selecting the Perform button (or pressing Alt+Shift+R) or pressing Enter.

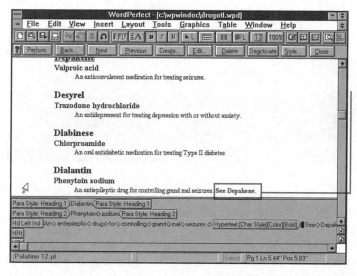

To make a hypertext jump, click somewhere in the hypertext link after activating the Hypertext feature.

After making a jump to a bookmark in the current or a different document, you can return to your starting place (that is, the hypertext link) by pressing Alt+Shift+B or clicking the Back button on the Hypertext Feature Bar. If you're in a different document window that WordPerfect for Windows had to open at the time you selected the Back button, the program will automatically put away the file and close the document before returning to the hypertext callout from which you made the jump. If you made changes to the document with the bookmark before you chose the Back button, the program will prompt you to save your changes before closing the document window.

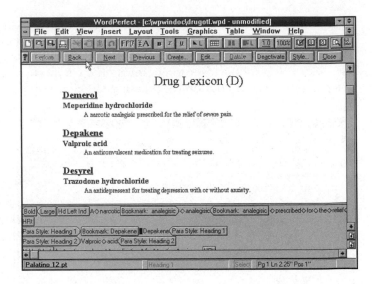

Press Alt+Shift+B or click the **B**ack button to return to the point of origin.

Instead of going back to the hypertext link from which you made the jump, you can move to the next hypertext link in the document by choosing the **N**ext button (Alt+Shift+N), or you can move to the previous link by choosing the **P**revious button (Alt+Shift+P) on the Hypertext Feature Bar. After you have selected the link, you can have it perform the action that you have defined for it or you can edit the link (see the next section).

Editing a Hypertext Link

You can edit a hypertext link at any time after adding it to a document. You can change either the action that the link performs when selected or the way it appears in the document. To edit a link, open the Tools menu and choose the **H**ypertext command to display the Hypertext Feature Bar. Then, move the insertion point to the link you want to change and press Alt+Shift+E or click the **E**dit button on the bar. The Edit Hypertext Link dialog box appears. In the dialog box, you can change the Action or Appearance as needed. When you have finished modifying these options, choose the OK button or press Enter to close the Edit Hypertext Link dialog box and put your changes into effect.

When you use the Text Appearance option to display the hypertext link in the document, you can change the attributes that WordPerfect for Windows applies to this text (by default, the program displays this text underlined in bold and in green). To change the appearance of the hypertext link, open the **T**ools menu and choose Hypertext to display the Hypertext Feature Bar, and then press Alt+Shift+S or click the Style button to display the Styles Editor dialog box, which shows the current settings for the Hypertext style.

To modify the contents of this style, delete the codes that you don't need (for example, you can remove the [Color: Green] code by pressing the Del key or dragging the code out of the Contents box). To add new attributes for displaying hypertext links, choose Layout in the Styles Editor dialog box, and then choose Font. Change the attributes in the Font dialog box to add the code to the Contents box. When you finish modifying the attributes used to display the hypertext links as text, choose the OK button or press Enter to close the Styles Editor and update the appearance of the hypertext links in your document.

Adding Footnotes and Endnotes

Footnotes and *endnotes* provide a standard way to cite references or to give the reader parenthetical information about a topic in the text. Footnotes appear throughout the text at the bottom of the page; endnotes appear together at the end of a section within the document or the end of the document itself. WordPerfect marks both types of notes in the text with a number or character that you specify.

Creating a Footnote or an Endnote

Creating a Footnote or an Endnote

1. Position the insertion point at the place in the text where you want the footnote or endnote number to appear.

2. Open the Insert menu, choose Footnote, or Endnote, and then choose Create.

   WordPerfect for Windows displays the Footnote or Endnote Feature Bar at the top of the document window.

   continues

continued

When you create a footnote, WordPerfect inserts the next available footnote number (using the superscript attribute) at the bottom of the page and waits for you to enter the note text.

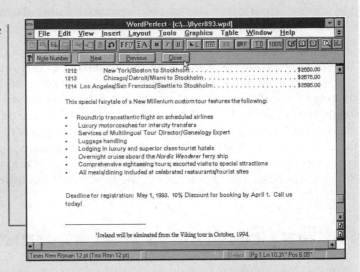

When you create an endnote, WordPerfect inserts the next available footnote number at the end of the document and waits for you to enter the note text.

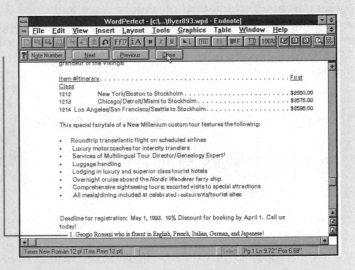

3. Enter the text of your footnote or endnote. You can use most WordPerfect editing and formatting features, including the Speller and the Thesaurus, when entering the text of your note.

4. Press Alt + ⇧Shift + C or choose the Close command to hide the Footnote or Endnote Feature Bar and return to the note number.

WordPerfect inserts the footnote or endnote number in the text at the place of the insertion point, using the superscript Place attribute. The program also places a [Footnote] or [Endnote] code in the document. This code contains information on the formatting of the note number and text.

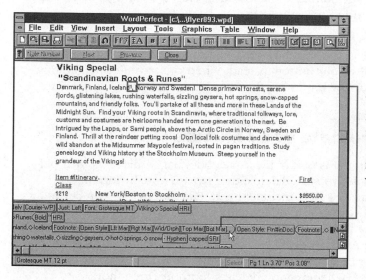

The superscript footnote number is in the text and its [Footnote] code is in the Reveal Codes window.

When you create a footnote, the program draws a separator line and places the footnote text below this line at the bottom of the page. When you create an endnote, WordPerfect automatically places the endnote text at the end of the document. If you want your endnotes to appear on a separate page, insert a hard page break at the end of the document by pressing Ctrl+Enter.

Editing a Footnote or an Endnote

You can edit the text of a footnote or endnote at any time and from any place in the document. To edit the text of a footnote or endnote, open the Insert menu, choose Footnote, or Endnote, and then choose Edit. WordPerfect for Windows displays an Edit Footnote or Edit Endnote dialog box showing the number of the next note in the text. If this is the number of the note you want to edit, choose OK or press Enter. Otherwise, type the correct note number in the Footnote Number or Endnote Number text box before you choose OK or press Enter.

WordPerfect for Windows places the insertion point at the beginning of the note you selected and again displays the Footnote or Endnote Feature Bar. You can then edit the note text as you would any other document text. If, while editing the note text, you inadvertently delete the note number, place the insertion point at the beginning of the text and select the Note Number button on the Footnote or Endnote Feature Bar.

To save your changes to the note and proceed to the next footnote or endnote in the document, select the Next button. To edit the preceding footnote or endnote, select the Previous button instead. When you have finished editing the notes, select the Close button on the Footnote or Endnote Feature Bar.

Deleting a Footnote or an Endnote

Because the note number is part of the same code that contains the text of a footnote or an endnote, you can delete either type of note by locating and deleting its note number in the document text. First, locate the number of the footnote or endnote you want to delete from the document (you can use the Find feature to locate the number quickly by searching for the [Footnote] or [Endnote] code). Open the Reveal Codes window and delete the footnote or endnote code (either by dragging it out of the Reveal Codes window or pressing Del or Backspace). Whenever you delete a footnote or endnote, WordPerfect automatically renumbers all remaining notes in the document.

Changing the Footnote or Endnote Numbering

WordPerfect automatically numbers your footnotes and endnotes starting with the number 1. You also can restart the numbering sequence for your footnotes or endnotes at any place in the document. To renumber your notes, position the insertion point in front of the first note number in the text to be renumbered, open the Insert menu, choose Footnote, or Endnote, and then choose New Number. WordPerfect for Windows displays a Footnote Number or Endnote Number dialog box.

To increase the note number by 1, make sure that the Increase radio button under Existing Number is selected, and then choose OK or press Enter. To decrease the note number by 1, choose the Decrease radio button instead. To enter the new starting number, choose the New Number option, type the number in its text box, and choose OK or press Enter.

Using Footnote and Endnote Options

You use the options in the Footnote or Endnote Options dialog box to change the numbering method, the style used to print the note reference and note text, the spacing and positioning of the notes on the page, and so on.

To change the Footnote or Endnote options for your document, position the insertion point at the place in the document where you want the changes in footnote or endnote formatting to begin.

To open the Footnote Options dialog box, open the Insert menu, choose Footnote, and then choose Options.

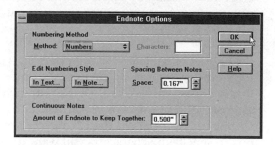

To open the Endnote Options dialog box, open the Insert menu, choose Endnote, and then choose Options.

Table 14.1 explains the usage of the various options you can select when modifying the appearance of the footnotes and endnotes in your document.

Table 14.1   Footnote and Endnote Options

Option or Button	*Function*
Numbering Method	
Method	The default method of numbering for footnotes and endnotes is Numbers, which numbers notes consecutively from the number 1. To change the type of numbering, select Lowercase Letters, Uppercase Letters, Lowercase Roman, Uppercase Roman, or Characters in the Method pop-up list box.
	If you select Lowercase Letters or Uppercase Letters, WordPerfect letters your footnotes or endnotes consecutively from a (A) through (z) Z (the program doubles letters—aa, bb, and so on—if you have more than 26 footnotes or endnotes). If you select Lowercase Roman or Uppercase Roman, the program numbers your footnotes consecutively from i (I) on.
	If you select Characters, WordPerfect marks footnotes or endnotes with asterisks (the first with one asterisk, the second with two asterisks, and so on). When you select Characters, you can use the Characters text box to specify the characters you want to use.
Characters	If you change the Method option from Numbers to Characters, enter in the Characters text box up to five different characters (without any spaces between them) that you want to mark footnotes and endnotes. After using all the characters, WordPerfect

Option or Button	Function
	doubles them, triples them, and so on. If, for example, you enter ! and # as the characters, WordPerfect uses them in this order:

First Note	!
Second Note	#
Third Note	!!
Fourth Note	###
Fifth Note	!!!!
Sixth Note	#####

Edit Numbering Style

In Text: The default style for indicating footnote or endnote numbers in the text of the document is with superscript numbers. To change the way the footnote or endnote number appears in the document, modify the formatting codes in the Contents box of the Styles Editor dialog box. To delete codes, drag them out of the Contents box or press Del or ◄Backspace. To add codes, choose the appropriate commands on the Styles Editor pull-down menus.

In Note: The default style for indicating footnote numbers in the footnote text is with superscript numbers. The default style for indicating endnote numbers in the endnote text is with note numbers followed by periods. To change the way the footnote or endnote number appears in the note, modify the formatting codes in the Contents box of the Styles Editor dialog box. To delete codes, drag them out of the Contents box or press Del or ◄Backspace. To add codes, choose the appropriate commands on the Styles Editor pull-down menus.

continues

Table 14.1 Continued

Option or Button	Function
Spacing Between Notes	
Space	By default, the program uses a line height of 0.167 inch between each note (comparable to the height of a typical 12-point font). To change this distance, enter the new spacing value in this text box.
Position	
Place Notes Below Text	(Footnote Options only.) Prints footnotes immediately below the text on each page.
Place Notes at Bottom of Page	(Footnote Options only.) Prints footnotes at the bottom of the page even when the text does not fill the page.
Separator Button	
Separator	(Footnote Options only.) By default, WordPerfect prints a two-inch line to separate text from the footnotes on a page. In the Line Separator dialog box that opens when you select this button, you can change space above and below the line along with the place, length, and style of the line to be used.
Continued Footnotes or Continuous Notes	
Amount of (Footnote) Endnote to Keep Together	Initially, WordPerfect keeps at least .5 inch of the text of a note together on the bottom of a page. To change the amount of the note the program keeps together, enter the new note height value in this text box.

Option or Button	Function
Insert (continued...) Message	(Footnote Options only.) If a footnote is too long, the program continues its text on the next page. To print *(continued)...* on the last footnote line of the first page and *...(continued)* on the first footnote line of the next page, select this check box.

> *Note:* If you use both footnotes and endnotes in a document, be sure to modify the Numbering Method for one or the other. Otherwise, WordPerfect numbers both the footnotes and endnotes starting with the number 1, and your reader will not be able to tell which numbers refer to footnotes on the page and which refer to endnotes at the end of the chapter.

Changing the Location of Endnotes in the Document

WordPerfect groups endnotes together at the end of the document unless you specify a different location. To specify a different location, you first need to place the insertion point at the place in the document where you want WordPerfect to print the endnotes. Open the Insert menu, choose Endnote, and then choose Placement.

WordPerfect displays the Endnote Placement dialog box containing two radio button options: Insert Endnotes at Insertion Point (the default) and Insert Endnotes at Insertion and Restart Numbering. If your document contains several discrete sections and you want the note numbers in each section to begin with 1, select the Insert Endnotes at Insertion and Restart Numbering option before you choose OK or press Enter.

Using WordPerfect's Other Reference Features

Footnotes and endnotes aren't the only automatic references you can generate in your document. WordPerfect includes several automated referencing features that you can use to create and maintain lists of figures, tables, graphs, and so on; generate a table of contents and an index; and maintain cross-references to specific information in the document. For detailed information on how to use these specialized referencing tools, refer to Que's *Using WordPerfect 6 for Windows,* Special Edition.

Summary

In this chapter, you learned how to use WordPerfect for Windows' annotating capabilities. You learned how to number the lines in a document, add comments (both visual and audio), create bookmarks and hypertext links to them, and create footnotes and endnotes. In addition, you learned about the other sophisticated reference features of WordPerfect, including tables of contents, indexes, lists, tables of authorities, and cross-references.

In the next chapter, you learn how to use WordPerfect's powerful Table feature. As you will see, you can use this feature to set up almost any type of table that you may need to create in your documents. You learn how to set up text in a table and ways that you can set calculations between its values as well.

Creating Tables

15

Understanding table basics

Creating tables

Editing the table structure

Formatting cells, columns, and rows

Creating formulas to calculate new values

T he Table feature is one of the most powerful and versatile features in WordPerfect. Tables created with the Table feature are more like worksheets rather than WordPerfect tables composed of tabbed columns or parallel text columns. Like spreadsheets, these tables are composed of individual cells located at the intersections of the columns and rows in the table. In fact, in WordPerfect 6.0 for Windows, the Table feature offers full spreadsheet capabilities, including the capability to create formulas in cells that include sophisticated built-in functions. If you already have some experience using spreadsheet programs, such as Microsoft Excel, Lotus 1-2-3 for Windows, or PlanPerfect, you already understand the underlying structure of WordPerfect tables and their basic usage.

You can use the Table feature to create almost any kind of table in your WordPerfect document. Tables created with this feature can replace parallel columns used to set columnar material with variable numbers of lines so that the material remains grouped. The Table feature is also perfect for creating tables in newsletters and flyers.

This chapter shows you how to create, format, and edit the structure and contents of a table. First, you learn how to set up the original table structure and add your data to it. Then, you learn how to edit the table structure and modify its contents.

Key Terms in This Chapter

Cell

The intersection of a column and row in a table or spreadsheet. The cell reference is composed of the column letter plus the row number. Cell A1, for example, is the intersection of column A and row 1 of the table.

Cell format

The appearance and size attributes, alignment, and justification applied to the text and numbers entered into the cells of a table.

Columns

Vertical stacks of cells in a table or spreadsheet, named from left to right with letters of the alphabet. The first column is A, the second B, and so on.

Rows

Horizontal lines of cells in a table or spreadsheet, numbered from top to bottom starting with 1.

Spreadsheet

Table containing text, numbers, and formulas created with special spreadsheet software programs, such as Microsoft Excel or Lotus 1-2-3 for Windows. WordPerfect tables can import spreadsheets from all the major spreadsheet publishers. You can link tables and spreadsheets so that changes made to the spreadsheet are automatically made in the WordPerfect table.

Table structure

The physical layout of the table, describing the size of the columns and rows, as well as the type of borders and grid lines used.

Understanding Table Basics

When you create a table, WordPerfect creates a grid of empty boxes, called *cells*, at the insertion point's position in your document. Vertical stacks of cells in the grid make up the columns. Columns are named from left to right with letters of the alphabet, beginning with *A*. A table can have a maximum of 32 columns. Because the alphabet has only 26 letters, however, WordPerfect must begin doubling letters after the 26th column (Z) so that the 27th column is AA, the 28th is BA, and so on (to FA for the 32nd column). Horizontal lines of cells make up the rows in the grid. Rows are numbered from top to bottom, beginning with 1. A table can have a maximum of 32,765 rows.

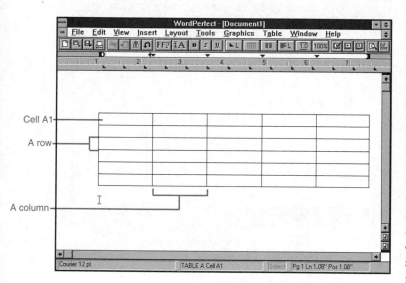

A cell is formed at the intersection of every column and row in the table. Each cell takes its name from its column letter and row number; the cell at the intersection of column A and row 1 is cell A1. The program displays the name of the table followed by the address of the current cell on the status bar as you move the insertion point from cell to cell.

Creating a Table

Creating a Table with the Power Bar's Table Button

1. Position the insertion point on a new line at the place in the document where you want the table to appear.

2. If the Power Bar is not displayed, open the View menu and choose Power Bar.

3. Click the Table button on the Power Bar to display the tiny table grid. Drag to the right to select the columns, and drag down to select the rows you want in the table.

The number of rows and columns for the table are selected on the grid and indicated on the Power Bar.

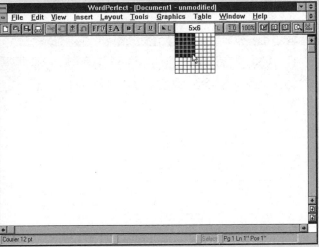

4. When you have selected the desired table size on the grid, release the mouse button.

Creating a new table is simple in WordPerfect. The Power Bar contains a Table button, which shows a miniature version of a table with eight cells (four columns in two rows). When you click the Table button, a tiny grid of cells appears. To indicate how many columns and rows you want in your table, drag the mouse over the columns and rows in this grid. When you release the mouse button, WordPerfect immediately inserts a table with the selected number of columns and rows in the document at the insertion point's position.

After creating the table structure, notice that the table borders are drawn with a single line and that the table is given a name (TABLE A, TABLE B, and so on). This name appears on the Status bar along with the address of the first cell (Cell A1).

If you display the ruler (by pressing Alt+Shift+F3), you will also notice that the triangular-shaped icons that point downward now appear on top of the Ruler. These are the *column-margin icons* that indicate the widths of the columns in the table. The two inward-pointing brackets at the top of the ruler indicate the location of the table's left and right edges.

WordPerfect inserts a [Tbl Def] code with the name of table in the document where you create the table. It inserts [Row] codes to indicate the beginning of each new row and [Cell] codes to indicate the beginning of each new column in the table.

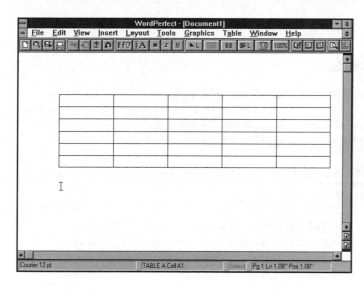

The empty table containing the number of columns and rows selected on the grid attached to the Table button.

You also can create
a table with the
Create Table dialog
box in which you
specify the table
size in the **Columns**
and **Rows** text
boxes.

To display the Create Table dialog box, open the T**a**ble menu (F12) and choose
Create. You also can double-click the Table button on the Power Bar.

After you enter the number of columns and rows for the table in the **Columns**
and **Rows** text boxes, select OK or press Enter. WordPerfect draws the table
structure.

Moving in a Table

To locate the insertion point in a cell of the table, you can use the direction
keys, or you can click a cell with the I-beam pointer. After the insertion point is
located in a table, you can use a combination of keys to move to different cells.
Table 15.1 lists a few of the basic keys you can use to navigate in a table.

Table 15.1   Navigating in a Table with the Keyboard

Key(s)	Movement
Tab	Moves the insertion point forward or Alt + → (right) to the next cell. If the insertion point is located in a row's rightmost cell, Tab moves the insertion point to the first cell in the row below. When the insertion point is in the bottom right cell of the table, Tab adds a blank row to the end of the table.
Shift + Tab	Moves the insertion point backward or Alt + ← (left) to the previous cell. If the insertion point is located in a row's leftmost cell, Shift + Tab moves the insertion point to the rightmost cell in the row above. If the insertion point is in the top left cell, Shift + Tab has no effect.

Key(s)	Movement
Alt + ↑	Moves the insertion point up one cell in a column.
Alt + ↓	Moves the insertion point down one cell in a column.
Esc Esc	Moves the insertion point to the rightmost cell in the row.
Home Home	Moves the insertion point to the leftmost cell in the row.

Entering Text in a Table

Entering Text in a Table Cell

1. Move the insertion point to the cell where you want to enter your text.

2. Type the text for that cell.

   If your line of text is longer than the width of the table column, WordPerfect expands the height of the cells in the row and wraps the text to a new line.

   To format your text on several short lines, press ↵Enter as you normally do to start a new line.

3. To enter text in the next cell to the right, press Tab↹ and begin typing the entry for the column.

   When you advance the insertion point to the next cell, the insertion point is once again positioned at the beginning of the first line of the cell—even when the row has been expanded by a multi-line entry in a previous cell. The text aligns in each row of the table in the same way as the text in parallel columns.

   continues

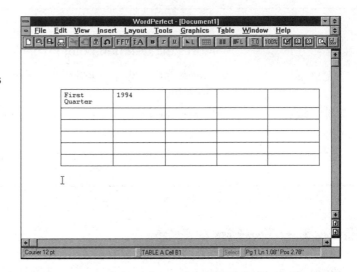

WordPerfect wraps text that is too wide to a new line and expands the height of the row to accommodate the extra line in this cell.

By using Tab, you can make entries across and down the columns and rows of the table. When you finish entering text in a cell in the last column of the table and press Tab, WordPerfect advances the insertion point to the beginning of the cell in the first column of the row below.

To start a new line of text in a cell entry, press Enter just as you do when entering regular document text. To indent an entry with a tab, however, you must press Ctrl+Tab. If you just press Tab, WordPerfect moves the insertion point to the next cell to the right. To indent the lines of text in a cell entry on the left, press the Indent key, F7. To release the tab stop or indent with the margin release, press Ctrl+Shift+Tab. Remember that if you press just Shift+Tab, WordPerfect moves the insertion point to the previous cell in the table.

By default, WordPerfect left-aligns each line of text in the cell. To center- or right-align your text as you enter it, press the Center key combination, Shift+F7, or press the Flush Right key combination, Alt+F7, and then type the entry.

In multi-line entries that wrap to new lines of the cell, notice that WordPerfect left-justifies the text in the cells. To use center-, right-, or full-justification for your text in a particular cell, choose **J**ustification on the **L**ayout and select the **R**ight (Ctrl+R), **C**enter (Ctrl+E), or **F**ull (Ctrl+J) command, and type your entry. You also can change the justification in a cell with the pop-up menu attached to the Justification button on the Power Bar.

Tip: You also can change the justification for a whole column or range of cells in the Format Column or Format Cell dialog box (see "Formatting Cells" and "Formatting Columns" later in this chapter for details). This method is more efficient when you need to change the justification for entire columns, rows, or a group of cells. It also enables you to choose decimal-align as the justification (in addition to left, right, center, and full) to right-align numbers on the decimal point.

Editing Text in a Table

Editing text in a table is like editing text in a regular document. To insert new characters in the text, make sure that you're in Insert mode; then position the I-beam pointer at the place where you want the new characters to appear. Click the mouse to place the insertion point, and begin typing. To delete individual characters, position the insertion point after the last character you want to erase and press Backspace, or position the insertion point before the first character you want to erase and press the Del key.

To erase more than a few characters in a cell, select all the text with the mouse or keyboard, and then press either Backspace or Del. To delete a word in a line, press Ctrl+Backspace. To delete to the end of the line in a cell (not to the end of the row), press Ctrl+Del.

If you need to erase text in a range of cells, select all the cells before you press Del. To delete the contents of an entire row or column, select that row or column and press Del. This procedure erases only the text in the cells in that column or row, not the cells themselves.

Selecting Cells with the Mouse

When editing or formatting tables, WordPerfect enables you to select single cells, entire columns and rows, groups of cells made up of partial columns and rows (referred to as *cell ranges*), or all the cells.

To select a single cell, place the I-beam pointer on one of the edges of the cell you want to select, then, when the I-beam pointer changes shape to an arrow pointing either to the top or left border of the cell, click the mouse button to select the cell.

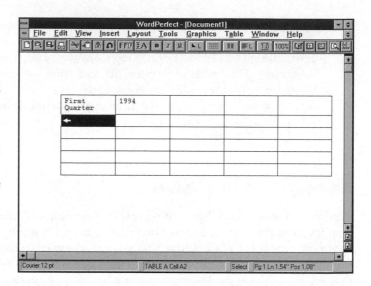

The highlighted cell has been selected by clicking the mouse button after the pointer changes to the arrow pointing toward the left edge of the cell.

To select more than one cell, repeat the preceding procedure with one difference: instead of clicking the mouse button, click and drag the pointer until all the cells you want to use are highlighted. To select an entire row of the table, double-click the mouse button after the pointer changes to an arrow pointing to the left. To select an entire column of the table, double-click the mouse button after the pointer changes to an arrow pointing up. To select all the cells in a table, triple-click the mouse button after the pointer changes either to an arrow pointing left or up.

Remember that any formatting changes you make to the table's structure or contents are applied to all currently selected cells. Make sure that you select the area of the table you want to apply a command to before you choose the command.

> *Tip:* When selecting more than one cell of the table by dragging through the cells of the table, you can place the I-beam anywhere in the first cell, and then drag the pointer to the last cell. You don't have to touch one of the cell's borders or wait until the I-beam changes to an arrow pointing up or to the left before you begin highlighting the cells.

Selecting Cells with the Keyboard

You also can select the cells in a table with the keyboard. Table 15.2 shows the various key combinations and the number of cells each key combination selects. Before you can use these keys, you must place the pointer in one of the table cells. You can position the pointer with the cursor-movement keys or by clicking the cell with the I-beam pointer.

Table 15.2   Selecting Cells in a Table with the Keyboard

Keys	Cells Selected
⬆Shift + F8	Selects the current cell and turns on Select mode.
⬆Shift + Arrow key	Extends the selection one cell, column, or row in the direction of the arrow, depending on what cells are selected at the time.
⬆Shift + Home ⬆Shift + Home	Extends the selection to the beginning of the current row.
⬆Shift + Esc ⬆Shift + Esc	Extends the selection to the end of the current row.
Ctrl + → or Ctrl + ←	Extends the selection to include the current row.
Ctrl + ↑ or Ctrl + ↓	Extends the selection to include the current column.

Cutting and Copying Cells

Cutting or Copying Cells

1. Select the cells in the table that contain information you want to cut or copy to a new place in the table.

2. To move the cells, open the Table QuickMenu and choose **Cut** or open the **Edit** menu and choose **Cut** (or press Ctrl + X). To copy the cells, open the QuickMenu and choose **Copy** or open the **Edit** menu and choose **Copy** (or press Ctrl + C).

continues

continued

WordPerfect displays the Table Cut/Copy dialog box with the **Selection** radio button selected.

Tip: Don't confuse the Text QuickMenu with the Table QuickMenu. The Text QuickMenu appears when you click on the text in a cell that isn't selected with the secondary mouse button (and its menu contains commands like **P**aste, **f**ont, **Q**uickFormat, and so on). The Table QuickMenu appears after you've selected a cell or a group of cells and then clicked the selection with the secondary mouse button (and its menu contains commands like **C**ut, **C**opy, **P**aste, and so on).

3. To cut or copy the information in all rows that contain selected cells, choose the **R**ow radio button. To cut or copy all columns that contain selected cells, choose the **C**olumn radio button. To copy the current cell to another single cell in the table, choose the **C**ell radio button. To copy the current cell down the column so many cells, choose the **C**ell radio button. Choose the **D**own option, and enter the number of cells to copy down in the Times text box. To copy the current cell across the row so many cells, choose the **C**ell radio button, and then choose the **R**ight option. Enter the number of cells to copy in the Times text box.

4. Select the OK button or press ⏎Enter to cut or copy the designated information into the Clipboard.

5. To paste the information into a new place in the table (or a new table in the document), place the insertion point in the first cell, and then open the Table QuickMenu or the **E**dit menu and choose **P**aste (or press Ctrl + V).

The process for cutting, copying, and pasting cells is very similar to the one you use to move and copy regular text in a document. Select the cells either with the mouse or keyboard as described earlier. Open the Table QuickMenu or the **E**dit pull-down menu and choose the **C**ut or **C**opy command, and indicate whether you want to use the selection as highlighted in the table or extend it to include the entire row or column. Finally, place the insertion point in the first cell of the range in which the information is to be moved or copied. Open the Table QuickMenu or the **E**dit pull-down menu, and choose the **P**aste command (or use the Ctrl+V shortcut).

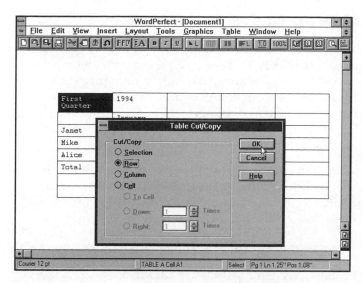

In this example, you select a cell in the first row, and then select the **R**ow radio button in the Table Cut/Copy dialog box.

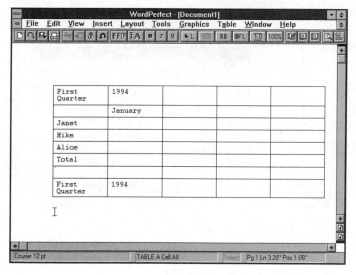

This is the pasted information in its new place.

Using Drag and Drop to Cut and Copy

In addition to the traditional method of cutting and copying text, you can use the use drag-and-drop method as well. To move a cell selection with drag and drop, click the selection and hold down the mouse button until the pointer changes to the drag-and-drop pointer (indicated by a small rectangle with a dotted shadow beneath the regular arrow pointer). Then, drag the pointer until the insertion point is located in the first cell into which you want to move the selection and release the mouse button.

The procedure for copying with drag and drop is almost identical except that you hold the Ctrl key as you click and drag the selection. The drag-and-drop pointer for copying is similar to the one for moving a cell selection except that the rectangle has a dark shadow rather than a dotted shadow.

In this example, you hold down Ctrl as you click the cell selection to copy the names of the months.

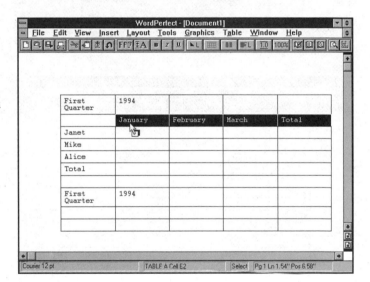

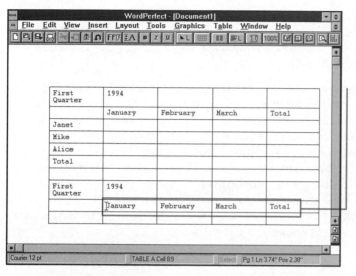

You see the copied information in row 9 after placing the insertion point in cell B9 and releasing the mouse button.

Deleting a Table

To delete a table, you must select all the cells in the table and press the Del key or open the Table QuickMenu and choose **D**elete (remember, you can select all the cells in a table quickly by triple-clicking). You cannot delete a table by locating and selecting and deleting the [Tbl Def] code that defines the structure for the table in the Reveal Codes window.

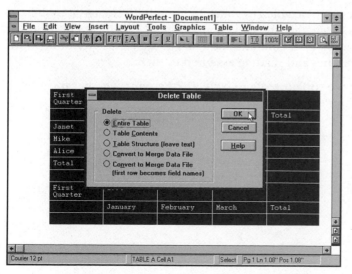

When you press Del after selecting all the cells in a table, WordPerfect displays the Delete Table dialog box.

The Delete Table dialog box prompts you to indicate whether you want to delete the whole table, the table's contents, or the structure, or whether you want to convert the table data to a text data file for merging (see chapter 11 for details on table and text data files used in merge).

To delete both the structure and the text in a table, select the Entire Table radio button. To erase the text and leave the table's structure intact, select the Table Contents button. Or, to delete the structure and leave the text, select the Table Structure (leave text) radio button. When you select this radio button, WordPerfect places tabs between the entry in each column after removing the table grid. To convert a table data file to a text data file with ENDFIELD and ENDRECORD merge codes, choose the Convert to Merge Data File radio button. To convert a table data file to a text data file with FIELDNAMES, ENDFIELD, and ENDRECORD merge codes, choose the Convert to Merge Data File (first row becomes field names) radio button.

> *Caution:* After you select the appropriate radio button in the Delete Table dialog box, WordPerfect for Windows does not ask you to confirm your deletion. Therefore, if you select the wrong option, choose Undo on the Edit menu or press Ctrl+Z immediately to restore the table to its previous state.

Editing the Table Structure

You can edit the structure of a table any time after you have created it in the document, regardless of whether the table contains text. Editing at the structural level affects the number of columns and rows in the table, their width and height, and the border lines and shading assigned to them.

The steps for altering the structure of the table are the same whether the table is empty or contains entries.

Changing the Column Widths

When you first create the table, WordPerfect establishes equally spaced columns. To create these columns, WordPerfect divides the distance between the left and right margins by the number of columns you specify. To modify the width of a column, place the mouse pointer on the column border, and then drag the border when the pointer changes to the *table-sizing arrow* (a double-headed arrow pointing opposite directions). If the ruler is displayed, you can also drag the column-margin icons to change to the column width (when you drag a column-width icon, WordPerfect for Windows displays a dashed, column guide line from the downward-pointing arrow to the column border you're adjusting.

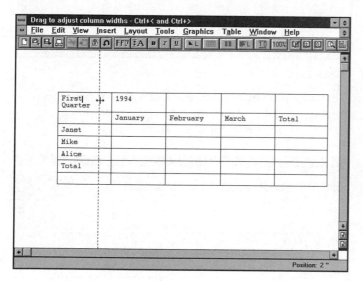

You narrow the First Quarter column (and increase the January column without changing the table width) by dragging the border between it and the 1994 column.

To change the width of a column and, at the same time, the width of the table, you vary the preceding procedure somewhat. This time, hold down the Ctrl key as you drag the appropriate table-sizing arrow.

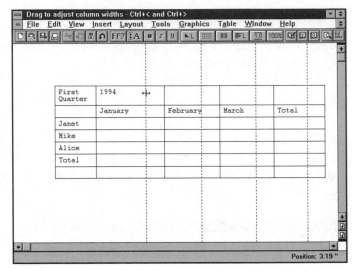

You narrow the January column and the overall width of the table at the same time by pressing Ctrl as you drag the table sizing arrow.

To adjust the width of a column and change the width of adjacent columns to the right without affecting the overall width of the table, you hold down Alt+Shift as you drag the table sizing arrow for the column.

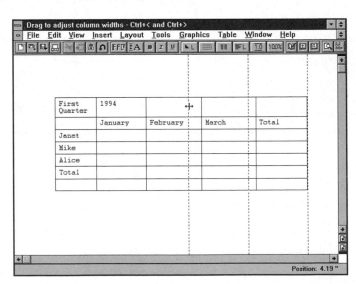

You adjust the width of the February, March, and Total columns without affecting the size of the table by holding down Alt+Shift as you drag the table sizing arrow.

You can increase or decrease the overall width of a table by manipulating the width of the first or last border of the table.

Inserting Columns and Rows

Inserting New Columns and Rows in a Table

1. Place the insertion point in the cell in the column or row of the table where you want to insert the new row(s) or column(s).

2. Open the Table QuickMenu or the Table pull-down menu, and choose the **Insert** command to open the Insert Columns/Rows dialog box.

3. Choose the **Columns** or **Rows** radio button, and enter the number of columns or rows to insert in the associated text box.

4. Choose the **Before** or **After** radio button.

5. Choose OK or press 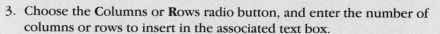Enter.

You can always add blank columns or rows to a table any time after creating its original structure. Remember that you can add a new row to the end of the table simply by pressing Tab when the insertion point is in the last cell. To insert rows in the midst of the table or new columns, you follow the steps outlined.

> *Tip:* WordPerfect for Windows also offers two keyboard shortcuts you can use to insert a single row in a table: Press Alt+Ins to insert a new row before the row containing the insertion point. Press Alt+Shift+Ins to insert a new row after the row containing the insertion point.

Deleting Columns and Rows

Deleting a Column or Row in a Table

1. Place the insertion point in one of the cells in the column or row you want to delete.

2. Open the Table QuickMenu or the Table pull-down menu, and choose **Delete** to display the Delete dialog box.

3. Choose the **Columns** or **Rows** radio button.

4. Enter the number of columns to the right of the insertion point or rows below the insertion point you want to delete.

5. Choose OK or press ⏎Enter to remove the designated columns or rows.

The procedure for deleting columns and rows from a table is similar to the one used to insert them. When you delete a column or row from a table, you remove it from the table's structure along with any information in that column or row.

Tip: To delete the current row, you can press Alt+Del. You can also display the Delete dialog box to remove multiple columns or rows by pressing the Del key after selecting the first column or row to be removed. The entire column or row must be highlighted at the time you press the Del key. Otherwise, WordPerfect for Windows will delete the contents of the cells selected in that column or row without displaying the Delete dialog box.

Joining Cells

Joining Adjacent Cells into One Cell

1. Select all the cells you want to join into one.

2. Open the Table QuickMenu and choose the **Join Cells** command, or open the Table menu and choose **Join** and then **Cell**.

   WordPerfect joins all the cells you have highlighted into one cell.

You can join, or combine, cells to make a larger cell. Before you join the cells, however, you must select them with the mouse or the keyboard. To enter a title for your table that you later center, for example, you could join all the cells in the first row, and then turn on centering and enter the text of the title.

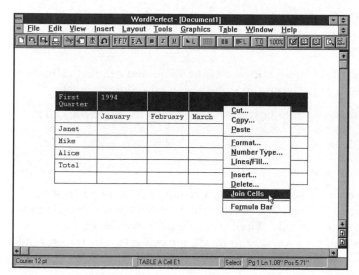

In this example, you want to combine the five selected cells in the first row into one to hold the centered title for the table.

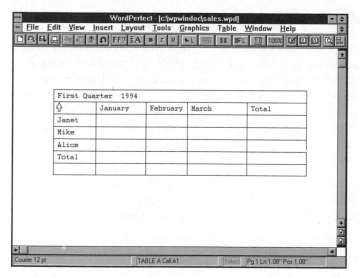

After opening the Table QuickMenu and choosing **J**oin Cells, WordPerfect immediately joins all the selected cells into one larger one.

Splitting a Joined Cell

Splitting a Joined Cell

1. Place the insertion point in the joined cell you want to split.

2. Open the Table QuickMenu and choose S**plit** Cell, or open the **Table** pull-down menu and choose **S**plit and then **C**ell to open the Split Cell dialog box.

3. Choose the **C**olumns radio button to split the joined cell vertically, or choose the **R**ows radio button to split the joined cell horizontally.

4. Enter the number of columns or rows into which to divide the cell in the associated text box.

5. Choose OK or press ⏎Enter.

WordPerfect not only enables you to combine a group of cells into a larger one but also to split a larger cell (created from the union of cells in several columns or rows) into smaller, separate cells. When you split a cell combined from smaller cells, you must indicate whether to divide the cell vertically into several columns or horizontally into several rows.

Joining or Splitting Tables

In addition to joining and splitting cells, you can join and split tables. To join two separate tables in a document into one larger table, the tables must have the same number of columns and you must remove all text and hidden codes between the two tables. In other words, before you try to join two tables, you need to make sure that there are no text or codes between the [Tbl Off] code for the first table and the [Tbl Def] code for the second table. Then, you simply place the insertion point in the first cell in the last row of the first table, open the Table menu, choose **J**oin, and choose **T**able.

To split a table that has been joined, you place the insertion point in the first cell of the row that will become the first row of the new table when the split occurs. Open the Table menu, choose **S**plit, and choose **T**able.

Tip: After splitting one table into two tables, you can separate the tables with text or blank lines. Open the Reveal Codes window (press Alt+F3) and position the cursor in the Reveal Codes window so that it is in front of the [Tbl Def] code that defines the second table. Then start typing your text or press Enter to insert hard returns.

Modifying the Border Lines or Fill Patterns

Changing the Border Lines or Fill Patterns for a Table

1. Select all the cells that contain borders you want to modify. To modify only the borders of a single cell, put the insertion point in that cell. To modify the borders for the entire table, you can place the insertion point in any cell in the table.

2. Open the Table QuickMenu or the Table menu and choose Lines/Fill (or press ⇧Shift+F12) to open the Tables Lines/Fill dialog box.

3. To change the borders lines for the current cell or cell selection, leave the Current Cell or Selection radio button selected. To change the borders for the entire table, choose the Table radio button.

4. If you selected the Current Cell or Selection radio button, select the desired line style for appropriate sides. To select the style by example, click the button next to the Line Styles option for the particular side you need to change, and select the sample of the style in the pop-up list. To select a line style by name, click the drop-down list button and choose the style name in the drop-down list box.

5. If you selected the Table radio button, you choose the Line Style option under Default Line Style and select a new line style to modify the column and row borders in the table. You choose the outside Border option under Border Lines and select a new line style to modify the outside borders of the table.

   To make the line style you selected for the table the new default, choose the Use as Default button.

6. To select a new color for the border lines, click the button to the right of the Custom Color check box, and select the new color you want to use in the palette.

continues

427

continued

7. To select a new fill style, choose the desired fill style for selected cells. To select the fill style by example, click the button next to **F**ill Style and select the sample of the style in the pop-up list. To select a fill style by name, click the drop-down list button and choose the fill style name in the drop-down list box.

8. When you have finished specifying the new line, color, and fill styles for the selected cells or table, choose OK or press ⏎Enter.

A table is visually defined by a grid of border lines. Border lines print with a document only if your printer can print graphics images. The Table Lines/Fill dialog box enables you to edit the type of lines that define the table. You can choose from a wide variety of line styles for the cell or table borders, including single and double lines of various thicknesses as well as dashed, dotted, and thick lines. If your table doesn't require any lines, you also can remove them entirely. When editing the lines in a table, keep in mind that you are really modifying the borders of the cells you have selected.

Use the following Line Styles options to change cell borders. These options are available only when the Current Cell or Selection radio button is selected in the Table Lines/Fill dialog box.

- **L**eft to change the left edges of all selected cells.

- **R**ight to change the right edges of all selected cells.

- **T**op to change the top edges of all selected cells.

- **B**ottom to change the bottom edges of all selected cells.

- **I**nside to change the borders of all the cells inside the selected block.

- **O**utside to change all the outside edges of the selected block.

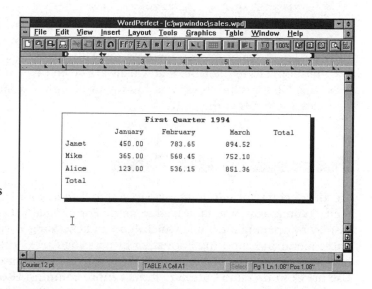

In this figure, you see a table after removing all the inside lines and creating the drop-shadow effect by choosing <None> as the Default Line Style and Shadow as the Border Lines style.

> *Tip:* Removing the border lines around cells with the options in the Tables Lines/Fill dialog box does not have the same effect as joining the cells. When you select <None> as the line option, the borders between cells remain even though the borders are now invisible. When you join cells, however, WordPerfect actually removes the borders between them.

WordPerfect for Windows includes a wide variety of fill patterns that you can apply to a cell selection. The most basic fill patterns are simply shading based on the percentage of gray to be used (these range from a 10% Fill to a 100% Fill, which is equivalent to black). Instead of simply shading the cell selection, you can choose a different fill pattern based on various line patterns (such as Horizontal Lines, Vertical Lines, or a number of Diagonal Lines) or a gradient fill pattern where the shading gradually goes from light to dark in a particular pattern (you can choose between a rectangular or circular pattern of gradient fill).

By default, WordPerfect uses a gray color for the dots of lines used to create the fill pattern on a white background. If you have a color monitor or printer, you can spruce up the fill pattern you've selected for your tables cells by changing the Foreground (the color used for the dots or lines in the pattern) and/or the Background color. When choosing new foreground and background colors, be sure that you use highly contrasting colors (one light and the other very dark). Otherwise, you will end up with a muddy effect that washes out the pattern.

> *Tip:* Be very judicious with your choice of fill pattern when the cells you're applying them to contain text or numerical entries. Reserve the heavy shading (anything over 20% Fill), line fills, and gradient fills for cells in the table that will always be empty. Use no more than 10% Fill for cells whose data you want to emphasize such as subtotals and totals in the table.

Formatting the Table

WordPerfect 6.0 for Windows enables you to format your tables on four levels (cell, column, row, and table), all from the Format dialog box (which you display by opening the Table QuickMenu and choosing Format, opening the Table menu and choosing Format, or by pressing Ctrl+F12). Use the Cell radio button in the Format dialog box to format only the current cell or cell selection. Use the Column radio button to format entire columns. Use the Row radio button to modify the number of lines in a row as well as the row height and row margins. Use the Table radio button to modify the formatting for the entire table.

Selecting Fonts for a Table

Before you learn about the various formatting changes you can assign to cells, columns, rows, or the entire table, you need to learn how to assign different fonts in a table. First, you need to keep in mind that you don't assign fonts to the cells of your table with the options in the Format dialog box you are about to explore.

 In WordPerfect, fonts are not assigned to the table structure that holds your text, but to the actual text, you enter into the table structure. To change the font, you must select the text in a cell rather than the cell itself, and then choose the new font with the Font button on the Power Bar or with the Font dialog box. The only attributes you can assign to entire columns or groups of selected cells are appearance and text size attributes such as Bold, Underline, Superscript, and the like.

To select the font you want to use for the text of an entire table, all you have to do is place the insertion point in front of the first cell of the table, and then choose your new font using the Font and Size buttons on the Power Bar or the Font dialog box. If, however, you need to use a different font or point size in different cells, you must select the text in each cell and make the font change. You must repeat this procedure of selecting all the text in every single cell that needs a new font; you cannot select a group, column, or row of cells with the I-beam because this selects the cells as well as the text they contain.

> *Tip:* The easiest way to change the size of the text in a table is to select the initial font and size you want used for most of your text (such as 10-point Times Roman) at the beginning of the table. Then use the size options (**Fine, Small, Large, Very Large,** and **Extra Large**) in the Format dialog box to change the size of the selected cells. The actual point size assigned to the text in the selected cells when you choose a text size attribute is then tied directly to the point size of the initial font for the table. You will see the new font size in the table; the Status bar continues to show the initial font as you move the insertion point through the table.

Formatting Cells

Formatting the Current Cell or Cell Selection

1. Select the block of cells you want to format.

2. Open the Table QuickMenu and choose **Format**, or open the Table menu and choose **Format** or press Ctrl + F12.

3. Select the Cell radio button.

continues

431

continued

WordPerfect displays cell options in the Format dialog box.

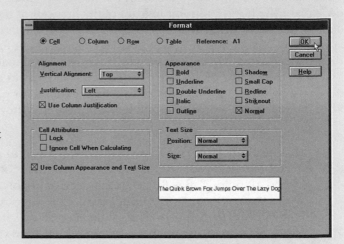

4. Change all the settings you want for the selected cell(s) by modifying any of the options.

5. Select OK or press ⊂Enter⊃ to put the formats you have selected into effect in the table.

You can use the options in the Format dialog box after selecting the **Cell** radio button to assign appearance and size attributes or new justification to just those cells that you have selected. If you have already formatted a column with another of these attributes, you can decide whether the column settings should override the cell settings. In addition, you can set the vertical alignment of the text in the selected cells, lock the cells so that they cannot be changed, or indicate that their contents should not be used in any math calculations you perform.

The options in the Format Dialog box are as follows:

*   To change the vertical alignment of the text in the cells, select the appropriate option (**T**op, **B**ottom, or **C**enter) in the **V**ertical Alignment pop-up list.

*   To change the justification of the columns, select the appropriate option (**L**eft, **R**ight, **C**enter, **F**ull, **A**ll, or **D**ecimal Align) in the pop-up list. Select the **D**ecimal Align option if you will be entering numbers in the column and want to align them on the decimal point.

- To lock the cells so that no further changes can be made to their contents or formatting, choose the Lock option to place an × in its check box.

- To have WordPerfect disregard numbers in the selected cells when performing calculations involving the cells, choose Ignore Cell When Calculating to place an × in its check box.

- To add enhancements to the text in columns, place a check in all the appropriate Appearance and Text Size check boxes.

Formatting Columns

Formatting Columns

1. Place the insertion point in one of the cells in the column you want to format.

   To format multiple columns, select a group of cells that includes all the columns you want to format. To format all the columns in a table, select an entire row of the table.

2. Open the Table QuickMenu and choose Format, or open the Table pull-down menu and choose Format, or press Ctrl + F12.

3. Select the Column radio button.

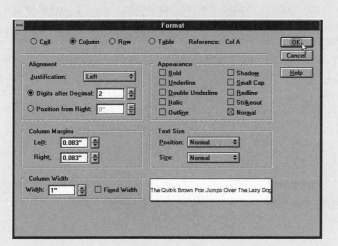

WordPerfect displays column options in the Format dialog box.

continues

continued

4. Change all the settings you want for the selected column(s) by modifying any of the options.

5. When you have finished selecting all the column format settings, choose OK or press ⏎Enter to put the formats you have selected into effect in the table.

Column formatting includes the justification of the text, the number of decimal points in numbers in the columns, the exact position of the column margins, appearance and size attributes, and the type of justification for all the cells in the selected columns. In addition, if you enter numbers in a column and align them on the decimal point, you can control how many decimal places are displayed on a single line of each cell.

The options in this format dialog box are as follows:

- To change the justification of the columns, select the appropriate Justification option (**L**eft, **R**ight, **C**enter, **F**ull, **A**ll, or **D**ecimal Align) in the pop-up list. Select the **D**ecimal Align option if you will be entering numbers in the column and want to align them on the decimal point.

- By default, WordPerfect displays only two decimal places on a single line when you enter numbers in cells that use decimal-align justification. It also restricts the decimal places to two in calculated results in cells. To change the number of places in the column, enter a number other than 2 in the Digits after Decimal text box. To change the position of the numbers from the right edge of the column, enter a new dimension in the Place from Right text box as well.

- To change the position of the left and right margins in the selected columns, select the Left or Right options and enter the distance from the left or right edge of the column and the column margin. To change the width of the column (or the first column if more than one is selected), enter a new width in the Width text box. To prevent anyone from changing the column width further, choose the Fixed Width option to put an × in its check box.

- To add enhancements to the text in columns, place a check in all the appropriate appearance and text size check boxes.

Formatting Rows

Formatting Rows of a Table

1. Place the insertion point in a cell in the row you want to format. To format multiple rows, select a group of cells that includes all the rows you want to format. To format all rows in the table, select all the cells in a single column.

2. Open the Table QuickMenu and choose Format, or open the Table pull-down menu and choose Format, or press Ctrl + F12.

3. Select the Row radio button.

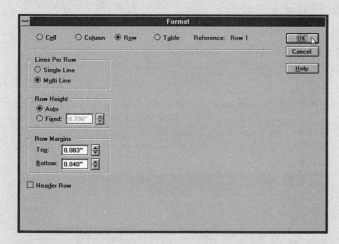

WordPerfect displays row options in the Format dialog box.

4. To limit the number of lines in the row to 1, select the Single Line radio button under Lines Per Row.

5. To fix the row height to a specific height, select the Fixed option button under Row Height, and then enter the maximum height in the Fixed text box.

6. To set the top and bottom margins for the cells in the selected rows, choose the Top or Bottom options and enter the distance from the top or bottom edge of the row and the row margin.

7. To make the selected rows header rows that are printed at the top of each page when the table spans multiple pages in the document, choose the Header Row option to put an × in its check box.

8. Select OK or press ↵Enter to put your row formatting changes into effect in the table.

435

As you learned earlier, WordPerfect automatically expands the height of the cell to accommodate multiple lines of text. The program also automatically increases the height of the row if you increase the size of the text in one of its cells. Although most of the time you will want to use this automatic expansion in the number of lines and the row height, you can use the options in the Format dialog box after you choose the Row radio button to limit the lines per row or fix the maximum height for the row. You can also use these options to change the top and bottom margins of the selected rows and to designate the rows as header rows to be printed at the top of each page when the table spans more than one page.

Formatting the Entire Table

Formatting the Entire Table

1. Place the insertion point in any one of the cells in the table that you want to format.

2. Open the Table QuickMenu and choose Format, or open the Table menu and choose Format, or press Ctrl + F12.

3. Select the Table radio button.

WordPerfect displays table options in the Format dialog box.

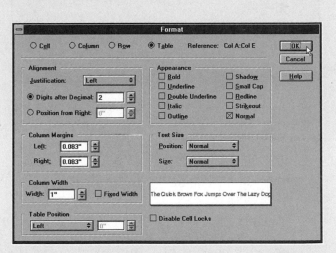

4. Make all the necessary changes to the Table options.

5. Select OK or press ⏎Enter to put your table formatting changes into effect.

When you select the Table radio button in the Format dialog box, WordPerfect for Windows offers several options that affect the entire table. You can use these options to change the settings to suit the style of your table and the amount of information you have to fit in the table you're creating. These settings include the alignment and width of all cells, the position of the entire table in relation to the left and right document margins, the appearance and text size options applied to all cells, and temporarily disabling protection for all locked cells.

The options for formatting the entire table in the Table Format dialog box are as follows:

- To change the justification of all the cells, select the appropriate Justification option (Left, Right, Center, Full, All, or Decimal Align) in the pop-up list. Select the Decimal Align option if you will be entering numbers in the column and want to align them on the decimal point.

- By default, WordPerfect displays only two decimal places on a single line when you enter numbers in cells that use decimal-align justification. It also restricts the decimal places to two in calculated results in cells. To change the number of places in the cells, enter a number other than 2 in the Digits after Decimal text box. To change the position of the numbers from the right edge of the cells, enter a new dimension in the Place from Right text box as well.

- To change the position of the left and right margins in all columns in the table, select the Left or Right options and enter the distance from the left or right edge of the column and the column margin. To change the width of the column (or the first column if more than one is selected), enter a new width in the Width text box. To prevent anyone from changing the column width further, choose the Fixed Width option to put an × in its check box.

- To change the position of the table in relation to the left and right margins of the document, select the appropriate option as follows:

  Left to align the table with the left margin.

  Right to align the table with the right margin.

  Center to center the table between the margins.

  Full to expand the table in the margins.

From Left Edge to specify the distance that the table should be indented from the left margin. Enter the amount that the table should be indented in the text box to the right of this Table Place option.

- To add enhancements to the text in columns, place a check in all the appropriate appearance and text size check boxes.

- To turn off protection to all locked cells temporarily, choose the Disable Cell Locks option to place an × in its check box. This enables you to make editing changes in locked cells without having to change their locked status. After making your changes, you can return to the Format dialog box and remove the × in this check box to once again protect the cells from further changes.

Performing Calculations in a Table

Entering a Simple Formula in a Table Cell

1. Place the insertion point in the cell that is to contain the calculated result.

2. If the Cell Formula Entry mode is turned on, type the formula— including the cell references and mathematical operator(s)—directly in the cell.

   If the Table Formula Feature bar is displayed, you can enter your formula in the Formula bar as follows: click the text box to place the insertion point in it, click the first cell you want to refer to, type the mathematical operator, click the second cell you want to refer to, and finally, click the button with the check mark to insert the formula in the current cell and calculate the result (click the button with the × in it to cancel the formula entry).

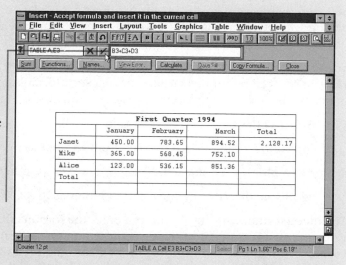

You can enter your formula in the Formula bar, and then calculate the result by clicking the button with the check mark.

3. If you entered the formula directly into the table cell, choose the Calculate command on the Table menu, choose the Calc Table button or choose the Calculate button on the Table Formula Feature bar (if it's displayed) to calculate the formula and display the result in the current cell.

   If you made a mistake when building or entering the formula, WordPerfect for Windows will display ?? instead of the expected answer. If this is the case, you must edit the formula, and then recalculate the table.

WordPerfect for Windows makes it possible to enter formulas that perform simple to quite complex calculations, using the values in your table. When you create a formula in a table, you refer to the cells that contain the numbers you want to use rather than entering the numbers themselves. If, for example, you want to divide the number 100 (entered in cell A2) by the number 5 (entered in cell B2) and have WordPerfect enter the answer in cell C2, you would enter

A2/B2

into cell C2 rather than enter the formula 100/5. Of course, either formula gives you the same answer of 20). By building the formula with cell references rather than numbers, you retain the possibility of modifying the answer without having to change the formula. If, for example, you replace 100 in cell A2 with

500, and then have WordPerfect for Windows recalculate the table, the program will update the answer in cell C2 to 100 without requiring any editing of the original A2/B2 formula.

You can create simple formulas that add, subtract, multiply, and divide the value in one cell by another. When creating such formulas, you use the following mathematical operators between the cell addresses:

- + to add the values in the cells as in A2+A3.

- – to subtract the value in one cell from another as in A2–A3.

- * to multiply the value in one cell by another as in A2*A3.

- / to divide the value in one cell by another as in A2/A3.

To enter a formula into a cell, you can enter the formula directly into the cell when the Cell Formula Entry mode is turned on, or you can display the Table Formula Feature bar and enter the formula into the Formula bar. To tell whether the Cell Formula Entry mode is turned on, you open the Table pull-down and check whether the Cell Formula Entry command has a check mark in front of it. If not, you can turn on this mode by choosing this command.

Note that when you enter a formula directly into a cell when Cell Formula Entry mode is active, you still have to recalculate the table either by choosing the Calculate button on the Table Formula Feature bar (if it's displayed) or by opening the Table menu and choosing Calculate, and then choosing the Calculate **T**able or Calculate **D**ocument button.

To display the Table Formula Feature bar to enter a formula in the Formula bar, open the Table QuickMenu and choose Formula Bar, or open the Table pull-down menu and choose Formula. After displaying the formula bar, you can enter the formula by clicking the Formula bar text box where you build the formula. After you have completed the formula entry, you insert and calculate the formula by clicking the button with the check mark.

> *Tip:* For more information on creating formulas in tables and using the other built-in functions besides SUM, see Que's *Using WordPerfect 6 for Windows,* Special Edition.

Using Data Fill

Creating a Series of Numbers or Names

1. Enter the first entries in the series you want to create in adjacent cells in the same column or row (such as Jan and Feb when you want to enter a series of the 12 months, or 100 and 200 when you want to create the number series 100, 200, 300, 400, and so on).

2. Select the cells with the sample series entries along with all the blank cells in the same column or row that you want to fill with the remainder of the series.

3. To fill all the empty cells in the selection with the remainder of the series, open the Table menu and choose Data Fill, or press Ctrl + ⇧Shift + F12, or choose the Data Fill button on Table Formula Feature bar.

Data Fill

You can use the new Data Fill command on the Table menu to have Word-Perfect for Windows finish out a series of numbers or entries such as the a list of days of the week or the months of the year. To use the Data Fill feature, enter the first couple of entries in the series, and then select these cells plus all the blank cells in the same column or row where you want the program to fill out the series.

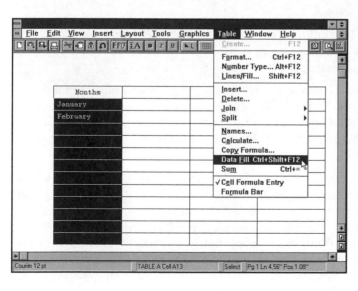

To create a series with the name of the 12 months, you enter *January* and *February* in two adjacent cells, and then select them plus all the blank cells where the other 10 months are to appear.

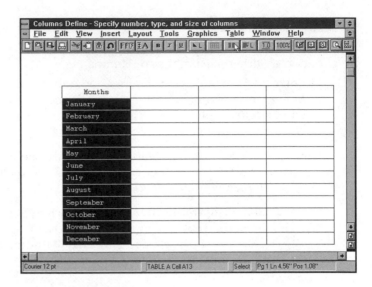

After you open the Table menu and choose Data Fill, WordPerfect fills in the other months for you.

Using the Sum Function

Totaling a Range of Cells with the SUM Function

1. Select all the cells in a column or across the row that you want to sum plus the single blank cell below or to the right where you want the total to appear.

2. Open the Table menu and choose Sum or press Ctrl + = to create the SUM formula. You can also choose the Sum button on the Table Formula bar, if it's displayed.

3. If you open the Table menu and choose Sum instead of pressing Ctrl + =, you must open the Table menu and choose Calculate. Then choose the Calc Table button or choose the Calculate button on the Table Formula Feature bar, if it's displayed.

Without a doubt, the most commonly used function is the SUM function, which totals all the values in a range or list of cells. To create a SUM function in a table cell, you simply select the cells to be totaled plus the empty cell to hold the answer and press Ctrl+=. You can also sum a column or row of numbers by positioning the insertion point in the empty cell at the bottom of the column or in the row to the right of the values where the total is to appear, and then pressing Ctrl+= or opening the Table menu and choosing Sum. After creating the SUM function in the cell, you still have to open the Table menu and choose Calculate and choose the Calc Table button to have WordPerfect compute the total and place the sum in the selected cell.

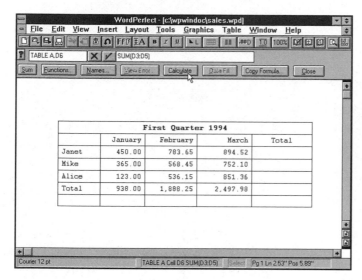

To total the monthly sales for January, February, and March, you select all the cells with the sale figures plus the blank cells where the totals are to appear, and then press Ctrl+= or choose the Sum and Calculate buttons on the Table Formula Feature bar.

Summary

In this chapter, you learned how to use WordPerfect tables to set all types of text and perform simple calculations. You learned how to create the table structure, enter table data, format your data, and create and calculate formulas.

In the next chapter, you learn about using columns and graphics in a document. You learn how easy it is in WordPerfect to set text in columns as well as to spruce up a document with graphic images, borders, and lines.

16

Using Columns and Graphics

WordPerfect for Windows makes it easy to set up columns and add graphics to your documents. With the Columns button on the Power Bar, you can instantly set your document text in two, three, four, or five columns. Graphics that you bring into your documents remain visible on-screen at all times. To reposition or resize graphics, there is no need to switch to a special graphics editing mode—you can size and move graphics directly in the document window. If you use WordPerfect for desktop publishing, you will appreciate the capability to mix graphics and text, and you will appreciate the ease with which you can use columns.

In this chapter, you will learn how to set text in columns, retrieve and manipulate graphics images, and draw borders and graphics lines in your documents.

Defining columns

Understanding graphics in WordPerfect

Inserting, repositioning, and resizing a graphics image

Adding a caption to a graphics image

Editing a graphic with the Image Tools palette

Using borders and graphics lines

Key Terms in This Chapter

Borders

Graphics lines drawn around a para-graph or page or between or around newspaper columns in a document. Borders automatically expand and contract to suit changes made to the paragraph text or the formatting of the page or columns to which they are applied.

Graphics box

A box defined to hold a figure, a table, text, user-defined elements, or an equation, and to have certain characteristics, such as border style and caption style.

Graphics lines

Horizontal or vertical rules of various weights and lengths that you can directly move and size with the mouse.

Newspaper columns

Columns in which text flows from the top of a column to the bottom of the column and then wraps to the top of the next column, as in newsletters.

Text columns

Newspaper or parallel columns created with the **Columns** command on the **Layout** menu or the Columns button on the Power Bar as opposed to tabular columns set up on-the-fly by pressing the Tab or Indent (F7) key.

Defining Columns

Defining Newspaper Columns with the Columns Button

1. Position the insertion point at the place in the document where you want the columns to begin.

2. Click the Columns button on the Power Bar, drag to the appropriate columns command (2 Columns, 3 Columns, 4 Columns, or 5 Columns) in the pop-up menu, and then release the mouse button.

WordPerfect for Windows supports four types of columns: newspaper, balanced newspaper, parallel, and parallel with block protect. In standard newspaper columns, text flows down the first column, and then wraps at the bottom of the page and starts the next column. In balanced newspaper columns, WordPerfect wraps the columns wherever necessary to make sure that they always line with each other at the top and bottom. In parallel columns, text flows across the page. In parallel columns with block protect, WordPerfect makes sure that all text within each parallel column always stays together on the page.

Newspaper and parallel columns are known as *text columns* in WordPerfect to differentiate them from *tabular columns* (columns created with tabs). Newspaper columns are used in magazine articles, newsletters, and brochures. Parallel columns are used in inventory lists, itineraries, and schedules.

This document uses two balanced newspaper columns where text flows from the bottom of one column to the top of the next column. You can define Newspaper columns before or after you enter the text.

With the Columns button on the Power Bar, you can set up to five standard newspaper columns. If you want to set up more than five newspaper columns (the program supports a maximum of 24 columns) or if you want to define balanced newspaper columns or either type of parallel columns, you need to use the options in the Columns dialog box.

To open the Columns dialog box, you double-click the Columns button on the Power Bar or select the Define command on the pop-up menu that appears when you click this button. If you prefer to use the keyboard, you can open this dialog box by opening the **L**ayout menu, choosing the **C**olumns command, and then choosing the **D**efine command on the cascading menu.

You can define two, three, four, or five standard newspaper columns for a document by selecting the Columns button on the Power Bar.

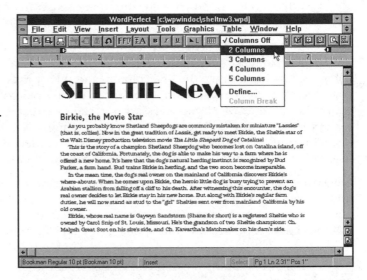

In this example, regular newspaper columns were creating by selecting the 2 Columns command on the pop-up menu attached to the Columns button on the Power Bar.

After you define the number and type of columns for your document, you can return to normal text at any place in the document by turning off the Columns feature. When you define columns, WordPerfect inserts [Col Def] codes at the insertion point's position in the document. To turn off the Columns feature, you can select the Columns Off command on the pop-up menu that appears when you click the Columns button on the Power Bar; or you can open the **Layout** menu, choose Columns, and then choose **Off** on the cascading menu.

Defining Columns in the Columns Dialog Box

Defining Columns in the Columns Dialog Box

1. Position the insertion point at the place in the document where you want the columns to begin.

2. Double-click the Columns button or select the Define command on its pop-up menu. If you prefer using the keyboard, open the **Layout** menu, choose Columns, and then choose **Define**.

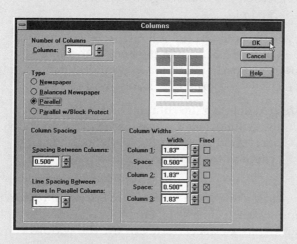

WordPerfect displays the Columns dialog box.

3. By default, WordPerfect selects the setting for creating two columns. To increase the number of columns, enter a new number (up to 24) in the **Columns** text box.

4. By default, the program selects Newspaper as the type of columns to create standard newspaper columns. To create balanced newspaper columns, choose the **Balanced Newspaper** radio button under Type.

continues

449

continued

To create standard parallel columns, choose the **P**arallel radio button. To parallel information together on a page, choose the **P**arallel w/Block Protect radio button.

5. By default, WordPerfect divides the line length into columns of equal size with a distance of one-half inch between columns. To change the amount of space between each column (this space is known as the *gutter*), enter a new value in the **S**pacing Between Columns text box or click the up- and down-arrow buttons to increase or decrease the value in the text box.

6. Make any needed changes in the Column Widths area of the dialog box. To vary the size of the columns, enter the new column width in the text box. To vary the gutter space between a pair of columns, enter the new Space settings. To allow WordPerfect to adjust the dimensions of a column width or gutter space if needed, remove the × from the Fixed check box. To make sure that WordPerfect does not make adjustments to a column width or gutter space, select the Fixed check box to place an × in it.

7. If you're creating parallel columns (of either type) and you want to use spacing other than single spacing in the lines of text in each column, choose the Line Spacing Between Rows in Parallel Columns option and enter the new line spacing in its text box.

8. When you have finished defining the columns, check the layout of the sample page in the Columns dialog box. If everything looks all right, choose the OK button or press ⏎Enter to define and simulta-neously turn on the columns in your document.

You must use the Columns dialog box when you want to create more than five standard newspaper columns, balanced newspaper columns, or parallel columns (either standard or with block protect). You can use the options in the Columns dialog box to vary the widths of the columns or to change the amount of space between each pair of columns. The Column Widths options are:

- *Width.* To vary the size of the columns, enter the new column width in the text box of the appropriate column under Column Widths.

- *Space.* To vary the gutter space between a particular pair of columns, enter the new settings.

- *Fixed.* To allow the program to vary the dimensions that you enter for a particular column width or gutter space if necessary, remove the × from the associated Fixed check box. To make sure that no adjustment is ever made to a particular column width or gutter space, select the associated Fixed check box to place an × in it.

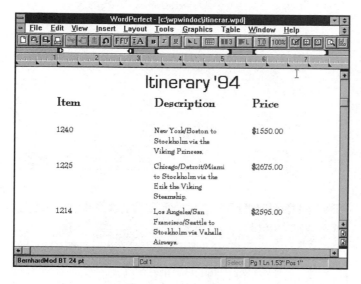

In this figure, you see text set in three parallel columns created with the options in the Columns dialog box.

Adjusting Widths of Newspaper Columns from the Ruler

WordPerfect makes adjusting the width of any type of text columns from the Ruler easy. To change the width of a column, position the insertion point at the place in the text where you want to adjust the column's width. Then drag the appropriate Column-Margin icon to the desired position on the Ruler. To adjust the size of two adjacent columns without changing the size of the gutter, click the gutter area (the gray area between the Column-Margin icons) and drag it to a new position on the tab ruler.

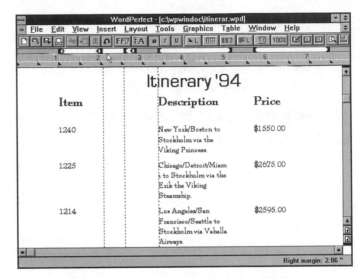

In this example, you decrease the size of the first column and simultaneously increase the size of the second one by dragging the gutter to the left.

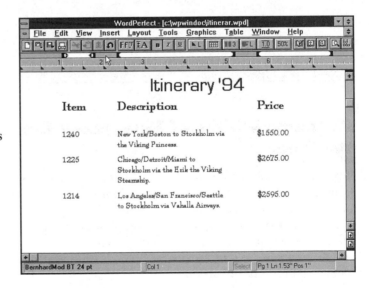

When you release the mouse button, WordPerfect reflows the text according to the new sizes of the columns.

Tip: Before you start adjusting the widths of columns in your document, make sure that the Auto Code Placement feature is on. This ensures that WordPerfect updates the [Col Def] code at the beginning of the columns instead of adding a new definition in the document.

Entering Text in Columns

You can define text columns and turn them on before entering text; or, you can enter all the text before defining the columns. When you create newspaper columns, it is easier to type the text and then define and turn on the columns. When you create parallel columns, the opposite is true: it is easier to define the columns and then turn them on before entering the text.

After defining and turning on newspaper columns, enter text as you normally would. Press Enter to terminate paragraphs in each column. When you reach the bottom of a column, WordPerfect moves the insertion point to the top of the next column. If you want to end a column before you reach the bottom of the page and move to the top of the next column to enter text, press Ctrl+Enter or open the Layout menu, choose Columns, and then choose Column on the cascading menu to insert a column break [HCol] code. When you reach the end of the page in the last column, WordPerfect moves the insertion point to the top of the first column on the next page.

When entering text in parallel columns, use Ctrl+Enter or the Column Break command to terminate each column entry and to move to the next column. When you press Ctrl+Enter or this command at the end of the last parallel column entry on the right, WordPerfect moves the insertion point to the first column in the next row. This row is two lines down from the longest entry in the previous row of parallel columns.

When you are editing text, you can move the insertion point to a new location by clicking in the text you want to edit. If you prefer using the keyboard, press Alt+← to move the insertion point to the next column on the left; or, press Alt+→ to move the insertion point to the next column on the right. To move the insertion point to different columns, you also can use the Go To dialog box (accessed by pressing Ctrl+G or opening the Edit menu and choosing Go To).

After defining and turning on columns in a document, WordPerfect displays new options on the **Position** pop-up list in the Go To dialog box. Use these options to move between columns.

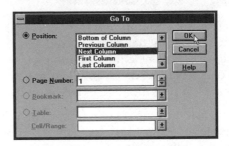

As mentioned earlier, you can turn off columns whenever you want the text formatted into a single column that spans the entire width of the left and right margins. You can turn off the columns either by choosing the Columns Off command on the Columns button pop-up list on the Power Bar or by opening the **Layout** menu, choosing **Columns**, and then choosing **Off** on the cascading menu.

Understanding Graphics in WordPerfect

In WordPerfect 6.0 for Windows documents, you can place graphics images in one of four types of graphics boxes: figure, equation, text, or custom. After you create a graphics box, you can insert text, graphics, charts, or graphs created with other external programs such as CorelDRAW!, DrawPerfect, Excel, or Lotus 1-2-3. You can place graphics boxes in the body of a document as well as in headers, footers, footnotes, or endnotes.

If you are setting equations, you can use WordPerfect's special Equation Editor to create them in an equation box. You also can draw horizontal or vertical graphics lines (also known as *rules*) or place borders around paragraphs or pages of text or between columns in a document. You can retrieve from outside WordPerfect other types of graphics, such as charts, clip-art drawings, and scanned images created for Windows. You can insert these graphics directly into a WordPerfect document.

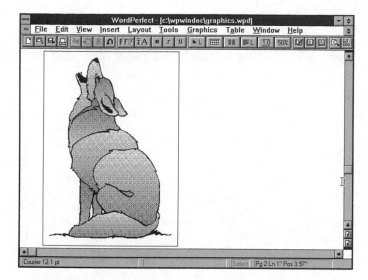

This is a sample figure box containing a drawing supplied with WordPerfect for Windows.

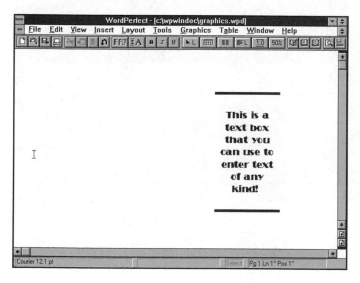

This is a sample text box created with WordPerfect for Windows.

This is a sample equation box containing an equation created with the Equation Editor.

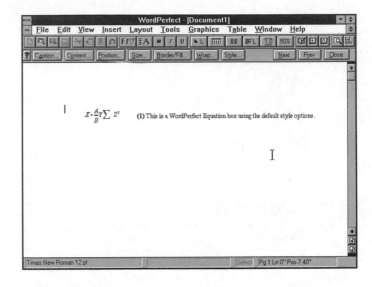

This is a custom graphics box containing a WordPerfect graphics image; the graphics image uses the Button box style.

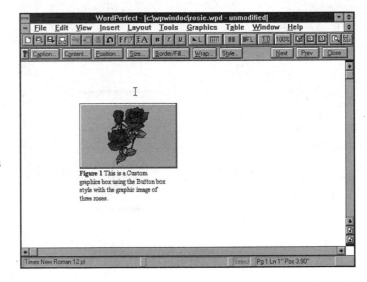

When you retrieve a compatible graphics image with the **Figure** command on the **Graphics** pull-down menu or paste an image from the Clipboard into your document, WordPerfect creates a figure box to hold the graphics image. You then can move and size this figure box on the page by using the mouse.

You can combine a variety of graphics on a page. The following newsletter, created in WordPerfect, mixes several different types of graphics.

Volume II No. 9 June, 1994

SHELTIE News

Birkie, the Movie Star

As you probably know Shetland Sheepdogs are commonly mistaken for miniature "Lassies" (that is, collies). Now in the great tradition of *Lassie*, get ready to meet Birkie, the Sheltie star of the Walt Disney production television movie *The Little Shepard Dog of Catalina!*

This is the story of a champion Shetland Sheepdog who becomes lost on Catalina island, off the coast of California. Fortunately, the dog is able to make his way to a farm where he is offered a new home. It's here that the dog's natural herding instinct is recognized by Bud Parker, a farm hand. Bud trains Birkie in herding, and the two soon become inseparable.

In the mean time, the dog's real owner on the mainland of California discovers Birkie's where-abouts. When he comes upon Birkie, the heroic little dog is busy trying to prevent an Arabian stallion from falling off a cliff to his death. After witnessing this encounter, the dog's real owner decides to let Birkie stay in his new home. But along with Birkie's regular farm duties, he will now stand as stud to the "girl" Shelties sent over from mainland California by his old owner.

Birkie, whose real name is Gaywyn Sandstorm (Shane for short) is a registered Sheltie who is owned by Carol Snip of St. Louis, Missouri. He's the grandson of two Sheltie champions: Ch. Malpsh Great Scot on his sire's side, and Ch. Kawartha's Matchmaker on his dam's side.

In This Issue

- ▶ Birkie, the Sheltie Movie Star
- ▶ Training Your Sheltie
- ▶ Great Sheltie Sires and Dams
- ▶ Ancestors of the Shetland Sheepdog

Seahaven Sass-Me-Back (Ginger for short)

Training Your Sheltie

Shelties are among the most intelligent breeds. As a result, they are one of the easiest dogs to train. The obedience-trained Sheltie performs well in almost every social situation and is a real joy to be around. At the very least, your Sheltie should know how to sit, stay, and come, and be lead trained. This training could save his life in a panic situation.

Training should begin as soon as you bring your Sheltie home.

However, remember to keep all training sessions short. A few minutes every day is much better than working a hour or so once every week. Especially when the pup is very young, it is easy for him to become distracted. To prevent this from happening, you will want to break off the training monment that the puppy becomes at all distracted or tired.

(continued on page 4)

The first page of this newsletter combines newspaper columns, a text box with a table, figure boxes with a scanned image, WordPerfect clip art, and several graphics lines.

Tip: In WordPerfect 6.0 for Windows, graphics has become a diverse subject. Many of the intricacies of graphics are beyond the scope of this book. This chapter teaches the basics of working with graphics in figure boxes and creating graphics lines and borders. To learn more about the graphics capabilities of WordPerfect 6.0 for Windows, including the powerful WordPerfect Draw for Windows utility, see Que's *Using WordPerfect 6 for Windows*, Special Edition.

Inserting a Graphics Image into a Document

Placing a Graphics Image into a Document

1. Position the insertion point at the place in the document where you want the graphics image to appear.

2. Open the Graphics menu and choose Figure.

WordPerfect displays the Insert Image dialog box, and displays the contents of the \GRAPHICS directory.

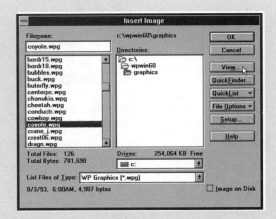

3. If the graphics file is in a different directory, select that directory in the Directories list box; then select the graphics file in Filename list box, or enter the file name in the Filename text box.

4. By default, the program displays only WordPerfect graphics files (with the extension WPG) in the Filename list box. To list other types of graphics files, choose the List Files of Type option, and then select the type of files to use in its text box (to display the list of file types in a list box, click the drop-down list button next to this option).

5. If you want to preview the image in the graphics file to make sure that it is indeed the one you want to retrieve, select the file name in the Filename list box, and then choose the View button to open the Viewer window.

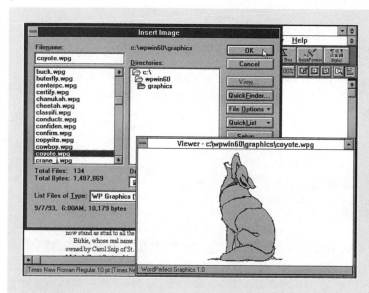

In this example, you use the Viewer to preview the COYOTE.WPG graphics file prior to inserting it in a document.

6. After you have selected the graphics file you want to use, choose OK or press ↵Enter to insert the graphics image into the document.

   WordPerfect returns you to the document window and inserts the graphics image in a figure box at the location of the insertion point.

You can insert almost any graphics image created in another program into a WordPerfect document. To insert an entire graphics file into your document, open the **Graphics** menu and choose the **Figure** command. To preview the contents of the graphics file and make sure that its format is compatible with WordPerfect's, you can view the contents of the graphic in a Viewer window attached to the Insert Image dialog box.

If you want to use only a portion of a graphic, you can use a separate Windows graphics program such as CorelDRAW! or PaintBrush to select the part of the image you want to use, and then copy the selection to the Clipboard with the Copy command on that program's **Edit** command (Ctrl+C). Then return to WordPerfect for Windows and paste the selected portion of the image directly into your document with the **Paste** command on WordPerfect's **Edit** menu (Ctrl+V).

Tip: If you insert the wrong graphics image into your document, you can delete it simply by pressing the Del key as long as the image is still selected (indicated by the sizing handles—or small rectangles—around the figure's border. If the image is no longer selected, you can do this by clicking the figure box anywhere with the mouse.

Repositioning a Graphics Image

Moving a Graphics Image in the Document

1. Position the pointer anywhere in the graphics box and click the primary mouse button.

When you click a graphics image, WordPerfect selects the graphic, the pointer changes to a four-headed arrow, and sizing handles appear around the graphics box.

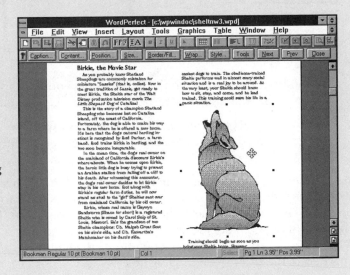

2. Drag the graphics box with the four-headed arrow pointer to the desired location on the page. (You will actually drag the dotted outline of the graphics box; WordPerfect will not redraw the picture until you release the mouse button.)

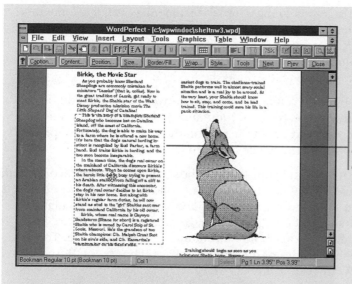

Drag this dotted outline to the desired position on the page.

3. Release the mouse button when the graphics box is in the desired position on the page.

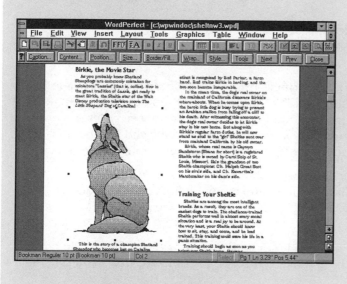

As soon as you release the mouse button, WordPerfect redraws the picture and wraps any existing text around the repositioned graphics box.

4. Click the pointer somewhere on the page outside the graphics image to deselect the graphics box.

Any time you retrieve a graphics image into a document, you can use the mouse to fine-tune the graphic's position or move it to a new position on the page. If you position a graphics image in the middle of the page in a single column layout, WordPerfect does not split the text around the left and right side of its graphics box but wraps all the text around the left side.

To wrap text around both the left and right side (as well as on top and below) of a graphic that is centered on the page, you must either change the way text wraps around the graphics box or set the text on the page in two newspaper columns before you position the image between them.

To change the text flows around your graphics box, choose the **Wrap** command on the Graphics QuickMenu. When the Wrap Text dialog box appears, choose the desired Wrapping Type and Wrap Text Around radio buttons. To make the text wrap around the shape of the graphics image rather than the figure box that holds it, choose the **C**ontour radio button under Wrapping Type. To make the text contoured on both sides of the graphics shape, choose the **B**oth Sides radio button under Wrap Text Around as well.

Resizing a Graphics Image

Resizing a Graphics Image in a Document
1. Position the pointer within the graphics box and click the primary mouse button.

   The mouse pointer changes from an arrowhead to a four-headed arrow, and sizing handles appear around the sides of the graphics box (now shown by dotted lines). When the mouse pointer is positioned in a graphics box, the graphics box type and number is displayed on the status bar at the bottom left corner of the screen.

2. To change the size of a graphic, position the I-beam pointer on the appropriate sizing handle until the pointer changes to a double-headed arrow. Then drag the handle until the graphics box is the size you want.

   To make the image wider or narrower, drag the sizing handle on the right side of the graphics box to the left or to the right. To make the image shorter or taller, drag the sizing handle on the bottom side upward or downward. To change both the width and length of the graphics image at the same time, drag the sizing handle in the lower right corner diagonally upward or downward.

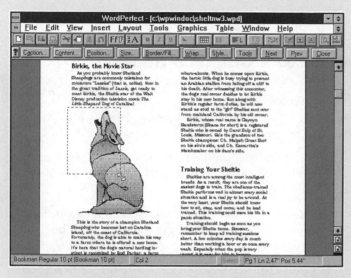

In this example, you drag the sizing handle in the lower right corner of the graphics box up toward the left to make the image smaller.

3. When the image is the size you want, release the mouse button and click the pointer outside the graphic to deselect the graphics box.

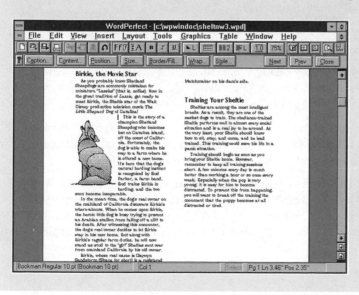

When you release the mouse button, WordPerfect redraws the graphics box along with its image; existing text reflows around the new size.

WordPerfect makes it easy to resize a graphic after you place it on the page. Simply select the graphic, position the mouse pointer on a side or corner, and then drag the mouse to modify the size (and shape) of the graphics box; the shape of the graphics image inside changes. When you change the size of a graphic, WordPerfect rewraps existing text to conform to the new shape of the graphic, depending upon what Text Wrap options are in effect for that graphics image.

Adding a Caption to a Graphics Image

Adding a Caption to a Graphics Image

1. Click the figure box containing the graphics image for which you want to add a caption. This action selects the figure box.

2. Choose the Caption command on the Graphics QuickMenu; or choose the Caption button on the Graphics Feature Bar. The Box Caption dialog box appears.

3. Change any of the Caption options you want to modify, including the position of the caption in relation to the graphics box and the rotation of the caption text.

4. Choose the Edit button to have WordPerfect close the Box Caption dialog box. In the figure box, insert the next available figure number (for example, type Figure 1) in the caption, and position the insertion point after this figure number.

   To remove the figure number from your caption, simply press `◆Backspace` to delete it.

5. Type the text of your caption, and then click the pointer somewhere outside the figure box to deselect it.

WordPerfect for Windows makes it easy to add captions to graphics boxes. The program automatically and sequentially numbers each type of graphics box. You can use this figure number or enter a caption of your own.

If you need to edit the caption you have added to a figure, choose the Edit Caption command on the Graphic QuickMenu to position the insertion point after the figure number at the beginning of the caption text. When you have finished editing this text, click the pointer anywhere outside the graphics box to deselect it.

Editing a Graphic with the Image Tools Palette

WordPerfect enables you to edit graphics images directly in the document with the Image Tools palette. You can use its tools to crop an image within its graphics box; rotate, invert (flip), or scale an image; and reset the brightness and contrast for an image.

To display the Image Tools palette, click the graphics box with the secondary mouse button and then choose the Image Tools command on the Graphics QuickMenu.

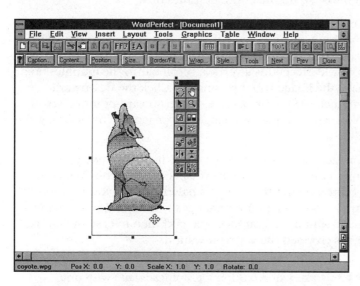

When you select Image Tools on the Graphics QuickMenu, the Image Tools palette appears in its own window next to the graphics box.

Because the Image Tools palette is displayed in its own window, you can move it around the document editing window. Simply drag it by its title bar. You cannot, however, resize the Image Tools palette; its buttons always remain in two columns arranged in three groups of four and one group of two. To find out the function of a particular button in the Image Tools palette, position the mouse pointer on the tool. WordPerfect then displays a short description of the tool's function on the title bar of the WordPerfect program window. When you are finished with the Image Tools palette, double-click its tiny Control menu box, or click the Control menu box and select the Close command in its pull-down menu.

Scaling or Cropping a Graphics Image

After you have displayed the Image Tools palette, you can enlarge the figure in its graphics box by scaling it; you can also crop the figure by moving it within its graphics box so that only part of the total image is seen.

To scale a graphics image, click the Scale Image button (the one with the magnifying glass) to display three icons to the right of the button. To enlarge just a part of the image, click the magnifying glass icon with the + symbol inside it to change the pointer to a magnifying glass with cross-hairs. Then, use this pointer to drag a bounding box around the part of the graphics image you want to enlarge. As soon as you release the mouse button, the part of the image you selected is enlarged to take up the entire graphics box.

To enlarge or decrease the size of an image in its graphics box, choose the second icon (the one with the up and down arrows) that appears to the right when you click the Scale Image button on the Image Tools palette. As soon as you click this button, WordPerfect adds a vertical scroll bar to the graphics box that you can use to make the image larger or smaller. Click the downward-pointing scroll arrow to increase the image size or the upward-pointing scroll arrow to decrease it. You can also quickly change the image size by dragging the scroll box in this scroll bar.

Instead of scaling an image, you may want to crop the image by moving it within the graphics box so that only part of it is displayed. To crop an image, click the Move Image button on the Image Tools palette. When you position the pointer within the graphics box, the pointer changes to a hand. Use the hand pointer to drag the image within the graphics box, and then release the mouse button when the image is cropped the way you want it.

Tip: If you make a mistake when editing a graphics image with one of the buttons on the Image Tools palette, you can restore the image to its original appearance by clicking the Reset button on the Image Tools palette.

Rotating or Flipping a Graphics Image

You can rotate a graphics image or flip it so that the mirror image appears in the graphics box. To rotate an image, click the Rotate button on the Image Tools palette. WordPerfect will then display rotation handles at each of the inside corners of the graphics box. Click one of these rotation handles and drag in the direction you want to rotate the graphics image (clockwise or counter-clockwise). As you drag, the program will indicate the degree of rotation on the status bar. When you release the mouse button, the program will redraw the image rotated the desired amount.

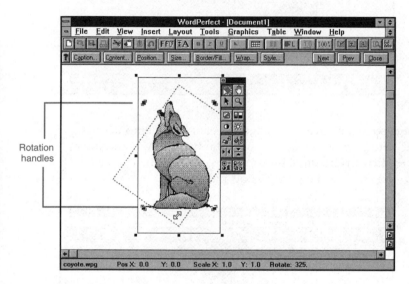

Rotation handles

To rotate an image, click the Rotate button on the Image Tools palette, and then drag one of the rotation handles.

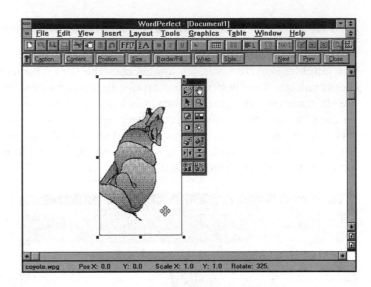

When you release the mouse button, WordPerfect redraws the image rotated the desired amount.

To flip a graphics image so that a mirrored image appears in the graphics box, click either the Mirror Vertical button (the one with the two arrows pointing to the vertical line) or the Mirror Horizontal button (the one with the two arrows pointing to the horizontal line) on the Image Tools palette.

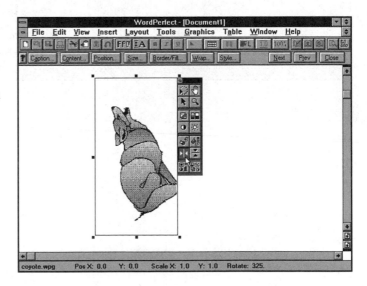

In this example, you click the Mirror Vertical button to make the coyote point toward the right instead of the left.

Using Borders and Graphics Lines

WordPerfect comes with many decorative borders that you can add to your documents. These ready-made designs are perfect additions for announcements or invitations, or you can use them to set off text within other documents. You can also add lines of varying weights and styles to complete the professional (or whimsical) look of a document.

Adding Borders to a Document

Adding Borders to Paragraphs, Pages, or Columns

1. Position the insertion point in the first paragraph, page, or column that you want to surround with a border.

2. To create a paragraph border, open the **Layout** menu, choose **Paragraph**, and then choose **Border/Fill**.

   To create a page border, open the **Layout** menu, choose **Page**, and then choose **Border/Fill**.

   To create a column border, open the **Layout** menu, choose **Columns**, and then choose **Border/Fill**.

   After you choose one of these commands, WordPerfect displays a Border dialog box.

3. Choose a border style either by example or by name. To choose a style by example, click the button to the right of the **Border Style** option and then click one of the border styles in the displayed palette. To choose a style by name, click the button next to the **Border Style** text box and select the style name in the drop-down list.

4. To add a fill style to the paragraph, page, or column border, choose a fill style by clicking the button to the right of the **Fill Style** option and then clicking one of the fill styles in the displayed palette. To choose a style by name, click the button next to the **Fill Style** text box and select the fill style name in the drop-down list.

5. When the border appears as you want in the example box, choose OK or press ⏎Enter to return to your document and apply the selected border and fill style to the current paragraph, page, or column and all those thereafter.

WordPerfect 6.0 for Windows makes it easy to add borders to the paragraphs, pages, or borders in your document with the Border/Styles command. When you add a border around text with this command, WordPerfect automatically redraws the borders to suit the size of the paragraph, page, or column.

When you add paragraph, page, or column borders, WordPerfect inserts a [Para Border], [Pg Border], or [Col Border] code to the document that adds the selected border and fill style to the current paragraph, page, or column as well as all subsequent paragraphs, pages, or columns in the document. To turn off a border at a particular paragraph, page, or column, position the insertion point somewhere in that paragraph, page, or column and then repeat the procedure for adding the appropriate type of border, this time selecting None as the border style.

Tip: When adding a paragraph border, you can restrict the border to a particular paragraph or group of paragraphs by selecting the paragraphs before you undertake the procedure for adding the paragraph borders. WordPerfect will automatically set the paragraph border style to None thereby turning off the paragraph borders at the end of the selection.

Creating Horizontal and Vertical Graphics Lines

Adding a Horizontal or Vertical Graphics Line to a Document

1. Position the insertion point in the document where you want the graphics line to appear.

2. To draw a horizontal line, open the **Graphics** menu and choose **H**orizontal Line; or press Ctrl + F11. To draw a vertical line, open the **G**raphics menu and choose **V**ertical Line; or press Ctrl + ⇧Shift + F11.

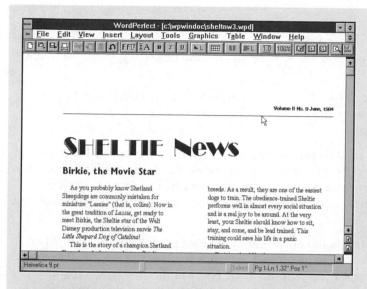

When you select **Horizontal Line** command on the **Graphics** menu, the program draws a single horizontal line the width of the current left and right margin settings.

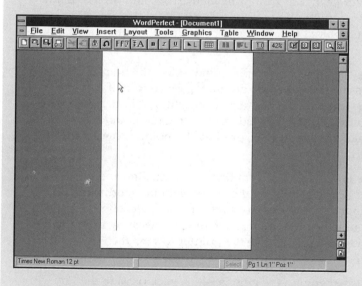

When you select the **Vertical Line** command on the **Graphics** menu, the program draws a single vertical line the length of the current top and bottom margins.

3. If you want to change the default settings for your horizontal or vertical graphics line, double-click the line or click it with the secondary mouse button. Then choose **E**dit Horizontal Line or **E**dit Vertical Line command on the Graphics Line QuickMenu (depending upon the type of graphics line) to open the Edit Graphics Line dialog box.

continues

continued

4. Change all of the default options you want to modify, including Line Style, Position/Length, Spacing (above and below the line), color, and thickness.

5. Choose OK or press ⏎Enter to return to your document and put your changes to the default line style into effect.

With WordPerfect, you can create vertical and horizontal graphics lines and place them anywhere on the page. A graphics line can be any color or length in various weights. After you have drawn a graphics line in a document, you can move or size it directly in the document with the mouse by using the following techniques:

- To move a graphics line, position the I-beam pointer on the line. When the I-beam changes to an arrowhead, click the line to select it (sizing handles will appear around the line). Position the pointer on the line until the pointer changes to a four-headed arrow, and then drag the line to its new position on the page. Keep in mind that text does not wrap around graphics lines. If you place a vertical or horizontal graphics line in the middle of text, the line will print over the text.

- To change the thickness of a graphics line, select the line and position the pointer on the sizing handle on the top or bottom of a horizontal line or on the sizing handle on the left or right of a vertical line. The pointer becomes a double-headed arrow. Drag the pointer away from the line to make the line thicker; or, drag the pointer toward the line to make the line thinner.

- To modify the length of a graphics line, select the line and position the pointer on the sizing handle on the left or right of a horizontal line, or on the sizing handle on the top or bottom of a vertical line. The pointer becomes a double-headed arrow. Drag the pointer away from the line to make the line longer; or, drag the pointer toward the line to make the line shorter.

When you have finished editing the graphics line, click outside the line to deselect it.

Summary

In this chapter, you learned how to enhance your documents with columns and graphics. You learned how to set up to five newspaper columns directly from the Power Bar as well as the other types of text columns with the options in the Columns dialog box. You also learned how to insert a graphics image from a compatible program and place the graphic directly into a WordPerfect document. In addition, you learned how to move and resize graphics, and how to enhance graphics in your documents with horizontal and vertical graphics lines.

In the next chapter, you will learn how to customize WordPerfect for Windows by using the Button Bar feature. You also will learn how to modify the Button Bars supplied with the program and how to create custom Button Bars of your own.

17

Creating and Using Button Bars

Editing a Button Bar

Creating a custom Button Bar

Setting up a Button Bar library

Button Bars enable you to perform routine tasks in WordPerfect simply with a click of the mouse. In almost all situations, you will find clicking a button on a Button Bar faster than selecting an equivalent command sequence from the appropriate pull-down menus either with the mouse or keyboard.

The assortment of buttons that appear on the various Button Bars that come with WordPerfect 6.0 for Windows is by no means static. You can create a button for any WordPerfect command on the pull-down menus as well as create buttons that insert standard text, launch other programs, and play any of the macros you have created (see chapter 10).

In this chapter, you learn how you can customize the Button Bars that come with WordPerfect as well as create custom Button Bars of your own design. As part of this process, you learn how to add, remove, and reorder buttons on the Button Bar. At the end of the chapter are step-by-step instructions for creating some Button Bars that you can include in your own Button Bar library.

Key Terms in This Chapter	
Button	Special icon that performs a particular task such as executing a particular WordPerfect command or playing back a macro when you click the button with the mouse.
Button Bar	Series of buttons that can be displayed anywhere in the current document window in a floating palette or around the sides of current document window, at the top, bottom, left, or right side. You can create and save Button Bars of your own design.

The Button Bars in WordPerfect for Windows

Selecting a New Button Bar

1. If necessary, display the current Button Bar by opening the View menu and choosing **B**utton Bar or by clicking the Display Button Bar button on the Power Bar.

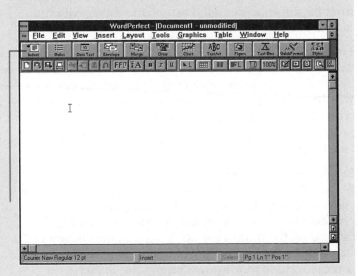

By default, the program displays the WordPerfect Button Bar when you open the **Vi**ew menu and choose **B**utton Bar.

2. Click anywhere on the displayed Button Bar with the secondary mouse button to display the Button Bar QuickMenu. (Be sure that you click the secondary and not the primary mouse button because clicking the primary button might select a button on the Button Bar rather than display the Button Bar QuickMenu.)

To select another Button Bar, you choose it in the Button Bar QuickMenu.

3. Drag to the name of the Button Bar you want to select, or click it in the Button Bar QuickMenu.

   WordPerfect displays the Button Bar you selected on the QuickMenu in the same position and style as the Button Bar it is replacing.

continues

continued

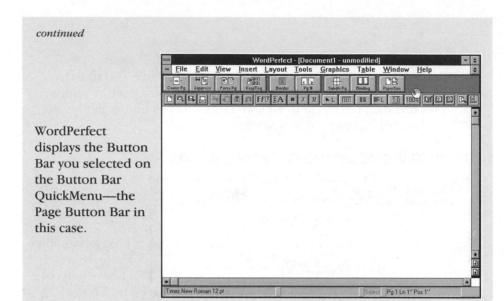

WordPerfect displays the Button Bar you selected on the Button Bar QuickMenu—the Page Button Bar in this case.

WordPerfect for Windows comes with a variety of preconfigured Button Bars that you can use as is or customize to suit your needs. Remember that after selecting a Button Bar, you can modify its position and button style (see "The Button Bar" in chapter 2 for details on how to do this). To select a button and perform its action, you must click the button with the primary mouse button.

Editing a Button Bar

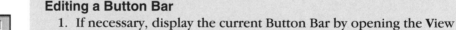

Editing a Button Bar

1. If necessary, display the current Button Bar by opening the **V**iew menu and choosing **B**utton Bar or by clicking the Display Button Bar button on the Power Bar. To edit a different Button Bar, open the Button Bar QuickMenu with the secondary mouse button, and then choose the name of the Button Bar you want to edit.

2. Open the Button Bar QuickMenu and choose **E**dit to open the Button Bar Editor dialog box for the selected Button Bar.

   WordPerfect displays the Button Bar Editor dialog box. Note that all the buttons in the selected Button Bar are activated—even those that are usually dimmed, such as the Cut and Copy buttons (these buttons are normally active only when text is selected).

3. To add a button to the Button Bar, choose the appropriate radio button under Add a Button To: Activate a Feature radio button to add a menu command, Play a **K**eyboard Script radio button to insert text, **L**aunch a Program radio button to start a new program from WordPerfect for Windows, or Play a **M**acro radio button to execute a macro.

   As soon as you choose **A**dd Button or press ⏎Enter, WordPerfect inserts at the very end of the Button Bar a new button for the feature, keyboard script, program, or macro you selected.

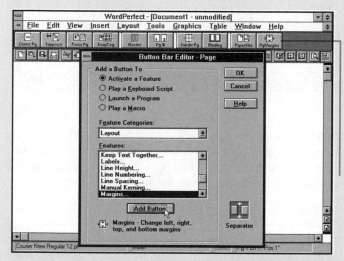

In this figure, the PgMargins button has been added to the end of the Page Button Bar.

4. To move a button to a new location on the Button Bar, drag the button until you have positioned it at the place in the Button Bar where you want it to appear, and then release the mouse button.

   To insert a button between two others on the bar, position the button between the two then release the mouse button.

continues

continued

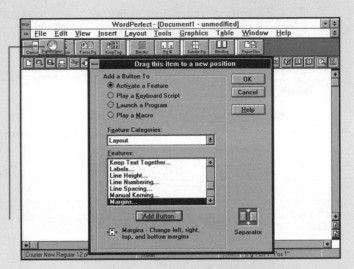

In this example,
the new
PgMargins
button is being
repositioned
between the
Center Pg and
Suppress buttons
at the left end of
the Page Button
Bar.

5. To insert a separation between a pair of buttons to group them
   together, click the Separator area of the Button Bar Editor dialog box.
   When the pointer changes to a hand holding a separator, drag this
   pointer until it's between the buttons on the bar that you want to
   separate.

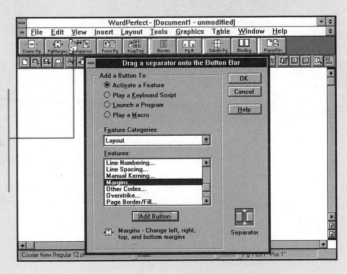

In this example, a
separator is being
added between
the PgMargins and
Suppress buttons
on the Page
Button Bar.

6. To remove a button or a separator from the Button Bar, drag the icon off the Button Bar, and then release the mouse button.

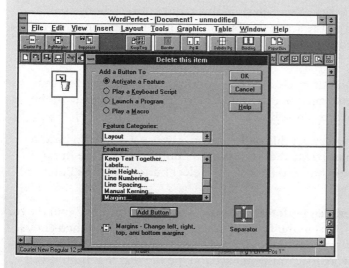

In this example, the new Force Pg button is being removed from the Page Button Bar.

7. When you have finished adding, moving, and deleting buttons from the Button Bar, choose the OK button to close the Button Bar Editor dialog box and save your changes to the current Button Bar.

The procedure for editing a Button Bar is quite easy. Select the Button Bar, open the Button Bar QuickMenu, and choose Edit. After that, it is a simple matter of adding, moving, and deleting buttons until you have them the way you want them.

When adding buttons, you have a choice between adding a button that performs a menu command or WordPerfect feature, enters some stock text (like the company or firm name), launches a program, or plays a macro that you have recorded (see chapter 10 for details). These options are as follows:

- Activate a Feature: After selecting this option, choose the pull-down menu that contains the command for which you want to add a button in the Feature Categories list box. Then choose the particular command or feature in the Features list box and choose Add Button or press Enter. Note that instead of choosing Add Button or pressing Enter, you can also drag the Button icon representing the feature or command you have selected in the Features list box directly to the place on the Button Bar where you want it added.

- Play a **Keyboard Script**: After selecting this radio button, choose the option called "Type the script this button will play." Then type the text you want inserted when you click the button and choose **Add Button** or press Enter.

- **Launch a Program**: After selecting this option, choose **Select File**, and then select the program file that you want the button to execute in the Select File dialog box. Press Enter.

- Play a **Macro**: If you select this radio button, choose **Add Macro** button. Next, select the macro file that you want the button to execute in the Select Macro dialog box and choose the **Select** button or press Enter or choose OK.

When you add a button that performs a feature, you first choose the pull-down menu (such as **File** or **Edit**) in the **Feature Categories** list box, and then choose the command that you want played in the **Features** text box. When you add a button that plays a keyboard script, you have to type the text that button will insert in the document when you select it.

When you add a button to launch a program when you click it, you must select the program file that starts the program (such as EXCEL.EXE in the \EXCEL directory) in the Select File dialog box. Note that when you launch a program from WordPerfect for Windows with one of these buttons, you are returned directly to WordPerfect for Windows when you exit the program.

When you add a button that plays a macro, you must type the macro file name in the Select Macro dialog box or use the List file pop-up button to display the Select File dialog box in which you choose the desired macro file.

> *Tip:* The Undo feature cannot undo changes made to the buttons on the Button Bar. If you move a button to the wrong place on the bar, you must then move it back to its previous position with the same drag-and-drop technique that you used to move the button to the wrong place on the bar. If you delete a button in error, you must go through the procedure of adding it again to restore it to the Button Bar.

Creating a Button Bar

Creating a New Button Bar

1. If necessary, display the current Button Bar by opening the View menu and choosing **B**utton Bar or by clicking the Button Bar Display button on the Power Bar.

2. Open the Button Bar QuickMenu and choose **P**references to open the Button Bar Preferences dialog box.

3. Choose the C**r**eate button to open the Create Button Bar dialog box.

4. By default, WordPerfect for Windows stores the new Button Bar with the current template. To store the Button Bar with whatever template is the default (Standard unless you have changed it), choose the **T**emplate button, and then choose the Store with **D**efault Template radio button in the Button Bar Location dialog box. Choose OK or press ⏎Enter.

5. Enter a name for your new Button Bar in the **N**ew Button Bar Name text box, and then choose OK or press ⏎Enter.

6. To add a button to the Button Bar, choose the appropriate radio button under Add a Button To: Activate a Feature radio button to add a menu command, Play a **K**eyboard Script radio button to insert text, **L**aunch a Program radio button to start a new program from WordPerfect for Windows, or Play a **M**acro radio button to execute a macro. These options are explained in the preceding section, "Editing a Button Bar."

7. Repeat step 6 until you have added all the buttons you want on the new Button Bar.

8. To move a button to a new location on the Button Bar, drag the button until you have positioned it at the place in the Button Bar where you want it to appear, and then release the mouse button.

9. To insert a separator between a pair of buttons to group them together, click the Spacers area of the Button Bar Editor dialog box. When the pointer changes to the Separator button, drag this button until it's between the buttons on the bar that you want to separate with a separator.

continues

483

continued

10. When you have finished adding buttons and arranging them on the new Button Bar, choose OK to close the Button Bar Editor dialog box and return to the Button Bar Preferences dialog box where your new Button Bar appears in the Available Button Bars list box.

11. To select the new Button Bar, choose Select in the Button Bar Preferences dialog box. To leave current whatever Button Bar was selected at the time you created the new Button Bar, choose the Close button instead.

The procedure for creating a new Button Bar is very similar to that for editing a Button Bar. You follow the same steps for adding and moving buttons on the new Button Bar as you do when adding or moving buttons on the Button Bar you're editing (see the previous section for details). WordPerfect automatically saves the new Button Bar as part of the current template (unless you save it as part of the default template—note, however, that these are both the same Standard template unless you have selected another template when creating the current document), meaning that this Button Bar is available for selection in every document that uses the template.

Creating a Library of Custom Button Bars

This section describes how to create several custom Button Bars that you can add to your own Button Bar library. You will find step-by-step instructions for creating the following Button Bars:

- An Editing Button Bar for general document editing

- A Bookmark Button Bar for adding comments and bookmarks to the document

- A Document Button Bar for setting up a new document

After creating these three Button Bars, you learn how to create macros and attach them to buttons that link these Button Bars. Then you can select either of the other two Button Bars with the click of a button on the current Button Bar.

The Editing Button Bar

Follow these steps for creating the Editing Button Bar:

1. If necessary, display the current Button Bar by opening the View menu and choosing **B**utton Bar or by clicking the Display Button Bar button on the Power Bar.

2. Open the Button Bar QuickMenu and choose **P**references to open the Button Bar Preferences dialog box.

3. Choose the C**r**eate button to open the Create Button Bar dialog box.

4. Type Editing as the Button Bar name, and then press ⏎Enter or choose OK.

5. Choose Edit in the F**e**ature Categories list box.

6. Choose Find in the **F**eatures list box, and then press ⏎Enter or choose **A**dd Button to add the Find button to the new Button Bar.

7. Choose Find Next in the **F**eatures list box, and then press ⏎Enter or choose **A**dd Button to add the Find Next button to the new Button Bar.

8. Choose Find Previous in the **F**eatures list box, and then press ⏎Enter or choose **A**dd Button to add the Find Prev button to the new Button Bar.

9. Add a separator to the Button Bar after the Find Prev button.

10. Choose Replace in the **F**eatures list box. Press ⏎Enter or choose **A**dd Button to add the Replace button to the new Button Bar.

11. Add a separator to the Button Bar after the Replace button.

12. Choose Initial Capitals in the **F**eatures list box. Press ⏎Enter or choose **A**dd Button to add the Initial Caps button to the new Button Bar.

13. Choose Uppercase in the **F**eatures list box. Press ⏎Enter or choose **A**dd Button to add the Uppercase button to the new Button Bar.

14. Choose Lowercase in the **F**eatures list box, and then press ⏎Enter or choose **A**dd Button to add the Lowercase button to the new Button Bar.

15. Choose Case Toggle in the Features list box, and then press ⏎Enter or choose Add Button to add the CaseToggle button to the new Button Bar.

    To increase the versatility of your Editing Button Bar, you will now add the two last buttons: one to turn on and off the Ruler's display and another to turn on and off the Reveal Codes window.

16. Add a separator to the Button Bar after the Case Toggle button.

17. Choose View in the Feature Categories list box, and then choose Ruler Bar in the Features list box. Press ⏎Enter or choose Add Button to add the Ruler Bar button to Button Bar.

18. Choose Reveal Codes in the Features list box. Press ⏎Enter or choose Add Button to add the RevCodes button to the Button Bar.

19. Choose the OK button to close the Button Bar Editor for the Editing Button Bar.

Your new Editing Button Bar should look like this one. Choose Select to make Editing the current the Button Bar.

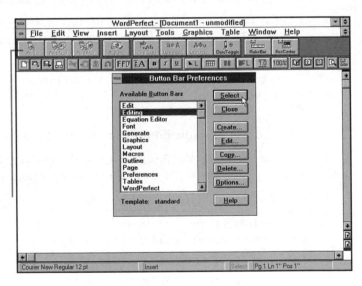

Experiment with your Editing Button Bar by clicking the RulerBar and RevCodes buttons to display and hide the Ruler and the Reveal Codes bar. Then type some sample text all in lowercase letters, such as this is a test, and select the text. Click the Initial Caps button to convert the line of text to *This Is a Test*. Click the Uppercase button to convert the selection to *THIS IS A TEST*. Click the lowercase button to convert the selection to *This is a test*. Then, click the CaseToggle button twice in a row: the first time to convert the selection to *THIS IS A TEST* and the second time to change it back to *This is a test*. Finally, click outside the selected text to deselect it.

The Bookmark Button Bar

To create the Bookmark Button Bar, follow these steps:

1. Open the Button Bar QuickMenu and choose **Preferences**.

2. Choose Create, type Bookmark in the **New Button Bar Name** text box, and press ⏎Enter.

3. Choose Insert in the **Feature Categories** list box.

4. Choose Abbreviations in the **Features** list box, and then press ⏎Enter or choose **Add Button** to add the Abbreviation button to the new Button Bar.

5. Choose Abbreviations Expand in the **Features** list box, and then press ⏎Enter or choose **Add Button** to add the ExpandAbrv button to the new Button Bar.

6. Add a separator to the Button Bar after the ExpandAbrv button.

7. Choose Comment Create in the **Features** list box, and then press ⏎Enter or choose **Add Button** to add the Comment button to the new Button Bar.

8. Choose Comment Edit in the **Features** list box, and then press ⏎Enter or choose **Add Button** to add the CommentEd button to the new Button Bar.

9. Choose Convert to Text in the **Features** list box, and then press ⏎Enter or choose **Add Button** to add the CommentCvt button to the new Button Bar.

10. Add a separator to the Button Bar after the CommentCvt button.

11. Choose Bookmark in the **F**eatures list box. Press ⏎Enter or choose **A**dd Button to add the Bookmarks button to the new Button Bar.

12. Choose QuickMark Set in the **F**eatures list box. Press ⏎Enter or choose **A**dd Button to add the SetQuikMrk button to the new Button Bar.

13. Choose QuickMark Find in the **F**eatures list box. Press ⏎Enter or choose **A**dd Button to add the FindQuikMrk button to the new Button Bar.

14. Add a separator to the Button Bar after the FindQuikMrk button.

15. Choose Tools in the **F**eature Categories list box and choose Hypertext Create in the **F**eatures list box. Press ⏎Enter or choose **A**dd Button to add the HypertextCr button to the new Button Bar.

16. Choose HyperText in the **F**eatures list box. Press ⏎Enter or choose **A**dd Button to add the Hypertext button to the new Button Bar.

17. Choose the OK button to close Button Bar Editor for the Bookmark Button Bar.

Your new Book-mark Button Bar should now look like this one. Choose **S**elect to make Bookmark the current Button Bar.

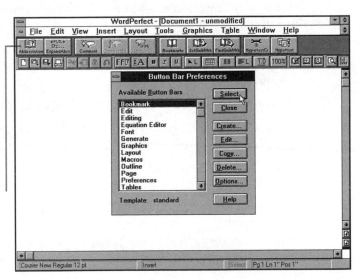

Practice using your new Bookmark Button Bar by creating and expanding an abbreviation. Type your full name on a new line. Select the text and click the Abbreviation button on the Bookmark Button Bar to open the Abbreviations dialog box. Press Enter or choose **Create** to open the Create Abbreviation dialog box in which you type your initials and press Enter or choose OK. Choose the **Close** button in the Abbreviations dialog box, and then type your initials and click the ExpandAbrv button on the Bookmark Button Bar to insert your full name.

The Document Button Bar

Follow these steps to create the Document Button Bar:

1. Open the Button Bar QuickMenu and choose **Preferences**.

2. Choose **Create**, type Document in the **New Button Bar Name** text box, and press ⏎Enter.

3. With File selected in the **Feature Categories** list box, choose Close in the **Features** list box, and then press ⏎Enter or choose **Add Button** to add the Close button to the new Button Bar.

4. Choose Document Summary in the **Features** list box. Press ⏎Enter or choose **Add Button** to add the Summary button to the new Button Bar.

5. Add a separator to the Button Bar after the Summary button.

6. Choose Print Document in the **Features** list box. Press ⏎Enter or choose **Add Button** to add the PrintDoc button to the new Button Bar.

7. Add a separator to the Button Bar after the PrintDoc button.

8. Choose Template in the **Features** list box. Press ⏎Enter or choose **Add Button** to add the Template button to the new Button Bar.

9. Choose Layout in the **Feature Categories** list box, and then choose Initial Codes Style in the **Features** list box. Press ⏎Enter or choose **Add Button** to add the Init Style button to the new Button Bar.

10. Choose Initial Font in the Features list box. Press ↵Enter or choose Add Button to add the Initial Font button to the new Button Bar.

11. Add a separator to the Button Bar after the Initial Font button.

12. Choose Page Border/Fill in the Features list box. Press ↵Enter or choose Add Button to add the Border button to the new Button Bar.

13. Choose Paper Size in the Features list box. Press ↵Enter or choose Add Button to add the PaperSize button to the new Button Bar.

14. Choose Paragraph Border/Fill in the Features list box. Press ↵Enter or choose Add Button to add the Border button (with the ¶ symbol in the page icon) to the new Button Bar.

15. Choose Paragraph Format in the Features list box. Press ↵Enter or choose Add Button to add the ParaFormat button to the new Button Bar.

16. Add a separator to the Button Bar after the ParaFormat button.

17. Choose File in the Feature Categories list box, and then choose Document Info in the Features list box. Press ↵Enter or choose Add Button to add the DocInfo button to the new Button Bar.

18. Choose the OK button to close the Button Bar Editor for the Document Button Bar.

Your new Document Button Bar should now look like this one. Choose Select to make Document the current the Button Bar.

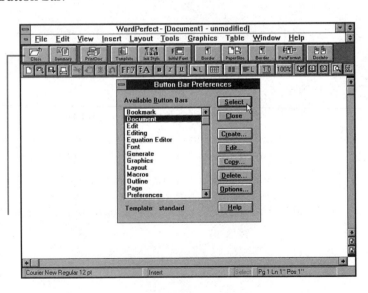

The last Button Bar you created contains a number of buttons that you can use when creating a new document. You can use its buttons to select new settings for the document (such as a new template with the Template button or new initial settings with the Init Style and Initial Font buttons). Use the Border button to add page or paragraph borders to your document, Paper Size to select a new paper size, and ParaFormat to change the way your document's paragraphs are formatted. When you're finished, you can use the PrintDoc button to print the entire document and the Close button to save and put away your document in preparation for starting a new one.

Linking the Button Bars

Now that you have created these three useful new Button Bars, you can link them to make it easier to select which Button Bar is displayed. Follow these steps to link the Button Bars:

1. Open the **Tools** menu and choose **Macro**. Choose **Record** or press Ctrl + F10.

2. Type editbar as the name for the macro in the **Name** text box, and then choose **Record** or press ⏎Enter.

3. Open the Button Bar QuickMenu and choose the Editing Button Bar. Open the **Tools** menu, choose **Macro**, and then choose **Record** or press Ctrl + F10 again to save and compile the macro.

   Now you're ready to record the second macro that selects the Bookmark Button Bar.

4. Open the Tools menu and choose **Macro**, and then choose **Record** or press Ctrl + F10.

5. Type bookmrk as the name for the macro in the **Name** text box, and then choose **Record** or press ⏎Enter.

6. Open the Button Bar QuickMenu and choose the Bookmark Button Bar. Open the **Tools** menu, choose **Macro**, and choose **Record** or press Ctrl + F10 again to save and compile the macro.

   Now, you're ready to record the last macro that selects the Document Button Bar.

7. Open the **Tools** menu, choose **Macro**, and choose **Record** or press Ctrl + F10.

8. Type docbar as the name for the macro in the **Name** text box, and then choose **Record** or press ⏎Enter.

9. Open the Button Bar QuickMenu and choose the Document Button Bar. Open the **Tools** menu, choose **Macro**, and choose **Record** or press Ctrl + F10 again to save and compile the macro.

   Now, you're ready to add these buttons to the appropriate Button Bars.

10. With the Document Button Bar selected, open the Button Bar QuickMenu and choose **Edit**.

11. Choose the Play a **Macro** radio button, and then choose the **Add Macro** button.

12. Type editbar in the **Name** text box and choose **Select** or press ⏎Enter to add an editbar button to your Button Bar.

13. Choose the **Add Macro** button again, type bookmrk in the **Name** text box, and choose **Select** or press ⏎Enter to add a bookmrk button to your Button Bar.

14. Choose OK to close the Button Bar Editor for the Document Button Bar.

15. Click the down-arrow button at the end of the Button Bar to display the Editbar and Bookmrk buttons. Click the Editbar button to display the Editing Button Bar.

16. Open the Button Bar QuickMenu and choose **Edit**. Then choose the **P**lay a Macro radio button and use the Add Macro button to add buttons to play both the bookmrk and the docbar macros. Choose the OK button.

17. Click the Bookmrk button on the Editing Button Bar to select the Bookmark Button Bar.

18. Open the Button Bar QuickMenu, choose **Edit**, choose the **P**lay a Macro radio button, and use the Add Macro button to add buttons to play both the editbar and the docbar macros. Choose the OK button.

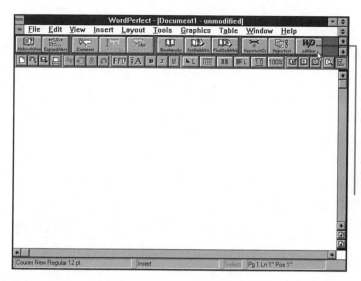

Here, you see the Bookmark Button Bar after adding the editbar and docbar (not visible in this figure) macro buttons.

Now, all three of your custom Button Bars are linked to one another, enabling you to select any of the other two by clicking the appropriate button rather than having to select them from the Button Bar QuickMenu. Go ahead and experiment with selecting the various Button Bars by clicking the Editbar, Bookmrk, and Docbar buttons.

Summary

In this chapter, you learned how to modify any of the predefined Button Bars that come with WordPerfect 6.0 for Windows as well as create custom Button Bars that contain just the buttons you need to accomplish a particular task. Keep in mind when editing or creating a Button Bar that you can add buttons that choose particular menu commands and features, insert text, launch other programs, or play macros you have recorded.

Index

A

abbreviations, 121-123
Abbreviation button, 487
Abbreviations (Ctrl+A) shortcut key, 55
Abbreviations command (Insert menu), 121
Abbreviations dialog box, 121-123, 489
About Help command (Help menu, Help window), 60
About WordPerfect command (Help menu), 59
abstracts of documents, 272
Activate a Feature radio button, 479, 481, 483
Add Printer dialog box, 253
Add QuickList Item dialog box, 278
Additional Installation Options dialog box, 252
Address Font dialog box, 337
Advance dialog box, 223
Advance option, positioning text, 223-224

alignment, 188-193
  vertical, 432
Alpha sort key, 346-348
alphanumeric keys, 54
Alternate key, 54
Always on Top command (Help menu), 60
AND (&) search operator, 293
Annotate command (Edit menu), 60
antonyms, 142, 158-161
Any Single Character (?) search operator, 293
applying styles, 247-248
arrow keys, 83-84
arrows, tables, 421
ascending sort order, 345
Assign Macro to Menu dialog box, 302
assigning passwords, 267-268
Associate command (File Manager File menu), 97
attributes, 196-200
  redline or strikeout, 135-139
auto code placement, 168, 174-175

B

Back Help command button, 61
Back Tab key, 54
Backspace key, 54
backups, 99-101
balanced newspaper columns, 449
bar codes, 82
binding offset, 220-221
Binding Options dialog box, 220
BK! (WordPerfect backup file), 96
blank lines, 123
Block Protect option, 237-238
blocks of text, 16
body text, 362-363
Bold (Ctrl+B) shortcut key, 55, 199
bold text attribute, 199-200
Bookmark button, 488
Bookmark command (Insert menu), 388
Bookmark dialog box, 389
Bookmark menu, Help window, 60
bookmarks, 376
    hypertext links
        creating, 390-392
        editing, 394-395
        jumping, 392-394
    inserting, 388-389
    QuickMark, 389-390
Border button, 490
Border dialog box, 469
Border Style command (Border dialog box), 469-470
borders, 446
    adding, 469-470
    modifying lines, 427-430
    pages, 231
bottom margins, 221-222
Box Caption dialog box, 464
bullets, 205-207, 366

Bullets & Numbers command (Insert menu), 205-206
Bullets & Numbers dialog box, 205-206
Bullets and Numbers (Ctrl+Shift+B) shortcut key, 55
business letters, 79-80
Button Bar command (View menu), 20, 32-35, 304, 476, 478, 483, 485
Button Bar Editor dialog box, 304, 478, 481, 483
Button Bar Location dialog box, 483
Button Bar Preferences dialog box, 34, 483-485
Button Bar QuickMenu, 477
Button Bar Setup dialog box, 33-34
Button Bars, 20-22, 27, 32-35, 87, 171, 476
    creating, 483-484
    custom library, 484
        Bookmark, 487-489
        Document, 489-491
        Editing, 485-487
    editing, 478-482
    linking, 491-493
    macros, adding, 304-305
    Power Bar, 20
    selecting, 476-478
buttons, 476
    Button Bar
        adding, 479, 482-491
        changes, undoing, 482
        removing, 481
        repositioning, 479-480
        separating, 480
    Maximize, 28, 47
    Minimize, 28, 47
    mouse, 41
    radio, *see* radio buttons
    Restore, 28, 47

C

Calculate command (Table menu), 439-443

calculations, tables, 438-443

capitalization (Speller), 156-157

Caption command (Graphics QuickMenu), 464

captions (graphics images), 464

Cascade command
  Program Manager Window menu, 67
  Windows menu, 116

cascading
  menus, 87
  windows, 116-118

case of text
  converting, 201
  Speller, 156-157

CaseToggle button, 486

Cell Formula Entry mode, 438, 440

cells, 406
  borders, 428-429
  cutting/copying, 415-416
  formats, 406, 431-433
  joining, 424-426
  justification, 412-413, 437
  locking, 433
  naming, 407
  ranges, 413, 442-443
  selecting, 413-415
  table
    formulas, entering, 438-440
    text, entering, 411-413

Center (Ctrl+E) shortcut key, 55

center justification, 186

Center Line (Shift+F7) shortcut key, 188-189

centering
  between margins, 188-189
  on specific point, 189
  vertically on pages, 222-223

character alignment, 192

Character command (Insert menu), 206-208

character strings, 148-151

character transposition macro, 312-313

characters, 206-208
  erasing, 413
  footnotes/endnotes, numbering, 400-401
  inserting in text, 413
  wild-card, 147

check boxes, 90

clicking mouse, 42

Clipboard, 66
  copying/pasting, 104-106

Close button, 489

Close command (File menu), 101

Close Document (Alt+F4) shortcut key, 95

closing windows
  document window, 101-102, 118
  Help window, 63
  Reveal Codes window, 39

Coach command (Help menu), 58, 62

codes
  auto code placement, 174-175
  finding, 144-145
  formatting, 77
  hidden, 39, 132-135
  replacing, 148-151

Codes dialog box, 145, 147

Column radio button, 430

column sorts, 356

column-margin icons, 409

columns, 406-407
  borders, 469-470
  deleting, 424
  formatting, 433-434
  inserting, 423
  justification, 432-434

newspaper, 446
  defining, 447-451
  text, entering, 453-454
  widths, adjusting, 451-452
parallel, 450-451
sizes, 450-451
tabular, 446-447
text, 446-447
widths, 421-423
Columns command (Layout menu),
  446, 448-449, 453-454, 469
Columns dialog box, 448-451
commands
  canceling, 94
  Edit menu
    Annotate (Help window), 60
    Convert Case, 201, 312
    Copy, 104-106, 127-132, 415-416
    Cut, 105-106, 127-132, 415-416
    Find, 142-147
    Go To, 85
    Go To Last Position, 146
    Paste, 105-106, 127-132, 416,
      459
    Replace, 148-151
    Undelete, 126
    Undo, 125-126, 351, 420
  File menu
    Close, 101
    Compare Document, 138
    Document Summary, 270-276
    Exit, 102, 388
    New, 71, 79, 115
    Open, 22, 80
    Preferences, 306
    Preferences, Display, 31, 39, 41,
      73, 77, 169
    Preferences, Environment, 135
    Preferences, File, 99, 101
    Preferences, Keyboard, 53,
      306-307

Preferences, Status Bar, 31
Preferences, Summary, 275-276
Print, 259-264
QuickFinder, 286-293
Save, 71, 94, 100, 343, 388
Save As, 23, 71, 94, 343
Select Printer, 250-258
Template, 72
File Options pop-up menu, 280-285
Graphics menu
  Figure, 458-459
  Horizontal Line, 470
  Vertical Line, 471
Help menu
  About Help, 60
  About WordPerfect, 59
  Always on Top, 60
  Coach, 58, 62
  Contents, 58
  How Do I, 58
  How to Use Help, 60
  Macros, 310
  Search for Help On, 58
  Tutorial, 58
  What Is, 59
Insert menu
  Abbreviations, 121
  Bookmark, 388
  Bullets & Numbers, 205-206
  Character, 206-208
  Comment, Convert to Text, 384
  Comment, Create, 380, 384
  Comment, Edit, 383
  Date, 79
  Endnote, Create, 395
  Endnote, Edit, 397
  Endnote, New Number, 398
  Endnote, Options, 399
  Endnote, Placement, 403
  File, 115-116

Footnote, Create, 395
Footnote, Edit, 397
Footnote, New Number, 398
Footnote, Options, 399
Sound, 384, 387
Layout menu
  Columns, 446, 448-449, 453-454, 469
  Document, Initial Codes Style, 75
  Document Redline Method, 136
  Envelope, 80, 216-218
  Font, 197-198, 314
  Font, Bold, 199
  Font, Italic, 199
  Font, Redline, 137
  Font, Strikeout, 137
  Header/Footer, 226-232
  Justification, 187, 412
  Labels, 338-339
  Line, Center, 188-189
  Line, Flush Right, 190-191
  Line, Flush Right, 79
  Line, Height, 203-204
  Line, Hyphenation, 209-212
  Line, Numbering, 377
  Line, Other Codes, 192, 209
  Line, Tab Set, 179-181, 192-193
  Line Spacing, 202
  Margins, 173, 221-222, 313
  Page, 469
  Page, Binding, 220-221
  Page, Border/Fill, 231
  Page, Center, 222-223
  Page, Force Page, 239-240
  Page, Keep Text Together, 237-239
  Page, Paper Size, 215-216, 218-220
  Page, Subdivide, 240-242
  Page, Suppress, 234-235

Page Numbering, 232-234
Paragraph, 469
Paragraph, Double Indent, 183-184
Paragraph, Hanging Indent command, 184-185
Paragraph, Indent, 182-185
QuickFormat, 204-206
Styles, Apply, 247-248
Styles, Create, 245-246
Styles, Options, 246-247
Styles, Quick Create, 243-244
Typesetting, Advance, 223-224
Watermark, 229-232
menu, selecting, 43-45
Preferences menu, 382
selecting
  QuickMenu, 88-89
  with keyboard, 87-88
  with mnemonic keys, 54
Table menu
  Calculate, 439-443
  Data Fill, 441-442
  Format, 430-436
  Join/Cell, 424
  Join/Table, 426
  Lines/Fill, 427
  Split/Cell, 426
  Split/Table, 426
  Sum, 442-443
Tools menu
  Grammatik, 162-166
  Hypertext, 390, 392, 394
  Macro, 297, 303, 491-492
  Macro, Edit, 308
  Macro, Pause, 299
  Macro, Play, 297, 300-301, 311, 314
  Macro, Record, 297, 299, 311-313
  Merge, 320-339

Outline, 365, 369-370
Sort, 343, 348, 356
Speller, 151-157
Thesaurus, 157-161
View menu
Button Bar, 20, 32-35, 304, 476,
478, 483, 485
Draft, 77
Page, 79, 264
Power Bar, 74, 408
Reveal Codes, 39, 133, 135
Ruler, 38-39, 74
Ruler Bar, 123, 171
Show, 77
Windows menu
Cascade, 116
Tile, 116
Comment button, 487
Comment command (Insert menu)
Convert to Text option, 384
Create option, 380, 384
Edit option, 383
Comment Feature Bar, 380, 383
CommentCvt button, 487
CommentEd button, 487
comments, 376
converting text to/from, 383-384
editing, 383
inserting, 380-382
sound clip
adding, 384-385
playing, 385-386
recording, 387-388
Common User Access (CUA), 10, 12
keyboards, 51-53
Common User Interfaace (CUA)
keyboards, 16
Compare Document command (File
menu), 138
comparison operators in selection
statements, 358-359

compatibility of macros, 296
compiling macros, 296
conditional page breaks, 238
Contents command (Help menu), 58
Contents Help command button, 61
context-sensitive help, 59
Control key, 54
Control menu commands
Minimize, 48
Restore, 48
Convert case (Ctrl+K) shortcut key,
56
Convert Case command (Edit menu),
201, 312
Copy command (Edit menu), 104-106,
127-132, 415-416
Copy to Clipboard (Ctrl+C) shortcut
key, 55
copying
cells, 415-416
documents between programs,
104-106
printer drivers, 257
text, 127-128
between WordPerfect
documents, 132
in same document, 128-130
with drag-and-drop feature,
130-131
Create Abbreviation dialog box, 489
Create Bookmark dialog box, 388
Create Button Bar dialog box, 483, 485
Create Comment window, 380
Create Data File dialog box, 321
Create Envelope Definition dialog
box, 217
Create Hypertext Link dialog box,
390-392
Create in the Style List dialog box,
245-246

Create Merge File dialog box, 338-339
Create Paper Size dialog box, 218
Create Table dialog box, 410
cropping graphics images, 466
cross-references, Help topics, 59
Ctrl+Backspace key combination, 413
Ctrl+Shift+Tab key combination, 412
    keyboards, 16, 51-53
CUA (Common User Access), 10-12
cursor-movement keys, 57
cursor movement, 66, 82
        with arrow keys, 83-84
        with Home and End keys, 85
        with keyboard, 83
        with mouse, 83
        with PgUp/PgDn keys, 84
Cut command (Edit menu), 105-106,
    127-132, 415-416
Cut to Clipboard (Ctrl+X) shortcut
    key, 56
cutting
    cells, 415-416
    drag-and-drop method, 418
    text, 127-128
        between WordPerfect
            documents, 132
        in same document, 128-130

D

Dash Character (Ctrl+-) shortcut key,
    209
data files, 318-329
    records
        editing, 326-327
        selecting for merges, 333-336
    table, 320-323
        converting to text, 420
    text, 323-324
Data Fill command (Table menu),
    441-442

Date code (Ctrl+Shift+D) shortcut
    key, 55
Date command (Insert menu), 79
Date text (Ctrl+D) shortcut key, 55
dates in comments, 380
decimal alignment, 191-192
decimal places (in cells), 434, 437
Default Directory For Saving Indexes
    dialog box, 286
default settings, 73-75
Delete File dialog box, 282
Delete Table dialog box, 420
deleted text, restoring, 126
deleting
    endnotes, 398
    footnotes, 398
    headers/footers, 229
    hidden codes, 135
    passwords, 269
    printer drivers, 257
    tables, 419-420
    tabs, 177-180
    text
        with redline or strikeout
            attribute, 138-139
        with shortcut keys, 124-125
demoting, 362
    headings, 369
    levels, 365
descending sort order, 345
dialog boxes, 44
    Abbreviations, 489
    Assign Macro to Menu, 302
    Bookmark, 389
    Border, 469
    Box Caption, 464
    Button Bar Editor, 304, 478, 481,
        483
    Button Bar Location, 483
    Button Bar Preferences, 483-485

Columns, 448-451
Create Abbreviation, 489
Create Bookmark, 388
Create Button Bar, 483, 485
Create Hypertext Link, 390-392
Create Table, 410
Delete Table, 420
Edit Endnote, 397
Edit Footnote, 397
Edit Graphics Line, 471
Edit Hypertext Link, 394
Edit Macro, 308
Endnote Number, 398
Endnote Options, 399
Endnote Placement, 403
Environment Preferences, 380, 382
Font, 395, 431
Footnote Number, 398
Footnote Options, 399
Format, 430, 432
Format Cell, 413
Format Column, 413
Go To, 453
Insert Image, 458
Insert Sound Clip into Document, 384
Keyboard Editor, 306-307
Keyboard Preferences, 306-307
Line Numbering, 377, 379
Line Separator, 402
Macro Facility Syntax Error, 310
Macro Location, 298, 300-301, 308
options, 89
Play Macro, 297, 301-303
Preferences, 307
Record Macro, 296-297, 299
Save As, 388
Select File, 300, 482
Select Input File, 349
Select Macro, 302, 304, 307

Select Output File, 349
Sort, 353-356
Sound Clips, 384
Styles Editor, 395, 401
Table Format, 437
Tables Lines/Fill, 427-429
Wrap Text, 462
dictionaries, 142, 157
dimmed commands, 44
directories
    files, saving, 95
    \GRAPHICS, 458
    opening, 109
Display Preferences dialog box, 31, 73, 77, 169
DocInfo button, 490
document dictionaries, 157
Document command (Layout menu)
    Initial Codes Style option, 75
    Redline Method option, 136
document summaries, 266
    entering information, 270-272
    preferences, 275-276
    printing, 272-273
    saving, 272-274
Document Summary command (File menu), 270-276
Document Summary dialog box, 271-276
document window, 26, 35
    closing, 101-102, 118
    Reveal Codes window, 39-41
    Ruler Bar, 38-39
    scroll bars, 36-38
    viewing, 116
documents, 71
    backups, 99-101
    business letters, 79-80
    copying between programs, 104-106
    formatting with styles, 242-248

opening, 108-111
  at WordPerfect startup, 69
  multiple, 115-116
  new, 115
passwords
  assigning, 267-268
  deleting/changing, 269
  opening protected files, 268-269
pasting between programs, 104-106
printing, 259-264
replacing text and codes, 148-151
saving, 94-96, 98
templates, 72
viewing, 111-112
watermarks, 229-232
dot leaders, 177, 181
Double Indent Paragraph
  (Ctrl+Shift+F7) shortcut key, 183
double words, 156
double-clicking with mouse, 13, 15, 42
Draft command (View menu), 77
Draft mode, 77-79
  comment text, 381-382
Draft mode (Ctrl+F5) shortcut key, 77
dragging and dropping with mouse,
  15, 42, 130-131, 418
drivers, *see* printer drivers
drop-down list boxes, 89

E

Edit Caption command (Graphics
  QuickMenu), 464
Edit Endnote dialog box, 397
Edit Footnote dialog box, 397
Edit Graphics Line dialog box, 471
Edit Hypertext Link dialog box, 394
Edit Macro dialog box, 308
  Annotate, 60
  Convert Case, 201, 312
  Copy, 104-106, 127-132, 415-416

Cut, 105-106, 127-132, 415-416
Find, 142-147
Go To, 85
Go To Last Position, 146
Paste, 105-106, 127-132, 416, 459
Replace, 148-151
Undelete, 126
Undo, 125-126, 351, 420
Edit QuickList dialog box, 113
Edit QuickList Item dialog box, 278
editing
  Button Bars, 478-482
  comments, 383
  endnotes, 397-398
  footnotes, 397-398
  graphics images, 465-468
  headers/footers, 228-229
  macros, 308-310
  outlines, 369
  QuickList, 276-278
  records in data files, 326-327
  styles, 245-246
  table structure, 420
    border lines/fill patterns, 427-430
    cells, 424-426
    column widths, 421-423
    columns/rows, 423-424
    joining/splitting, 426-427
    text, 413
ellipses(...), 44
End key, 85
Endnote command (Insert menu)
  Create option, 395
  Edit option, 397
  New Number option, 398
  Options option, 399
  Placement option, 403
Endnote Feature Bar, 395-397
Endnote Number dialog box, 398
Endnote Options dialog box, 399

Endnote Placement dialog box, 403
endnotes, 376, 395
    creating, 395-397
    deleting, 398
    editing, 397-398
    location of, 403
    numbering, 396, 398
    numbering methods, 400, 403
    options, 399-403
    spacing between, 402
    see also footnotes
Enter key, 54
Envelope command (Layout menu),
    80, 216-218
Envelope dialog box, 216-218
envelopes, 80-82, 216-218, 337-338
Environment command (Preferences
    menu), 382
Environment Preferences dialog box,
    210-212, 380, 382
environments, 103
equation boxes, 454-456
Equation Editor, 454-456
errors (macros), 309-310
Esc key, 94
EXE (Program or executable file), 96
Exit command (File menu), 70, 102,
    388
exiting WordPerfect, 101-102
ExpandAbrv button, 487

F

families (outlines), 362, 371-372
Feature Bars, 20-22
    Comment, 380, 383
    Macro, 308, 310
    Outline, 365, 368, 370-372
    Sound, 385-386
fields, 318, 342-343
Figure command (Graphics menu),
    458-459

File command (Insert menu), 115-116
File Manager
    Associate command, 97
    Exit command, 70
    starting WordPerfect for Windows,
        70-71
File menu (Alt+F) shortcut keys, 29
File menu commands
    Associate (File Manager), 97
    Close, 101
    Compare Document, 138
    Document Summary, 270-276
    Exit, 102, 388
        File Manager, 70
    Help window, 59
    New, 71, 79, 115
    Open, 22, 68, 80
    Preferences, 306
    Preferences, Display, 31, 39, 41, 73,
        77, 169
    Preferences, Environment, 135
    Preferences, File, 99, 101
    Preferences, Keyboard, 53, 306-307
    Preferences, Status Bar, 31
    Preferences, Summary, 275-276
    Print, 259-264
    QuickFinder, 286-293
    Run, 68
    Save, 71, 94, 100, 343, 388
    Save As, 23, 71, 94, 343
    Select Printer, 250-258
    Template, 72
file names, 66, 96-97
    extensions, 96-97
    headers/footers, 228
File Options pop-up menu, 280-285
File Preferences dialog box, 99
File Viewer, 111-112
files
    compatibility with Versions 5.1 and
        5.2, 22-23

data, 318-329
   editing records, 326-327
   selecting records for merges,
     333-336
   table, 320-323
   text, 323-324
finding with QuickFinder, 289-293
form files, 318-333
indexing with QuickFinder, 286-288
management options, 280-285
opening, 112-113
PRINTER.TST, 257-258
QuickList, 279
saving document summary, 272-274
table data, 420
fill patterns, 427-430
Find and Replace Text dialog box,
  148-151
Find button, 485
Find command (Edit menu), 142-147
Find dialog box, 143-147
Find Next button, 485
Find Prev button, 485
Find QuickMark (Ctrl+Q) shortcut
  key, 56
Find Text dialog box, 143-147, 326
finding
   files (QuickFinder), 289-293
   Help topics, 61-62
   text, 142-147
FindQuikMrk button, 488
flipping graphics images, 467-468
Flush Right (Alt+F7) shortcut key,
  190-191
flush right alignment, 190-191
FON (Windows font file) file name
  extension, 96
Font (F9) shortcut key, 197
Font command (Layout menu),
  197-198, 314

Bold option, 199
Italic option, 199
Redline option, 137
Strikeout option, 137
Font dialog box, 395, 431
Font Underline shortcut key, 199
fonts, 168, 193-197
  attributes, 196
  changing, 197-198
  initial, 254
  selecting, 430-431
footers/headers, 214, 226-227
  deleting, 229
  editing, 228-229
  file names, 228
  page numbers, 227
  placement, 228
Footnote command (Insert menu)
  Create option, 395
  Edit option, 397
  New Number option, 398
  Options option, 399
Footnote Feature Bar, 395-397
Footnote Number dialog box, 398
Footnote Options dialog box, 399
footnotes, 376, 395
  continued onto next page, 402-403
  creating, 395-397
  deleting, 398
  editing, 397-398
  locating, 402
  numbering, 396, 398
  numbering methods, 400, 403
  options, 399-403
  spacing between, 402
  see also endnotes
Force Page dialog box, 239
form files (merges), 318-333
Format Cell dialog box, 413
Format Column dialog box, 413

Format command (Table menu),
  430-431, 433, 435-436
Format dialog box, 430, 432
formats
  cells, 406
  sound, 385
formatting
  columns, 434
  documents, 242-248
  page numbers, 232-234
  pages, suppressing, 234-235
  tables, 436-438
    cells, 431-433
    columns, 433-434
    fonts, selecting, 430-431
    levels, 430
    rows, 435-436
  text with QuickFormat, 204-206
formatting codes, 77
full justification, 186
Full justification (Ctrl+J) shortcut key,
  56
function keys, 51-53

G

global find/replace option, 150-151
global selection statements, 359
Go To (Ctrl+G) shortcut key, 56
Go To button, 62
Go To command (Edit menu), 85
Go To Data shortcut key, 328
Go To dialog box, 85-87, 453
Go To key, 85-87
Go To Last Position command (Edit
  menu), 146
gradient fill patterns, 429
Grammatik command (Tools menu),
  162-166
Grammatik dialog box, 162-166
Graphical User Interface (GUI), 10-11,
  41

graphics, 17-22, 454-457
graphics boxes, 446
  moving, 460-462
  resizing, 462-464
  types, 454, 456
\GRAPHICS directory, 458
graphics images
  captions, adding, 464
  editing, 465-468
  inserting, 458-460
  modifications, undoing, 466
  moving, 460-462
  resizing, 462-464
  rotating/flipping, 467-468
  scaling/cropping, 466
Graphics Line QuickMenu, 471
graphics lines, 446
  adding, 470-472
  moving, 472
Graphics menu commands
  Figure, 458-459
  Horizontal Line, 470
  Vertical Line, 471
Graphics QuickMenu
  Caption command, 464
  Edit Caption command, 464
  Image Tools command, 465
  Wrap command, 462
gray commands, 44
Group (( )) search operator, 293
GUI (Graphical User Interface), 10-16,
  41
gutters, 450-451

H

Hanging Indent Paragraph (Ctrl+F7)
  shortcut key, 184
hanging indents, 184-185
hard hyphens, 209
hard page breaks, 214, 235-236

hard returns, 66
hard spaces, 208-209
header rows, 435
Header/Footer command (Layout
  menu), 226-232
headers/footers, 214, 226-227
  deleting, 229
  editing, 228-229
  file names, 228
  page numbers, 227
  placement, 228
Headers/Footers dialog box, 226
headings (outlines), 366
  converting to body text, 369
  moving, 369, 372
  promoting/demoting, 369
headwords (Thesaurus), 142
Help
  closing, 63
  on-line, 58-59
  searching for topics, 61-62
Help menu commands, 58-60
  About Help, 60
  About WordPerfect, 59
  Always on Top, 60
  Coach, 58, 62
  Contents, 58
  How Do I, 58
  How to Use Help, 60
  Macros, 310
  Search for Help On, 58
  Tutorial, 58
  What Is, 59
hidden codes, 39, 132-135
History Help command button, 61
HLP (Help file) file name extension, 96
Home key, 85
horizontal graphics lines, 470-472
Horizontal Line command (Graphics
  menu), 470
How Do I command (Help menu), 58

How to Use Help command (Help
  menu), 60
Hypertext button, 488
Hypertext command (Tools menu),
  390, 392, 394
Hypertext Feature Bar, 390
hypertext, 376
  bookmarks, 390-395
  macros, creating, 392
HypertextCr button, 488
Hyphenation feature, 208-212
Hyphenation Prompt setting, 210-212

I-beam pointer, 26
icons, 10, 12-14, 409
Ignore Cell When Calculating
  command (Format dialog box), 433
Image Tools command (Graphics
  QuickMenu), 465
Image Tools palette
  displaying, 465
  graphics images
    rotating/flipping, 467-468
    scaling/cropping, 466
images, graphics, *see* graphics images
Indent Paragraph (F7) shortcut key, 182
indents
  paragraphs, 182-185
  releasing, 412
indexes, 286-289
INI (Windows initial settings file) file
  name extension, 96
Init Style button, 489
Initial Caps button, 485
initial caps macro, 312
Initial Font button, 490
initial fonts for printers, 254
Insert Field Name or Number dialog
  box, 338-339

Insert File dialog box, 115
Insert Image dialog box, 458
Insert menu commands
   Abbreviations, 121
   Bookmark, 388
   Bullets & Numbers, 205-206
   Character, 206-208
   Comment, Convert to Text, 384
   Comment, Create, 380, 384
   Comment,Edit, 383
   Date, 79
   Endnote, Create, 395
   Endnote, Edit, 397
   Endnote, New Number, 398
   Endnote, Options, 399
   Endnote, Placement, 403
   File, 115-116
   Footnote, Create, 395
   Footnote, Edit, 397
   Footnote, New Number, 398
   Footnote, Options, 399
   Sound, 384, 387
Insert mode, 108, 119-121, 182
Insert Sound Clip into Document
  dialog box, 384
inserting
   blank lines, 123
   spaces, 123
   tabs, 123
   text with abbreviations, 121-123
insertion point, 57, 66
Installation Type dialog box, 252
installing printer drivers, 252
Italic (Ctrl) shortcut key, 56, 199
italic text attribute, 199-200

J-K

Join Cells command (Table
  QuickMenu), 424
Join/Cell command (Table menu), 424

Join/Table command (Table menu),
  426
jumps (hypertext), 392-394
justification, 185-187
  cells, 437
  columns, 432, 434
Justification command (Layout menu),
  187, 412

Keep Text Together dialog box,
  237-248
key combinations
  assigning macros to, 307
  cell selection, 415
  Ctrl+Backspace, 413
  Ctrl+Shift+Tab, 412
  Shift+Tab, 412
  tables, navigating, 410-411
keyboard
  macros, assigning, 306-307
  selecting cells with, 415
  tables, navigating, 410-411
Keyboard Editor dialog box, 306-307
Keyboard Preferences dialog box, 53,
  306-307
keyboards, 50
  commands, selecting, 87-88
  Common User Interface (CUA), 16
  deleting text, 124-125
  QWERTY, 54
  selecting text, 120-121, 124
keys
  alphanumeric, 54
  arrow, 83-84
  cursor-movement, 57, 83
  End, 85
  function, 51-53
  Go To, 85-87
  Home, 85
  mnemonic, 54-55
  PgUp/PgDn, 84

sort, 342
    defining, 346
    specifying for column sorting, 356
    specifying for line sorts, 351-353
    specifying for merge record
      sorting, 354
    specifying for paragraph sorts, 353
    specifying for table sorting,
      355-356
    types, selecting, 346-348
    see also shortcut keys
keystroke abbreviations, 122
keywords, 272

L

labels, 338-339
Labels command (Layout menu),
  338-339
Labels dialog box, 338-339
Landscape mode, 215
Launch a Program radio button, 479,
  482-483
Layout menu commands
    Columns, 446, 448-449, 453-454,
      469
    Document, Initial Codes Style, 75
    Document Redline Method, 136
    Envelope, 80, 216-218
    Font, 197-198, 314
    Font, Bold, 199
    Font, Italic, 199
    Font, Redline, 137
    Font, Strikeout, 137
    Header/Footer, 226-232
    Justification, 187, 412
    Labels, 338-339
    Line, Center, 188-189
    Line, Flush Right, 190-191
    Line, Flush Right, 79
    Line Height, 203-204

Line, Hyphenation, 209-212
Line, Numbering, 377
Line, Other Codes, 192, 209
Line Spacing, 202
Line, Tab Set, 179-181, 192-193
Margins, 173, 221-222, 313
Page, 469
Page, Binding, 220-221
Page, Border/Fill, 231
Page, Center, 222-223
Page, Force Page, 239-240
Page, Keep Text Together, 237-239
Page Numbering, 232-234
Page, Paper Size, 215-216, 218-220
Page, Subdivide, 240-242
Page, Suppress, 234-235
Paragraph, 469
Paragraph, Double Indent, 183-184
Paragraph, Hanging Indent
  command, 184-185
Paragraph, Indent, 182-185
QuickFormat, 204-206
Styles, Apply, 247-248
Styles, Create, 245-246
Styles, Options, 246-247
Styles, Quick Create, 243-244
Typesetting, Advance, 223-224
Watermark, 229-232
left justification, 186
Left justification (+L) shortcut key, 56
legal numbering, 367
letter (new) macro, 313-314
letters, 79-80
levels
    outlines, 362-366
      headings, moving, 369, 372
      promoting/demoting, 365
      viewing, 370-372
    table format, 430
LEX (WordPerfect spelling dictionary)
  file name extension, 96

libraries
  custom Button Bars, 484-493
  macros, 310-314
line breaks, 208-212
Line Center command (Layout menu), 188-189
Line command (Layout menu)
  Flush Right option, 79, 190-191
  Numbering option, 377
  Other Codes option, 192, 209
  Tab Set option, 179-181, 192-193
line height, 168, 203-204
Line Height command (Layout menu), 203-204
Line Height dialog box, 203-204
Line Hyphenation command (Layout menu), 209-212
Line Numbering dialog box, 377, 379
Line Separator dialog box, 402
line sorts, 351-353
line spacing, 201-202
Line Spacing command (Layout menu), 202
Line Spacing dialog box, 202
lines
  inserting, 123
  numbering, 377-379
  separating text from footnotes, 402
Lines/Fill command (Table menu), 427
linking
  bookmarks by hypertext, 390-395
  Button Bars, 491-493
list boxes, 89
list buttons, 91
locking cells, 433
Look Up option (Thesaurus), 161
Lowercase button, 485
lowercase text
  converting to uppercase, 201
  Speller, 156-157

M

Macro command (Tools menu), 297, 303, 491-492
  Edit option, 308
  Pause option, 299
  Play option, 297, 300-301, 311, 314
  Record option, 297, 299, 311-313
Macro Facility Syntax Error dialog box, 310
Macro Feature Bar, 308, 310
macro libraries, 310-311
  character transposition, 312-313
  company name/address, 311
  initial caps, 312
  new letter, 313-314
Macro Location dialog box, 298, 300-301, 308
Macro menu
  assigning assigning, 301-303
  removing macros, 303
macros, 296
  Button Bars, linking, 491-493
  character transposition, 312-313
  company name/address, 311
  compatibility, 296
  compiling, 296
  creating, 297
  document, 296
  editing, 308-310
  errors, 309-310
  hypertext link, 392
  initial caps, 312
  naming, 298
  new letter, 313-314
  playing, 300-307
  quick, 296
  recording, 297-300
  removing from menu, 303
Macros command (Help menu), 310

Mailing Address Font dialog box, 337
mailing labels, 338-339
managing
    files, 280-285
    QuickFinder indexes, 288-289
margins, 171-173
    positions, changing, 434, 437
    top and bottom, 221-222
Margins (Ctrl+F8) shortcut key, 173
Margins command (Layout menu),
    173, 221-222, 313
Margins dialog box, 172-173, 221-222
marking text (redline/strikeout),
    137-138
Maximize button, 28, 47
measurement units, 31, 169-170
Menu Bar (Alt or F10) shortcut key, 87
menu bars, 26, 28-29
Merge command (Tools menu),
    320-329, 330-339
Merge dialog box, 320-329, 330-339
merges, 318-329
    addressing envelopes, 337-338
    form file to data file, 329-333
    printing mailing labels, 338-339
    record sorts, 354
Microsoft Windows, 11
MIDI (Music Instrument Digital
    Interface) format, 385
Minimize button, 28, 47
Minimize command (Windows
    Control menu), 48
Mirror Horizontal button, 468
Mirror Vertical button, 468
mnemonic keys, 54-55
modes
    Cell Formula Entry, 438, 440
    Draft, 77-79
    Insert, 108, 119-121, 182
    Page, 79

    paper, 215
    Read-Only, 111
    Select, 124
    Typeover, 108, 119, 123
    WYSIWYG (What-You-See-Is-What-
      You-Get), 17
monospaced fonts, 193
mouse, 10, 41
    clicking, 42
    double-clicking, 13, 42
    drag-and-drop, 130-131, 418
    dragging, 42
    moving
      cursors, 83
      windows, 47-50
    pointers, 14-15, 26
    recording macros, 300
    selecting
      cells, 413-414
      commands, 43-44
      QuickMenu commands, 45
      text, 45-47
    speeds of double-clicking and
      tracking, 43
    sizing windows, 47-50
Move Image button, 466
moving
    cursors, 82
      with arrow keys, 83-84
      with Home and End keys, 85
      with keyboard, 83
      with mouse, 83
      with PgUp/PgDn keys, 84
    text, 128-131
    windows with mouse, 47-50
Multiple Pages dialog box, 261

N

names
  columns, 407
  files, 96-97
  inserting in comments, 380, 382
  macros, 298
  series, creating, 441
navigating tables, 410-411
New command (File menu), 71, 79, 115
New Document (Ctrl+N) shortcut
  key, 56
new letter macro, 313-314
newspaper columns, 446
  balanced, creating, 449
  defining
    Columns button, 447-449
    Columns dialog box, 449-451
  text, entering, 453-454
  widths, adjusting, 451-452
non-Windows programs, 10
NOT (!) search operator, 293
numbering
  footnotes/endnotes, 396, 398, 400,
    403
  legal, 367
  lines, 377-379
  pages, 232
    formats, 232-234
    headers/footers, 227
numbers, 205-206
  ignoring with Speller, 155
  series, creating, 441
  sorting, 348
  superscript, 401
Numeric sort key, 346-348

O

object-action model, 16
on-line Help, 58-59

Open command (File menu), 22, 68, 80
Open document (Ctrl+O) shortcut
  key, 56
Open File (Ctrl+O) shortcut key, 80
Open File dialog box, 80, 108, 111-113
opening
  documents, 108-111
    at WordPerfect startup, 69
    multiple, 115-116
    new, 115
  files
    options, 112-113
    password-protected, 268-269
operators
  comparison, 358-359
  search, 292-293
option buttons, 90
OR (|) search operator, 293
original backups, 100
orphan/widow protection, 239
orphans, 214
Other Codes dialog box, 192
Outline command (Tools menu), 365,
  369-370
outline families, 362, 371-372
Outline Feature Bar, 365, 368, 370
  collapsing/expanding
    families, 370-372
    outlines, 370-372
  moving headings, 369, 372
Outline styles (Ctrl+Shift+O)
  shortcut key, 56
Outline view, 369
outlines, 362-364
  collapsing/expanding, 370-372
  creating, 365-367
  editing, 369
  headings, 366
    converting to body text, 369
    moving, 369, 372
    promoting/demoting, 369

levels, 362-363, 365-366
    promoting/demoting, 365
    viewing, 370-372
styles, 362, 366, 368
text, 362-363

P

page breaks, 235-236
    conditional, 238
    hard, 236
    odd/even, 239-240
    widow/orphan protection, 239
Page command (Layout menu), 469
    Binding option, 220-221
    Border/Fill option, 231, 469
    Center option, 222-223
    Force Page option, 239-240
    Keep Text Together option, 237-239
    Paper Size option, 215-216, 218-220
    Subdivide option, 240-242
    Suppress option, 234-235
Page command (View menu), 79, 264
Page Format dialog box, 221
Page mode, 381-382
Page mode (Alt+F5) shortcut key, 79
Page number display (Ctrl+Shift+P)
    shortcut key, 56
Page Numbering command (Layout
    menu), 232-234
Page Numbering dialog box, 233
page numbers (headers/footers), 227
Page View (Alt+F5) shortcut key, 264
pages
    borders, 231, 469-470
    margins, 221-222
    numbering, 232-234
    positioning text with Advance
        option, 223-224
    printing, 259-263
    Speller, 152-154

subdividing, 240-242
suppressing formatting, 234-235
text
    Block Protect option, 237-238
    centering vertically, 222-223
    Thesaurus, 157-161
Paper Size dialog box, 215, 218-220
paper sizes, 215-221
    binding offset, 220-221
    new, 218-221
PaperSize button, 490
ParaFormat button, 490
Paragraph command (Layout menu),
    469
    Border/Fill option, 469
    Double Indent option, 183-184
    Hanging Indent option, 184-185
    Indent option, 182-185
paragraphs
    borders, 469-470
    indenting, 182-185
    sorting, 353
parallel columns, 446
    creating, 450-451
    text, entering, 453-454
passwords
    assigning, 267-268
    deleting/changing, 269
    opening protected files, 268-269
Paste command (Edit menu), 105-106,
    127-132, 416, 459
Paste from Clipboard (Ctrl+V)
    shortcut key, 56
pasting
    documents between programs,
        104-106
    drag-and-drop method, 418
    text, 127-128
        between WordPerfect
            documents, 132
        in same document, 128-130

pausing macro recording, 299
Perform Merge dialog box, 330-339
Perform Merge Options dialog box, 331
PgUp/PgDn keys, 84
PIF (Windows program initiation file) file name extension, 96
Play a Keyboard Script radio button, 479, 482-483
Play a Macro radio button, 479, 482-483, 492
Play Macro dialog box, 297, 301-303
playing macros, 300-301
    Button Bar, 304-305
    keyboard, 306-307
    macro cascading menu, 301-303
point-and-click with mouse, 15
pointers, 14-15, 26
points, 194
pop-up list buttons, 91
Portrait mode, 215
position indicators, 30-31
POSTNET bar code, 82
Power Bar, 20, 26-27, 30, 171
    selecting commands, 87
    tables, creating, 408-410
Power Bar command (View menu), 74, 408
Preferences command (File menu), 306
    Display option, 31, 39, 41, 73, 77, 169
    Environment option, 135, 382
    File option, 99, 101
    Keyboard option, 53, 306-307
    Status Bar, 31
    Summary option, 275-276
Preferences dialog box, 31, 169, 307
previewing documents, 264
primary files, *see* form files
primary mouse button, 41
Print shortcut key, 259

Print command (File menu), 259-264
Print Help command button, 61
Print Output Options dialog box options, 260
Print page (Ctrl+P) shortcut key, 56
PrintDoc button, 489
printer drivers, 216
    copying/deleting, 257
    updating, 257
    Windows, 250
    WordPerfect, 250, 252
Printer Information dialog box, 254
Printer Setup dialog box, 256
PRINTER.TST file, 257-258
printers, 250-251
    adding, 253-254
    initial fonts, 254
    testing, 257-258
    WordPerfect setup options, 255-256
printing
    document summaries, 272-273
    documents, 259-264
Program Manager
    starting WordPerfect for Windows, 67-68
    Window menu commands
        Cascade, 67
        Tile, 67
program window, 26, 27
    Button Bar, 32-35
    menu bars, 28-29
    Power Bar, 30
    status bars, 30-32
    title bars, 28
programs
    copying/pasting between, 104-106
    non-Windows, 10
    switching between, 103-104
    Windows, 10

promoting, 362
 headings, 369
 levels, 365
proportionally spaced fonts, 193
pull-down menus, 43-45, 54

Q

Quick Data Entry dialog box, 325-327
quick macros, 296, 298
QuickFinder, 266
 files
  finding, 289-293
  indexing, 286-288
 indexes
  editing, 288
  managing, 288-289
QuickFinder command (File menu),
 286-293
QuickFinder dialog box, 286-293
QuickFormat, 204-206
QuickFormat command (Layout
 menu), 204-206
QuickList, 113-114, 266, 276
 editing, 276-278
 files, 279
QuickMark, 389-390
QuickMenu, 19
 commands, 45, 88-89
QWERTY keyboard arrangement, 54

R

radio buttons, 90
ranges, cell, 413
 totalling, 442-443
Read-Only mode, 111
Record Macro dialog box, 296-297, 299
recording macros, 297-299
 pausing, 299
 with mouse, 300

records, 318, 342-343
 data files, 333-336
 selecting, 357-359
 sorting, 348-356
redline attribute, 108, 136-138
Replace shortcut key, 148
Replace button, 485
Replace command (Edit menu),
 148-151
replacing text and codes, 148-151
Restore button, 28, 47
Restore command (Windows Control
 menu), 48
restoring deleted text, 126
RevCodes button, 486
Reveal Codes command (View menu),
 39, 133, 135
Reveal Codes window, 39-41, 108,
 132-133, 398
right alignment, 190-191
right justification, 186
Right justification (Ctrl+R) shortcut
 key, 56
Rotate button, 467
rotating graphics images, 467-468
Row radio button, 430
rows, 406
 formatting, 435-436
 inserting/deleting, 423-424
Ruler, 19-20, 168, 170-171
 margins, 171-173
 tabs, 176-181
 units of measure, 169
Ruler (Alt+Shift+F3) shortcut key, 38,
 74
Ruler Bar, 38-39
Ruler Bar (Alt+Shift+F3) shortcut
 key, 123
Ruler Bar command (View menu),
 123, 171

Ruler command (View menu), 38-39, 74
RulerBar button, 486
rules, 454
Run command (Windows File menu), 68-69
Run dialog box, 68-69

S

sans serif fonts, 194
Save (Ctrl+S) shortcut key, 56
Save As command (File menu), 23, 71, 94, 343
Save As dialog box, 94-95, 98, 388
Save command (File menu), 71, 94, 100, 343, 388
Save Data File As dialog box, 322
Save File (Ctrl+S) shortcut key, 100
saving
    document summaries, 272-274
    documents, 94-96
        with new name, 98
        with passwords, 266-269
Scale Image button, 466
scaling graphics images, 466
scroll bars, 26
    windows, 36-38
Search for Help On command (Help menu), 58
Search Help command button, 61-62
searching, *see* finding
secondary files, *see* data files
secondary mouse button, 41
security (passwords), 266-269
Select Data File to Associate dialog box, 328
Select Directory dialog box, 256
Select File dialog box, 300, 482
Select Fonts dialog box, 256
Select Input File dialog box, 349

Select key (F8), 124
Select Macro dialog box, 302, 304, 307
Select mode, 124
Select Output File dialog box, 349
Select Printer command (File menu), 250-258
Select Printer dialog box, 216, 250-258
Select Printer Directory dialog box, 252
Select Records dialog box, 333-336
Select Sheet Feeder dialog box, 256
series, creating, 441
serif fonts, 194
Set QuickMark (Ctrl+Shift+Q) shortcut key, 56
SetQuikMrk button, 488
Shift key, 54
Shift+Tab key combination, 412
shortcut keys, 55-57
Show command (View menu), 77
Show Topics button, 61
Show View shortcut key, 77
sizes
    columns, 450-451
    gutter, 450-451
    text, 431
sizing windows with mouse, 47-50
Soft Hyphen (Ctrl+Shift+-) shortcut key, 209
soft page breaks, 214, 235-236
soft returns, 66
Sort command (Tools menu), 343, 348, 356
Sort dialog box, 353-354, 356
sort keys, 342
    column sorting, 356
    defining, 346
    line sorts, 351-353
    merge record sorting, 354
    paragraph sorts, 353

table sorting, 355-356
types, selecting, 346-348
sorting, 342-343
methods, choosing, 343
numbers, 348
orders, choosing, 345-346
records, 348-351
column sorting, 356
line sorts, 351-353
merge record sorts, 354
paragraph sorts, 353
table sorting, 355-356
sound clip comments
adding, 384-385
playing, 385-386
recording, 387-388
Sound Clips dialog box, 384
Sound command (Insert menu), 384, 387
Sound Feature Bar, 385-386
sound formats, 385
Sound Recorder utility, 387
space bars, 123
spaces, inserting, 123
special characters, 206-208
Speller
alternative spellings, 153-154
options, 154-155
Speller command (Tools menu), 151-157
Split Cells command (Table QuickMenu), 426
Split/Cell command (Table menu), 426
Split/Table command (Table menu), 426
spreadsheets, 406
Standard paper size, 216
starting WordPerfect for Windows
from File Manager, 70-71
from Program Manager, 67-68
from Windows File menu, 68-69

Status Bar Options dialog box, 32
Status Bar Preferences dialog box, 31-32
status bars, 30-31
customizing, 31-32
units of measure, 169
Strikeout attribute, 108, 137-139
strings, 142, 148-151
structures, table, 406, 420-430
Style List dialog box, 244, 246-247
Style Quick Create option, 243-244
styles, 168, 214
formatting documents, 242-248
outline, 362, 366, 368
Styles command (Layout menu)
Apply option, 247-248
Create option, 245-246
Options option, 246-247
Quick Create option, 243-244
Styles Editor, 75, 245-246
Styles Editor dialog box, 245, 395, 401
Styles Quick Create dialog box, 244
Subdivide Page dialog box, 240
subdividing pages, 240-242
subscript text, 200
Sum command (Table menu), 442-443
SUM function, 442-443
Summary button, 489
superscript numbers in footnotes/endnotes, 401
superscript text, 200
Suppress dialog box, 234
synonyms, 142, 158-161

T

Tab key, 54
text, inserting, 412
Tab Set dialog box, 179-181, 192
tab stops, 412
tabbed tables, 351
Table button, 408-410

Table Format dialog box, 437-438
Table Formula Feature bar, 438, 440
Table menu commands
    Calculate, 439-440, 442-443
    Data Fill, 441-442
    Format, 430-431, 433, 435-436
    Join/Cell, 424
    Join/Table, 426
    Lines/Fill, 427
    Split/Cell, 426
    Split/Table, 426
    Sum, 442-443
Table QuickMenu, 416, 419
table-sizing arrow, 421
tables
    border lines, 427-430
    calculations, 438-443
    characteristics, 407
    columns
        deleting, 424
        formatting, 433-434
        inserting, 423
    creating, 408-410
    data files, 320-323, 420
    deleting, 419-420
    fill patterns, 427-430
    formatting, 436-438
        cells, 431-433
        fonts, selecting, 430-431
        levels, 430
    formulas, 438-440
    joining/splitting, 426-427
    navigating, 410-411
    rows
        deleting, 424
        formatting, 435-436
        inserting, 423
    sorts, 355-356
    structure, 406
        editing, 420-430
        deleting, 419-420

text
    editing, 413
    entering, 411-413
Tables Lines/Fill dialog box, 427-429
tabs, 176-177
    adding, 178-179
    deleting, 177-180
    dot leaders, 181
    inserting, 123
    nonuniform, 181
    types, 178
    uniform, 180-181
tabular columns, 446-447
Template (Ctrl+T) shortcut key, 56,
    72
Template button, 489
Template command (File menu), 72
templates, 72
Templates dialog box, 72
testing Button Bars, 487
text
    attributes, 199-200
        redline or strikeout, 135-139
    body, *see* body text
    converting to/from comments,
        383-384
    copying, 127-128
        between WordPerfect
            documents, 132
        in same document, 128-130
    cutting, 127-128
        between WordPerfect
            documents, 132
        in same document, 128-130
    deleting with shortcut keys, 124-125
    dragging and dropping with
        mouse, 130-131
    editing in tables, 413
    entering, 75-77
        in columns, 453-454
        in tables, 411-413

finding, 142-147

formatting with QuickFormat, 204-206

pasting, 127-128
  between WordPerfect documents, 132
  in same document, 128-130

positioning with Advance option, 223-224

replacing, 148-151

restoring deleted, 126

selecting
  with keyboard, 120-121, 124
  with mouse, 45-47

special characters, 206-208

subscript/superscript, 200

see also blocks of text

text boxes, 89

text columns, 446-447

Text QuickMenu, 416

text-wrapping
  altering flow, 462
  newspaper columns, 447-454

Thesaurus, 142, 157-158
  alternate words, 159-160
  Look Up option, 161
  replacing words, 158-159

Thesaurus shortcut key, 157

Thesaurus command (Tools menu), 157-161

THS (WordPerfect thesaurus) file name extension, 97

Tile command (Window menu), 67, 116

tiling windows, 58, 116-118

time, inserting in comments, 380

timed backups, 99-101

title bars, 26, 28

Tools menu commands
  Grammatik, 162-166
  Hypertext, 390, 392, 394

Macro, 297, 303, 491-492
  Edit option, 308
  Pause option, 299
  Play option, 297, 300-301, 311, 314
  Record option, 297, 299, 311-313

Merge, 320-329, 330-339

Outline, 365, 369-370

Sort, 343, 348, 356

Speller, 151-157

Thesaurus, 157-161

top margins, 221-222

tracking speeds of mouse, 43

Tutorial command (Help menu), 58

Typeover mode, 108, 119, 123

Typesetting, Advance command (Layout menu), 223-224

U

Undelete (Ctrl+Shift+Z) shortcut key, 57

Undelete command (Edit menu), 126

Underline (Ctrl+U) shortcut key, 56, 199

underlining text attribute, 199-200

Undo (Ctrl+Z) shortcut key, 57, 125

Undo command (Edit menu), 125-126, 351, 420

units of measure, 3, 169-170

uppercase, 156-157, 201

Uppercase button, 485

USPS POSTNET bar code, 82

V

vertical alignment, 432

vertical centering of pages, 222-223

vertical graphics lines, 470-472

Vertical Line command (Graphics menu), 471

View menu commands
    Button Bar, 20, 32-35, 304, 476,
        478, 483, 485
    Draft, 77
    Page, 79, 264
    Power Bar, 74, 408
    Reveal Codes, 39, 133, 135
    Ruler, 38-39, 74
    Ruler Bar, 123, 171
    Show, 77
viewing
    documents, 111-112
    multiple document windows, 116
volume (sound clips), 387

W

Watermark command (Layout menu),
    229-232
watermarks, 214, 229-232
WAV format, 385
WCM (WordPerfect for Windows
    macro file) file name extension, 97
What Is command (Help menu), 59
What Is Help (Shift+F1) shortcut key,
    59
widow/orphan protection, 239
widows, 214
widths
    columns, 421-423
    newspaper columns, 451-452
wild-card characters, 147
Window menu (Program Manager)
    commands
    Cascade, 67, 116
    Tile, 67, 116
Windows
    Control menu
        Minimize command, 48
        Restore command, 48
    environment, 103

File menu commands
    Open, 68
    Run, 68-69
    starting WordPerfect for
        Windows, 68-69
printer drivers, 216, 250
programs, 10
returning to, without exiting
    WordPerfect, 103-106
windows
    cascading, 116-118
    closing
        document, 101-102, 118
        Help, 63
    Create Comment, 380
    document, 26, 35
        Reveal Codes window, 39-41
        Ruler Bar, 38-39
        scroll bars, 36-38
        viewing multiple, 116
    Help, 59-60
    moving with mouse, 47-50
    program, 26-35
    Reveal Codes, 132-133, 398
    sizing with mouse, 47-50
    tiling, 58, 116-118
Windows Printers dialog box, 253
word wrap, 66
WordPerfect
    printer drivers, 216, 250, 252
    printer setup options, 255-256
    program window, 26-35
WordPerfect characters (Ctrl+W)
    shortcut kcy, 56
WordPerfect Characters dialog box,
    206-208
WordPerfect for Windows
    compatibility with Versions 5.1 and
        5.2, 22-23
    exiting, 101-102

starting
    from File Manager, 70-71
    from Program Manager, 67-68
    from Windows File menu, 68-69
WordPerfect Printer Drivers dialog
  box, 252
words
    replacing with Thesaurus, 158-159
    Speller, 152-154
    Thesaurus, 159-160
WPD (WordPerfect documents) file
  name extension, 97
WPG (WordPerfect graphics) file name
  extension, 97
WPM (WordPerfect macro) file name
  extension, 97
Wrap command (Graphics
  QuickMenu), 462
Wrap Text dialog box, 462
wrapping text
    altering flow, 462
    newspaper columns, 447-454
writing styles (Grammatik), 162
WWB (WordPerfect for Windows
  Button Bar) file name extension, 97
WWK (WordPerfect keyboard) file
  name extension, 97
WYSIWYG (What-You-See-Is-What-
  You-Get), 17, 167

X–Y–Z

Zero or More Characters (*) search
  operator, 293

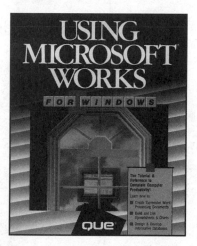

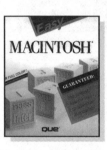

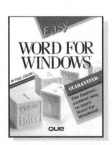